D1234097

MERGERS

MOTIVES
MODES
METHODS

Mergers

Motives
Modes
Methods

WALTER H. GOLDBERG
University of Gothenburg,
Sweden

PUBLICATION OF THE SCIENCE CENTER BERLIN
INTERNATIONAL INSTITUTE OF MANAGEMENT

EDITORIAL BOARD
Prof. Dr. Karl W. Deutsch
Prof. Dr. Meinolf Dierkes
Prof. Dr. Dennis C. Mueller
Prof. Dr. Frieder Naschold
Prof. Dr. Fritz W. Scharpf
Prof. Dr. Udo E. Simonis

NICHOLS

First published in the United States
of America in 1983 by
Nichols Publishing Company
Post Office Box 96
New York N.Y. 10024

Library of Congress Cataloging in Publication Data

Goldberg, Walter, 1924–
      Mergers: motives, modes, methods.

      Includes bibliographical references and indexes.
      1. Consolidation and merger of corporations.
2. Interorganizational relations. 3. Industrial
organization (Economic theory) I. Title.
 HD2746.5.G64 1983   658.1′6   83–2259
 ISBN 0–89397–155–3

Contents

PREFACE

The present volume is one in a series reporting about studies undertaken at and upon the initiative of the International Institute of Management of the Science Center Berlin (Wissenschaftszentrum Berlin). It deals with interfirm co-operation and mergers, their motives, modes and consequences, and with merger policy options. Substantive research on merger problems has been carried out at the above institute by industrial organization and competition economists. This volume is complementary to those studies, with contributions from behavioural scientists, business administrators, political scientists and economists. Whereas the economists' merger studies (Mueller, D.C. (ed.), 1980 - see Introduction - hereafter referred to as »Seven Countries Study») deal with the topic comparatively, looking for similarities and variations in merger motives and examining the effects and policies at national and industrial levels, the present volume explores the topic at the level of the organization involved in merger activities or interorganizational co-operation. It also investigates different modes of interfirm co-operation which precede merger activities or are chosen in lieu of merger. Furthermore, in an attempt to improve our understanding of processes which are still rather ambiguous, this volume also deals with interorganizational co-operation of non-business organizations.

The Wissenschaftszentrum Berlin expresses its appreciation to the authors-contributors and to the editor. We would also like to thank the European Institute for Advanced Studies in Management, the University of Gothenburg, Sweden, and the Social Science Research Concil of Sweden for their financial support to joint seminars, and Dr. Herman Daems of the European Institute for Advanced Studies in Management for his valuable advice to the editor.

The Science Center Editors

INTRODUCTION

1. Merger and Interorganizational Co-operation Research at IIM

When the International Institute of Management (IIM) developed its first mid-term research programme in 1973, it decided to address an issue which was expected to attract growing attention at the beginning of the 1980's. The programme attempted to develop scientific evidence, data, and instruments that would be of use to decision-makers on industrial policy issues in highly developed countries. At that time it was not foreseeable that the crisis following the oil price shock of October 1973 would so drastically increase the urgency of such evidence.

The programme envisaged research into problems of industrial structure and efficiency, and the participation of the industrial sector in public programmes on issues of employment, regional and sectoral development. The core of the programme was to consist of studies into the efficiency and change of industrial structures. The Institute, which awards contracts to its researchers only for limited periods of time, was privileged to have such eminent industrial organization economists as F.M. Scherer and D.C. Mueller on its international research staff.

When D.C. Mueller was hired as a senior research fellow to the institute, he brought with him a vested interested in merger research.[1] Because of his reputation and his position at the institute, he had the opportunity to establish teams for an international comparative merger study within the IIM international network of contacts with scientists and institutes. The topic was pursued at the level of industrial growth (by merger and other means), competition, and industrial policy research.

The reports from the comparative Seven-Countries Study are published under the following title:

Mueller, D.C. (ed.), *The Determinants and Effects of Mergers: An international Comparison.* Oelgeschlager, Gunn & Hain, Cambridge, Mass., 1980.

Because the Seven-Countries Study concentrated mainly on economic issues and methodology of mergers, studies focusing on interorganizational co-operation and mergers would complement the available evidence on merger motives, modes, and effects. The aim of such complementary research was to gather evidence on the *motives, modes,* and *processes* of interorganizational co-operation (of which merger is a particular case). The emphasis was to be on the methodology employed in organizational research, political science,

---

[1]   Mueller, D.C, (1969).

public administration, and business administration. In comparison to the resources employed in the Seven-Countries Study, the funds available for those studies were very modest. The level of aspiration had to be adjusted consequently. The research reported is thus not of hypotheses-testing but rather exploratory character. It does not aim at cross-cultural comparisons, i.e., it is not designed to differentiate between national idiosyncracies in interorganizational behaviour, even though such differences undoubtedly exist.

The findings emphasize the necessity of eclectic approaches in order to comprehend the complex and multi-facetted problems of interorganizational co-operation. Advice to utilize such approaches stems from researchers who have gained deep insights into the matter through studies of their own (such as the IIM team), or from evidence available from pertinent research.[1]

It should be pointed out, however, that multi-factor models often render ambiguous results, at least in this field. In this respect, they are hardly superior to few-factor models, which tend to produce inconclusive, but highly unambiguous, results. Nevertheless, when research is aimed as results for policy considerations, the eclectic approach can be justified. If reality is so variable that it cannot simply be explained (i.e. if mergers, cartels, and other modes of interorganizational co-operation cannot be classified by means of unambiguous and unobtrusive parameters and variables), a more complex, flexible, costly, and time-consuming control mechanism and procedure is called for. The decision-maker involved must judge each individual case on its own conditions and merits.

Indeed, the complexity and ambiguity of interorganizational behaviour models is demonstrated by *Hughes, Mueller, and Singh* in the Competition Policy Chapter of the Seven-Countries Study. They demonstrate how different modes of merger policy can be applied to achieve results contrary to the intended ones.

2. Interorganizational Co-operation and Merger

As mentioned above, the research reported here deals with phenomena which cover but also go beyond mergers in a strict sense. Whereas merger research usually reports on one to one acquisitions and merger, i.e. one enterprise assimilating another one $(1 + 1 = 1)$, this volume also reports cases where:

a. more than two enterprises merge into one $(1 + n = 1)$

b. enterprises give up their decision-making prerogatives on certain important issues to a joint organization, yet at the same time, remain intact in other capacities (joint ventures, consortia, interlocking directorates, etc.).

---

[1] Steiner, P.O. (1975).

4

The non-merger forms may be pre-merger arrangements, i.e. they may be applied before a formal merger is decided upon. Such forms may also be implemented without the intent of merger.

Poensgen[1] distinguishes a hierarchy of more or less coupled »systems», ranging from the closely tied family or hunting band (i.e., the primary or secondary group held together by non-economic as well as economic goals), to the market system. In between these types are the peer groups (for the pursuit of economic objectives), the hierarchical organization, and other associations or federations of peer groups or of hierarchically organized entities. The order (from family to market) reflects a decreasing strength of *bonds* of the persons involved, a decreasing length of *time* of association, a decreasing number of *needs* satisfied by the association, and an increasing *substitutability* of one partner for another.

A view advocated frequently in this volume is based on the organizational interdependence philosophy as proposed in organization theory (e.g. Aldrich, Pfeffer, 1976; Pfeffer, Salancik, 1978; Aldrich, 1979). Organizations are engaged in exchange[2] with the environment. At the border of the organization (which may be a »sharp» dividing line, or a »diffuse zone» - cf. Goldberg in this volume on the situation of personnel managers in SSAB) the organization's control over its activities decreases, and the control of other organizations (etc.) increases. The organization becomes subject to influence, usually from several sources. The organization may want or need to reduce the resulting uncertainty by altering its situation of interdependence through use of internal measures, by attempts to extend its domain of control into vital areas, or by decreasing its dependence on critical exchanges. Agreements, federations, and mergers are one cluster of means to achieve the above, withdrawal is another.

Merger as a means to eliminate the uncertainty created as a result of interdependence is discussed and tested in Pfeffer-Salancik (1978) with convincing results. Corroborating this interdependence hypothesis they confront it with three other merger »motives», which, however, are *rejected:*

a. mergers occur on a random basis (also Poensgen, 1980, op.cit., claims that this can hardly be the case. Merger activity increases strongly when the ratio of the market price of a firm's equity - capital, as well as book and replacement values - is low. It is then cheaper to buy the existing firm than to buy the equivalent substance piece by piece.);

b. profitable industries are more likely to attract potential speculators than non-profitable industries are;

c. merger is a way to circumvent barriers to entry into an industry.

The volume also deals with interorganizational co-operation and merger of non-profit organizations as well as of co-operatives. There are several reasons why we have used this widened scope:

---

[1] Poensgen, O.H. (1980).
[2] White, P.E., (1974).

5

a. merger motives are often similar to those of merging/co-operating economic entities, and may therefore be treated as if they were economic motives;

b. merger motives, irrespective if economic or non-economic in character, require varying approaches to merger management based on the individual case;

c. conflicts and conflict settlement in such organizations have relevance to economic merger study approaches as well.

3. Modes, Motives, Processes

The chapters in this volume are organized into three sections:

☐ *Modes* of Co-operation and Merger

☐ *Motives* to Co-operate/Merge

☐ *Processes* covering Pre-merger Decisions-making to Post-merger Integration.

However, the delineation into these three sections is not very stringent. In almost every chapter all three aspects are present, but to varying degrees. The ordering is based on the main emphasis of the chapter in question. Each section is preceded by a short introduction and overview, and if possible, also by conclusions.

4. Policy Considerations

This set of studies does not allow any general policy conclusions[1] and thus, differs only slightly from stringent merger research. However, it permits a range of conclusions to be drawn, which in many cases are complementary to those from economists' merger research. For example, findings are consistent with the evidence from other merger studies (the Seven-Countries Study included) that the pre-merger expectations regarding the gains associated with merger (as measured, for example, in longer range post merger stock market value of shares) are not immediately realized once the merger has been completed. Singh (1971), for instance, maintains that the merged organization needs to exist at least five years before expected gains begin to materialize. Obviously, only »unfriendly» mergers seem to render merger gains (cf. Kummer and Hoffmeister, 1973). Merger legislation, however, prohibits such mergers in many countries.

---

[1] Further policy implications will be briefly discussed in the introductions to each section.

6

The explanation this volumes offers may be summarized as follows:

a. It seems that merger decisions are often based on inconsistent and incomplete information of questionable validity and reliability, even in cases where otherwise competent decision-makers are involved.

b. Conflicting or incompatible motives are often suppressed during the pre-merger phases and come to surface only during the merging process phase which, as a result, is greatly disrupted by conflicts.

5. References

Aldrich, H.E., 1979
  Organizations and Environments. Englewood Cliffs: Prentice Hall.

Aldrich, H.E., Pfeffer, J., 1979
  »Environments of Organizations», *Annual Review of Sociology,* No. 2: 79-105.

Kummer, D.R., Hoffmeister, J.R., 1978
  »Valuation Consequences of Cash Tender Offers», *Journal of Finance,* XXXIII:505-16.

Mueller, D.C., 1969
  »A Theory of Conglomerate Mergers», *Quarterly Journal of Economics,* LXXXIII (Nov.): 643-59.

Pfeffer, J., Salancik, G.R., 1978
  The External Control of Organizations. New York: Harper & Row.

Poensgen, O.H., 1980
  Between Market and Hierarchy. Saarbrücken, (mimeo).

Singh, A., 1971
  Takeovers: Their Relevance to the Stock Market and the Theory of the Firm. London: Cambridge University Press.

Steiner, P.O., 1975
  Mergers, Motives, Effects, Policies. Ann Arbor: University of Michigan Press.

White, P.E., 1974
  »Resources as Determinants of Organizational Behavior», *Administrative Science Quarterly,* 19:366-379.

SECTION I: MOTIVES

1. Section Contents: An Overview

The economic literature on mergers deals with the topic of merger motives quite extensively. Basically, most studies have as their root the economic rationality assumption, i.e. that man will do what seems to him to be appropriate in order to further his own (economic) interests. Thus, motives are reflected by variables (or proxies) such as:

- size and growth

- economies of scale

- profitability, return on shares, profit variability

- market share, market power.

The objectives are often inseparable from the instruments used to obtain them. Profitability and size (dominance) are considered to be the basic merger motives. There are, of course, studies which cite a wider variety of motives, demonstrating the complexity of merger or co-operation objectives. Two such lists of motives may illustrate the diversity of merger motives:

Ansoff, Brandenburg, Portner, and Radosevich (1971) identified the following motives:

1. A desire to limit competition or achieve monopoly profits

2. A desire to utilize unutilized market power

3. A response to shrinking opportunities for growth and/or profit in one's own industry, due to shrinking demand or excessive competition

4. A desire to diversify, to reduce the risks of business

5. A desire to achieve a large enough size to realize an economical scale of production and/or distribution

6. A desire to overcome critical lacks in one's own company by acquiring the necessary complementary resources, patents, or factors of production.

7. A desire to achieve sufficient size to have efficient access to capital markets or inexpensive advertising

8. A desire to utilize more fully particular resources or personnel controlled by the firm, with particular applicability to managerial skills.

9

9.   A desire to displace an existing management

10.   A desire to utilize tax loopholes not available without merging.

11.   A desire to reap the promotional or speculative gains attendant upon new security issues, or changed price earnings ratios.

12.   A desire of managers to create an image of themselves as aggressive managers who recognize a good thing when they see it.

13.   A desire of managers to manage an ever-growing set of subordinates.

Practically important merger (or acquisition) motives beyond those found by Ansoff et al. are:

- Buying equity is often a *cheaper* and *faster* means of entering markets, than establishing subsidiaries *ex ovo,* i.e. by building up so called greenfield plants from scratch.

- Merger requires different managerial skills, integration and change oriented ones, rather than entrepreneurial ones needed to launch new ventures. As the former skills seem to be more frequently available than entrepreneurial ones, merging may be a more attractive alternative.

- Merging with (or acquiring) indigenous firms is a method quite frequently used by foreign firms to enter new markets, i.e. to internationalize their operations (further).

The multivariate nature of merger motivation is also illustrated by Steiner (1975), who depicts mergers being contingent of actors, climates, motives, and participants:

I.   *Actors*
      Stockholders of affected companies
      Managers of affected companies
      Investors generally
      Speculators
      Financial community
      Antitrust authorities
      SEC (Securities and Exchange Commission)
      Congress
      Courts
      President and Executive branch
      Lobbyists
      Political parties
      Public interest groups
      Press

II.   *Climates*
      States of economy

Stock market
Legal
Regulatory
Tax
Accounting

III. *Types of Motivation for and against Mergers*

   A. Profit increasing for the firm:
       Achieving real efficiencies
       Increasing market power
       Tax and accounting opportunities

   B. Growth as a goal

   C. General (external) speculative goals

   D. Insider opportunities:
       to stockholders
       to acquiring managements
       to acquired managements
       to financial groups

   E. Deterrents:
       Antitrust law enforcement
       Securities law and enforcement
       Transactions cost
       Public and Congressional opinion

IV. *Participants in Individual Merger*

   A. Bidders - classified by

       Type

       Success in attempt

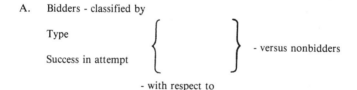 - versus nonbidders

                 - with respect to

       Industry, extent of diversification, size, managerial or ownership control,
       growth, profitability, liquidity, stock market performance, etc.

   B. Targets - classifid by

       Resistance
                                          - versus nontargets
       Outcome

                 - with respect to

11

Industry, extent of diversification, size, managerial or ownership control, growth, profitability, liquidity, stock market performance etc.

C.   Financial institutions:
Brokers
Banks
Mutual funds
Others

However, for a number of reasons, such enumerations do not help the researcher a great deal:

a.   Most mergers are controlled by multiple motives rather than by a single one, because several parties are involved, each of them usually having several different objectives in mind to be achieved by means of merger.

b.   Many motives can be characterized either as being of a »hidden agenda» type (i.e. not expressed overtly) or as fake motives (intended to mask the real ones). The use of fake motives cannot unequivocally be considered as cheating. Rather, they substitute for objectives which actors do not want or dare to expose.

c.   Motives/objectives are not always consistent over time, but rather shift, change character, emphasis, and priority in the course of events.

d.   Motives must not necessarily be congruent or non-conflicting. This is particularly true in cases where several parties are concerned. Each single participant in the merger may want to pursue internally inconsistent goals as well.

e.   Objectives may not be susceptible to operationalization, and thus cannot be measured.

f.   Rich, many-facetted models in economic and social research are not necessarily good models (cf. Starbuck's expression »The Bonini Syndrome»).

g.   Finally, as Steiner (1975, pp. 31ff) points out, one must not only know the motives and classify them into broader categories (such as anti-competitive considerations, search for efficiencies, for speculative gains, satisfaction of managerial objectives, etc.). Above all, one must be able to determine which motives are decisive in accounting for the various levels of merger activities.

Why, then, does this volume emphasize merger motives as an important issue? Several factors play a role in the decision to deal with this topic:

a.   There seems to be a tendency by researchers to reproduce, or at best, marginally improve older models of research. There should be more considerations on real and dominant motives.

b. There are important motives which control merger behaviour, but which have not yet been investigated by economists. Several reasons account for this neglect:

  • Economists have largely ignored such motives because they are inconsistent with the economic rationality assumption.

  • Data, information, and suitable proxies are assumed to be lacking on the phenomenon in question (such assumptions may or may not be correct).

  • The information that is to be attained, is only available via »soft» research (rather than via »hard» data).

The chapters in this section list some important motives which have had definite and substantive bearing on decisions to co-operate/merge. In their study of merger motives in farmers' co-operatives, *Nyström-Utterström* stress the importance of socio-political motives in relation to techno-economic ones. They maintain that such motives are at least as important as, if not more so, than the techno-economic aspects. Indeed, they found that in the absence of (further) techno-economic justifications, important merger decisions were made strictly on the basis of socio-political factors.

The socio-political motives are internally complex. Whereas some are rational social goals or »musts», some of them are simply prevailing values, or »myths» dominant at a certain point in time. Together they control and justify choices of alternative courses of action. Nyström-Utterström claim that when the techno-economic and socio-political dimensions meet (or are made to meet), certain decisions are made or brought to maturity.

The Nyström-Utterström proposals are in accordance with the so-called ecological approaches of e.g. Aldrich (1979) or, as represented in this volume, by Pennings. Nyström-Utterström also stress the importance of change agents, in particular in the phases of problem identification, development of visions, and establishment of ideology. They demonstrate the impact of myths as mediating mechanisms, which, employed by change agents, make possible the acceptance of ideologies as necessary conditions for decision-making, when techno-economic rationality is not applicable as motive.

Cable stresses the information motive in search processes for investment opportunities, i.e. using mergers as a means to gain access to information which otherwise would not be available.

Edström, Norbäck and Högberg demonstrate the use of co-operative strategies by holders of complementary resources as well as by competitors, when both groups are motivated by the opportunity through joint co-operation:

a. to gain access to scarce resources,

b. to reduce uncertainty stemming from the environment, or

c.   to maintain their action potential or power in risky situations where they by acting each at their own would have to commit or reserve a much higher share of their critical resources. If the negative effects possible in a risky situation are fully realized, they might be detrimental to a single organization. Thus chosing a co-operative strategy is similar to buying an insurance certificate.

The most surprising conclusion is that even otherwise competing organizations may find it worthwhile and rewarding to enter into co-operative ventures.

Goldberg (in Section III, Processes) calls attention to a valid merger motive, which has been widely neglected in the economic literature, viz., merging in order to reduce (over-) capacity in an industry (here, in the steel-making industry. Cf. also Edström-Alarik in the process section on the capacity reduction motive). Capacity reduction by merger often takes place under either pressure from or participation by the public sector in one way or another. Important objectives other than capacity reduction are loss minimization, job protection (or rather, long-range job security), and the establishment of a highly competitive remaining industry. In the case discussed here another objective was to achieve maximum employee co-determination.

Merger as a means to cope with stagnation or recession differs substantially from merger for growth, the latter being the most popular subject of economists' merger studies.

Uncertainty avoidance or risk minimization/neutralization has already been mentioned as a major merger objective. Economic literature deals with risk as a merger motive in a different manner, viz., diversified investment or conglomerate merger is viewed as a means of spreading risks. Blois (1980) discusses the uncertainty stemming from an organization's environment and the attempts organizations make in order to cope with or manage this uncertainty.

The literature suggests three principal mechanisms for dealing with environmental uncertainty:

a.   altering the internal structure of the organization

b.   adjusting the boundaries of the organization (e.g. through merger), and

c.   negotiating with the environment (co-optation, contracts, agreements, joint ventures, etc. cf. Pfeffer, 1972)

Management of risk and uncertainty as a merger motive appears in all three of the principal merger modes:

a.   vertical integration is used as a means to control production processes (or to protect the technical core of an enterprise, cf. Thompson, 1967), material flows, distribution and marketing processes, all of them being

14

subject to risk and uncertainty, and thus to disturbances (symbiotic interdependence, as Pfeffer, 1972, labels it). If the expected cost of risk and uncertainty is higher than the expected net cost of acquisition, the firm may decide to acquire sources of supplies and/or channels of distribution and marketing.

b. Horizontal merger is used to reduce the uncertainties stemming from activities of competitors. This motive is then labelled as power or monopolization motive (the case of competitive interdependence, Pfeffer, 1972).

c. Conglomerate mergers are used to put a corporation's eggs in several baskets, instead of only into one.

Economic theory claims that shareholders can spread their holdings themselves, in order to spread their risks according to their own needs and expectations, and that risk spreading by conglomerate merger is therefore done in the interest of managers rather than in the interest of the shareholder. This train of thought assumes that only shareholders' interests are important. In Europe, however, shareholders as well as managers are held socially responsible beyond their strict financial interest (cf. Goldberg and Nyström-Utterström). They are thus expected to behave in ways which avoid the risk of close-down and consequent unemployment, as well as the risk of deterioration not only of shareholder equity, but also of public investment into infrastructure (which, often to a considerable extent has been made to cater for efficient conduct of industrial activities).

Brenner and Shapira investigate »upstream» and »downstream» (i.e. vertical) mergers undertaken to reduce uncertainty, based on the hypothesis that the propensity to merge vertically increases with an increase of symbiotic interdependence and uncertainty.

2. Policy Considerations

Because merger motives are complex and diverse, and because they change over time, merger policy can hardly be established upon findings based only from economic research. Merger in a socially oriented and controlled market economy most likely will not be solely motivated by strictly economic reasons, but will be influenced by various social factors.

Each merger case should thus be individually assessed upon multiple techno-economic as well as socio-political criteria. Checklists rather than strict guidelines seem to be commendable for merger control, particularly because both the techno-economic and the socio-political conditions will shift. Thus, the stability and consistency of merger policy is subject to erosion.

Analyses of national merger policy regularly undertaken by the Europan Communities as well as by OECD indicate that national policies with a few exceptions gradually have become less liberal. On one side, mergers of big enterprises in some countries have become subject to close scrutiny, on an individual basis, in order to prevent erosion of competition. On the other side, in some countries (Italy in particular) small and medium size enterprises are subject to »merger protection», if bids are made by large corporations.

Whereas about ten years ago only a few European countries regulated merger, the•second half of the 1970's brought about explicit or implicit merger control in practically all industrialized countries of Europe. From having been an instrument of competition control, merger policy has become more complex. It is quite commonly used as an instrument of labour market (safeguarding employment by merger) or industrial structural policy (controlled capacity reduction, improved competition). In most countries, however, the conditions and potential consequences of individual mergers are looked into by Cartel or Competition Boards or Commissions.

3. References

Aldrich, H.E., 1979
    Organizations and Environments. Englewood Cliffs: Prentice Hall

Ansoff*, I., Brandenburg, R.G.,
Portner, F.E., and Radosevich, H.R., 1971
    Acquisition Behavior of U.S. Manufacturing Firms, 1946-1965. Nashville, Tenn.: Vanderbilt Univ. Press.

Blois, K.J., 1980
    »Quasi-Integration as a Mechanism for Controlling External Dependencies», *Management Decisions,* XVIII: 55-63.

Pfeffer, J., 1972
    »Merger as a Response to Organizational Interdependence», *Administrative Science Quarterly,* XVII: 382-394.

Steiner*, P.O., 1975
    Mergers, Motives, Effects, Policies. Ann Arbor: University of Michigan Press.

Thompson, J.D., 1967
    Organizations in Action. New York, London: McGraw-Hill.

* Copyright permit for quotation kindly granted by the publishers.

1. A SEARCH THEORY OF DIVERSIFYING MERGER*

John Cable
International Institute of Management, Berlin
and University of Warwick, Coventry, England

* *An extended version of an article in* **Recherches Economiques de Louvain,** *vol. 43, No. 3, pp. 225-243, with permission.*

1. Introduction

The chapter argues that gaining information on potential investment opportunities can be a sufficient motive for the acquisition of a firm, at least in conglomerate merger cases. It suggests that search via merger can be efficient and hence rational behaviour under more-or-less standard assumptions. Some support for a merger-as-search hypothesis exists in the presently available evidence on merger activity, though the relative incidence of search motivated merger is not clear. A potential welfare gain is identified concerning the flexibility of capital transfer in the economy, but this may be offset by an impairment to the long-run corporate competitive process. At the practical policy level the arguments support the use of non-discretionary rules rather than case-by-case review.

Existing theories of conglomerate or diversifying merger date mostly from the US merger boom of the late nineteen- sixties.[1] At that time much attention was focused on the conglomerate phenomenon, popularly seen as waves of acquisitions by a number of corporations, some initially quite small and quasi-financial in character, and producing enterprises with an elusive industrial logic. Interest had shifted away from the less dramatic issue of why established industrial firms enter new areas by external growth from time to time in the course of their development. Although a long-recognised phenomenon (e.g. Penrose, 1963), and despite the theoretical and empirical work occasioned by the most recent U.S. merger boom,[2] much remains unknown about the circumstances in which this occurs. Amongst other things this results in uncertainty over the appropriate stance for antitrust policy towards mergers.

---

[1] See particularly Mueller (1969), Gort (1969), Levy and Sarnat (1970). A comprehensive survey of theoretical explanations is contained in Steiner (1975).

[2] For a recent review of the empirical literature, see Mueller (1977).

For European countries the issue is becoming more urgent. Whereas the conglomerate nature of the merger wave of 1966-1971 was confined to the U.S., there are now signs of an increasing incidence of diversifying mergers in Europe. Up to 1970 eighty per cent or more of mergers in Britain, France, West Germany and other, smaller European countries were horizontal. But in Britain, for example, the number of mergers officially classified as diversifying rose from 12.5 % of the total from 1965-70 to 24.4 % in 1971-75. And in 1972 one half of the total gross assets involved in all mergers were accounted for by diversifying mergers.

A convincing account of diversifying merger in the present context must explain the original urge to diversify, the choice of external growth over *de novo* expansion, and, where diversification is into more profitable areas, as is often the case, how a more profitable firm can be acquired at a price which makes the acquisition itself profitable. Given the well documented existence of product and industrial life cycles in the face of changing tastes, technology and world economy development, the need for companies to diversify and so dissociate their corporate life cycles from those of their existing activities is perhaps the least difficult aspect to account for. If, further, it is recognised that knowledge of alternative production possibilities among existing firms is incomplete, search - acquiring the information capital required to undertake »new» activities - is evidently an essential feature of the diversification process.

The present paper puts forward a new theory of diversifying merger as search for investment opportunities. The fact that diversification occurs sometimes, but not always, by merger is explained by the costs and attractiveness of merger as a search mode, relative to other methods. The profitable acquisition of more profitable firms by less profitable ones, is shown to be possible because different values can be placed on given information by acquired and acquiring firms who begin searching from diverse starting points. In effect the theory shows that information (of a particular kind) can be a sufficient motive for merger *per se*. [1] The possibility of other motives is not denied, and the present contribution should be seen as supporting rather than rebutting the call for an eclectic approach to the merger problem (Steiner, 1975).

The theoretical arguments are put forward in section 2. Section 3 considers some empirical evidence, drawn mainly from existing studies but supplemented by information on diversifying mergers in the U.K. Welfare and policy implications are discussed in section 4 and found to be complex. On the one hand they concern the demise of viable economic entities which in the long run might have challenged the usually larger, entrenched firms which acquired them. On the other hand, search motivated merger is seen to contribute positively to the efficiency of capital transfer via internal (intra-firm) capital markets.

---

[1] Arrow (1975) has shown that informational factors can explain an equilibrium in which up- and downstream activities in the same production chain are vertically integrated. However, it does not necessarily follow that vertical merger must occur to bring this equilibrium about.

2. Merger as Search

At any given time an established firm possesses a certain knowledge of production opportunities, enabling it to undertake specific, real investments. This will have accumulated mainly from past production, together with past, associated search. Hence the stocks held by firms with different production histories will differ in quality, extent and content. The firm also has a given financial record and a corresponding capital-market status and supply of internal funds. In a market economy the firm's task is to seek and implement, period-by-period, investment plans which satisfy long-run capital market criteria. For analytical purposes we later assume that firms maximise a two parameter profit objective.

The external market is seen to operate on the basis of historical prices or earnings, plus other publicly available information (announcements of annual results, stock splits etc.). The internal information held by firms on real investment possibilities, however, is not publicly available in a systematic way, although a small part of it may be known to the external market. This asymmetry of information between firms and the market does not imply an inefficient capital market, in the sense used by Fama (1970) and others.[1] It does, however, entail a two-stage allocation process. Thus the external market makes allocations among firms based on inferences, drawn from the information it holds, about the quality of unknown company investment plans. Firms carry out internal allocations among projects as dictated by the information available to them.

The firm's search and investment planning procedures are conceived as follows. The initial knowledge held at any given time provides a stock of »accessible» investment opportunities, i.e. projects capable of immediate implementation without search, including replacement. Some combination of accessible projects would constitute an initial, optimal investment plan which maximises expected return under the initial state of knowledge. Successful search expands the firm's investment opportunity set in such a way that the expected return of the optimal plan increases. Optimising behaviour requires that search continue until the increase in the value of the optimal plan for that period equals the marginal cost of search.

The process can be examined more closely in the framework of portfolio theory, if certain assumptions are made.[2] If there are constant returns and

---

[1] Certainly under the more common *weak* and *semi-strong* tests, which require that the market fully adjusts to information on historical prices and other »obviously public» information respectively (Fama, 1970, p. 383). Significantly, however, the monopolistically held information of corporate insiders is one of the established examples of inefficiency under the *strong-form* test, and the asymmetry noted would imply an inefficient market on a *super-strong* test, requiring that all existing information on future investment plans, including internal information, be made use of. The asymmetry of information between firms and the market is merely noted at this stage.

[2] I am indebted to Marshall Sarnat who inspired the application of portfolio theory to the present problem. The theory was recently surveyed by Jensen (1972).

19

no interdependencies among projects, the set of efficient investment plans derivable from a particular firm's accessible project set may be represented by the frontier FEM in figure 1.1. Specifically, FEM shows the maximum return for a given degree of risk $\sigma^2(R)$ from all possible combinations of accessible projects.

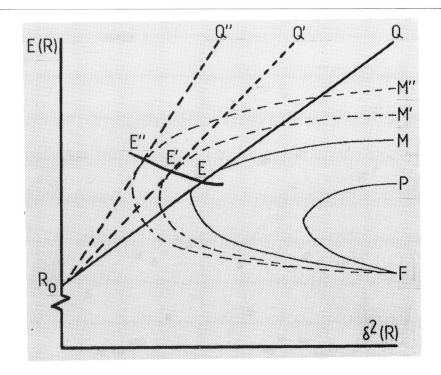

Figure 1.1

Since firms also have access to information available to shareholders, the accessible set includes both internal investment opportunities, known only to the firm, and portfolio holdings in other firms.[1] In the presence of a risk-free asset and drawing on the Sharpe-Lintner market equilibrium model[2] R_oEQ is the boundary of the attainable set before search begins, and an expected-return maximizing firm would implement the efficient combination of its internal investment opportunities E, and invest risk-free, in a ratio dic-

---

[1]   The intra-firm covariances subsumed in the frontier FEM are relevant for capital budgeting decisions under the asymmetry of information assumed earlier. Since information on individual projects is »impacted«, it is only firms, and not security holders in the (financial) capital market, who can optimise over this opportunity set.

[2]   Sharpe 1964, Lintner, 1965.

tated by its degree of risk aversion. Note that not every known project necessarily features in the optimal investment plan.[1]

Successful search will shift out the frontier FEM, and trace out a locus of points E, E', E''. The firm's decision process can now be envisaged in a manner analogous to that adopted in models of job- and price-search. Assume that the firm holds some *ex ante* notion of the probability distribution of values of investment programmes in general, based on the historical profit performance of industry as a whole, or of some more relevant peer-group of firms, e.g. some relevant sector or industry. Experience of search outcomes as search proceeds yields more information to the firm on search costs and the distribution of potential investment returns. Search continues until the expected value of the best plan known to the firm (less search cost) equals its revised, expected value for investment programmes in general, e.g. at point E''.

The search process itself can be looked at as the acquisition of new information sets, beginning from the firm's initial knowledge set K and reaching out towards new activities represented by the information sets S_1, S_2, ... S_n. The sets K, S_i are are finite sets in which the elements are individual indivisible particles of knowledge, and are distinct from the physical resources required for production. Each defines a particular activity in that no two different activities would have the same information set.[2] Two elements in search are distinguished: an »insight» or perception component, in which a basic idea, or awareness of the existence of a new activity is created; and a »deliberative» element, in which the original perception is explored, refined and simplified by the exclusion of extraneous details. In terms of information sets, the insight component involves perceiving some subset $I \subset K \cap S$ (figure 1.2). That is, a part of the firm's existing knowledge triggers awareness of some other, previously unrecognised activity. The deliberative element in search involves assembling the complete set S, by finding and arranging $S - I$ given that I and K are known. This process is deliberative because the set S_i describes a production activity and so has elements which are linked by

---

[1]   The locus of efficient points (plans) is found by deriving the investment proportions x_i which minimize the variance of, in this case, the plan for given expected rates of return. Formally, this involves finding the vector X which minimizes the objective function C:
$$C = X'\Sigma X$$
subject to: $x_i 0$ $(i = 1,2,..,n)$
            $X'R = E$
            $X'1 = 100$
where: x_i denotes the share of the i'th project in the plan, and Σ denotes the variance-covariance matrix of the rates of return for projects i, j $(i, j = 1,2,...,n)$, and R_i denotes the average rate of return on project i so that $X'R$ represents the return on the investment plan with a given vector of project shares X. Thus the possibility of some $x_i = 0$ is quite explicit.

[2]   In practice different manufacturers of, say, shoes are very likely to hold somewhat different information so that »the» shoemaking set is ill-defined. However, we assume that competition will limit the degree of informational differences, at least sufficiently for the purpose of distinguishing shoemaking from, say, hatmaking.

causal and technological relationships. Hence *systematic* search procedures can be applied, guided by the normal rules of logic.

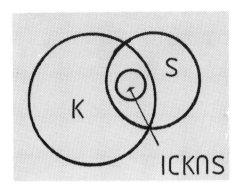

Figure 1.2

Utilising this framework, the total cost of carrying out a completed search for some S_i may be written:

$$C = f\,(d,m,s)$$

with $f_d, f_s > 0$ and, over some range, $f_m < 0$.

C is search cost; d is the disparateness of the initial and sought activities, reflected in the size of the intersection between the sets K and S;[1] s is the size and complexity of the sought activity which for clarity of exposition is assumed to be, related to the absolute size (order) of the set S; and m similarly, captures the size and diversity of the initial knowledge set K, size and diversity again being assumed to go together.

The justification for $f_s' > 0$ is obvious. $f_m < 0$ over some range because the larger and more complex is the firm's initial knowledge set K the larger will be the probability of some overlapping activity being perceived within a given time and cost horizon. However, the ability of the firm to process internal information efficiently will decline as m increases, and it is possible that the system can be overwhelmed at some stage. Hence it may be reasonably expected $f_m' > 0$ with a possibility that beyond some point $f_m > 0$. The expectation $f_d > 0$ has a twofold basis. First, the smaller is $K \cap S_i$ for a given search set i, the smaller is the probability of some $I \subset K \cap S_i$, being perceived. Secondly, the larger is $S_i\text{-}K$, both absolutely and in relation to $K \cap S_i$, the less efficient the second-stage, deliberative part of the search is likely to be. For more of the firm's search is then taking place outside rather than inside the firm's existing area of expertise.

---

1) The concept of disparateness is somewhat analogous to Narver's »degree of node commonality», except that Narver's concept concerns the overlap of resource rather than information sets (Narver, 1969, p. 4).

Merger ranks as a mode of search since, among other things, it involves the acquisition of information embodied in a firm. In comparison with other methods, searching by merger has two distinctive features. Firstly, it permits the acquisition of *complete* information sets: the merger of firms A and B is the union of their information set $K_A \cup K_B$ Other search options will typically involve the piecemeal accumulation of knowledge, whether this is done purely by »internal» search processes, or by hiring key personnel. Secondly, the merger search cost is likely to contain a relatively large fixed element, in comparison with other methods, due to the existence of acquisition-price premia and transaction costs (e.g., the cost of harmonising internal accounting systems, etc.).

The cost functions for merger-search and alternative methods will therefore tend to differ in the following way. Although the »fixed cost» elements in merger search are not pre-determined and will in fact vary from case to case, they may reasonably be expected to generate a higher intercept for merger-search than for the alternative. But a significantly smaller gradient may be expected for merger search in the d and s planes, arising from the fact that the search set is acquired as a whole. Under the alternative modes of search, the search set must be both perceived and then assembled piecemeal in the course of the second »deliberative» search phase. As the size and complexity of the search set rises, and as its disparateness from existing knowledge increases, relatively rapid increases in »deliberative» search costs are to be expected. But the acquisition of the complete set through merger more or less fully avoids the deliberative search stage and its associated costs, depending on the organisational structure of the firm. If the merged entity is run on divisionalized M-form lines and the resource set of the acquired firm is left intact, centralisation of information on the acquired firm's technology and operational matters is not involved. Hence the »deliberative» search process is avoided completely, leaving only the perception cost elements, which are common to all search alternatives.[1] The mitigation of deliberative search costs will, however, be much less complete in a functionally organised firm, where the technology of the acquired firm must be absorbed at a high level in each department of the acquiring firm, and its operational control procedures applied to the new production activity.

The necessary condition for merger search to dominate other search modes on cost grounds is therefore that the relative slopes of the relevant cost functions in the C,d and C,s planes differ sufficiently to offset the larger intercept in the merger search function, and produce an intersection as in figure 1.3. Whether or not such an intersection will occur is ultimately an empirical question. But the theoretical arguments presented above indicate there are factors operating towards this end.

The theoretical possibility of searching by merger can now be shown. Consider first two firms in the same industry. Their initial knowledge sets (K) will be identical or at least very similar. Hence, they begin their respective

---

[1] The process differs, however. In merger it is a suitable take-over candidate which is perceived whereas under other options it is a new production opportunity to be explored. On previous arguments it is the C,m plane of the cost function which is mainly affected. For both merger and other methods the overall slope of the function in this plane is likely to be negative over some range, and for the same reason, but the relative gradient is uncertain.

23

searches for investment opportunities from the same base, say, the accessible plans denoted by FEM in figure 1.1, and they face the same search costs. Except by chance, they will tend to progress roughly in steps along the search curve and arrive, in equilibrium, at the same point on it, say E''. In such a case a merger motivated by search is unlikely to occur.

But when we consider firms with different existing activities, the initial knowledge sets differ in content, size and complexity. Consequently the accessible project sets will differ, e.g., due to dissimilar profit and growth prospects affecting the returns to reinvestment in the firms' respective industries. Moreover, the differences in the initial knowledge sets result in the firms facing different search environments and costs. Now let there be a firm A with relatively good accessible investments, denoted by FEM in figure 1.1, and another firm B with inferior accessible opportunities FP. It is obvious that both initially and in subsequent stages of the search process, A has knowledge of investment opportunities which is of value to B. But as long as the projects in question enter into A's currently-held optimal plan, and are fully reflected in the market price of A, B would have to pay more for the information than its present value (because of the premium and transaction costs of merger). However, if at any stage in the search process (including the initial state and also the state where A has reached equilibrium at, say E'', but B has not) there exists a project which attracts a zero weight in A's optimal investment plan but would shift B's inferior efficient investment frontier, then a differential valuation of the information will arise in the two firms. Provided the discrepancy is large enough to cover the costs of merger and provided also firm B could not discover the information more cheaply by internal search, the necessary conditions for search via merger are met.

Suppose, moreover, that firm A is also more advantageously placed for search than firm B, e.g., because its initial knowledge set is larger, or less disparate from the sets describing other investment opportunities offering high returns and/or low risk. It is now possible that at any stage, but especially if A has reached equilibrium at E'' while B is still searching, *further* search by A will not shift its own investment frontier, or cause it to revise its opinion of E'' as the maximum attainable risk/return combination, but would still produce results having these effects for B. In this case, again provided that the gain to B exceeds the costs (which now include merger costs and the cost of additional search based on firm A), a motive exists for B to acquire A not for the sake of information already held but as a way of improving its own search base, and this is possible because further search is apparently unprofitable to A.

These conclusions depend crucially on the fact that firms' search begins not *in vacuo* but from a fixed base determined by existing knowledge. As a result both search costs and the value of a given discovery can differ among firms. In everyday terms this assumes no more than that both the costs of learning and the benefits obtained depend on what is already known. The absence of a frictionless market for information as a commodity is a further necessary assumption.[1] However, the analysis does not require that firms behave in a

---

[1]   The imperfection of the market for information as a commodity has been stressed by Arrow (1962). The outcome is a non-optimal allocation of resources to »invention» under competition but this needs not, of course, imply non-existent information markets.

myopic or non-optimising fashion; or that there must be interfirm differences in expected maximum investment returns; or that the market value of the acquired firm is below its true present value. If any or all of these latter conditions were in fact met, the possibility of merger motivated as search would increase rather than decline.

3. Some Empirical Evidence

Firms resorting to merger in their search for investment opportunities will be experiencing difficulties in finding satisfactory projects. Since the better projects are most probably to be found where existing profitability is high, we should therefore observe less profitable firms acquiring relatively higher profit firms. For this to be possible the acquiring firm will generally need to be relatively large. However, since the firm's internal information system can be overwhelmed by size and diversity beyond some point, *very* small acquisitions may not be worthwhile because the opportunity costs of management time are too great to warrant application to very small, albeit promising activities. Hence we might expect that acquisitions have to reach some threshold size, which is presumably larger for large firms.

Existing evidence offers some support for these propositions. In particular, Weston and Mansinghka (1971) found that companies heavily involved in the conglomerate merger wave of the 1960's earned lower returns on capital than a random sample of industrials prior to the merger wave, and roughly the same returns after it. Analysing the characteristics of some 700 acquired firms over the period 1948-68, Boyle (1970) found that the acquired firms in conglomerate mergers had higher levels and growth of profits than in horizontal and vertical cases, and characterised the conglomerate merger process as the acquisition of strong and financially viable firms by larger corporations. Unfortunately for the present purpose, the relative profitability of the acquirers was not reported. On the other hand, Conn (1976) has recently reported no significant difference in the mean profitability of acquired and acquiring firms involved in 56 pure conglomerate mergers in the period 1960-69. But comparison of group means is not conclusive if there are two sorts of merger process simultaneously at work, one in which firms diversify by acquisition into more profitable areas, the other in which failing firms are absorbed by their more efficient competitors in the market for corporate control (Dewey, 1961, Manne, 1965). In this situation data on individual cases is required.

Data for a sample of 37 U.K. mergers in the period 1965-70, officially listed among a total of 50 diversifying cases, shows that in 14 cases (37.8%) the acquired firms earned significantly higher profit rates in the five years preceding the merger than the firms which acquired them, and were on average 10.8% more profitable.[1] In a subset of 15 unambiguously diversifying cases where the parties had no (roughly 3-digit) industry in common, 53.3% of the

---

[1]   The data source for this and for subsequent analyses of the U.K. sample was a data tape made available by Douglas Kuehn (see Kuehn, 1975).

acquired firms were earning more than their acquirers.

The U.K. data also shows a strong tendency for the acquired firms to be smaller, with only 7 exceptions overall of which 2 were in the subsample, in which the acquired firms were on average only 8.1% as large (in terms of assets) as the acquirers. To test for a possible threshold size for acquisition the 37 cases were divided into six classes according to the size of the acquiring firm, containing roughly equal numbers. The minimum acquisition size was then found for each. As a percentage of the class mean, the smallest acquisition fell very sharply, from nearly 50% in the smallest size class, but at an exponentially decreasing rate, apparently approaching an asymptote of between 1 and 2%. While it is clearly hazardous to draw firm conclusions, this asymptote value might be regarded as a reasonable minimum for the marginal activity of a firm bearing in mind prospects for its future growth, and that the average division size could be much larger.

The merger-as-search hypothesis is consistent with a number of other observed or discoverable aspects of diversification and mergers. First, since the motive is the acquisition of information which is embodied in the acquired firm's personnel and other resources, it is to be expected that the existing management of the acquired firm will be retained. And the tendency for acquired firms to be left to operate as autonomous divisions, often under the existing management, has been widely noted (e.g., Mueller, 1969). Secondly, the theory links the firm's search process closely to its investment planning, so that the frequency of mergers prompted as search should vary directly with the level of pressure to invest in the economy. Again, the correlation between merger intensity and the level of business activity seems firmly established (e.g., Nelson, 1959, Hannah, 1974). Thirdly, the merger search hypothesis implies that diversification will be purposeful rather than random, i.e., will display some underlying logic in terms of production technology, marketing, R + D and so on. And this has been noted in the observed pattern of diversification and diversifying merger (Reid, 1968, Narver, 1969, Gorecki, 1975). Fourthly, the search cost function on which the hypothesis hinges is such that the first investment opportunities to be considered will be those closest to existing activities. By definition, both horizontal and vertical mergers involve the firm more deeply in its existing activities of technically related areas, i.e. in »close» activities involving total or substantial overlap of the relevant information sets. Thus we should not find diversifying mergers being initiated by firms operating in unconcentrated markets, or where there are few forward and backward linkages, *cet par.* Similarly, reinvestment in existing activities is by definition the closest possible opportunity available, so that firms initiating the sort of merger and consideration should tend not to be operating in rapidly growing industries. These expectations are wholly consistent with the evidence of Gort (1962, 1969).

Two further, more specific predictions can be spelled out from the search hypothesis. One is that, since merger search dominates other search modes, if at all, only beyond some critical level of disparateness, diversification by merger rather than *de novo* expansion should increase with some (proxy) measure of disparateness. A direct test was attempted using data on product acquisitions and additions among pairs of industries and the product structure of manufacturing firms by industry as reproduced in Wood (1971). The dependent variable (Y) was simply the ratio of product acquisitions to total product additions for any given pair of industries, i.e., the proportion of diversification activity from industry i to industry j in which merger was involved. The independent variable (X) was defined as $(1-p)$ where p is an estimate of the proportion of firms active in industry i who were also active in j.[1] X was interpreted as a proxy for the disparateness of the industries, on the grounds that, insofar as firm's product structures evolve in a rational, cost-minimizing way, the disparateness of the activities involved will be revealed in a diversification matrix which shows the proportion of firms that have actually bridged the distance from a given industry to some other. A semi-logarithmic equation yielded a highly significant relationship of expected sign:

$$\log Y = -0.49 + 0.66\,X \qquad R^2 = .27$$
$$(t = 3.71) \qquad F = 13.79$$

although the result should be regarded as preliminary, in view of data limitations.

The second prediction is that M-form firms should be the first to initiate diversifying mergers *cet par*. Whereas the multi-divisional firm can readily absorb a newly acquired unit, the U-form firm must either reorganise along M-form lines or accomplish the more difficult task of integrating the new firm into the existing, functionally arranged hierarchy. The consequently lower transactions cost for the multidivisional firm implies a downward shift in the merger search-cost function in figure 1.3 and a point of intersection to the left of d'. Data on the organizational form of the acquiring company was available for all but one of the 37 U.K. conglomerate merger cases.[2] Twelve (33.3%) were pure M-form at the time of the merger; seven (19.4%) were transitional M-form (M'); and a further nine (25.0%) corrupted M-form ($\overline{M}$). Of the remainder five were holding companies (H-form) and two were unitary (U-form) firms.

Since it is the ability of the firm to add extra quasi-autonomous units which is presently at issue, a case may be made employing a broad definition of M-form, including M' and $\overline{M}$. And purely from an ease of expansion standpoint the H-firm may share the M-form's advantages to some degree. On this basis the predominance of the appropriate organizational form in the sample is overwhelming. In any event, the fact that there were only two U-form firms is striking.

The bulk of the existing evidence not so far considered consists of studies of conglomerate merger performance, many utilising the capital-asset-pricing model. These have mostly produced neutral or negative findings (Mueller, 1977). Of itself this neither contradicts nor supports the merger search hypothesis. A successful search-motivated merger will by definition improve

---

[1] The derivation was as follows. The original matrix gave the number of firms in each industry (n) and the number of products in the basic industry (p_0) and in each other industry ($p_i, i = 1,2,\ldots n$). Given that the number of firms active in the basic industry was by definition n the probable number of *firms* active in each other industry was estimated as (np_i/p_0).

[2] The classification by organizational form is due to Peter Steer (1973), who kindly extended his original sample at the author's request. The various firm types are distinguished by Williamson and Bhargava (1972).

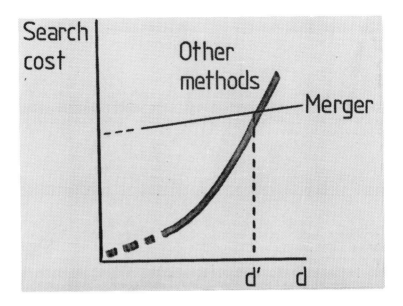

Figure 1.3

the profitability of the acquiring firm. But if initiated against a background of internally perceived, diminishing profit expectations, due to lack of investment openings, the improvement can be consistent either with a rise or decline in externally observed earnings, or with unchanged financial results. At the same time, the merger results in the acquired firm: information on existing and potential investment opportunities which does not improve its own prospects but is of value to the acquiring firm. As a number of merger studies have shown, for the acquiring firm the cumulative average residual (between *ex post* security returns and the estimated equilibrium returns predicted from the capital-asset-pricing model) is not greatly affected by merger, whereas for the acquired firm the residual rises sharply 9-12 months before the merger, when the news leaks out (Halpern, 1973, Mandelker, 1974, Ellert, 1976). While there are many possible explanations, this could reflect realisation of a unique, informational resource held by the acquired firm at the time of the merger.

4. Welfare and Policy Implications

A possible welfare gain may arise from the transfer of capital that is involved in search-motivated, diversifying mergers. While the same reallocations could eventually come about via the external markets, merger can foreshorten the transfer process. According to the hypothesis advanced earlier, search leading to merger follows recognition of declining investment opportunities in the initiating firm. Because of the asymmetric information held by firms and by the market, correction via the external market would take place only after the dwindling investment opportunities had fed through into reported profits. In view of the typical life-span of investment projects, and the relatively small impact of a deteriorating future on any one year's returns, this lag could be long. Hence, by removing the lag, search motivated mergers can contribute to the dynamic flexibility of the system.

The merger-as-search arguments also complement the affirmative case made out for conglomerates by Williamson, 1970, 1975), resisting on the claimed superiority over the external capital market of a system of capital transfer via miniaturized, internal capital markets in appropriately organized (M-form) diversified firms. Williamson's analysis treats the reallocation of funds within individual conglomerate firms whose boundaries are taken as given.[1] However, for a global optimum, capital transfer *across* as well as within corporate boundaries is important. Moreover the very factors which confer advantages on the M-form firm as an allocative instrument - superior access to information and reduced intervention costs - also give rise to a bias in favour of internal investment. Hence, if the boundaries of conglomerate undertakings were irrationally drawn, from a capital transfer point of view, or were inflexible once drawn, the overall allocative efficiency of the economy could diverge markedly from the global optimum, despite efficient funds-metering within sectors. But where mergers act as a form of corporate search for external investment opportunities, as presently mooted, they help mitigate the risk of such a state of only local sub-optimality. Moreover, to the extent that conglomerates are formed by mergers of this type, their boundaries will not be irrationally drawn from a capital transfer point of view.

On the other hand, the typical circumstances envisaged for mergers motivated as search involve the demise of viable firms as separate, independent entities. The theoretical arguments of section 2 show that information gain alone can be a sufficient motive for merger. Thus it cannot be relied upon that choice of external growth as a means of diversification is confined to circumstances in which there also exist potential size economies or other synergistic gains, or the acquired firms is failing (and hence its assets are undervalued by the market), or its growth is blocked by a discontinuity in the supply of finance, etc. In the absence of such circumstances all that happens is that the life cycle of one firm - typically already large and well established - is extended at the expense of another - typically younger and smaller. The short run effect is an increase in overall concentration, with attendant, incremental growth in the problem of maintaining the balance of economic and political power in society, against which must be set only the possible gain in the efficiency of capital transfer previously discussed. Moreover, in the longer term the balance of social gain and loss is more adverse in that, as Boyle (1970) has noted, it is the relatively young, profitable, small but growing concerns being acquired that might have risen to challenge the positions of large entrenched corporations which acquire them. Thus, insofar as it shows that the acquired

---

[1]   Williamson discusses the role of conglomerates as displacement agents, but sees the motivating gain in the potential for reorganizing acquired U-form along M-form lines.

firms in diversifying merger cases can be successful concerns, under no threat to their continued life and growth other than from takeover, the merger-search theory lends support to the view that conglomerate mergers can impair the long-run corporate competitive process.

At the practical policy level the analysis points towards the use of non-discretionary rules: non-intervention or an outright ban rather than case-by-case review. First, the principal welfare effects identified (the possible gain via capital transfer and loss of overall competition) arise at the systems level and depend not so much on the impact of individual mergers as on the cumulative effect of the merger process over time. Hence, they are not susceptible to evaluation in individual cases at firm level. Secondly, search-motivated mergers innocent of monopolistic intent could be hard to distinguish *ex ante* from other, more sinister cases. In particular, they may closely resemble mergers in which firms with dominant positions in existing markets, but of limited expected duration, diversify by acquisition with a view to cross-subsidising their new activities before their existing monopoly positions are finally eroded, and by eliminating competitors engineer new situations of market dominance to replace the old. It is true that differences in the structural and performance conditions of the two cases may exist, particularly with respect to the acquiring firm's market share and profitability, and the height of entry barriers and seller concentration levels in the acquired firm's industries. But even where this is so, the depth of analysis required to permit reliable inferences of motive and projections of future behaviour is unlikely to be possible in the limited time available to any review body.

The analysis also highlights some possible but otherwise unexpected consequences an outright merger prohibition might have. Precluding merger as a search option will divert some firms to the alternative, internal search, involving higher resource cost in circumstances where, for reasons outlined by the theory, merger search would otherwise be chosen. In addition, reducing the ease of exit from existing activities in this way would increase the incentive for firms to seek ways of reviving the fortunes of these activities. Thus a merger ban could lead to defensive strategies involving intensified advertising, product differentiation, lobbying for protection and so forth. While these effects would not in themselves necessarily make prohibition inappropriate, they should of course be weighed in the choice of overall merger policy.

5. Conclusions

Theoretical arguments have been presented which show that conglomerate mergers may occur as a form of corporate search. Moreover this is under assumptions which depart only slightly from those of received microtheory, mainly by recognising that knowledge of all production opportunities cannot be taken for granted and that information is not costless to acquire. The theory is consistent with a fairly wide range of known and demonstrable aspects of diversification and merger. On the basis of the evidence reviewed, it seems that a capital transfer mechanism involving merger does exist, in which large established firms can acquire firms which are smaller but more profitable than themselves, so enhancing their own investment potential and extending their corporate life-cycle. This mechanism is quite distinct from the one in which more efficient firms devour their less efficient competitors.

Search-motivated mergers can improve the flexibility of capital transfer within the economy, but involve the demise of viable firms as independent entities, impairing overall competition. Whilst this ambivalence superficially suggest a flexible policy approach would be desirable, other considerations point towards the use of non-discretionary rules. But overall merger policy must be framed with reference to all merger situations, of which search-motivated mergers may form only a subset. To aid the formulation of policy, and given the many alternative merger theories that exist, there is a pressing need for further empirical research to determine the proportion of merger activity that is accounted for by each.

6. References

Arrow, K.J., 1962
»Economic Welfare and the Allocation of Resources for Inventions.» In *The Rate and Direction of Inventive Activity,* NBER. Princeton, N.J.: Princeton University Press.

Arrow, K.J., 1975
»Vertical Integration and Communication.» *The Bell Journal of Economics,* Vol. 6, No. 1 (Spring) pp. 173-183.

Boyle, S.E., 1970
»Pre-Merger Growth and Profit Characteristics of Large Conglomerate Mergers in the United States 1948-68.» *St. John's Law Review,* Special edition 44 (Spring) pp. 152-170.

Conn, R.L., 1976
»The Failing Firm/Industry Doctrines in Conglomerate Mergers.» *Journal of Industrial Economics,* Vol. 24 (March) pp. 181-187.

Cyert, R.M., March,J.G., 1963
A Behavioral Theory of the Firm. Englewood Cliffs, N.J.: Prentice Hall.

Dewey, D., 1961
»Mergers and Cartels: Some Reservations about Policy.» *The American Economic Review,* Vol. 61, (May), pp. 255-262.

Ellert, J.D., 1976
»Mergers, Antitrust Law Enforcement and Stockholder Returns», *The Journal of Finance,* Vol. 31, No. 2, (May), pp. 715-732.

Fama, E.F., 1970
»Efficient Capital Markets: A Review of Theory and Empirical Work», *Journal of Finance,* Vol. 25, pp. 383-417.

Gorecki, P.K., 1975
»An Inter-Industry Analysis of Diversification in the U.K. Manufacturing Sector», *Journal of Industrial Economics,* Vol. 24, (December), pp. 131-146.

Gort, M., 1962
Diversification and Integration in American Industry. Princeton, N.J.: Princeton.

Gort, M., 1969
»An Economic Disturbance Theory of Mergers», *The Quarterly Journal of Economics,* Vol. 83, No. 4, (November), pp. 624-642.

Halpern, P.J., 1973
»Empirical Estimates of the Amount and Distribution of Gains to Companies in Mergers», *The Journal of Business,* Vol. 46, No. 3, (October), pp. 554-575.

Hannah, L., 1974
»Mergers in British Manufacturing Industry 1980-1918», *Oxford Economic Papers,* Vol. 26.

Jensen, M.C., 1972
»Capital Markets: Theory and Evidence», *The Bell Journal of Economics,* Vol. 3, No. 2, (Autumn), pp. 357-398.

Kuehn, D.A., 1975
Takeovers and the Theory of the Firm. London: McMillan.

Levy, H., and Sarnat, M., 1970
»Diversification, Portfolio Analysis and the Uneasy Case for Conglomerate Mergers», *Journal of Finance,* Vol. 25, (September), pp. 795-802.

Lintner, J., 1965
»Security Prices, Risk and Maximal Gains from Diversification», *The Journal of Finance,* Vol. 20, No. 4, (December), pp. 587-616.

Lintner, J., 1965
»The Valuation of Risky Assets and the Selection of Risky Investments in Stock Portfolios and Capital Budgets», *The Review of Economics and Statistics,* Vol. 47, No. 1, (February), pp. 13-37.

Mandelker, G., 1974
»Risk and Return: The Case of Merging Firms», *The Journal of Financial Economics,* Vol. 1, No. 4, (December), pp. 303-335.

Manne, H.G., 1965
»Mergers and the Market for Corporate Control», *The Journal of Political Economy,* Vol. 73, No. 1, pp. 110-120.

Mueller, D.C., 1969
»A Theory of Conglomerate Mergers», *The Quarterly Journal of Economics,* Vol. 83, No. 4, pp. 643-659.

Mueller, D.C., 1977
»The Effects of Conglomerate Mergers: A Survey of the Empirical Evidence», *Journal of Banking and Finance,* Vol. I, December: 315-347.

Narver, J.C., 1969
Conglomerate Mergers and Market Competition, Berkeley: University of California Press.

Nelson, R.L., 1959
Merger Movements in American Industry 1865-1956, Princeton University Press.

Penrose, E.T., 1963
The Theory of the Growth of the Firm. Oxford: Basil Blackwell.

Radner, R., 1975
»A Behavioural Model of Cost Reduction», *The Bell Journal of Economics,* Vol. 6, No. 1, (Spring), pp. 196-215.

Reid, S.R., 1968
Mergers, Managers and the Economy, New York, McGraw-Hill.

Rothschild, M., 1973
»Models of Market Organization with Imperfect Information», *The Journal of Political Economy,* Vol. 81, No. 6 (Nov.-Dec.), pp. 1283-1308.

Sharpe, W.F., 1964
»Capital Asset Prices: A Theory of Market Equilibrium under Conditions of Risk», *The Journal of Finance,* Vol. 19, No. 3, pp. 425-442.

Simon, H.A., 1955
»A Behavioral Model of Rational Choice», *The Quarterly Journal of Economics,* Vol. 69, (February), pp. 99-118.

Steer, P., 1973
»An Investigation into the Managerial Organization of Firms», unpublished M.A. thesis, Coventry: University of Warwick.

Steiner, P.O., 1975
Mergers: Motives, Effects, Policies. Ann Arbor: University of Michigan Press.

Weston, J.F., and Mansinghka, S.K., 1971
»Tests of the Efficiency Performance of Conglomerate Firms»,
The Journal of Finance, Vol. 26, No. 4, pp. 919-936.

Williamson, O.E., 1970
Corporate Control and Business Behaviour. Englewood Cliffs,
N.J.: Prentice Hall.

Williamson, O.E., 1975
Markets and Hierarchies: Analysis and Antitrust Implications.
New York, N.Y.: Free Press.

Williamson, 0.E., and Bhargava, N., 1972
»Assessing and Classifying the Internal Structure and Control
Apparatus of the Modern Corporation», in K.G. Cowling (ed.)
Market Structure and Corporate Behaviour, Gray-Mills, London.

Wood, A., 1971
»Diversification, Merger and Research Expenditures: A Review
of Empirical Studies», in Marris, R., and Wood, A. (eds.) *The
Corporate Economy,* Harvard University Press, Boston.

2. MYTH, ISSUE AND IDEOLOGY - REORGANIZATION BY MERGER AMONG FARMER CO-OPERATIVES IN SWEDEN

Harry Nyström and Carl Utterström
Swedish Agricultural University
Department of Economics and Statistics
Uppsala, Sweden

1. Background and Purpose

Most studies of mergers emphasize economic factors connected with their causes and effects. The present study, however, utilizes a much wider framework and includes both techno-economic and socio-political factors in analysing mergers among farmer co-operatives in Sweden.

Since the 1930's, farmer co-operatives have been of dominating importance in the food industry and in the farm supply sector of this country. For instance, 100% of the Swedish dairy industry is currently co-operatively owned by the farmers themselves, and 60% of the farm supply business is under their control.

An important element in the changing structure of the farm co-operative sector has been mergers between independent regional co-operative societies. This was particularly the case during the 1960's when a number of very large co-operatives were established through mergers. As a result, the number of independent co-operatives in the three main areas - meat, dairy products, and farm supplies - diminished from 316 in 1960 to 66 in 1973. The majority of the mergers took place in the dairy industry (72%).

In Sweden most farmers are organized in local or regional co-operatives, joined together in national co-operative federations. One example is the Swedish Dairy Association (SMR), whose main purpose is to represent its member organizations in farm price negotiations with government. It also gives technical assistance and acts as a consultant to its member organizations in questions concerning production and administration. Other national co-operative federations perform similar functions for their member organizations. All national co-operative federations belong, in turn, to the Federation of Swedish Farmers (LRF), which was the result of a merger between the National Farmers' Union (RLF) and the Federation of Swedish Farmers' Associations (SL) in 1970.

The Swedish agricultural policy in the 1960's emphasized efficient production and cost reduction (Swedborg, 1968). As a result, a larger number of

Table 2.1   Number of mergers between farmer co-operatives 1960-1975. (Dairy, meat marketing and farm supply co-operatives)

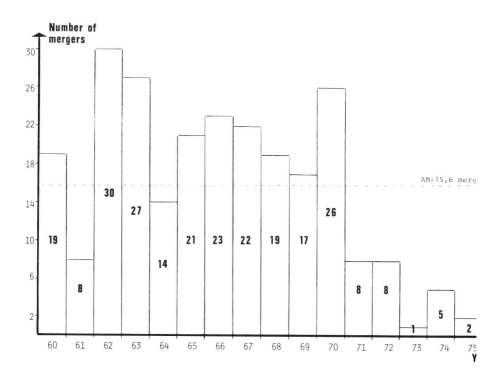

mostly small farmers went out of business, and agricultural production shifted towards areas suited for large scale production. This led, for instance, to a decrease in the total supply and an anticipated shortage of milk and dairy products, and created problems for the dairy co-operatives in co-ordinating production and distribution. At the same time, farmers were greatly concerned about existing low milk prices and pessimistic about the future.

In the early 1970's, the political and economic situation affecting farmers and the co-operative movement changed. The trend towards centralization and efficiency based on large scale economics turned into a greater emphasis on the need for smaller units and decentralized influence on decision-making. At the same time, prices of agricultural products reached more satisfactory levels, and farmers became more optimistic about the future. (Statens Offentliga Utredningar, 17, 1977). Mergers were no longer viewed as necessary or desirable steps in reorganizing the structure of the co-operative industry.

2. Research Methodology

As we have noted above, mergers have been a frequent and important element in the reorganization of farmer co-operatives in Sweden, which has taken place during the last decades. These mergers are the result of important social, economic and technical changes which have greatly influenced the future of the companies and the performance of the industry.

In order to analyse this development, we found it useful to employ a combined economic and sociological framework. To make such an analysis possible, we need to consider changes over time in technical and economic factors, and in prevailing orders and values, at both societal and organizational levels.

It is our belief that a purely economic or sociological type of analysis is inadequate for understanding this tendency. Instead, an approach is needed which combines the two perspectives and emphasizes both the relative independence of and the interaction between the two (Weber, 1947).

Since understanding merging situations demands complex consideration of multiple factors, we found it necessary to use many different sources of data (Denzin, 1970). Our main data were collected by intensive personal interviews with the leading decision-makers most actively involved in the mergers. This was supplemented by secondary data from company documents, periodicals and other publications.

The merger cases investigated were selected to be as representative as possible of the types of mergers carried out among Swedish farmer co-operatives since 1960. A preliminary extensive study of the total range of mergers provided a basis for starting empirical studies. A number of variables, which then appeared to be significant aspects of the merger situation, were used as the basis for choosing the cases. By maximizing the differences between the cases along these dimensions, (Glaser and Strauss, 1967) an attempt was made to provide broad coverage of the problem area and to investigate the relative importance of these variables in different merger situations. The first case was selected because it was an example of a merger between two large regional dairy co-operative companies, together covering the most important markets in Sweden. As we have noted above, the most frequent mergers have taken place in the dairy industry, making it natural to start with this industry.

The second case was selected after the results of the first case had been analysed.

In contrast to the first case involving only two co-operatives, both belonging to the dairy industry, the second case is more complex, and involves a large number of co-operatives of various sizes and active in different lines of business.

The result of the merger in the second case was thus a large diversified company, while in the first case the result was a large company with basically a single line of business.

The third case was selected to further clarify and substantiate our understanding of the merger processes. It took place between four small and local dairy co-operatives and at an earlier point in time than the other two. The complexity of the merger appears in this instance to have been greater than in the first case, but less than in the second.

For instance, the number of companies taking part in the merger was four, compared to two in the first case and twelve in the second. The decision-making process in the third case also lasted longer and involved more conflicts than in the first merger case, but less so than in the second.

The interviews with leading decision-makers who had been active and influential in the merger processes were carried out in 1977-1978. The interviews, some of which were taped, lasted from 1-5 hours each, and were carried out with one respondent at a time. Both authors, one of which has a background in agricultural economics and the other in business administration, took part in each interview. This led to a broader coverage of the problem area, and was also advantageous in accurately recording the interviews and interpreting and checking the data.

25 individuals were interviewed, some more than once (to provide additional information), or, as in four instances, because the respondent was involved in more than one of the merger situations. The first person interviewed in each case was chosen because his position at the time of the merger indicated that he played a leading role. In most instances this person was the Managing Director. The remaining respondents were selected on the basis of accumulated information from the interviews, which indicated that they had also played an important role in the merger. In each case, when we were convinced that we had included in our sample all persons who could significantly contribute to our knowledge of the merger process, no further interviews were carried out.

Since the purpose of the interviews was to generate new knowledge, rather than test propositions, no structural questionnaire was used. Instead, the discussion was guided by our evolving understanding of the merger situations and by the reactions of the respondents to our questions.

3. Case Studies

In this section we will describe the three merger cases as a basis for our interpretation and analysis in the next section. The cases are presented in the order in which the interviews were carried out, which is not the same as the order in which the mergers took place.

3.1 Case one: The Milk Co-operative Arla

The »Farmers' Milk Co-operative» (LMC) was formed in 1934 by joining two dairy co-operatives in the Gothenburg area. In Western Sweden a Regional Federation of Dairy Co-operatives (VMC) was created at about the same time, and LMC became one of the members. In the 1960's almost all the member co-operatives in VMC merged with LMC to become Sweden's second largest dairy co-operative. This merger process was completed in 1967.

The »Milk Co-operative» (MC) was founded in 1915 to supply the Stockholm market. It expanded by acquiring other companies distributing milk products in the Stockholm area, and became Sweden's largest dairy co-operative by far. During the sixties MC started to expand outside the Stockholm area and acquired 43 local companies. In February 1971 a merger between LMC and MC took place. In the early 1970's a number of other regional co-operatives merged with MC and the new organization (Arla) dominated the Swedish dairy industry, holding a 60% share of the market.

In order to understand these mergers, we need to discuss the role of national co-operative federations, particularly the Swedish Dairy Association (SMR). SMR appointed a planning committee in 1959 to study the future structure of the dairy industry in Sweden. At this time the co-operatives were faced with serious problems. Milk supply was decreasing due to low prices to farmers, while at the same time co-operatives experienced distribution problems in supplying the growing urban areas with milk and dairy products.

After thoroughly analysing the situation, the Planning Committee suggested a new industry structure in 1965, which would be comprised of 5 regional companies instead of the existing 174.

In May 1966 this proposal was accepted by the Annual Meeting of SMR. A number of mergers subsequently took place between Dairy Co-operatives all over Sweden. The Planning Committee continued its work and presented an outline for the future marketing organization of the five Regional Companies. In this process the idea of a single marketing organization for the five companies was suggested. Continued discussions and analysis of this alternative led to a reevaluation of the original idea of having five regional companies. Instead, the idea of *one, countrywide* company for processing and distributing dairy products in Sweden emerged.

The new, one-company idea was presented at a special meeting with leading representatives of the industry, and was unanimously agreed upon as a guideline for future policy. A recommendation to this effect was put forward at a general meeting of SMR in 1970 and was accepted by a majority of the delegates. This made possible more total mergers involving regional companies. Some mergers took place, such as the one between LMC and MC. In promoting the one-company idea, SMR played an important role. When interviewed, a leading representative for SMR said:

»I was made responsible by the Annual Meeting and the board for carrying out the one-company idea, and I did not hesitate in doing so... the sole motive for the LMC-MC merger was to carry out the one-company idea, nothing else. No strong opposition was voiced against the merger proposition, either among the members or among their elected representatives. At the Annual Meeting of LMC one single representative expressed some reservation. He felt very much alone. The merger question was too big for the members. It was dead silent. The question had been settled at the national level and nobody in Gothenburg could do anything about it.»

Leading representatives for MC and LMC strongly supported the one-company idea, and actively worked for a merger between the two companies.

In October 1970 the boards of both MC and LMC held a joint meeting and decided to go ahead with the merger. However, according to LMC's General Manager, »... no specific economic and technical analysis of the consequences of the merger were carried out.» The other participants in the interview were in agreement with his judgement.

The details for the merger were quickly agreed upon. A proposal was put forward to the members and discussed at member meetings in early 1971, and in February of that year the General Meeting of the elected representatives of LMC voted unanimously to accept the merger proposal. Since MC's Board of Directors had been in favour of it all along, the merger then took place in September 1971.

3.2 Case two: The Mixed Merger, NNP

Nedre Norrlands Producentförening is the result of a merger between six small co-operatives, three of which were dairy co-operatives, one a co-operative meat packing firm, one a farm supply co-operative and one a combined dairy and farm supply co-operative. The actual planning and analysis phase of the merger process was extensive, covering a period of more than four years from September 1965 to January 1, 1970, at which time the NNP merger was completed. At the beginning, twelve co-operatives were involved in the merger discussions, but only six took part in the final negotiations.

Of the three dairy co-operatives, Jämtlands Läns Mejeriförening was the largest, with a well developed distribution system. It had also been active in developing and marketing new products, and in entering new areas, such as baking and selling bread. The other two co-operatives were much smaller and concentrated more on traditional dairy production.

The meat packing firm and the farm supply co-operative taking part in the merger were active in the same geographical area as Jämtlands Läns Mejeriförening. They were both traditionally oriented farmer co-operatives, working along relatively narrow and established lines of business. Sundsvalls Mjölkcentral, the sixth company taking part in the merger, was itself the result of an earlier merger in the 1940's between a dairy co-operative and a farm supply co-operative.

In the case of the NNP merger, the resulting new company was thus much less homogeneous than in the Arla case, covering the whole range of dairy and meat products and farm supplies.

From a market point of view NNP is therefore much less dominant in its total area of operation than Arla, since there is greater competition in meat packing and farm supplies than in the dairy industry. NNP is actually the only case of a truly »mixed farm co-operative» in Sweden - that is, of a multipurpose type of co-operative working in radically different product areas.

The *idea* of a mixed company, however, has a long historical background in the co-operative movement, particularly as an alternative for companies working in geographically dispersed areas, such as Northern Sweden. In Jämtland, for instance, the mixed company idea was introduced at a Farmers' Union Meeting in the late 1940's. In Sundsvall, as we have noted above, the idea was even realized to some extent in the merger between a dairy and a farm supply co-operative in 1948.

The general pessimism around 1965 among farmers in Sweden was particularly strong in Northern Sweden, because of the naturally prevailing marginal farming conditions. Representatives for twelve farm co-operatives therefore met in 1965 to discuss the future of farming in the area.

In this connection an outside consultant was brought in to explore the implications of different regional organization structures for the co-operatives. The two main alternatives were to create one large regional co-operative in each product area or to form mixed co-operatives serving more limited geographical areas. In 1965 a report on the economic consequences of the two main alternatives was presented by the consultants to the board members of the twelve co-operatives, and was then discussed at member meetings. During this year a heated debate took place between different fractions with opposing viewpoints.

In December 1965, six of the co-operatives decided that they did not want to continue the negotiations for a possible merger. The other six favoured a merger and went on to discuss the details. The final proposal was presented to the members in 1969 and, despite some opposition, was accepted. The new company, NNP, began operation on January 1st, 1970.

3.3 Case three: Värmlands Mejerier, A Merger of Four Local Dairy Co-operatives

In the Swedish province of Värmland, four local co-operatives were joined together in 1965 to form Värmlandsmejerier. The largest of these co-operatives was Karlstadsortens Mejeriförening, which through earlier mergers in the 1940's had grown to become the largest dairy co-operative in the area. The other co-operatives in Värmland viewed the growth of Karlstadsorten as a threat, and a number of smaller mergers took place in the 1950's to try to maintain the economic independence of the other co-operatives in Värmland. These mergers led to a regional structure in Värmland of four dairy co-operatives, which later merged to become Värmlandsmejerier.

These four dairy co-operatives were all members of a regional dairy federation, Värmlands Mejeriförbund. At the annual meeting of this federation in 1959, a committee was appointed to study the economic consequences of a merger between the four co-operatives. This led to a recommendation, which was accepted by the Federation, that closer co-operation between the co-operatives should be initiated.

However, the major problems facing the co-operatives could not be solved by this type of co-operation between independent firms. A new investigation of the consequences of a regional merger was therefore initiated in 1965. This study indicated that substantial economic savings would result from a merger, due mainly to the fact that three dairy plants out of eight could then be closed down without restricting production.

The merger proposal was presented at member meetings of the four co-operatives in the fall of 1966. In three of the co-operatives there was little member opposition, while in the fourth it was more difficult to gain acceptance. The merger decision then became final, and Värmlandsmejerier was established as a company on January 1st, 1967.

4. Interpretation and Analysis

In this section we will present an interpretation and analysis of our data. To begin with, an overall framework will be developed which emphasized the techno-economic and socio-political factors described in the introduction. By employing collective and individual concepts of social order, such as myths, organizing visions and ideologies, we will then try to combine the different perspectives in an attempt to understand the merger decision processes.

4.1 Techno-Economic and Socio-Political Changes in the Environment of the Farmer Co-operatives

Central to our overall explanatory framework is the development of two basic dimensions over time. The first, the techno-economic dimension, deals with supply and demand, and the mechanisms for producing and distributing the products involved. The second, the socio-political dimension, has to do with the underlying rationale and the social justifications for choosing different courses of action (Figure 2.1).

We will regard these two dimensions as largely independent processes with different determining factors. From time to time, however, there are points of contact which offer possibilities for action affecting both the techno-economic performance and the socio-political basis for decision making. On such occasions, if leading actors are present who interpret the situation correctly (Nyström, 1970) and who want to assume the role of change agents, decisions may be made which radically alter both the social order and economic functioning of the system.

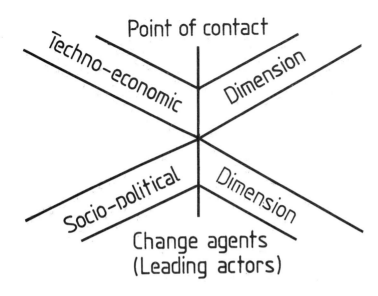

Figure 2.1   General framework.

In the merger situations we are interested in, a number of techno-economic changes took place in the environments of the co-operative firms. As we have noted in the introduction, for example, profitability in the farm sector was low during the 1960's and led to a decrease in the supply of farm products as well as to increasing pessimism among farmers. At the same time, dominant political values in Swedish society and the co-operative ideology in the farming community emphasized centralization as a desirable feature in economic policy. These developments brought forward the issue of mergers as a desirable means of reorganizing the structure of farm co-operatives in Sweden.

In other words, the techno-economic and socio-political dimensions found a point of contact in the merger issues, and in both areas a need for change was perceived by the leading actors and by influential bodies of decision makers.

After 1970, however, radical changes took place in the Swedish farm economy, profitability went up, and farmers became more optimistic. Independent of this trend, there was also a change in societal values in Sweden, favouring smaller units and decentralized decision making. Changes thus took place in both the techno-economic and socio-political dimensions which virtually excluded mergers from consideration. There was no longer any point of contact between the two dimensions, and in fact, very few mergers have taken place since then among farm co-operatives in Sweden.

In all instances it is necessary to consider both the techno-economic and socio-political factors in order to understand why a merger took place. The relative importance of these two main dimensions in creating a favourable merger situation varies, however, from case to case.

In the case of Arla, the socio-political dimension was of major importance, and the economic and technical consequences of a merger for the companies concerned was given very little attention. No special study of these consequences was carried out as a basis for the decision.

On the other hand, the preliminary merger discussions were based on detailed economic calculations in the NNP case. Later in the process, however, socio-political considerations were of major importance in determining the outcome. For instance, after six co-operatives had decided not to participate, the final merger situation was not studied at all with regard to its economic consequences. Instead, the idea of a mixed regional merger in itself was sufficient to achieve agreement on the merger issue. In the words of one of the respondents:

> »... the idea of a mixed merger became a religion - a belief. Some persons thought that all problems would be solved in such a co-operative.»

In the case of Värmlandsmejerier, the merger decision was almost completely based on techno-economic considerations. Economic investigations which clearly indicated the desirability of a merger were carried out, and the results of these investigations were generally accepted as a sufficient basis for the merger decision.

4.2 Myth, Issue and Ideology in the Decision Making Process

To understand how and why these merger decisions were taken, we will now present a model of decision making which deals with collective and individual concepts of social order. This model will then be applied to our empirical data.

In our model of decision making, *organizational visions* are defined as images of preferred future states, which are suggested by individuals or small ad hoc-groups in search of support from leading actors in the organization.

Ideologies are organizational visions which have found support in established interest groups.

Issues are solutions to problems in search of an ideology.

Myths are viewed as enabling conditions for ideologies. They are characterized by being comprehensive in their objects, inclusive in their subjects, decentralized in their control, unconsciously held, and ambiguous in their meaning (Dale and Spencer, 1976).

In our analysis, the function of a myth is to render possible agreement between individuals whose various perceptions and evaluations of reality on complex issues create conflicting points of view. Such agreement is made possible through the ambiguity of meaning, which permits different interpretations of an issue, yet at the same time provides a common sense of direction. This pervasive nature of myths makes them an important element in our model of decision making, since they enable the development and acceptance of ideologies.

Decisions, then, may be viewed as the meeting between issues and ideology, as mediated by the *leading actors* and accepted by the governing bodies of the organizations. These leading actors are thus change agents, which play various roles in linking together the techno-economic and political dimensions.

Our approach to decision making thus differs from the usual, rational model of organizational decision making, which concentrates on organizational means and objectives, and views ideologies as not constraining, externally given and constant over time. Instead it resembles the type of organizational decision making discussed by March and Olsen (1976).

We will now use the explanatory framework to analyze our three merger cases. In the Arla case the *five regional companies idea* and the *one company idea* had been competing for support for many years. The first vision to be accepted as an ideology was the *five regional companies idea,* which in effect, prevented an early merger between LMC and MC. Instead, a number of smaller mergers took place as a means towards realizing this ideology. However, while the five regional companies idea was being implemented, there were growing doubts about its desirability.

In 1970 the Annual Meeting of SMR changed its position and advocated the one company idea with the support of both MC and LMC. This competing vision had thus been accepted as the prevailing ideology instead of the five regional companies idea. In contrast to the five regional companies idea, the one company idea was compatible with a merger between LMC and MC, and this resulted in the merger decision.

In NNP's case, the organizational vision of forming regional co-operatives also occurred at an early stage of the decision making process. In contrast to Arla, however, three different lines of business were involved. In the dairy co-operatives, the five regional companies idea was an early organizational vision, which in this case competed with the mixed company idea. In the meat packing and farm supply co-operatives we also find the organizational vision of forming regional companies competing with the mixed company idea, but not necessarily involving five regional companies.

In the Arla case the same organizational vision (the one-company idea) became firmly established as an ideology in both companies involved in the merger discussions. In the NNP case, however, neither of the main organizational visions achieved dominant support in the governing bodies of all the companies discussing a merger.

The mixed company idea was accepted by six companies as the ideological basis for the resulting merger. The other six companies could not accept this organizational vision and, in spite of the fact that investigations had indicated that such a merger would be economically advantageous, dropped out of the discussions.

45

In the case of Värmlandsmejerier, the organizational vision of creating one regional dairy co-operative in Värmland had existed since the 1940's, but had never gained support from leading decision makers. However, strong ideological support was not necessary to achieve a merger, since no competing organizational visions were introduced during the discussions. Instead, the techno-economic reasons for a merger were so strong and generally accepted that, in the absence of ideological opposition, they alone were sufficient motivation for a decision in favour of a merger.

In all the merger cases a prevailing myth facilitated the ideology formation process by making certain that organizational visions were acceptable to both professional management in the co-operative and to member farmers. According to this myth, which was constantly reflected in the co-operative press and their educational programs, it is possible to combine economic efficiency with member influence and control in co-operative enterprises, regardless of size. In other words, the myth maintains that there is no basic conflict between traditional business management and co-operative ideology in managing business firms.

What remains to be discussed is the active part played by the change agents (the leading actors) in the decision process. These change agents are needed to mediate between issues and ideologies, and they play various roles in the linkage of the techno-economic and political dimensions (Merton, 1957). These roles, of course, are idealizations of actual behaviour. In reality all roles will be mixed, and several people may carry out the same role in various combinations. However, we will try to identify the main roles played by different persons in the merger.

To begin with, there is a need to identify and evaluate problems in the techno-economic environment. This is usually regarded as the main task of management (Simon, 1960). For important issues, such as the question of mergers, the General Manager is a likely candidate for this role. We will call this role *problem identification and evaluation.*

A second role concerns the *development of organizational visions,* i.e., alternatives for the future. This role may be carried out by many different individuals, within or outside of the organization, which makes it difficult to associate the role with specific official responsibilities in the oganization structure. Nevertheless, it is an important role, especially for the type of organization we are interested in, in which ideology is an important determinant of many decisions.

The third role is more directly concerned with ideology. It involves choosing among different, often competing, organizational visions, expressing these visions more clearly, and working for their general acceptance in the organization. This role we will call *establishing ideology.*

The final role in our organizational analysis deals with recognizing points of contact between the techno-economic and political dimensions of organizational change, and joining together issues and ideology - in other words, the *co-ordination of issues and ideology.*

From the interview data, it appears that the role of problem identification and evaluation in the Arla Merger was performed to a large extent by the Managing Director of LMC. He said that at a very early stage he raised the merger issue as a possible solution to LMC's problems. This was quite natural for him in his capacity as top manager of the company, most drastically affected by the Arla merger. His previous experience with mergers in other dairy co-operatives, where he was also Managing Director, must have sensitized him to this type o problem.

In the NNP case, the role of problem identification and evaluation was played by several different executives in the companies involved. At the outset, the Managing Director of the largest company played an important part by raising the merger issue. Later in the merger decision process, the Managing Directors of the other companies also came to view the merger as a solution to company problems, and took active part in the evaluation process.

In the case of Värmlandsmejerier, the head of the Organization Department at SMR was most influential in identifying and evaluating the problems of the four dairy co-operatives in Värmland, which later merged and formed Värmlandsmejerier.

The role of developing organizational visions is much more difficult to pinpoint. The clearest instance of role differentiation is found in the NNP case. In the 1940's the organizational vision of a mixed co-operative was proposed by the Managing Director of the largest company and by the Chairman of the Board in one of the other companies taking part in the merger. This was also the case in the formation of Värmlandsmejerier, in which the organizational vision, which later became the ideological basis for the merger,' was introduced during the 1940's by the Managing Director of one of the dairy co-operatives in Värmland. In the Arla case, however, it is more difficult to identify specific individuals playing the major role in the development of organizational visions. In this case, the one-company idea was first mentioned as an ideological alternative in a report by a planning committee appointed by SMR to study the future of the Dairy Industry in Sweden.

The most clear instance of role differentiation in establishing ideology is again in the NNP case. Here the Chairman of the Board of the second largest co-operative was very active in this capacity during the merger discussions. In the Arla case, the Managing Director of MC played a leading part in formulating the one-company idea, while the leaders of SMR worked most actively for its general acceptance. As noted above, there was no clear ideological basis for the merger decision in the case of Värmlandsmejerier, and therefore this role did not become influential.

The final role of co-ordinating issues and ideology is again of interest only in the Arla and NNP-cases, where ideology was of major importance for the merger decisions.

In the Arla case, the Managing Director, whom we have identified above as playing the major role of problem identification and evaluation, also appears to have been most influential in co-ordinating issues and ideologies. In the NNP case, the Chairman of the Board of the second largest co-operative, to whom we earlier attributed the role of ideology establisher, was also most influential in co-ordinating issues and ideologies.

5. Conclusion

Our analysis of the three merger cases strongly suggests that it is necessary to use a broad and varied framework in order to understand the complexity and uniqueness of individual merger situations. If we instead try to use a more general type of analysis focusing on one explanatory factor, we run the risk of overlooking what is most important in a specific instance. In the Arla case it is quite clear that techno-economic reasons are inadequate to explain the merger decision. It is also necessary to consider socio-political factors, such as the need for establishing ideology in an organization and the role of leading actors. We have argued that these were the main explanatory variables in the Arla case.

The case of Värmlandsmejerier, however, decisively shows that in some instances it is extremely important for proponents of a merger to be able to justify it economically. Finally, in the NNP merger, both techno-economic and socio-political factors were highly important in determining the decision, and it is difficult to attribute a dominant influence to either one.

6. References

Dale, A. and Spencer, L., 1976
    Sentiments, Norms, Ideologies and Myths: Their Relation to the Resolution of Issues in a State Theatre Company. Working Paper. Brussels: European Institute for Advanced Studies in Management.

Danielsson, C., 1974
    Studier i företags tillväxtprocess, Linköping.

Denzin, N., 1970
    The Research Act. Chicago.

Glaser, R. and Strauss, A., 1967
    The Discovery of Grounded Theory: Strategies for Qualitative Research, Chicago.

March, J.G. and Olsen, J., 1976
    Ambiguity and Choice in Organizations. Oslo.

Merton, R.K., 1957 *Social Theory and Economic Organization,* New York.

Normann, R., 1976
    Creative Management, London.

Nyström, H., 1974
»Uncertainty, information and organizational decision making. A cognitive approach.» *Swedish Journal of Economics,* Vol. 76.

Simon, H., 1960
The New Science of Management Decisions, New York.

Stymne, B., 1970
Values and Processes, Stockholm.

Swedborg, E., 1968
Jordbrukspolitiken 1967. Bakgrund, riktlinjer, tillämpning, Stockholm.

Weber, M., 1947
The Theory of Social and Economic Organization, New York.

Statens Offentliga Utredningar (SOU), 1977:17
Översyn av jordbrukspolitiken. Betänkande av 1972 års jordbruksutredning, Stockholm.

3. ENVIRONMENTAL UNCERTAINTY AS DETERMINING MERGER ACTIVITY

Menachem Brenner and Zur Shapira
School of Business Administration
Hebrew University
Jerusalem, Israel

1. Introduction

Based upon economic considerations of profit maximization and on organizational conceptualization of uncertainty avoidance, a merger is defined as a strategy whose objective is to minimize uncertainty subject to a given level of expected profits. Data on vertical mergers were analyzed from several aspects including time series trends and risk and return characteristics of firms engaged in mergers. The analyses suggest that vertical mergers can be described as a measure to reduce the uncertainty embedded in a company's relationship with both its suppliers and customers. The normative theory of the firm has undergone many changes since its basic »ought to» maximize profits was established. The owner-managed firm has turned into a managers-managed firm and the objective of utility maximization has become the desired norm. The managers of the modern corporation, the owners' agents, ought to make decisions that will lead to maximization of the utility of the owners. Economic theorists have simply replaced the profit maximization objective by the utility maximization objective, where utility is usually defined over two parameters that characterize the future uncertain profits (e.g., expected profits and their variability).

Behavioural economists, however, claim that actual behaviour of corporate managers does not coincide with owners utility maximization. Some (e.g., Williamson, 1970) have tried to describe the motives that underly the many decisions taken by the corporate managers by some constrained maximization of the manager's utility. The constraints are usually placed to satisfy the owners and the utility function is defined over pecuniary and non-pecuniary compensations.

Organizational theorists (see, e.g., March & Simon, 1958; Cyert & March, 1963) have carried this argumentation even further by suggesting that other parties such as employees, suppliers, customers and governmental agencies can affect the objectives of the firm. In contrast to the principle of maximization, they have proposed the principle of satisfying (cf. Simon, 1955) as more accurately describing the ways in which organizational decisions and goals are set.

Organizational theorists maintain that environmental uncertainty is a major factor in determining firm strategy. Cyert and March argued that organizations deliberately attempt to avoid uncertainty: »Our studies indicate quite a different strategy.... Organizations avoid uncertainty.... they avoid the requirement that they anticipate future reactions of other parts of their environment by arranging a negotiated environment» (1963, p. 119). Hence, according to Cyert and March not only do organizational objectives differ from profit maximization due to the satisfying principle. They even suggested that organizational decision making is based on this environmental uncertainty rather than on profit maximization. This idea, which is one of the cornerstones of modern organizational theory, was further developed by other organizational theorists (see, e.g., Thompson, 1967; Weick, 1969, 1979).

It is usually argued that the organization's decision makers (e.g., managers) would tend to undertake less risky decisions than the owners would, since they cannot diversify their risks in the manner in which the owners do. This, however, does not mean that they only make riskless decisions, since this may cause elimination of all possible profits. Obviously, it is assumed that the corporation would like to maintain its productive activities and therefore must maintain some level of risk. However, the organization must obey some constraints placed by outside parties. For example, the dominant constraint placed on a large non-regulated corporation is by the owners, who require a minimum level of realized profits. We can therefore restate the uncertainty avoidance motive as follows:

»Minimize uncertainty subject to a given level of expected profits.»

Once achieved, this combination of risk and expected profits will usually differ from the combination dictated solely by the owners utility function. It will usually contain a lower expected profit and a lower level of risk. Initially the corporation may be at a higher level of expected profit and risk, or at the given level of expected profit but at a higher level of risk. While in the first case the corporation will make decisions that affect both the expected profit and risk, in the second case the decisions made will be those that only reduce risk.

2. The Merger Decision: A Theoretical Discussion

An infrequent but major decision made by organizations, namely the decision to acquire another corporation, will be analyzed here in the framework of uncertainty reduction.

At this point we should distinguish among the different types of mergers: horizontal, vertical, and conglomerate. Industrial economists have maintained that monopoly power and economies of scale were the reasons behind horizontal mergers, and transaction costs savings was the main factor in vertical mergers. They regard diversification as the motive behind conglomerate mergers, although Mueller (1969) has proposed the familiar growth motive as the main determinant for conglomerate mergers. However, theoretical arguments and empirical evidence (see, e.g., Scherer, 1970) have challenged these classical explanations. As Scherer stated, for example,

»... the desire to build monopoly or oligopoly power has diminished in importance as a motive for merger.» (1970, p. 116).

The proposed reductions in costs due to vertical integration are doubtful (see, e.g., Williamson, 1975) for large corporations where the transactions cost savings may be offset by loss of control. Many economists also consider the explanation of a diversification motive being behind conglomerate merger as nonsensible, since stockholders can diversify themselves.

The motive of uncertainty avoidance, as stated by Cyert and March (1963), plays a major role in recent analyses of merger activity. Scherer (1970) stated that »vertical integration may give producers enhanced control over their economic environment.» He went on to explain that this control will lessen the probability of foreclosure by buyers or of price squeeze by sellers (cf. Williamson, 1970). We may expand this argument to include both parties in the merger. In other words, both downstream and upstream firms may resolve their uncertainty by merger. This local uncertainty is pertinent to the industries of the respective firms, and the way to handle them is to acquire and absorb the source of uncertainty. The uncertainty avoidance technique may explain two types of conglomerate mergers: those that do not affect expected (a) profits, (b) uncertainty (i.e. mergers with firms in different risk classes).

A similar analysis of merger activity was undertaken by organizational theorists. Behavioural scientists viewed mergers as a means of managing environmental interdependence (cf. Pfeffer, 1972; Thompson, 1967). The open systems framework for organizational analysis emphasizes the importance of the environment in determining organizational structure. Different authors have suggested the concepts of the *interorganizational network* (cf. Aldrich, 1976, 1980; Benson, 1975), the *organizational set* (cf. Evan, 1966) and the *task environment* (cf. Thompson, 1967) to describe the relevant domain of interorganizational relations. This environment is composed mainly of suppliers, customers and competitors, and is characterized by shortage of resources and by competition.

Modern organization theory treats the environment as a major source of uncertainty for organizations. This uncertainty stems from such factors as the heterogeneity of the environment, its instability, and its complexity.

Cyert and March (1963) were among the first authors to note the importance of environmental uncertainty in determining organizational behaviour and structure. They suggested that organizations should attempt to avoid uncertainty by arranging a negotiated environment. Other authors have proposed a more active model of coping with environmental uncertainty. They suggest that organizations actively search for ways of reducing this uncertainty (cf. Thompson, 1967; Weick, 1969, 1979). Such methods generally involve attempts by organizations to manage their dependencies on other organizations and control their environments. Several authors (cf. Benson, 1975; Schmidt & Kochan, 1977; Thompson, 1967) have distinguished between competitive and co-operative strategies for gaining power over the environment, and thus reducing the dependence on it. Among others, co-operative strategies include the following methods: co-opting, contracting, coalescing, joint programs and joint ventures (Pfeffer & Nowak, 1976).

The organizational literature has focused more on analyzing interorganizational relations in the non-profit sector (see, e.g., Benson, 1975; Schmidt &Kochan, 1977). rather than in the profit sector. Thompson (1967) and Pfeffer (1972) were among the few which dealt with merger activities as a strategy of managing environmental uncertainty of profit organizations.

Thompson (1967) suggested that organizations' environments can be characterized by constraints and by contingencies which the organization has to meet. He proposed that organizations »seek to place their boundaries around those activities which, if left to the task environment, would be crucial contingencies» (1967, p. 39). He further suggested that the organization's technology would determine the specific form of merger which the organization will engage in.

Pfeffer (1972) has elaborated on these ideas by empirically testing various hypotheses pertaining to the different types of mergers. In analyzing data on mergers collected by The Federal Trade Commission, he concluded that merger could be explained as a response to organizational interdependence, whereby vertical mergers were undertaken to absorb symbiotic interdependencies, horizontal mergers to reduce competitive interdependencies. Conglomerate mergers could be partially explained by the motive for diversification.

The economic and organizational analyses thus suggest that uncertainty avoidance is a major determinant of merger activity, especially in its vertical and conglomerate forms. The present study deals with vertical mergers.

Using finance literature terminology, all corporations can be characterized by two parameters: risk and return. Applied to organizations, the uncertainty avoidance argument suggests that the decision makers (e.g., management) will choose a level of expected profits and minimize uncertainty subject to this constraint. In other words, management will make decisions which achieve as quickly as possible the target combination of risk and return. Uncertainty avoidance dictates a combination of both, which is usually lower than the owners of such a company would desire. This target can be achieved by internal expansion into other activities, but the practice of absorbing other activities by acquisition accomplishes the goal more quickly. Companies that have not achieved their target combination will engage in different types of mergers, where under certain circumstances one type of merger will be preferred over another. Companies with high uncertainty due to supply or demand uncertainty will tend to integrate vertically.

The above discussion can be summarized by the following testable *hypothesis:* The larger the uncertainty of company i in industry j is (due to the supply from upstream firms and/or the demand of downstream firms), the greater the tendency of company i to acquire companies in the upstream and/or downstream industries.

The hypothesis deals with a cross-section of industries and maintains that, due to a chain reaction, the reduction of uncertainty motive causes companies with high uncertainty to engage in vertical acquisitions.

3. Data

The present study employed three main sources of data: The Federal Trade Commission (1973) statistical report on mergers and acquisitions, the Department of Commerce (1975) input-output tables describing transactions among different sectors in the U.S. economy, and measures of risk and return of the different firms, which were based on rates of return data available on the University of Chicago Center for Research in Security Prices (CRSP) tape.

The FTC report covers mergers that took place in the period 1948-1972. Several interesting observations are included in the report: the acquiring firms were, for the most part, large, and the acquired firms were generally small. For example, in 1972, 75 per cent of the acquiring firms had assets valued at 10 million dollars or more, while 92.7 per cent of the acquired firms had assets valued at less than 10 million dollars (74 per cent were under one million dollars in assets value). We have focused on mergers where the acquired firm had assets of 10 million dollars or more, since much more detailed information was available for them in comparison with mergers where the acquired firm had assets of less than 10 million dollars.

The FTC report which deals with the large mergers provides the following data on each merger for both acquiring and acquired firms: name of firm, the firm's standard industrial classification (ISIC) code,[1] the firm's assets, the date of the merger, a distinction whether it was a whole acquisition or a partial acquisition, a distinction whether the merger was carried using cash or securities, and the type of the mergers.

The total number of large mergers in the years 1948-1972 was 1437. However, due to some missing data on 19 mergers the total number of mergers included in the present analysis was 1418. Out of these mergers 214 were horizontal, 162 were vertical, 665 were product extension conglomerates, 57 were market extension conglomerates and 320 were pure conglomerates. The input-output tables show the dollar value of the transactions that took place among producing industries and between producing industries, and the final markets of the American economy. Firms are classified into 21 industries according to their dominant ISIC classification. In addition, the tables include other sections such as purchases made by the government and the value added for each industry.

The rate of return data provided measures of risk and return for each acquiring company involved in mergers. Pertinent data were available for the period 1966-1972 only for acquiring companies. Thus, it covers about one half of all mergers in the entire period. The monthly rates of return for each

---

[1]   ISIC = International Standard Industrial Classification

company over the above period, denoted &, were used to estimate the risk measure, $\sigma(e)$, and the average rate of return, $\bar{R}$. The estimated risk, $\hat{\sigma}(e)$, was obtained from the regression of R for each company, with the rate of return on the Standard and Poors index. The estimated risk, $\hat{\sigma}(e)$, the residual variance, and $\bar{R}$ were then averaged across industries to obtain industrial risk and profitability measures.

In some tests we also used industry concentration measures taken from Weiss (1963).

4. Empirical Tests

4.1 Uncertainty Avoidance and Vertical Integration

The thesis purposed in this paper suggests that mergers are arranged in order to reduce or avoid uncertainty. The uncertainty which a firm faces involves two factors: the market uncertainty which relates to the economy in general, and the specific uncertainty of the firm itself. The uncertainty of firms with which the company has buyer-supplier relations can be of a market and/or specific nature. The upstream or downstream uncertainty has two main sources: the amount purchased or sold, and the degree of concentration of the upstream or downstream firms.

Although it has been suggested in the past that reduction of uncertainty is synonymous with the reduction of dependence, a distinction between the two is indeed necessary. Dependency is not the same as uncertainty, although it may serve as a proxy to measure uncertainty in specific cases. To illustrate this distinction, assume that firm A is the sole supplier of firm B, and firm B is the only client of firm A. Although these two firms are highly interdependent, the situation cannot be classified as one of uncertainty. On the contrary, one may argue that there is a great deal of certainty involved in this interdependence, since both firms are engaged in a highly stable relationship. It is thus hypothesized that in situations where there is a *mutual dependence* , no uncertainty can be removed by arranging a vertical merger.

To test this hypothesis, a measure of mutual dependence was constructed. The direct requirements (D) of industry i from all other industries were correlated with the sales (S) of that industry to all other industries. This correlation (denoted DS) serves as a measure of mutual dependence. A high correlation indicates that D and S are balanced, and hence, a mutual dependence exists between industry i and the other industries. For example, the electronics industry possesses a high mutual dependence (around .7) while the textile and apparel industry have little or no dependence. Next, this measure was correlated with the percentage of the number of vertical mergers (V) out of the total number of mergers (T). The correlation $\varrho(DS, V) = -.54$ is significant at the .05 level, and thus supports the hypothesis that mutual dependency is inversely related to the proportion of vertical mergers.

The direct requirements (D) of an industry i from other industries can naturally serve as a measure of dependency. The same applies to the sales (S) of industry i to all other industries. The correlations of D for industry i with the number of acquisitions (M) of industry i from industry j for all industries were calculated and are presented in Table 3.1. In classifying companies as acquiring or acquired we adopted the FTC classification that is based on the name of the surviving organization. In most cases this was also the larger corporation. This classification is largely correct and we can assume that the acquiring firm played an active role in the merger. The respective correlations between S and M for all industries are presented in Table 3.2.

Column 1 in Table 3.1 and column 1 in Table 3.2 presents correlations which generally support the hypothesis. That is, the larger D is of industry i from industry j, the more the acquisitions of firms in industry j done by firms in industry i.[1]

The correlations in column 1 of Table 3.1 and in column 1 of Table 3.2 include as well the D and S values and the number of mergers within industries. Because the D and M values within industries are quite high, the correlations reported in column 1 of both tables may be spurious. It should be noted, however, that these tables are based on the FTC data. The input-output (I-O) tables, and the classification of firms into different industries in the I-O tables involves extensive aggregation. That is, the I-O tables are comprised of firms which are classified according to their two-digit ISIC codes. However, several industries in the I-O classification include different two-digit ISIC groups. Furthermore, each two-digit ISIC group may include several different three and four-digit ISIC groups. This means that due to the aggregation levels in the I-O tables we may find different firms which are interrelated vertically (i.e., that one firm is the supplier of the other firm, for example) in the same industry. It is thus likely that by using the I-O tables, mergers which are classified as within industry are actually vertical acquisitions between two firms which have different three or four-digit ISIC's. The available data does not allow such a detailed analysis, but this possibility would help to explain the drop in correlation magnitudes between column 1 and 2 in each table, and lessens the chance that column 1's correlations are spurious.

In comparing the tables it seems that the correlations in Table 3.2 are higher than their corresponding correlations in Table 3.1. The differences between D and S lie mainly in the value added (VA). Since each industry adds some value to products which it purchases and then sells, S should be larger than D. This, in turn, means that the dependency on downstream firms is larger than that on upstream firms. Hence, according to hypothesis B there should be more vertical acquisitions of downstream firms as compared with acquisitions of upstream firms. The differences of the correlation magnitudes in the two tables seem to lend support to this hypothesis.

---

[1] In a different framework, Pfeffer (1972) utilized similar measures of dependency and obtained results which are similar to those in column 1 of Table 3.1 and column 1 of able 3.2.

Table 3.1   Correlations for Industry i of direct requirements of Industry j with number of acquisitions of Industry i from Industry
j, for all industries (upstream hypothesis).

Industry	Correlation coefficient[a]	Correlation coefficient[b]
Metal mining	.27	-.07
Petroleum & gas mining	.02	-.02
Other mining	.49*	-.11
Food & tobacco	.86*	-.20
Textile & apparel	.97**	-.42
Wood & furniture	.65**	.01
Paper, printing & publishing	.92**	.02
Chemicals	.79**	-.23
Petroleum & coal products	.72	.85**
Rubber, plastics & leather	.45**	.21
Stone, clay & glass	.61**	.15
Primary metals	.93**	.02
Machinery	.67**	.62**
Electrical equipment	.80**	.56**
Transport equipment	.69**	.42*
Other manufacturing	.38*	.30
Transportation	-.26	-.21
Electrical & gas services	-.01	.50*
Other services	-.15	.11

a) These correlations <u>include</u> industry i direct requirements
from itself as well as the mergers within industry i.

b) These correlations <u>exclude</u> industry i direct requirements
from itself as well as the mergers within industry i.

* $p < .05$
** $p < .01$

An attempt to detect whether some lawfulness exists in the relation of the
correlations for the same industry in each of the tables reveals some interesting patterns. For some industries the correlations drop significantly in both
tables, while for others they drop in only one of them, and so on, The larger
the drop in correlation value is, the more important the D, S and M values

Table 3.2   Correlations for Industry i of sales made to Industry j by Industry i with number of acquisitions of Industry i from Industry j, for all industries (downstream hypothesis).

Industry	Correlation coefficient[a]	Correlation coefficient[b]
Metal mining	.70**	.70**
Petroleum & gas mining	.57**	.87**
Other mining	.73**	.16
Food & tobacco	.99**	.36
Textile & apparel	.99**	.15
Wood & furniture	.77**	.88**
Paper, printing & publishing	.91**	.38
Chemicals	.77**	.12
Petroleum & coal products	.63**	.28
Rubber, plastics & leather	.74**	-.02
Stone, clay & glass	.93**	.32
Primary metals	.84**	.60**
Machinery	.90**	.53*
Electrical equipment	.85**	.68**
Transport equipment	.68**	.91**
Other manufacturing	.55**	.20
Transportation	.27	.29
Electrical & gas services	-.16	.23
Other services	-.28	-.22

a) These correlations <u>include</u> industry i sales to itself as well as the mergers within industry i.

b) These correlations <u>exclude</u> industry i sales to itself as well as the mergers within industry i.

* p < .05
** p < .01

within industry. A possible explanation for this occurrence lies in the technology which these industries employ. Thompson (1967) treated most manufacturing firms in terms of long-linked technology. Other authors differentiated between mass production, unit production, continuous process and other types of technology. A similar component of technology is the number of different stages in the production process. If the process is composed of many stages, we define it as a long linkage technology. If it is composed of one or very few stages, it is defined here as a short linkage.

It is conceivable that the linkage variable will bear some relationship to vertical merger activity along the lines earlier discussed regarding upstream and downstream dependencies. Specifically, it is suggested that the relevant vertical mergers for short linkage type industries are those with the immediate supplier or purchaser. In contrast, relevant vertical mergers for long linkage type industries can extend beyond the immediate industries. Take, for example, the food or textile industries, which can be classified as short linked technologies. For both, relevant mergers can take place with firms in very close, three or four-digit ISICs. If this was the case, the number of mergers within industry (using the I-O tables) would be quite large in comparison to long-linked technology industries, such as machinery or electrical equipment. We would then expect a larger drop in correlations of both D and S with M (comparing correlations which include respectively exclude D, S and M of the same industry) in the short-linked technology industries as compared with the long-linked type of technology. Both tables indicate that the drop in correlations for short-linked type industries (such as food and tobacco; textile and apparel; paper, printing and publishing) is much larger than the drop for long-linked type industries (such as machinery and electrical equipment).

In sum, the I-O tables allow for several different three and four-digit ISIC firms to be classified in the same industry. Short-linked technology firms are more likely to perform vertical acquisitions within the same industry (as defined by the I-O classification) than are long-linked technology firms. The patterns of correlations in both Table 3.1 and Table 3.2 tend to support this observation, and thus indicate the importance of including or excluding D, S and M values within industries (in the I-O classification) for the analysis of the determinants of vertical integration.

Finally, using industry concentration ratios (CR) the effect of the second source of uncertainty, degree of concentration, was tested. In an attempt to predict M, the CR's were run together with the D values using multiple regression. The addition of the CR values to the D values did not affect the prediction significantly (cf. Pfeffer, 1972). One must note, however, that matching the CR data with the I-O industry categories was not an easy task. Several two-digit industry CR values (weighted by size) were averaged together to meet the I-O classification. The result was that CR values were available for only 13 industries in the I-O data. The smaller number of observations and the reduction in concentration variability due to aggregation and averaging can, at least partially, explain the insignificance of the CR in predicting and explaining vertical merger activity.

Thus, these tests basically supported the earlier mentioned hypothesis, which suggested that the uncertainty of company i (derived from the upstream and the downstream firms) will be positively related to this company's tendency to acquire firms in the upstream and/or downstream industries.

4.2 A Time-Series Analysis of Vertical Integration

In the above analysis we used the I-O table of 1967 and all mergers in the period 1948-1972. To gain more insight into the effect of buyer-seller relations on merger activity we have split the period of analysis into two subperiods which include a similar number of mergers: 1948-1964 and 1965-1972. The I-O tables of 1958 and 1967 were related to the first and second subperiod, respectively.

Tables 3.3 and 3.4 present the correlations of D and S with M for the two subperiods. The change in the correlations from the first to the second subperiod is obtained by comparing columns 1 and 2 in each table, or alternatively columns 3 and 4. If only the correlations significant in at least one subperiod are compared, we find that with the exception of one industry (machinery) the correlations in the 1948-1964 period were higher than in the subsequent period. A similar pattern is obtained by comparing columns 3 and 4. In other words, the tendency of corporations in a certain industry to acquire companies in industries with which they have strong buyer-seller relationships has decreased over time. Indeed, the number of vertical mergers in the second subperiod is significantly smaller than the number of vertical mergers in the first subperiod. The uncertainty avoidance motive that mainly took the form of vertical mergers from 1948-1964 has been expressed by conglomerate mergers from 1965-1972, where uncertainty avoidance was achieved mainly through diversification. This trend is also seen in the sales figures which are presented in Table 3.4. While in the first subperiod, 16 out of 19 industries show highly significant correlations, only 12 industries show significant correlations in the second subperiod.

5. Conclusion

Uncertainty avoidance was defined as a major factor in the development of mergers. It suggests that, in order to cope with environmental uncertainty, the organization's decision makers set a *constraint minimization objective.*

The tests employed generally support this hypothesis, thus increasing our confidence in its validity. Further research should extend these results and apply them to other areas of managerial decision making.

Table 3.3   Correlations for Industry i of direct requirements of Industry i from Industry j, based on 1958 and 1967 input-output tables with number of acquisitions of Industry i from Industry j in the periods 1948-1964 (1) and 1965-1972 (2), respectively.

Industry	r_{ij} a) (1)	r_{ij} a) (2)	r_{ij} b) (1)	r_{ij} b) (2)
Metal mining	.41*	.21	.02	-.07
Petroleum & gas mining	-.05	.14	-.10	.16
Other mining	.71**	-.10	-.19	-.07
Food & tobacco	.87**	.83**	-.02	-.32
Textile & apparel	.96**	.96**	-.27	-.35
Wood & furniture	.66**	.59**	-.01	.13
Paper, printing & publishing	.95**	.90**	.05	-.08
Chemicals	.85**	.73**	-.26	-.16
Petroleum & coal products	.81**	.29	.92**	.34
Rubber, plastics & leather	.59**	.38*	.08	.27
Stone, clay & glass	.67**	.42*	.27	.03
Primary metals	.93**	.90**	-.10	.07
Machinery	.62**	.70**	.63**	.65*
Electrical equipment	.71**	.35	.52*	.22
Transport equipment	.79**	.05	.49*	.00
Other manufacturing	.01	.31	-.11	.42*
Transportation	-.18	-.14	-.16	-.11
Electrical & gas services	.09	-.16	.53**	-.12
Other services	-.05	-.17	.15	.08

a) These correlations include industry i direct requirements from itself as well as the mergers within industry i.

b) These correlations exclude industry i direct requirements from itself as well as the mergers within industry i.

* p < .05
** p < .01

Table 3.4   Correlations for Industry i of sales made to Industry j by Industry i based on 1958 and 1967 input-output tables with number of acquisitions of Industry i from Industry j in the periods 1948-1964 (1) and 1965-1972 (2), respectively.

Industry	r_{ij} a) (1)	r_{ij} a) (2)	r_{ij} b) (1)	r_{ij} b) (2)
Metal mining	.69**	.59**	.67**	.56**
Petroleum & gas mining	.75**	.10	.95**	.16
Other mining	.78**	,32	-.13	.58**
Food & tobacco	.99**	.97**	.57**	.12
Textile & apparel	.98**	.99**	.05	.26
Wood & furniture	.79**	.66**	.88**	.73**
Paper, printing & publishing	.90**	.85**	.19	-.20
Chemicals	.89**	.64**	.53**	-.22
Petroleum & coal products	.53**	.83**	.14	.61**
Rubber, plastics & leather	.94**	.32	.29	-.09
Stone, clay & glass	.97**	.69**	,39*	,23
Primary metals	.81**	.82**	.56**	.50*
Machinery	.88**	.90**	.49*	.57**
Electrical equipment	.94**	.51*	.74**	.62**
Transport equipment	.79**	.10	.68**	.36
Other manufacturing	.62**	.96**	.13	.22
Transportation	.29	.01	.26	.01
Electrical & gas services	-.12	-.16	.02	-.19
Other services	-.16	-.28	-.12	-.22

a) These correlations <u>include</u> industry i sales to itself as well as the mergers <u>within</u> industry i.

b) These correlations <u>exclude</u> industry i sales to itself as well as the mergers <u>within</u> industry i.

*   p < .05
** p < .01

6. References

Aldrich, H., 1976
»Resource Dependence and Interorganizational Relations.» *Administration and Society,* 7, 419-455.

Benson, J.K., 1975
»The Interorganizational Network as a Political Economy.» *Administrative Science Quarterly,* 20, 229-249.

Cyert, R. and March, J., 1963
A Behavioral Theory of the Firm. Englewood Cliffs, N.J.: Prentice-Hall.

Department of Commerce, Bureau of the Census, 1975
Historical Statistics of the United States. Washington, D.C.

Evan, W., 1966
The Organization Set: Toward a Theory of Interorganizational Relations.» In J.D. Thompson (ed.): *Approaches to Organizational Design.* Pittsburgh: University of Pittsburgh Press.

Federal Trade Commission, Bureau of Economics, 1973
Statistical Report on Mergers and Acquisitions. Washington, D.C.

March, J.G. and Simon, H.A., 1958
Organizations. New York: Wiley.

Mueller, D.C., 1969
»A Theory of Conglomerate Mergers.» *Quarterly Journal of Economics,* 83, 643-659.

Pfeffer, J., 1972
»Merger as a Response to Organizational Interdependence.» *Administrative Science Quarterly,* 17, 382-394.

Pfeffer, J. and Nowak, P., 1976
»Joint Ventures and Interorganizational Interdependence.» *Administrative Science Quarterly,* 21, 398-418.

Scherer, .M., 1970
Market Structure and Economic Performance. Chicago: Rand McNally.

Schmidt, S. and Kochan, T., 1977
»Interorganizational Relations: Patterns and Motivations» *Administrative Science Quarterly,* 22, 220-234.

Simon, H., 1955
»A Behavioral Model of Rational Choice.» *Quarterly Journal of Economics,* 69, 99-118.

Thompson, J.D., 1967
Organizations in Action. New York: McGraw-Hill.

Weick, K.E., 1969
The Social Psychology of Organizing. Boston: Addison Wesley.

Weick, K.E., 1979
The Social Psychology of Organizing, »2nd edition. Boston: Addison Wesley.

Weiss, L.W., 1963
»Average Concentration Ratios and Industrial Performance.» *Journal of Industrial Economics,* 11, 237-254.

Williamson, O.E., 1970
Corporate Control and Business Behavior. Englewood Cliffs, N.J.: Prentice Hall.

Williamson, O.E., 1975
Markets and Hierarchies: Analysis and Antitrust Implications. New York: The Free Press.

4. THE STRATEGIC ROLE OF INTERFIRM CO-OPERATION

*Anders Edström**
*Bengt Högberg***
*Lars Erik Norbäck***

* *Europan Institute for Advanced Studies in Management Brussels, Belgium, and the Stockholm School of Economics, Sweden*
** *University of Gothenburg, Sweden*

We gratefully acknowledge support for this study from the Bank of Sweden Tercentenary Foundation, The Swedish Council for Social Research, and the Adlerbert Research Foundation.

1. Introduction

This chapter re-evaluates some cases of interfirm co-operation reported elsewhere (Högberg, 1977; Edström and Högberg, 1977; Norbäck, 1978). The primary reason to re-evaluate them is another study by the present authors (Edström et al., 1981), who investigated the use of joint ventures and joint programs in a representative sample of Swedish manufacturing firms. Alternative theoretical explanations of interfirm co-operation were integrated in a framework of strategic roles of co-operation.

The cases reported here concern four Swedish companies which were exposed to changes in their environments. The changes were partly recognized as threats to the companies' survival and different methods were used when coping with the changes. The companies exhibited various efforts to expand, defend or retreat from parts of their existing domains. In these efforts they adopted several types of co-operative behaviour and non-co-operative activities like going it alone or acquisitions. The strategic role of co-operation is then defined as the domain strategy (expansion, defense, retreat) of which co-operation is a part.

Our purpose with this re-evaluation is to show that co-operative activities are best understood if the strategic roles they are supposed to fulfill are taken into consideration, and also to illustrate different strategic roles of co-operation.

We define interfirm co-operation as the relationships which develop between two or more, in terms of ownership, independent firms as a result of an explicit agreement on the future exchange of resources, concerted action, and/or joint decision making. Co-operation can take different organizational forms, such as contracts, joint programs, and joint ventures, which are of special interest in this study.

A contract is an agreement for the exchange of performances in the future (Thompson, 1967: 35). Contracts are often used to facilitate functional specialization. A firm which is producing a complete product may contract out part of the production to suppliers. Other types of contracts are those concluded with agents or licensees. In all cases the use of contracts permits the business firm to stabilize and formalize its relations to important organizations in its environment.

Another linkage mechanism is the joint program or project. It is a form of coalescing (Thompson, 1967) which involves a commitment to joint decision making. One can observe several varieties of such joint efforts, for instance, joint research and development projects with competitors, suppliers or other firms, or co-ordination of production plans between some of the firms in the same industry to achieve a more even utilization of their production capacities. Joint programs can be used to promote either functional integration or specialization. The decision making is done through direct contact between the partners or in a special task force or project group. A joint venture is a separate organizational unit which is jointly owned and controlled by the co-operating firms. The partners often have an equal share of the equity. In the joint venture resources are pooled together, while in the joint program resources remain with the co-operating companies.

The use of interfirm co-operation can be triggered by a desire to defend, extend or abandon part of an existing domain (Thompson, 1967), and consequently to manage existing interdependencies, create new interdependencies or get out of existing ones.

A decision to extend the domain of a firm can be implemented in essentially three different ways. One alternative is for the firm to rely entirely on its own resources, capital, personnel, and know-how. Another alternative is to buy another firm to gain access to its know-how, products and market position and hence complement the available internal resources. Both of these alternatives give the expanding firm complete control of new operations. A third alternative is to co-operate with another firm to complement its own resources and share the risks. This will also require the firm to share control of the joint operations with its partner.

It is also possible for a firm to partially retreat from a section of its domain by the use of a joint venture. One example is a company which was one of the first Swedish companies to enter into the computer business. It decided after a few years to sell out most of its operations in this industry but retained a specialized segment where a joint venture was formed in order to guarantee know-how and capital for the future. In this way the company could maintain a good return on its previous investments.

Whether interfirm co-operation will be used to deal with existing interdependencies or to create new ones, will depend to a large extent on the situation the firm is in. In the present study we set out to specify a few key dimensions of the situation or the strategic context in which the firm operates. Organization theory provides various explanations of why business firms create linkage mechanisms, such as joint ventures and joint programs for interfirm co-ordination and decision making. We maintain that existing theories largely disregard the strategic roles of those firms which make decisions about co-operation. Therefore, what seems to be conflicting explanations of the same phenomenon, are, according to our research, complementary explanations when considering the differences in strategic roles (Edström et al., 1981). We start our discussion with two of the main explanations of interfirm co-operation.

2. A Resource Interdependence View of Co-operation

The first explanation is based on the resource-dependence model (Yuchtman and Seashore, 1967; Aldrich, 1975), which has been the frame of reference for a number of empirical studies of linkages between organizations (Aldrich, 1975, 1976; Pfeffer, 1972; Pfeffer and Nowak, 1976; Pfeffer and Salancik, 1978). The basic reasoning is that specialization of production makes any manufacturing firm dependent on other firms for important resources and for disposal of its output. Resources are assumed to be scarce, and any firm has to compete for them with others. The firm's survival will depend on its ability to acquire resources. It will have to compete with other firms which are dependent upon the same resource (competitive interdependence) and it will have to negotiate with firms which control the allocation, access or use of a valued resource (transactional interdependence). Previous theories assume that firms seek to avoid uncertainty and reduce their dependence on contingencies (Cyert and March, 1963; Thompson, 1967). The more critical the resource is to a focal firm and the fewer the alternative suppliers, the more important it is to reduce uncertainty. One way of reducing uncertainty is to negotiate some form of co-operation.

Pfeffer and Nowak (1976: 402) stated that joint ventures are used to organize groups of companies to cope with competitive and transactional interdependence and tend to occur among either competitors or organizations which are in a buyer-seller relationship. Proceeding from the resource-dependence model, Pfeffer and Nowak (1976), tested the general hypothesis that the existence of resource interdependence will induce U.S. business firms to create domestic joint ventures to manage their mutual dependence. Their explanatory model accounted for 18 per cent of the variance in joint venture activities between individual industries.

The moderate explanatory power leaves room for alternative explanations. Pfeffer and Nowak considered some, such as the need for resources, but concluded (1976: 415):

> »The fact that the relationship among the parent organizations and the relationship between the parent organizations and the joint subsidiaries were related to resource interdependence measures as well as concentration - which is an indicator of the competitive relationship - leaves the argument that joint ventures are undertaken to take advantage of complementary strengths in doubt.«

They stated (1976: 407) that the rationale for transnational co-operation »is fundamentally different than that motivating linkages among domestic organizations».

In their study of 98 Swedish manufacturing firms, Edström et al. (1981) found that of the 35 cases of joint ventures or programs among these firms only a minority were with partners which were competitors, buyers or sellers. The majority of the cases concerned firms which extended their domains and co-operated with partners with whom they were neither in a transaction nor a competitive relationship.

3. A Structural Complexity View of Co-operation

Aiken and Hage (1968) studied the use of joint programs by health and welfare organizations in the United States. Their main argument was that internal organizational diversity stimulates innovation. To implement new ideas requires resources. In order to gain resources organizations seek co-operation. Aiken and Hage (1968: 916) also maintained that organizations which choose to co-operate

> »want to lose as little power and autonomy as possible in their exchange for other resources. This suggests that they are most likely to choose organizations with complementary resources, as Reid (1967) has suggested, or partners with different goals, as Guetzkow (1966) has indicated.»

While Pfeffer and Nowak argued that interdependence causes the creation of joint ventures (1976: 400) Aiken and Hage (1968: 913) argued that interdependence arises through joint co-operative programs.

Studies of multinational companies (Franko, 1971, 1976; Gullander, 1976; Stopford and Wells, 1972; Stopford and Haberich, 1976) have basically followed the lines of Aiken and Hage (1968) in that the need for resources was found to be the dominant reason for co-operation and that organizations want to lose as little power and autonomy as possible in their exchange for other resources. This is consistent with Pfeffer and Nowak's (1976) argument that the rationale for transnational and national co-operation is different.

Edström et al. (1981) found that complementary resources dominated when co-operation concerned domain expansion. When co-operation was used for activities within the firm's existing domain, contribution of similar resources dominated. Thus, what appear to be conflicting explanations of the same phenomenon are rather complementary explanations considering the differences in strategic role.

4. Research Design

Aiken and Hage (1968) and Pfeffer and Nowak (1976) used cross-sectional data. This precludes a dynamic interpretation of interorganizational co-operation. We have chosen a case-oriented approach in order to examine the use of interfirm co-operation within the context of the overall strategic development of the firm. This will make it possible to get a better understanding of how the propensity to co-operate can vary over time and how various contexts may influence the decision-making process.

To penetrate a firm's decision-making process is both a time-consuming and difficult task. The usual resource constraints for research will make a study of a large number of firms an unfeasible proposition. The exploratory nature of the research also makes it natural to study a limited number of firms. Furthermore, we will have to cover a considerable period of time in order to cover strategic development processes. We chose to follow in a detailed fashion the companies' development during the period 1974-76. In addition we tracked the companies' historical development during the preceding ten to fifteen years. During these periods each case of co-operation has been identified and data about it has been collected.

In view of the alternative theoretical explanations the companies have been chosen so as to contrast two companies, which use interfirm co-operation to deal with resource interdependencies, with two companies which use co-operation to establish interdependencies. The former two come from raw material-based industries while the latter come from the machinery industry. The characteristics of the firms are presented in Table 4.1.

In order to protect the companies involved we are using fictitious names throughout the report. Alpha and Beta are the two raw material based companies, and Gamma and Delta are the two companies from the machinery industry. All the companies have used interfirm co-operation during different phases of their development.

We have collected data by interviewing the managers who have taken up interfirm co-operation. Several decision-makers have been interviewed in each company and in most cases by two interviewers. This both facilitates the use of time and makes it possible to check interpretations between the interviewers. A large part of the interviews has been taped. The transcripts of the interviews have been sent to the interviewees for verification. The interviews have followed a general check list of issues but have been rather open in character. We have attempted not to force the respondents into a preconceived conceptual framework.

In addition to interview data we have had access to documents about the companies, and in some cases also to the contracts concluded between the co-operating firms. Documents about companies include their annual reports, newspaper clippings, and internal study reports. The publicly available documents have assisted us in formulating the checklists for the interviews.

71

Table 4.1   Firms studied.

Firm	Size		Environmental structure and interdependencies
ALPHA	Sales Employees	2 800* 6 000	OWN INDUSTRY High concentration, capital intensive, economies of scale CUSTOMER INDUSTRY High concentration, capital intensive, economies of scale INTERDEPENDENCIES Strong transactional interdependencies, technological interdependencies
BETA	Sales Employees	1 000* 2 900	OWN INDUSTRY High concentration, capital intensive, economies of scale CUSTOMER INDUSTRY Intermediate concentration INTERDEPENDENCIES Strong transactional interdependencies, technological interdependencies
GAMMA	Sales Employees	450* 2 800	OWN INDUSTRY High concentration CUSTOMER INDUSTRY Monopsonist INTERDEPENDENCIES Dependence on one customer
DELTA	Sales Employees	360* 2 200	OWN DOMAIN Multiple industries Heavily dependent on defense products

* in million Skr

5. The Cases

5.1 Alpha

During two decades (1955-75) Alpha grew rapidly. At the beginning of the period its operations were limited to the extraction of raw materials, some of which were further refined in Alpha's own refineries, but most were sold on the open market. At the end of the period, Alpha operated a rather diversified product line. Most of the new operations stem from successive steps of forward integration. To a considerable degree, Alpha has relied on joint ventures for its expansion.

The development pattern (Table 4.2) is characterized by periods of expansion of the domain (62-63; 70-73) followed by periods of consolidation and integration (65-70; 73-). These two phase cycles seem to dominate the two decades.

In the middle of the fifties, Alpha operated a large number of primary units (sources of raw-material extraction) many of which were too small to be run efficiently without central co-ordination. An effort was made to improve efficiency by co-ordinating the extraction, and to refine the major portion in a refinery in Sweden which had been expanded for that purpose. The sources of supply consisted of composite raw materials, i.e. several ingredients. The expanded refinery capacity led to an increased assortment of semi-finished products. The large investment in the refinery made the profitability of the operations increasingly sensitive to variations in production volume and to the marketing of by-products which were not further refined by Alpha. Consequently, there was increased pressure to reduce uncertainty in the disposal of outputs. Previously Alpha relied on delivery contracts for managing its relation to suppliers and customers. With the extended production capacity, stronger ties to the customers seemed necessary. Besides the need to market nonrefined by-products, and to buffer variations in demand, the technological interdependencies made it desirable to reduce uncertainty in the relationship with customers. The output from Alpha's refinery had certain particular characteristics which required special adjustments in the phase following the production sequence.

At the beginning of the sixties, Alpha made two major moves in order to assure the output of its products. Both resulted in joint ventures, wherein Alpha bought a substantial portion of shares in an existing firm. The moves can be seen as an attempt to secure the sales of important by-products from the pre-refining stage. In one case Alpha was able to buy a 50 per cent interest in a refinery. Alpha's partner in the refinery, an international holding company with interests in many industrial sectors, saw the joint venture as a means to secure input from its previous main supplier. The partner did not supply any raw materials to the refinery. For Alpha the decision to enter a joint venture rather than to go it alone was motivated by the disturbance it would have created on the market, the resources required and the added risk.

Table 4.2   Alpha's development pattern.

ALPHA (1955-1975)			
General development	Raw material extraction and refining	Chemicals	Machinery
1955-62 Internal co-ordination	1955 Investment in a new refinery in Sweden		
	1963 Jointly owned refinery in Scandinavia (50/50)	1963 Majority joint venture in chemicals	
		1963 Acquisition of chemical firms	
1968 New president			
1970-73 Expansion period			
1972 Divisionalized organization			1972 Acquisition of a company making machinery for raw material extraction
	1973 Jointly owned refinery within the European community (50/50)	1973 Joint venture production of a new chemical product (50/50)	

In addition the partner was not willing to sell 100 per cent of the equity. Instead both companies reduced uncertainty by formalizing their relationship.

One of the by-products from the pre-refinery stage was sold to the chemical industry. The variation in demand was considerable for this product too. Alpha bought an existing company in the chemical industry. Through this acquisition it became a partner in a joint venture in the same industry. At first the partners in the existing joint venture were not ready to sell or to cooperate. After Alpha had demonstrated its determination to go it alone if the negotiations were unsuccessful, it was able to acquire 33% of the shares. The joint venture now had three owners, two suppliers and one customer.

After the major acquisitions in 1962 and 1963 a period of integration and rationalization followed. The emphasis was on integrating the acquired firm and the jointly owned operations technologically and managerially with the rest of the operations. The emphasis on profitability and liquidity was heightened because it had been costly to finance the acquisitions. Toward the end of the sixties, however, profits started to diminish and sales began to stagnate, initiating a new period of change. A new president was appointed.

He introduced a multi-divisional structure instead of the previous centralized functional structure. In a memo he declared that Alpha would rely increasingly on co-operation with other firms.

The new period of change and expansion followed the pattern established earlier. Two new joint ventures were entered, one by the chemical division, and one by the extracting division. Two small chemical firms were acquired in the early seventies. Subsequently, it turned out that one of the products from the chemical production had an important potential as an ingredient in a newly developed process for metal production. The firm which had developed the new process was a large international metal producer. Alpha previously had contacts with this company for exchange of technical know-how. The two companies formed a joint venture in order to produce the input for the metal production process. The ownership was shared equally.

In the early seventies the long term prospects for one of the by-products from the refining operation were estimated to deteriorate. Since the output of this by-product was large, it was of major concern to the company to secure the market for it. Furthermore, the customs placed by the EEC on finished products made it important to own a refinery within the tariff barrier. One of the major customers, a German firm, was interested in running a joint refinery. The German firm had a narrow raw material base and had to buy considerable quantities on the open market. Again a 50/50 venture was formed.

Finally, as part of the expansion period, Alpha made a move into the machinery industry and acquired a firm which sold machinery equipment for the extraction of raw materials. The firm had previously been a supplier to Alpha. In addition, Alpha itself had developed a number of original machine designs for its own operations. For a summary of Alpha's strategic actions, see Table 4.3.

Comments. Alpha's operations are divided into three product lines, refining of raw materials, chemicals, which stem from forward integration from refinery, and machinery. The chemical actions were mainly motivated by a desire to find outlets for by-products which cannot be absorbed in Alpha's own refinery. This led to two joint ventures in the refinery stage, an acquisition of a chemical firm and a joint venture in the chemical industry.

It seems clear that the strategic moves were intended to reduce uncertainty within existing interdependencies. Alpha's position was threatened and it responded by extending its control of downstream operations. Joint ventures were formed with other big firms, while small ones were acquired. The joint ventures seem to be a logical outcome from a bystander's point of view: In all cases but one the partners were resourceful enough to defend their domains. Furthermore, there was a mutual interest to secure transactions of semi-finished products. Alpha did not want to acquire its customers, because this would have meant that it acquired new output uncertainty.

Alpha's development has, for the most part, followed the interdependencies which were conditioned by the technology and previous commercial relationships. The operations are characterized by a particularly inflexible base in terms of raw-material sites and high capital intensity which makes it very difficult to radically reorient operations. The strong interdependencies which exist constitute both constraints and a guide for the company's development.

Table 4.3   Alpha's co-operation agreements and acquisitions.

ALPHA (Development strategy - vertical integration)

Year	Form of co-operation	Partner(s)	Alpha's previous relation to partner
I. Refining of intermediate products			
1963	Joint venture (existing firm)	Belgian holding company	Supplier
1973	Joint venture (existing firm)	German firm	Supplier
II. Chemicals			
1963	Majority joint venture	2 Swedish firms	Supplier
1970	Acquisition of 2 chemical firms	-	Competitor
1973	Joint venture in chemicals	1 Swiss firm	Exchange of technical know-how
III. Machinery			
1972	Acquisition of 2 existing firms in machinery industry	-	Customer

There was both a strong technical interdependence and a limited number of customers and competitors which made interdependencies clear to all companies involved. The strategic vision guiding Alpha's development seems to have been heavily influenced by the pattern of these interdependencies. It is marked by a gradually increased control of a larger and larger part of the environment, but also by an increasingly positive attitude toward co-operation with other companies. Since the dominating vision has been remarkably stable, Alpha has been able to carefully plan, implement, and realize this vision.

5.2 Beta

Also Beta operates in a capital intensive industry. Its production is based on process technology. The degree of concentration in the industry is high. Beta's development is characterized by the same pulse as Alpha's with periods of expansion interspersed with periods of consolidation and rationalization. The major direction of growth is toward forward integration (Table 4.4).

Table 4.4   Beta's development pattern.

BETA (1960-1975)

General development	Forest	Packing materials
1962 Investment program	1963 Majority joint venture in Southern Europe	1965 New production facilities for intermediate product
1967 New president		1966 Search for co-operation partners
1970 Period of consolidation		1967 Co-operation agreement "umbrella"
		1968 Joint ventures with U.S. partners
1972 Reorganization multi-divisionalized structure adopted		1970 Acquisition in France

Beta's first strategic move abroad was to establish a majority joint venture in Southern Europe to assure its supply of raw materials. Through a management contract Beta was able to achieve operating control of the joint venture. Consequently, Beta's first joint venture did not imply joint decision making.

Beta's expansion started in the sixties with investments at home in the production of a semi-finished product. Already from the start it was realized that Beta needed to go still a step further in the production process to assure a stable volume of sales of the semi-finished product. The manufacturing of the end products needed to be located close to the markets because of high transportation costs. Beta did not have the know-how required for marketing and production of the end product. At this point of time a new president was appointed. He declared in the annual report that the industry needed to co-operate more (compare the comment made by Alpha's president a few years later). Beta started to search for a partner, guided by the following criteria: the partner should have the know-how for manufacturing and marketing the final product, produce the complementary input, and possess the financial strength to contribute on a 50/50 basis to acquire local firms manufacturing the end product.

In 1967, Beta concluded an agreement with a U.S firm. The U.S. firm had exchanged know-how with Beta for a number of years and contacts had been frequent prior to the agreement. The product group manager of Beta declared that

> »this firm worked on the same idea as we did, i.e., to integrate forward on the European market.«

The partners were to search jointly in Europe for possibilities to make joint investments in the production of the end product, because they needed local marketing know-how and access to distribution channels. Three joint ventures were established with the U.S. partner. The firms acquired were previous customers of the U.S. partner. Two of the joint ventures included a third, local, partner. In addition, Beta entered two joint ventures with local partners without participation of the U.S. firm and acquired 100 per cent of a French firm. In the latter case, the U.S. firm did not want to participate and in the two former cases the local partners did not want an American participation. In all three cases the firms were old customers of Beta (Table 4.5).

Beta's and its partner's insufficient experience of the local markets made their planning of the area diversification difficult. The choices of local partners were not as well-planned as the selection of the U.S.-firm. After only a couple of years Beta and its U.S.-partner withdrew from two of the local joint ventures, and revised their strategy. They decided to opt only for investments that gave them a dominating influence. They had the choice of either an ownership majority or an option to acquire such a majority. To quote the product-group manager:

> »It is difficult to control a joint venture if there are several partners and you are in a minority. It can be difficult enough to organize operations in which you hold a majority.«

Comments. The driving forces behind Beta's expansion were the fluctuating market for its intermediate product and increasing competitive pressures. Beta's response was to integrate forward. Beta shows a pattern of planned action similar to that of Alpha. The criteria for the search for a partner and the move to manufacturing in Europe was preceded by a formal planning process. Beta's strategic move implied a further departure from the existing domain than in the case of Alpha, because Beta also expanded to new markets. Beta did not have the experience of manufacturing and marketing in the local markets. The geographical expansion and, to a certain extent, the technical aspects in connection with the downstream integration led Beta to a learning process during which revisions of the strategy became necessary.

Table 4.5   Beta's co-operation agreements and acquisitions.

BETA (Development strategy - vertical integration and area diversification)

Year	Form of co-operation/ acquisition	Partner(s)	Beta's previous relation to partner
I. Packing materials			
1967	Informal co-operation	U.S. firm	Exchange of technical know-how
1968	3 joint ventures· with U.S. partner		
	1	U.S. firm	No previous relation
	2	U.S. firm/ Lebanese firm	No previous relation
	3	U.S. firm/ Spanish firm	No previous relation
1969	2 joint ventures with local partners		
	1	Swiss firm	Supplier
	2	Austrian/ Swiss firm	Supplier
1969	Acquisition		No previous relation

5.3 Gamma

Gamma is a producer of military equipment and as such it depends on government defense contracts for 90 per cent of its business. The number of employees were approximately 2800 in 1975. Around 50 per cent were technicians and engineers. Sales were Skr 450 million.

Already in the fifties the top management felt that Gamma's dependence on defense orders was unsatisfactory. Attempts were made to increase the product range. At the end of the fifties, printing machines were added to the product line. On two successive occasions in the early sixties, this product line was further extended. Each time Gamma acquired licenses. The early attempts to diversify operations were more the result of an apprehension concerning the future than of actual changes in defense orders. A more pronounced momentum toward diversification followed in 1967 in connection with a general crisis in the company. The crisis sparked entries into the hydraulic machine industry and the air cleaning equipment industry.

Table 4.6   Gamma's development pattern

GAMMA (1955-75)

General development	Defense products	Graphical machines	Hydraulic machines	Pollution control equipment
	1955 Defense products accounted for close to 100% of sales	1958 Addition of graphical machine		
1962-63 Search for new products		1962 Two licenses bought	1963 Joint research and development in hydraulic machines	
1967 Overall sales and profits started rapidly to decrease		1969 Graphical machines sold	1969 Marketing of hydraulic machines started through independent agents	
1970 New president			1970 Co-operation agreement and joint sales subsidiaries abroad	1972 New product-develoment together with cus ers sales with own sal engineers
1971 Renewed search for new products			1973 Co-operation agreement ended	1973 Co-operation agree ment (contract) with German firm
			1974 New co-operation agreement about R&D and sales	1974 Co-operation agree ment with Swedish firm
				1974 Co-operation offe by other firms
	1975 Defense products still account for approximately 65% of sales			

Hydraulic machines. Based on a market analysis a long-range plan was worked out in order to build up the hydraulic machine group. Previous efforts in product development had resulted in a new product. At first the new product was marketed in a rather primitive way. As a defense contractor Gamma did not have a wide-spread market organization, but relied on a small group of specialists. Two engineers »hunted representatives» as the head of the hydraulic-machine group expressed it. Before long the representatives complained that the assortment was too narrow. An additional complicating factor was that the machines were of an unnecessarily high quality and hence expensive (»the defense industry syndrom»). A complementary type of machine had to be developed only a year later in order to broaden the product line.

Sales and profits for the hydraulic machines did not develop in a satisfactory manner, and Gamma also had difficulties with its independent representatives. They often lacked the technical know-how required to deal effectively with the customers. In addition, since the representatives regarded Gamma's product range as too narrow, they were not willing to make the necessary marketing investments.

Towards the end of the sixties a change in strategy took place. Gamma founded subsidiaries on the most important foreign markets. After discussion with certain trade association members it turned out that two other firms had experienced similar problems and were willing to contribute resources and experience in order to solve the marketing problems. The three firms decided to found and operate jointly-owned sales subsidiaries in three European countries. The partners manufactured complementary products but of a kind which were also, to a certain degree, competing.

However, the joint efforts were not successful. Conflicts developed among the partners. It also turned out that the advantages of appearing as a group were rather limited, because in some main markets the customers did not want to buy complete systems. In 1973, the co-operation agreement was terminated.

Only a year later, a new co-operation agreement was signed with a Swedish producer of control systems for hydraulic machines. The new agreement was different from the previous ones in certain respects. It stated that on certain markets the partner's products would be sold through Gamma's outlets. Furthermore the agreement included research and development.

Pollution control equipment. Pollution control equipment was taken up following an order from a customer. The latter grappled with problems concerning disposal of smoke from its manufacturing process. The existing equipment on the market was not efficient enough. An application of the basic techniques that Gamma used in the defense sector was believed to offer a solution to the customer's problem. When the project was successfully terminated, the idea of marketing the same product to other customers was launched and accepted.

During the first year, the operations were performed on a rather small scale. The search for new orders was also rather unsystematic. A sales engineer visited potential Swedish customers. The first experience was that the product was not well adapted to the needs of the customers. Gamma also found that it lacked credibility with the potential customers because it had not proven that it possessed a competitive technology in this field.

As a result of this lack of references, Gamma entered into co-operation with an experienced German firm. The latter manufactured a component which considerably enlarged the potential area of application of Gamma's own system. Gamma and its German partner had well established contacts in other areas, which probably made the partner convinced of Gamma's competence.

The contract stipulated that Gamma would buy the above mentioned component from the German firm. The latter would supply the know-how and also participate in visits to potential customers. The German partner financed its part of the marketing efforts. Gamma was obliged to consult with and to offer participation to its partner in all projects where the partner's technology was applicable.

The first year of the co-operation was successful and half a dozen systems were sold. In 1974, difficulties appeared and no system at all was sold within the co-operation agreement. The reason was that the rapid technological development made the German firm's components less attractive to the customers, who started to request complete systems beyond those which Gamma could offer in co-operation with its partner.

In 1973, the marketing function expanded. The product group manager worked to establish co-operation with Swedish firms. The aim was both to increase the number of customer contacts and to acquire the necessary technical assistance to further adapt the product range to the needs of industrial customers. The three most important firms in the industry were contacted. The two largest ones were not interested. The product group manager confessed that »they did not believe that we had the necessary 'know-how'». The smallest of the three firms accepted the proposal to co-operate.

It soon became evident that the choice of partner was a mistake. The management of the pollution control group aimed to make use of the partner's sales organization abroad. These efforts failed because Gamma had overestimated its partner's knowledge of Gamma's own technology. It also appeared that the products were not perfectly complementary and hence lowered the partner's incentives to promote Gamma's products.

Comments. The decrease in defense orders and the change in defense policy made it necessary for Gamma to develop new markets, because it could not, as Alpha did, extend its control of its customers (Table 4.7). Rather, the tendency was to adapt existing technology to new products and markets (concentric diversification). Invariably, Gamma started to market its products alone and found that they were not well adapted to the customers' needs and that a broader product range was needed in order to be competitive.

Both the hydraulic and air-cleaning operations developed in what might be labelled a trial-and-error process. There was no clear knowledge of the market, and the resources were inappropriate. The vision that guided the development became invalid in the new situations. During the interviews, the responsible product-group managers expressed the uncertainty that was felt during the change process. Other firms were believed to possess the resources and the strategy that Gamma lacked, but comprehension of the exact nature of these resources was unclear to Gamma's decision makers.

Under such circumstances it is not surprising that the decisions were made ad hoc and that there were failures in the choice of partners. There are similarities when compared with Beta's development, but the piecemeal character of the actions was much more pronounced.

Table 4.7   Gamma's co-operation agreements and acquisitions

GAMMA (Development strategy - product development and product diversification)

Year	Form of co-operation	Partner(s)	Partner(s) product line	Gamma's previous relation to partner(s)
I. Hydraulic machines				
1963	Joint project in R&D	One Swedish firm		
1970	Joint program as "umbrella", joint sales subsidiaries abroad	Two Swedish firms	Complementary and partly overlapping	No previous relation
1974	Joint program covering sales and R&D	Swedish firm	Complementary	No previous relation
II. Pollution control equipment				
1973	Contract covering sales know-how	German firm	Complementary	Previous contacts
1974	Contract covering sales	Swedish firm	Complementary but partly overlapping	No previous relation

Why Gamma resorted to co-operation is not as clear as in the two preceding cases. It is true that Gamma was under a certain financial strain (which made it difficult to go it alone, or acquire other companies) and that the product lines were not well adapted to the needs of the customers. But the decisions to co-operate seem to be less founded on a clear evaluation of the new environment, its interdependencies, and demands on a supplier - than on the lack of capability to evaluate these interdependencies and demands. This is quite another type of uncertainty than that which stems from existing transactions or competitive interdependencies.

5.4 Delta

Delta, a company in the machinery industry, employed about 2200 people with sales of 300 million Swedish crowns in 1974. It operated four product lines - (1) engines, (2) transporation equipment, (3) generators and (4) graphical equipment. Delta specialized in high precision work on heavy work pieces. Some of the products have a world wide reputation for good quality. About 50 per cent of Delta's business was with the Swedish defense department. Traditionally, the emphasis has been on production technology and quality and less on marketing.

During the sixties, Delta and Gamma faced similar problems. A stagnation and even decrease in defense orders forced the firm to diversify its operations. During a ten year period defense orders fell to a level of about five per cent of Delta's annual sales. The decline in defense orders, starting in the late fifties, did not immediately result in an acute crisis, but Delta started to work for new products to compensate for the defense production (Table 4.8).

Between 1958 and 1963, two new products were adopted. In 1958 Delta started to produce equipment for nuclear power plants. In 1960 it signed a combined license and co-operation agreement with a major U.S. producer of graphical equipment.

In 1963, the decline in defense orders became acute and the sales of new products did not compensate for this loss. An action program which emphasized cost efficiency and a search for new products was put into effect. Two new products in the transportation field were introduced in 1964 and 1965. Furthermore, efforts to increase exports continued.

In 1967, Delta seemed to have recovered from the crisis. It reached the largest sales in the firm's history (at fixed prices), and, for the first time during the sixties, it showed a net profit. The annual sales continued to increase during the following years, but profits once again turned into losses. In 1968, the company was hit by the most severe crisis during the period studied.

The new crisis was met by a new round of rationalization and reorganization. Twenty per cent of the employees were laid off (mostly white collar workers). Some important replacements were also made in top management. In restructuring Delta, the president attempted to increase its market orientation. A concentration of the resources was also requested and the previous »expansion in all directions» was terminated. During 1973-75 annual sales increased rapidly and Delta was able to show net profits again.

Engines. A new line of engines had been acquired from a competitor in the late fourties. During the fifties, however, the engine gradually became obsolete and sales dropped rapidly. When the development of a small engine was started in the late fifties, the situation was bad.

The crisis in 1963 brought about a shift of managers of the product line. The new divisional manager's orientation was completely different from that of the previous one. According to comments: »He opened the window to the world». He found it necessary to broaden the product range and initiated a joint development project of a big engine with three other firms originally, two in the engine manufacturing business and one a large customer of big engines. A jointly owned firm was founded in 1967 to administer and control the effort. The development costs turned out to be higher than expected. For two of the participants, other alternatives appeared and they left the project in 1968. The financial burden for the two remaining partners therefore

Table 4.8   Delta's development pattern

DELTA

General development	Diesel engines	Generators	Transportation equipment	Graphical equipment
	1948 Engine acquired from competitor		1948 Contract/ license for new transmission	
	1958 Development of small engine started. limited co-operation			1960 License and co-operation agreement contracted by U.S. firm
1963 Crisis- rapid drop in defense orders Rationalization program				
1964 Organization according to product groups	1964 New manager	1964 Joint deliveries with a competitor	1964 New manager 1964 License and co-operation agreements	1964 Revision of contract
	1965 Development of new small engine finished			1966 Revision of contract
1968 New crisis Rationalization and reorganization	1966-67 Joint development of large engine			1968 U.S. partner bankrupt
1968 New president				1968 New product manager
1970 New organizational structure Concentration of resources	1970 New manager			1969 Supplementary line acquired
1972 New strategies requested. Concentration to a limited number of products	1971 Development of large engine collapsed	1971 New product group manager		1970 New U.S. partner
		1973 Development marketing and production of a new type of generator (same partner)		

increased. The remaining partner was taken over by a larger corporation in 1970, and the new owner decided to withdraw from the project in 1971. Delta could not continue the project on its own. It was estimated that Delta had lost 5-6 years in the development of a new line of engines.

When new strategies were requested by the president in 1972, it was decided that Delta would stay in the same capacity range as that represented by its small engine. It was further decided that granting licenses could be one way of expanding into new markets. Despite the costs for developing the big engine, the product group was showing handsome profits in 1972 and as the product manager expressed it: »When all things go well, you are less inclined to co-operate, you want to do everything yourself».

Generators. Delta also produced large and stationary generators. Annually, the generator group carried out a small number of big projects. For a firm which competed for large projects that are often decided upon by government authorities, it was necessary to have a well-functioning information system, based on well established contacts with buyers, consultants, and representatives in the respective countries.

During the fifties and the early sixties, in Sweden there was a rapid expansion in demand for the type of generators produced by Delta. The expansion attracted foreign competition. This happened at the same time as the defense orders started to decrease and Delta's profitability diminished.

In Sweden, the generator business was subject to competition from one domestic firm that faced the same problems as Delta. The parties discussed the possibility that one of the firms would take over the other's generator business. None of the firms, however, had the financial strength to do so. Instead, the discussion led to an agreement to co-operate on a project basis. The aim was to keep the foreign firms away from the Swedish market to smooth out the variations in the capacity utilizations, and to decrease the buyer's possibilities to play off one firm against the other.

The parties started to give joint tenders, both on the international and the domestic markets. Up to the end of the sixties, the joint deliveries amounted to 30-40 per cent of the partners' total sales of generators. Thereafter, almost all deliveries to the domestic market have been made jointly.

The project-based co-operation has led to a long-term agreement for the development, marketing, and production of a new line of generators. The new co-operation is based on a written contract and runs for a ten year period.

Transportation equipment. The background of the co-operation was a U.S. firm's desire to expand in the European market after the Second World War. However, its products were not adapted to European conditions, nor did the firm possess the necessary market know-how. It decided to expand through licensing in the respective countries. The potential licensees were firms that produced the same type of transportation equipment, but with less efficient transmissions. The U.S. firm would supply a license on the transmission and let the licensee use it in his own equipment. In the forties, Delta had carried out its own development work on a similar transmission, but had not been very successful. Therefore, the interest in a co-operation was pronounced at Delta.

Graphical equipment. The license and co-operation agreement with a U.S. manufacturer of graphical equipment in 1960 constituted a diversification of

Delta's operations. The diversification was the result of the search for new products during the late fifties. The U.S. manufacturer had received an inquiry from one of the largest Swedish newspapers that planned to invest in new equipment.

The Swedish newspaper, however, requested that the equipment should be produced in Sweden and also serviced by a domestic firm. The U.S. manufacturer contacted a few potential licensees, one of which had close ties with Delta and suggested that Delta would be a suitable partner. Delta's management knew very little about graphical equipment, especially the marketing side, but the products fitted well into the existing production facilities and it was decided to accept the U.S. firm's offer.

During the course of co-operation, Delta increased its marketing know-how and became less and less dependent on its licensor. The change in dependence is reflected in two revisions of the ten-year contract which gave Delta a succesively stronger position. The co-operation was suddenly interrupted by the licensor's bankruptcy.

Table 4.9   Delta's co-operation agreements and acquisitions

DELTA (Development strategy - product development and product diversification)

Year	Form of co-operation	Partner(s)	Partner(s) product line	Delta's previous relation to partner
I Diesel engines				
1966	Joint venture in R&D terminated 1971	Three Swedish firms	Complementary but partly overlapping	Two competitors and one customer
II Generators				
1964	Joint program covering sales	One Swedish firm	Overlapping	Competitor
1973	Renewal of contract, joint program in R&D	-"-	-"-	-"-
III Transportation equipment				
1948	License-based co-operation	One U.S. firm	Complementary	Exchange of know-how
1958	Renewal of contract again 1968	-"-	-"-	-"-
IV Graphical equipment				
1960	License-based co-operation revised 1964 and 1966	One U.S. firm	Complementary	No previous relation

Comments. The decrease in defense orders made it necessary for Delta to develop alternative sources of revenue. The pressure to find new products was strong. The guidance, or criteria for search, was mainly that new products should fit the existing production facilities. Hence no clear and accepted vision of the firm's future product-market scope existed. This lead to an expansion in »all» directions. The actual reorientation was completed in 1973 when a new vision and strategy for the firm had emerged. The strategic actions which included co-operation seem to have had three major directions, to defend existing product lines against aggressive foreign competition (generators), to strengthen existing product lines (transportation equipment and engines), and to develop new product lines (graphical equipment).

In two of the cases (generators and engines) Delta responded to external threats. It did not have the resources to go it alone. The joint program of the generator division was a successful attempt to fight off third parties and to increase the joint bargaining power towards the state monopsonist. For the most part the partners put in similar resources and their motives to co-operate remained stable. The joint development project in the engine division was a response to a similar situation. However, several partners were included, thereby increasing the risk of conflicts and co-ordination problems. Furthermore, developing a new product probably involves more uncertainty than defending an existing market.

In the two other cases (transportation and graphical machines) Delta responded to business opportunities (although the willingness to respond must have been influenced by the need for new products to compensate for the decline in defense orders). Since none of the co-operation agreements included joint operations (the licensor did not operate in Europe), the risk for conflicts of interests and co-ordination problems must have been reduced. However, an element of instability can be found in Delta's gradual learning of the graphical machine business. Delta's need for resources (technical and marketing know-how) was gradually reduced and called for revision of the initial agreement.

Compared with Gamma's development, Delta had opportunities both to defend its existing domain and to expand it. The overall change process seems to have been rather »chaotic» just as in Gamma, but the situations for the individual divisions were probably less difficult. The diversification was facilitated because the licensor could provide a market adapted product and a customer who had signed a purchase contract to start with.

6. Discussion

The analysis of the four companies' strategic actions illustrates that co-operation can be interpreted both as a means to control existing interdependencies, and, when they extend their domains (Table 4.10), as a means to acquire complementary resources, particularly product and market know-how.

From Table 4.10 we find that the raw material based firms developed through vertical integration and entered into co-operation mainly with their previous customers. A main purpose of the co-operation was to gain increased control over the disposal of the company's own output. The firms in the machinery industry co-operated with firms in their own industry but with whom they were not directly competing. They sought complementary resources and solutions to strategic problems.

Table 4.10   Summary of strategic action in the studied firms

Strategy/strategic action		Mechanism for implementing strategy	Previous relation to partner or acquired firm	Dominating motives
DEFENDING AN EXISTING DOMAIN				
1. Delta: Generators	1964 1973	Joint program	Competitor	Meet intensified foreign competition
FURTHER REFINEMENT OF EXISTING PRODUCTS				
2. Alpha: Refinery	1963	Joint venture	Supplier to partner	Increase control over sales interdependencies
3. Alpha: Refinery	1973	Joint venture	Supplier	Increase control over sales interdependencies
4. Alpha: Chemicals	1962	Acquisition	Supplier	Better economic results by integration spreading risks
5. Alpha: Chemicals	1963	Joint venture	Indirect supplier	Increase control over sales interdependencies
6. Alpha: Chemicals	1973	Joint venture	Exchange of know-how (Partner in the same industry but not competitor)	Complementary process know-how
7. Beta: Packaging	1965	Go it alone	-	Better economic result by integration
8. Beta: Packaging	1967	Joint program	Exchange of know-how	Increase control over sales interdependencies
FURTHER REFINEMENT OF EXISTING PRODUCT AND MARKET EXPANSION				
9. Beta: Packaging	1968	Joint venture	Supplier	Increase control over sales interdependencies
10. Delta: Engines	1966	Joint venture	Supplier and competitor	Complementary product know-how
11. Delta: Transport	1948	License/ contract	Exchange of know-how (Partner in the same industry but not competitor)	Complementary product know-how
DIVERSIFICATION				
12. Alpha: Machinery	1972	Acquisition	Customer of partner	
13. Gamma: Hydraulic	1970	Joint venture	Marginal competitors	Complementary products
14. Gamma: Hydraulic	1974	Joint program	No previous direct relation (partner in the same industry but not competitor)	Complementary resources and know-how
15. Gamma: Pollution control	1973	Contract	No previous relation with air cleaners, but in other fields	Complementary product and market know-how
16. Gamma: Pollution control	1974	Contract	No previous direct relation (partner in the same industry but not competitor)	Complementary market organization
17. Delta: Graphical	1960	License/ joint program	No previous direct relation (partner in the same industry but not competitor)	Complementary product and know-how

It is not surprising that in Sweden, a country with a relatively small domestic market and where foreign trade is extremely important, the distinction between national and transnational co-operation is not as clear as Pfeffer and Nowak (1976) stated. Alpha's transnational joint ventures in refining and

89

national joint venture in the chemical industry are both mechanisms to deal with existing transactional interdependencies. Likewise, Delta's national joint venture in the engine business and Gamma's joint sales subsidiaries are motivated by a need for complementary resources as well as cost sharing but not by existing resource interdependencies.

A number of co-operation agreements were entered primarily because of the need for complementary resources as previously suggested by Aiken and Hage (1968). However, their explanation only fits a part of the instances of co-operation presented here. For example, in the cases of diversification, the decisions to co-operate did not follow directly from the attempt to realize a business venture that initiated co-operation, but as a result of repeated failures.

Therefore, it is necessary to use a more sophisticated framework than either environmental characteristics and interdependencies or internal structural characteristics of the firm in order to understand interfirm co-operation. In this study we have added two components; the strategic role of co-operation and the strategic vision under which decisions to co-operate are made. We argue that there is a dynamic interaction between strategic vision, external, and internal variables which affect a firm's motives for co-operation and its willingness to continue that co-operation. The groups of variables are shown in Figure 4.1.

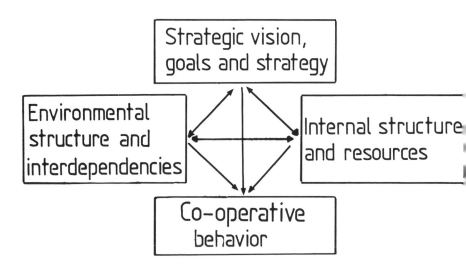

Figure 4.1 A framework for analyzing co-operative behaviour.

One of the striking differences between the cases is the existence of a strategic vision that may serve as a guideline for strategic action - the formulation of strategic goals and strategies to implement these goals. In the four companies studied the stability and articulation of the strategic vision seemed to be related to the structure of and interdependencies with the environment as well as the expansion of the company's domain. Furthermore, the change of domain required that new resources were developed, and hence affected the internal structure. The magnitude of these effects seemed to vary with the degree of domain expansion. Diversification led to more pronounced internal alterations than vertical integration did. This is quite natural, because diversification means that the company starts to operate with a new product in a new environment. Internal structure also includes the values and orientations of the organization's decision makers. The values and orientations are likely to interplay with strategic vision and external structure (Normann, 1976).

The context. The raw material based firms operated in highly concentrated industries and Alpha's customers were in similar environments, while Beta's customers operated in a moderately concentrated industry. Except for the dependence on a limited number of customers, there was also a strong technological interdependence between supplier and customer. This implies that a change of supplier or customer has technical consequences. The number of alternatives open are restricted by the environmental and internal constraints. The strategic action then became a means to change the control of environmental interdependencies. The situation which prevailed in Delta's generator division also has several of these characteristics.

When Beta and its partner expanded to new markets, the situation appeared less well structured and required fundamental changes in operations. The machinery companies were both faced with irreversible change in their relationships with the environment. Their ability to exercise control over the environment was much more limited than that of Alpha. On the other hand, these companies were not as restricted by technology and know-how as the raw-material based firms were. Their basic technology could be further developed and adapted to their needs (concentric diversification).

The diversification made the old dominating vision obsolete. This was realized by the top management, but they could not develop a successful alternative during a short period of time. Instead the developments of these firms were characterized by an unfocused search for new strategies and resources. In both cases these processes were lengthy and marked by crisis and repeated changes of key personnel and organizational structure.

The motives for co-operation. Clear strategic visions and considerable resources give the firm bargaining power to manage its strong interdependencies with the environment. This seems to make it inclined to increase its control over those elements in the environment that generate uncertainty. Alpha is a typical example of this situation. When the resources are insufficient to control the environment, the pooling of resources may be a means to improve the firms competitiveness. Delta's generator division experienced this situation. Co-operation then becomes a means to manage existing - transactional and competitive - interdependencies.

The managers who we interviewed also mentioned that an additional motive was to reduce costs either through technical integration or economies of scale. Such aims are understandable when nature products are under heavy competition.

Complementary resources become a dominant motive when the product-market scope is expanded further, and when the expansion also requires changes of the strategic vision, internal resources and structures. Co-operation becomes part of a trial-and-error process, and is not only motivated by a need for complementary resources, but is also expected to offer a solution to the problem of developing a viable strategy.

The decision to co-operate. A well-structured situation as the one which Alpha faced (and to a certain extent, Beta) facilitates the planning of strategic moves, whereas changes that lead to new types of environments and products might produce a traumatic process of organizational learning. The degree of expansion of the firm's product-market scope seems to affect whether co-operation is the result of a planning process or decided upon in an ad hoc manner. In the well-structured situation, co-operation usually becomes »*the* solution» to the problems of interdependence. When the planning conditions deteriorate, co-operation becomes a piecemeal decision. Each problem is treated as it appears, and successive revisions of the strategies are necessary.

Planned co-operation was characterized by conscious considerations of alternatives. The environmental structure and interdependencies, as well as the firm's own resources, seemed to create a situation where a joint venture was a natural solution, as in the case of Alpha. In the analysis of why co-operation became part of a traumatic change process, such clear cause-effect relations were not at hand. Rather the analysis must focus on understanding the change process and the strain it imposes on the decision makers. Co-operation was then one of several solutions, and often chosen merely because it appeared as an alternative, - the opportunity of finding a solution to »the unknown».

The choice of partner. The partners were often chosen within arm's length. Alpha managed its dependence on certain customers by co-operating with them. The choice of partner was quite evident: the customers were the sources of uncertainty which had to be controlled. Also Beta and the U.S.-firm mainly chose local customers as partners. The choice is less evident when a firm moves into a new environment. Even though Beta had 'established formal search criteria, it chose a firm with whom it already had an exchange of know-how. The diversifying firms tended to choose partners with whom they had no prior business relations. Still their choices were influenced by other relations to some of the partners: members of the same business association, companies which had relations with other units of the focal firm. The diversifying firms had few contacts within their new environments, and often enjoyed little prestige among the established firms, because they had not proven their competence. Hence, as with Gamma, the more prestigious firms did not want to co-operate.

The choice of partner also implies new uncertainty with respect to the potential partner's goals, competence, and way of operating. It seems as if firms -

the decision makers - place considerable importance on mutual trust as a means to reduce this type of uncertainty. In the two diversifying companies, where the task uncertainty was considerable, trust took a personal, or social, character. This was expressed by their choice of partners whom they already knew from elsewhere. In the raw material-based companies, where the planning conditions were good, and technical interdependencies were strong, the need for personal trust diminished. Instead it took a product-connected, technical character, based on past performance.

The viability of co-operation. Thompson (1967: 35) argued that co-operation means an exchange of commitments,

> »... commitments are obtained by giving commitments and uncertainty, reduced for the organization through its reduction of uncertainty for others.»

Stopford and Wells (1972) saw the decision to co-operate as a trade-off between the need for unilateral control and for resources. The firm reduces its control over a certain part of its operations in exchange for resources, or increased control over other parts of the operations.

When the firm's decisions about its own operations have little effect upon the environment - for example when there is a structural change in demand - unilateral control becomes an illusion. It then becomes important to extend the control of the sources of uncertainty. This type of trade-off was done in Alpha and Beta.

A firm may also open up when the dominant strategic vision has become obsolete, when new relations to the environment are sought, and when own resources are perceived to be insufficient. This happened during diversifications as well as when changes were made in top management.

If the initial motives for co-operation remain stable, it is likely that the joint program or venture can survive. As long as Alpha is dependent on its partners and they on Alpha, one would assume that the joint ventures have a fair chance to survive. But there will be pressures toward increased control when the strategic moves are completed, and attention is again shifted to operating efficiency. This is especially evident when co-operation is based on complementary resources, which can be acquired through learning. The initial motives then change, and the basis for co-operation may be disrupted. Beta revised its strategy for market expansion, and Delta's engine division preferred to go it alone »when everything works well».

A further reason for instability is that problems shift and that the choice of partners during the change processes are made ad hoc. When co-operation is a wrong decision, the partner is not the right one, or the nature of the problems changes, the stability of co-operation is likely to be limited.

93

7. Some Theoretical Implications

We have attempted to show that the resource-dependence and the structural-complexity models only provide partial explanations of interorganizational co-operation. Instead we argue that a contingency approach to understanding interorganizational co-operation would be more appropriate. The degree of domain expansion can serve as a contingency variable which enables us to differentiate between such strategic roles of co-operation as managing interdependencies and seeking complementary resources.

Both the resource-dependence and the structural-complexity models have deterministic traits. Co-operation follows from structural characteristics of the relations with the environment or of the firm. By using a case-oriented approach we can analyze, although to a limited depth, how the decisions to co-operate were made. There appears to have been a certain freedom of action (Child, 1972) in most cases. The firms did not always choose co-operation. Furthermore, the decisions to co-operate could become parts of a learning process. Then it was the decision makers' uncertainty about the nature of environmental interdependencies (and the appropriate strategy) that was to be reduced through co-operation.

Aldrich and Mindlin (1978: 161) made a similar distinction between a resource-dependence and an information-uncertainty perspective on the environment. They argued that »the decision makers' perceptions of their environments may be a key point at which the perspectives are joined» This can be seen as an argument for a subjectivist, purposive-action approach like the one presented by, for example, Weick (1969). We used the concept of strategic vision in order to differentiate between well-structured and ill-structured decision situations. When the firm acted within its existing domain, its ability to read the environment was much better than when it made considerable strategic changes. In the latter case the »objective» nature of the environment had little impact on the decisions, because the decision makers were uncertain about the nature. It is typical that the motives for co-operation often disappeared when the firm had increased its knowledge.

We would suggest three complementary models for analyzing interfirm co-operation with the degree of domain expansion serving as a contingency variable: *The resource-dependence model* suits situations where the firm operates in a well-known environment that exhibits strong interdependencies of a transactional or competitive nature. Co-operation would then be interpreted as a means to manage such interdependencies.

The structural-complexity model would be appropriate when the firm expands its domain and has a fairly clear vision of an appropriate strategy. Co-operation could be a means to acquire such resources that the firm does not possess itself. Co-operation may be both a temporary or a long-lived solution, partly depending on the firm's needs.

A trial-and-error learning model would be needed in order to understand how firms may seek co-operation in order to make up for their own lack of visions, or to create strategic goals. The decisions to co-operate are then likely to be made ad hoc and co-operation will often be unstable.

The models should not be interpreted as independent of each other. The cases indicated that they overlap to a considerable extent.

8. References

Aiken, M. and Hage, J., 1968
»Organizational Interdependence and Intra-organizational Structure.« *American Sociological Review,* 33: 912-930.

Aldrich, H., 1975
»Resource Dependence and Interorganizational Relations: Relations Between Local Employment Service Offices and Social Services Sector Organizations.« *Administration and Society* 7: 419-455.

Aldrich, H., 1976
»An Organizational Dependency Perspective on Relations Between the Employment Service and the Organization-Set.« In Kilmann, Pondy, and Slevin (eds.) *The Management of Organization Design.* Vol. II: 231-266, New York: Elsevier.

Aldrich, H., and Mindlin, S., 1978
»Uncertainty and Dependence: Two Perspectives on Environment.« In Karpik (ed.) *Organization and Environment.* Beverly Hills, California: Sage.

Child, John, 1972
»Organizational Structure, Environment, and Performance: The Role of Strategic Choice.« *Sociology,* 8: 1-21.

Cyert, Richard M., and March, James G., 1963
A Behavioral Theory of the Firm Englewood Cliffs, N.J.: Prentice-Hall.

Edström, A., and Högberg, B., 1977
»The Strategic Context of Interfirm Cooperation.« Working Paper No. 77-22. Brussels: European Institute for Advanced Studies in Management.

Edström, A., Högberg, B., Norbäck, L.E., 1981
»Alternative Explanations of Interorganizational Co-operation«. Paper No. 1981 - 172. Gothenburg: Department of Business Administration, University of Gothenburg.

Franko, L.G., 1971
Joint venture Survival in Multinational Cooperations. New York: Praeger.

Franko, L.G., 1976
The European Multinationals: A Renewed Challenge to American and British Big Business. London.

Guetzkow, H., 1966
»Relations among Organizations.» In Bowers, R. (ed.) *Studies on Behaviour in Organizations:* 13-44. Athens, G.A: University of Georgia Press.

Gullander, S., 1976
»An Exploratory Study of Interfirm Cooperation of Swedish firms.» Unpublished Ph.D. thesis, New York: Columbia University.

Högberg, B., 1977
Interfirm Cooperation and Strategic Development. Gothenburg: Business Administration Studies.

Norbäck, L.E., 1978
Relationer mellan samarbetande företag. Gothenburg: Business Administration Studies.

Normann, R., 1976
Management of Statemenship. Stockholm: SIAR Dokumentation AB.

Pfeffer, J., 1972
»Merger as a Response to Organizational Interdependence.» *Administrative Science Quarterly,* 21: 398-418.

Pfeffer, J., and Nowak, J., 1976
»Joint Ventures and Interorganizational Interdependence.» *Administrative Science Quarterly,* 21: 398-418.

Pfeffer, J., and Salancik, G., 1978
The External Control of Organizations. New York: Harper & Row.

Reid, W., 1967
»Interagency Coordination in Delinquency and Control.» *Social Service Review.* 38: 418-428.

Stopford, J.M., and Wells, L.T., 1972
Managing the Multinational Enterprise. New York: Basic Books.

Stopford, J., and Haberich, K., 1976
»Ownership and Control of Foreign Operations.» *Journal of General Management.* 4: 3-20.

Thompson, J.D., 1967
Organizations in Action New York: McGraw-Hill.

Weick, K.E., 1969
The Social Psychology of Organizing. Reading, Mass.: Addison-Wesley.

Yuchtman, E., and Seashore, S.E., 1967
»A System Resource Approach to Organizational Effectiveness.»
American Sociological Review 32: 891-903.

SECTION II: MODES OF INTERORGANIZATIONAL CO-OPERATION

1. Section Contents: An Overview

Organizational interdependence and co-operation may be managed in a variety of ways. For instance, the participating organizations may be left more or less intact or they may be replaced by a »new» organization. Merger is one extreme. It calls for a proprietary strategy (Aldrich, 1979), i.e., a strategy involving full ownership of and control over the resources. However, merger is not a unimodal method to define boundaries of the organization and to assign functions to it. Modal variety applies not only to market economies, where variability and flexibility are high, in fact almost unlimited in scope, but also to planned economies, where uniformity is high and superordinate to variability. But even there recognition of a changing environment requires organizational forms and modes of co-operation to be adapted to reality (see Kortan below). Variability in form is also requested in some sectors of public administration, as is demonstrated in the comparative analysis of Evan and Klemm.

Less definite modes of interorganizational co-operation (i.e., non-proprietary ones) are still richer in variety, as the contributions by Pennings on mergers and interlocking directorates (tight coupling) and the chapters by Edström, Högberg, and Norbäck on modes of co-operation (loose coupling) demonstrate. Aldrich, 1979, would use the term »Action set» for the forms chosen. Mattsson investigates modes to co-ordinate technology transfer projects in quasi-market situations.[1]

Daems develops a morphology for institutional organization of co-operation within industry to provide co-ordination, allocation, and monitoring (see Figure II.1).

He investigates why, under which conditions, and how the different modes appear in practice.

Pennings, analyzes the literature on merger and interlocking directorates as alternative means to manage interorganizational dependence. He compares and contrasts the two modes of co-ordination. He first defines his level of analysis. Whereas mergers at the *industrial* level have been abundantly researched, studies dealing with co-operating/merging *enterprises* still are rare. Research dealing with interlocking directorates is practically non-existent (Poensgen, 1980, provides the only empirical study in this area, supply-

---

[1] An investigation of related type of organizational forms for international industrial enterprises in socialist countries is reported upon in Goldberg, W.H., »Multinational Corporations in Socialist Countries», IIM/dp 80-7, Berlin, 1980, not included here.

Type of institution	Ownership	Returns	Supervision	Examples
Markets	Independent	No-pooling	No	Exchanges Contingent contracts
Federations	Independent Consolidated -> Independent	Pooling Pooling No-pooling	No No Yes	Cartels Industrial Groups Franchising Interlocking Directorship
Hierarchies	Consolidated ->	Pooling	Yes	Integrated and diversified companies

Figure II.1   Basic characteristics of markets, federations and hierarchies. Source: Daems.

ing evidence for the Federal Republic of Germany). Pennings proposes a number of conjectures regarding the efficiency and consequences of modes of interorganizational co-operation. He concludes that joint directors act as agents of co-operation/coercion in vertically integrated organizations, and as »common messengers» in horizontally integrated ones.

Kortan claims that economies of scale through concentration and specialization are the dominant merger motive in socialist countries. Improvement of planning is another motive mentioned. Distinguishing the varying functions to be performed by the management of enterprises, he identifies three different modes:

a.   industrial associations

b.   enterprise associations

c.   multiplant enterprises (which may also include vertical and horizontal combines).

Industrial associations are highly centralized and powerful. The participating enterprises are highly dependent; their decision-making power is very low. *Enterprise associations* are usually horizontally integrated enterprises. Their members are generally more independent than those of an industrial association. *Multiplant enterprises* apply centralization of functions to the enterprise level (directorate). Individual plants maintain only rudimentary management functions. Kortan reports that it is regarded necessary to go beyond

100

the fairly centralized types of large enterprises and to create looser modes of co-operation and co-ordination such as *associations of independent economic units* (quite similar to those investigated by Edström, Högberg, and Norbäck).

Evan and Klemm compare the effectiveness and consequences of four modes of interorganizational co-operation of hospitals: consortia, joint ventures, mergers, and corporate management systems. Their analysis departs from the environmental determinism and resource dependence models of Aldrich and Pfeffer (1967) as core determinants of organizational design. They thus adopt a contingency theory approach for a comparative study of varying forms of arranging for interorganizational co-operation. The *consortium,* an arrangement between non-profit organizations, is a very loose form of co-operation which leaves the participating institutes intact while offering joint services of some kind. If a consortium is arranged between hospitals operating on a profit basis, it is labelled as *corporate management system.* A *joint venture* is a separate facility organized under separate management by organizations remaining independent. Finally, Evan and Klemm discuss a regular *merger.* In Daems' terms the compared archetypes of interorganizational co-operations would be distinguished by the following properties:

Type of hospital organization	Ownership	Pooling of returns	Supervision	Example
Markets	Independent	Not applicable	No	Joint trade association at local, state or national level (mentioned by Evan and Klemm, but not part of their comparison).
Federations	Independent	Not applicable	Yes	Consortium of non-profit hospitals
	Independent	No	Yes	Corporate management systems, for-profit-hospitals.
Hierarchies	Consolidated	No	Yes	Joint venture
	Consolidated	Yes	Yes	Merged hospital(s)

Figure II.2   Daems' model applied to Evan and Klemm.

After elaborate analysis, the authors conclude that the formal organizational choices render greatly differing results. However, because of the complex goal structures of hospital systems, organizational (structural) variables do not follow strategy nearly as strongly and unambiguously as observed in industry (by Chandler, Channon, Rumelt and others). Nevertheless, strategy,

101

structure, and performance in multi-hospital systems are obviously and significantly interrelated in ways which lead to the conclusion that organizational and political alternatives and choices deserve much more attention from their constituencies than they enjoy today.

In the general setting of transfer of technology from developed to developing countries, *Mattsson* investigates the choice, performance, and efficiency of modes of interorganizational co-operation, as seen from the supplier's of technology point of view. The modes rank between the extremes

a. direct investment by and under the full control of sellers, and

b. dis-joint purchasing by the buyer.

In between these extremes fall turn key projects, joint ventures, production sharing, management contracts, service contracts, licensing, and other forms of mixed control by buyers and sellers over technology transfer projects.

After defining, delineating, and characterizing the various options, Mattsson concludes with an analysis of the relative efficiency of the different options in relation to the sellers' goal structure. He also takes the goals and situation of the recipient into account.

2. Conclusion

One can conclude from this section, as well as from sections I and III, that the typical conception of merger as bringing two organizations together $(1 + 1 = 1$, the larger acquires the smaller) reflects only a very small part of the entire picture of interorganizational co-operation. Indeed, a wide variety of motives for interorganizational co-operation exists, demanding a similar multitude of arrangements and modes. In most cases, a variety of structural and strategic options exist. Their relative merits ought to be assessed in relation to the motives and objectives of the particular case on one hand, but also with regard to the contingencies and the context in the resource dependence-environmental determinism dimension on the other hand. The process section below will further emphasize this statement.

3. References

Aldrich, H.E., 1979
    Organizations and Environments, Englewood Cliffs, N.J.: Prentice-Hall.

Aldrich, H.E., and Pfeffer, J., 1979
    »Environments of organizations.« *Annual Review of Sociology,* No. 2.

Chandler, A.D., 1966
  Strategy and Structure, New York: Anchor Books.

Channon, D.F., 1973
  The Strategy and Structure of British Enterprise, London: McMillan.

Goldberg, W.H., 1980
  »Multinational Corporations in Socialist Countries,» *IIM/dp 80-7,* Science Center, Berlin.

Poensgen, O.H., 1980
  Between Market and Hierarchy Saarbrücken (mimeo).

Rumelt, R.P., 1974
  Strategy, Structure and Economic Performance, Boston: Graduate School of Business.

5. MERGERS AND INTERLOCKING DIRECTORATES: CASES OF INTERORGANIZATIONAL CO-OPERATION

Johannes M. Pennings
Columbia University
New York, N.Y., U.S.A.

1. Introduction

This essay compares and contrasts mergers and interlocking directorates as alternative coordination devices for managing interorganizational interdependence. It presents a framework delineating interorganizational interdependence and its antecedents and suggests that organizations often may rely on interlocking directorates as an alternative to mergers. This choice is due to differences in flexibility and to differences in risk in evoking hostile environmental reactions. Interlocking directorates are relatively covert and difficult to monitor, while they also preserve the organization's autonomy. Both mergers and interlocking directorates may benefit the organizations involved. Similarly, they both may have public policy implications. This chapter lists some avenues of research that might identify the conditions under which such forms of inter-firm organizations promote organizational effectiveness, and whether they have implications for public policy. A dominant theme in the current organizational theory centers on how organizations are related to their environment. This theme concerns how organizations manipulate, control, and select their environments, as well as how they themselves are manipulated, controlled and molded by the environment. Organizations are often limited in their ability to generate the resources needed to survive, and they are thus forced to enter into exchange relationships with other organizations. They must negotiate in order to maintain the legitimacy of their existence. Their behavior is constrained by regulatory agencies, pressure groups, and other external interest groups. Furthermore, organizations compete for the acquisition of supplies and for the disposal of output, i.e., they are also interdependent with competing organizations with which they have no direct exchanges, but which can nonetheless affect the exchange relationships.

The present research on organization-environment relationships has evolved over a period of twenty years. Initially the focus was on individual organizations and the ways in which they were structurally designed in regard to environmental characteristics. For example, research by Dill (1958), Terreberry (1968), Lawrence and Lorsch (1967) dealt with focal organizations and how they cope with their particular environment, and try to determine how relationships between environmental and organizational variables relate to organizational effectiveness. Gradually, however, there has been a shift from this research on the focal organizational level to the supra-organizational level (e.g., Evan, 1973; Williamson, 1975; Aldrich, 1978; Hannan and Freeman, 1977; and Hirsch, 1975). The environment as a strategic arena becomes the unit of analysis and the focal organization is merely an actor in the arena. Apparently, the attempt to define organizational environments as well-bounded and tangible entities has resulted in a focus on significant agents in an organization's environment. Significant agents include individuals, groups, and organizations with which the focal organization is interdependent. The joint consideration of focal organizations and their interdependent actors in the environment has materialized in the above mentioned shift to study higher levels of organizations such as industries, markets, buyer-seller systems, or more generally, »action sets» (Aldrich, 1978). One outgrowth of this trend has been the analysis of inter-organizational relationships in their own right. The interorganizational relationships can also be studied as a set of external conditions that affect individual organizations.

Interorganizational relationships manifest themselves in various ways. The level of organization of such relationships can range from very formal, explicit, and overt structures, to rather informal, implicit, and covert structures, and include mergers, joint ventures, cartels, flows of personnel, interlocking directorates, and informal gatherings of members at various locations. Organizations may follow many different strategies in the management of their relationships with other organizations. Some of the above strategies reduce their autonomy from their environment to a greater extent than do others, i.e., some of them are »radical». For example, merger implies the amalgamation of two autonomous units into a larger organization, while flows of personnel and interlocking directorates preserve the organizations' autonomy. The difference in radicalism, however, may also imply differences in effectiveness, in that a merger is better suited for overcoming transactional difficulties between interdependent organizations.

This chapter compares and contrasts mergers (which involve the fusion of two or more organizations) and interlocking directorates (interorganizational linkages formed by directors who are members of two or more boards of directors) as modes of interorganizational coordination. These two modes have been chosen for comparison because they are among the more prominent ones, have been studied most frequently, and permit a juxtaposition with respect to their degree of radicalism.

In this chapter we treat mergers and interlocking directorates as expressions of interorganizational relationships. Therefore, we do not deal with more macroscopic approaches to these phenomena. For example, the waves of mergers have often been analyzed as a trend towards economic concentration, when fewer firms enjoy a greater share of economic activity (e.g., Berle and Means, 1932; Ijiri and Simon, 1973). Such trends have implications for society and its allocation of resources. Similarly, interlocking directorates have been the subject of societal considerations. For example, a popular assumption among many authors has been that interlocks are the cement which binds a monolithic corporate power structure, and reveals the existence of a cohesive, economic-political elite (Perrucci and Pilisuk, 1971; Domhoff, 1967). This research at the regional or societal level has little relevance to interorganizational relations, since it does not trace mergers or interlocks to the interorganizational interdependence. It may be relevant indirectly in that merger behavior or interlocking could facilitate access to scarce resources, but this relevance is usually not explicitly examined.

This chapter deals with mergers and interlocks as an expression of interfirm behavior. It outlines an interorganizational framework and discusses the pertinent literature. Mergers and interlocks may be contingent upon interorganizational interdependence; as coordination devices they may also contribute to organizational effectiveness.

2. Organizations vs Supra-Organizational Collectives

Before proceeding to a discussion of the interorganizational framework, it may be useful to specify the unit of analysis. The research on mergers and interlocks has been plagued by an uncertainty about levels of analysis. This difficulty has been elucidated by Hirsch (1975), who suggests that when the focus is on how organizations relate to their environment or on how collectives of organizations reveal patterns, organization-environmental research must be carried out on an interorganizational or institutional level. Such focuses cannot be studied from the vantage point of individual organizations and agencies organized around specific products or services.

While research on mergers has had a tendency to concentrate on dyadic entities, it has often relied on industrial characteristics, such as concentration and entry barriers, to explain merger behavior. In contrast, most research on interlocks has had a societal, macroscopic vantage point, with little attention given to dyadic and industrial level research.

Since the chapter deals with the interorganizational level of analysis, it should be pointed out that studies at the societal level have little relevance. Similarly, studies which take an explicit or implicit organizational vantage point are also inappropriate for understanding the relational structures and processes among strategically interdependent organizations. Research and theory that explore mergers and vertical integration from the point of view of a focal organization may not fully capture the dynamic interplay between that focal organization and other organizations. For example, research on business strategy that fails to incorporate the aspects of other organizations which are the subject of a firm's business strategy is too one-sided. Diversification (which represents a focal organization's absorption of relatively unrelated firms) also has little interorganizational relevance and is typically used as a strategy by a focal organization to disperse risk and uncertainty. Indeed, Williamson (1975) sees diversification arising out of the firm's need to circumvent capital market inefficiencies. Thus, merger through diversification cannot be considered a strategy for managing interorganizational interdependence. Research on the composition of boards of directors (Pfeffer, 1972; Helmich, 1977) also does not deal with the relational aspects between two or more organizations, because such research is biased toward a focal organization's perspective. For example, an outside director may be the result of either a cooptation or a coercion maneuver and may fail to identify the direction. An outside director could be regarded as an asymmetrical antenna which the focal organization has extracted from the environment. He represents an asymmetrical linkage in that there is no information on the other side of the dyad.

At the interorganizational level of analysis, it is useful to treat vertical mergers and vertical interlocks as a result of interfirm transactions, while horizontal mergers and horizontal interlocks are hypothesized to emanate from industries or what Aldrich (1978) refers to as »action sets». Within such action sets we may determine why firms differ in merger propensity, how merger activity modifies the structure of the action set, and the centrality of each of the participating organizations, depending on their direct or indirect linkages. The term centrality refers to the number of steps (direct or indirect) through which an organization must go in order to reach any of the organizations belonging to its action set. Apart from determining the position of a firm within the network of its action set, we may also determine the structural properties of the action set itself, including the degree to which the participating firms are interconnected by interlocking directorates. Presumably, the greater the density, the greater the degree to which they enjoy a »shared monopoly». Similarly, we may identify cliques of organizations. These considerations suggest that the level of analysis issue is somewhat fuzzy, but also that it is important to specify the level properly in order to make meaningful investigations about mergers and interlocking directorates as interorganizational phenomena.

3. An Interorganizational Framework

It is hypothesized that mergers and interlocks are most prevalent in cases where organizations are highly interdependent. Interdependence is either vertical or horizontal. *Vertical* interdependence exists among organizations which are located at adjacent stages of a production process. For example, steel firms receive iron ore and local coal from mining companies and dispose of steel products to automobile manufacturers, construction companies, and other customers. A rehabilitation agency receives its referrals from hospitals and its financial resources from the government, and releases its clients to half-way houses and other institutions. *Horizontal* interdependence exists among competing organizations, and is best illustrated by the concept of oligopoly, where organizations, because they are relatively few in number, recognize their interdependence and realize that their market behavior affects each other and is observed by each other. Vertical and horizontal interdependence are strategic in nature. *Symbiotic* interdependence (Pennings, 1978) is not strategic. It exists among organizations which complement each other in the rendering of services to individual clients. Such organizations have a functional relationship analogous to the interplay between subunits in functionally organized firms. For example, specialized engineering firms may each produce a specific component of a power plant, or several social agencies may provide complementary services such as family and legal counsel in adoption cases. Symbiotic interdependence is not considered strategic unless the complementary relationships become permanent, such that newcomers are prevented from replacing organizations in such an »organizational set» (Evan, 1973). Symbiotic interdependent organizations are also exposed to each others' complementary role and may be subject to a greater diffusion of innovation. In this regard, symbiotic interdependence may have strategic implications. However, such implications are relatively minor when compared with those of horizontal and vertical interdependence, and they will not be further discussed.

The magnitude of vertical interdependence is a function of the substitutability and criticalness of the resources involved. Criticalness refers to the importance of resources in the sense that discontinuation of their flows would impede the focal organization's functioning. If a resource is critical for an organization's performance and if there are no adequate substitutes, dependence on organizations which produce these resources will be great (Pennings and Goodman, 1977).

The magnitude of horizontal interdependence is a function of the number of competitors and the similarity of inputs or outputs for which they compete. Indices of concentration of an industry, market, or other »action sets» (Aldrich, 1978) reflect the amount of interdependence. If the concentration is of an intermediate level (i.e., the market share of the four or eight largest firms is neither »large» nor »small»), the member-firms experience the highest amount of mutual influence.

The strategic nature of horizontal interdependence is highest when concentration of a market or industry is intermediate. If the market is concentrated (»pure competition»), the behavior of its firms shows stochastic tendencies and there is little than any one of them can do to alter the market parameters, such as price. Firms in an intermediately concentrated industry, however, face an environment that is less stochastic and more difficult to predict. In such an environment, organizations are aware of each other's presence, and their behavior may appear volitional or quasi-erratic. When industries are extremely concentrated, such as is the case in monopolies or dominant firms, the highly institutionalized and patterned behavior is predictable. Indeed, when there are very few competitors there is little uncertainty. Some authors have therefore implied that the relationship between concentration and uncertainty or unpatterned variability is U-shaped, with the highest uncertainty in intermediately concentrated industries (Pfeffer, 1972; Stern, L.W., and Morgenroth, 1968).

The strategic nature of relationships between vertically interdependent organizations is more difficult to identify. When buyers and/or sellers are relatively few in number, they are horizontally interdependent; this interdependence may then affect their relationships on the supply or sales side. Such markets may be flawed to such a degree that organizations may integrate backwardly or forwardly. Such reasoning is prominent in the work of Williamson (1975), who claimed that vertical relationships are often problematic in bilateral oligopoly conditions.

The market imperfections due to »small numbers» and the corresponding flaws in such markets (imperfect, incomplete, and unevenly distributed information among actors) tend to aggravate the transactional difficulties between buyers and sellers. This vertical interdependence is very salient when a firm faces few buyers or sellers, and most prominent when a focal organization's resources from those buyers or sellers are critical and non-substitutable.

109

4 .Mergers and Interlocking Directorates

Organizations are more prone to merge and to establish interlocking directorates under conditions of high vertical and horizontal interdependence. In the case of mergers, we can distinguish between vertical mergers or *vertical integration* to manage vertical interdependence, and *horizontal mergers* to manage competitive interdependence. In the case of interlocking directorates, vertically interdependent organizations can be regarded as *cooptation/ coercion,* and horizontally interdependent organizations as *»common messengers».*

5. Mergers

Compared with interlocking directorates, mergers are a very radical and thorough solution to the problems associated with the management of interorganizational relationships. Vertical integration resolves the transactional difficulties by harmonizing the interest of two previously adversary firms. By grouping two firms into a single organization, transactional haggling, opportunism, and uncertainty that contaminates buyer-seller relationships are circumvented. Indeed, the new firm ensures more complete, accessible, and undistorted information among the previously transactionally interdependent partners and partially removes the uncertainty so that they obtain more complete control over the environment. It also removes the need for costly contract negotiations and renewals, and for the enforcement of the agreements. As Williamson (1975) has stressed, market inefficiencies, such as those of oligopoly, which aggravate the transactional difficulties among buyers and sellers, often dictate a choice in favor of coordinating decision making through internal, adaptive, and sequential processes rather than relying on the resource allocation in an open market. The decision to vertically integrate must be guided by the relative costs and benefits of market transactions versus internal allocative procedures.

Vertical mergers do not necessarily result in competition reduction or in improvement of market power. Comanor (1967) and Hawkins and Radcliffe (1973) argue that vertical mergers would affect competition only by virtue of its impact on entry barriers. When vertical integration prevents entry at a single stage, the potential competitor has to begin operations at two stages. Additionally, merged organizations necessarily limit their buying and selling relationships to internal components. Thus, vertical mergers may decompose the bilateral oligopoly into smaller segments. Williamson has expanded this argument. He maintains that vertical integration may affect competition insofar as new firms would have to enter at two stages, and since they lag behind in their learning curves in the backward or forward industry, they may have greater difficulty in gaining access to the capital market for financing operations in any of the two stages (Williamson, 1975: 110-113). Thus, vertical integration may have antitrust implications. Horizontal mergers have even greater antitrust implications and have been attacked more vigorously in the United States. There is some speculation that merger propensity is highest in industries with intermediate concentration, but Pfeffer (1972) was unable to substantiate such conjectures. Pfeffer explained his results by means of the fact that mergers tend to be inhibited by antitrust agencies. He also argues that when merger is proscribed, firms will rely on more acceptable collusion mechanisms, including interlocking directorates. It should be stressed, however, that Pfeffer compared industries, not organizations.

Weiss (1965) attempted to disaggregate his data. He corroborated Pfeffer's results, but also showed that mergers were more likely to occur at the eight-firm concentration level indices than at the four-firm level, and were even more probable at the 20-firm concentration ratio. Even though such evidence is rather »diffuse», it reveals a slight tendency for industries with intermediate concentration ratios to show higher merger propensity. It is also possible to conclude that firms of different sizes show varying inclinations toward merger behavior. Larger firms in an intermediately concentrated industry are less likely to merge than their somewhat smaller competitors.

Horizontal mergers may accrue benefits for the participating organizations because mergers may alter the market structure or because they perform an intelligence function for the organizations involved (see Cable's contribution in this book).

6. Interlocking Directorates

Compared with mergers, interlocking directorates are rather innocuous. They allow the focal organization to remain autonomous while potentially neutralizing vertical and horizontal interdependence. Interlocks among vertical organizations can be viewed as quasi-surreptitious attempts to alleviate transactional difficulties. It is often difficult to determine whether such interlocks were brought about by cooptation or coercion. Cooptation is a term coined by Selznick (1949), who noted in his TVA study that organizations confronted by advisory organizations were able to neutralize their potential disruption by making them part of the decision structure. Thus, cooptation implies that the recruitment initiative is vested in the focal organization. On the other hand, coercion implies that the selection originates from organizations to which the focal organization is related (e.g., banks). It is possible to determine the mode of an interlock by examining the principal affiliation of the linking director, if one exists. For example, if the director was employed by the focal organization, cooptation was the means of interlock. If he was employed by a supplier or buyer, coercion was the mode. Thus, interlocks represent an intermediate structure through which organizations preserve their autonomy, yet allow relevant outsiders into the internal decision making process. Vertical interlocks may therefore augment interdependence.

The interlocking directorates between competing organizations mitigates their strategic interdependence. As common messengers, they create prior knowledge which enables firms to forecast the otherwise unforeseen and possibly disruptive actions of competitors, and thus become a parameter in an organization's development of new strategies. Such interlocks also facilitate the surveillance of implicit collusive agreements and reinforce the propensity toward normative uniformity or competitive behavior. In comparison with mergers, interlocks probably have only relatively superficial effects (Williamson, 1975), but further research is needed before the significance of interlocks between horizontally interdependent organizations can be disregarded.

The research to date shows that vertical interdependence as defined in reference to banks is only slightly related to interlocking directorates (Pfeffer, 1972; Gogel et al., 1975; Allen, 1974; and Dooley, 1969). Vertical interdependence is measured with indices of capital structure, such as debt-equity ratio and solvency ratio. Horizontal interdependence has not often been related to interlocks. The only study which is indirectly relevant (Pfeffer and Nowak, 1976) measured board composition in relation to concentration of the firms' industry. Interlocks can be instrumental for organizational success; they are a device for achieving »political effectiveness» as distinct from »efficiency» (Katz and Kahn, 1978), and represent one method through which an organization can perform well politically even though it may be sub-standard on internal, efficiency criteria. Indeed, research that would contrast mergers and interlocking directorates should examine their relative efficiency in managing interorganizational relationships. This issue will be addressed shortly.

7. Mergers, Interlocking Directorates, and Organizational Effectiveness

Williamson implies that intermediate or invisible forms of interfirm organization, such as interlocking directorates, are highly deficient in overcoming transactional difficulties among interdependent firms, while mergers are very consequential as a cure for modifying strategic interdependence. In this regard, the comparison between mergers and interlocking directorates is of great interest. According to Williamson, interlocking directorates do not establish a common hierarchy among the joined firms, whereas mergers do. The common hierarchy replaces the markets with all their failures, and facilitates closer scrutiny of and information flow between the participants as well as the enforcement of contractual commitments. In comparison, interlocks are relatively ineffective in establishing a quasi-hierarchy and thus remain a poor alternative to mergers.

Williamson's (1975) assertions await further research and testing. From an interorganizational perspective it would appear that mergers can be regarded as a forestalling mechanism, and interlocking directorates as an information mechanism to manage interdependence. Mergers forestall environmental uncertainty in that they remove the unexpected or uncontrollable behavior of significant firms in an organization's environment. Interlocking directorates are an information mechanism in that they facilitate the procurement of relevant intelligence about other important organizations without altering the conditions that induce uncertainty. As stated earlier, mergers do and interlocks do not alter the structure of the market. Similarly, mergers nullify and interlocks preserve the organization's autonomy.

Mergers have implications in regard to the effectiveness of both the firms involved in merger activity as well as the total set of organizations with which the merging firms are strategically interdependent. Contributions from financial economics (e.g., Mandelker, 1974) reveal that acquired firms which initially have substandard performance tend to receive a booster as a result of merger. For example, Mandelker suggests that mergers are a vehicle through which incompetent management can be replaced. Unfortunately, however, effectiveness is expressed solely in terms of stock market indices in these studies. They also fail to distinguish between horizontal mergers, vertical mergers, and mergers for diversification.

By means of horizontal mergers, a firm's industry or market may become more concentrated (Weiss, 1965), so that indirect benefits can accrue to merging firms due to association between concentration and performance (Comanor, 1967; Lieberson and O'Connor, 1972; Weiss, 1965; and Mann, 1966) and other benefits such as higher price level (Bell and Murphy, 1969; Esposito and Esposito, 1961; and Scherer, 1972). Research which would examine to what extent such indirect benefits are incentives for individual firms to merge is currently needed.

Apart from the increase in market power and benefits which are enjoyed by all members of the action set, there are obviously also disadvantages associated with mergers. Mergers among competitively interdependent firms are subject to substantial integration costs and possible antitrust action, particularly in the United States. Since Western Europe is more tolerant toward horizontal mergers, European research that would investigate the consequences of horizontal mergers for a firm's organizational effectiveness as well as for degree of competition reduction and the public interest in general would be useful.

As indicated earlier, vertical mergers are sometimes seen as not affecting competition reduction and thus have no welfare consequences. Vertical integration is usually undertaken for the purpose of reducing transactional costs with buyers and sellers. Although the implications in regard to organizational effectiveness seem obvious, the evidence to date is equivocal and incomplete. Vertical integration does reduce transaction costs, including the cost of monitoring contractual commitments (Williamson, 1975). However, Rumelt (1974) has shown that excessively vertically integrated firms are among those which perform most poorly. Presumably, vertical integration can often result in the acquisition of firms about which the management of the acquiring firm may have little information and know how, thereby suffering from information deprivation. In other cases, vertical integration tends to highly specialize a firm, and to prevent it from dispersing its risk into different, but related areas of economic activity. Naturally, there are other considerations than transaction costs and risk dispersion, and they suggest that the implications of vertical mergers regarding effectiveness are complicated and require further research before the topic can be fully understood.

The advantages and disadvantages of mergers invite a comparison with interlooking directorates. Although interlocking directorates preserve partial autonomy and thus, the possibility of partial market failures, they nonetheless avoid the disadvantages associated with mergers. In general, it is plausible to assume that well interconnected organizations have better access to resources and can better communicate with competitors.

Due to the fact that measuring interlocking per se is problematic, and that there is a lack of information about the coordination process between organizations, it is rather difficult to determine whether interlocking directorates reduce opportunism and promote vertical integration among transactionally interdependent firms. Such information is not usually available since it is highly sensitive and confidential. Compared with the numerous quantitative techniques for analyzing interorganizational structure, there is virtually no attempt to measure and analyze the interlocking process. The research by Mintzberg (1973) is pioneering, but limits itself primarily to internal organizational processes. There are historical case studies, (e.g., Stern, F., 1976) which have explored the archival data, thereby uncovering outcroppings that reveal parts of interorganizational communication processes. Stern (1976), for example, was able to reconstruct the flows of information among banks of Bismarck Germany, and showed that these flows were more efficient than those of the formal diplomatic networks. At this stage such ideographic research may be most preferable.

There is virtually no quantitative empirical evidence on the relationship between interlocking directorates and organizational decision making. Pfeffer's study (1972) is the only investigation on the consequences of board composition, and thus on the consequences of interlocks. Pfeffer found that the discrepancy between a firm's predicted and actual percentage of inside directors was not related to income as a function of sales, nor as a function of equity. The predicted scores were derived from a regression equation in which the independent variables were the size of the firm and the debt-equity ratio, and the two dummy variables indicated whether or not the firm was nationally and regionally regulated. Since there are large differences between industries, Pfeffer (1972) supplemented the analysis with an industry-specific perspective. The performance measures were standardized with respect to the industry to which a firm belonged. Pfeffer found that the deviation from the predicted percentage of inside directors correlated respectively with the degree to which a firm deviated from the mean performance of firms belonging to its industry. The correlations were -0.30 (income-sales) and -0.295 (income-equity). This research provides modest support for the contention that organizations which develop an optimum number of outside directors are superior on »political effectiveness» (Katz and Kahn, 1978).

There are only two other studies that have tried to find effectiveness correlations of interlocking directorates, and they were unsuccessful (Bunting and Liu, 1977; Blankenship and Elling, 1962). Comparing data over seven time periods, Bunting and Liu found a very strong relationship between size (measured by total assets) and interlocking directorates for some types of industries (e.g., basic processing and machines and equipment), but even though their analysis was industry specific, they were unable to detect a relationship between interlocks and return on assets. Blankenship and Elling (1962), who studied nonprofit organizations, attempted to relate hospitals which are »central» in a local interorganizational network to the community legitimacy they enjoyed. They could not find any evidence to support the hypothesis that strongly tied hospitals extracted more resources from their environment (in dollars per bed).

The research to date has dealt with the effects of vertical and horizontal interlocks on organizational effectiveness. Thus, we do not know if well interconnected action sets are less competitive and their organizations better performers because the interlocking directorates meet their roles as common messengers and promote a more efficient exchange of information, or because of some other reason. Similarly, we do not know if vertical directors improve the intelligence among transactionally interdependent organizations, thereby reducing opportunism, contract breaching, and withholding of pertinent information. Such research is needed to evaluate the efficiency of »intermediate» forms of interfirm organization in comparison to more pronounced forms, such as mergers.

It is thus apparent that much more research dealing with the effectiveness of interlocking directorates is required before such interlocks can be compared with mergers. In general, there is a great need for comparison of the relative advantages and disadvantages of mergers versus less radical and less visible expressions of interfirm behavior. Economists today tend to discard interlocks as a device for dealing with interorganizational interdependencies (e.g., Williamson, 1975), and like Williamson, they underestimate the costs of mergers and accentuate their benefits. Research dealing with the effectiveness of interlocking directorates would thus be especially useful, as it might provide a viable alternative to mergers.

While the transactional costs will indeed diminish in the case of vertical integration, the costs associated with the need for increased coordination among intra-organizational units will increase. As a result of vertical integration, substantial sequential or serial interdependence will develop in the larger firm, and the resolution of conflict among its units seems to be much more difficult than economists such as Williamson suggests. In contrast, vertical interlocks may not yield the same informational benefits as vertical integration, but they will not require so much intra-organizational coordination. As we have indicated, it is not clear how effective interlocks are in alleviating informational deficiencies among vertically interdependent firms. For example, we do not know how successful a banking-industrial firm interlock would be in providing adequate intelligence to the bank in question. It is also not possible to determine to what extent such an interlocking directorate would suffer from »information impactedness» (Williamson, 1975), i.e., it is very difficult to investigate whether such a directorate would be at an informational disadvantage vis-à-vis the senior management of the industrial firm, as he does not have the inside knowledge of that firm's unique reality. Williamson himself clearly considers banks inferior to conglomerate firms, because unlike conglomerates, they do not have the same access to a firm's information system. He therefore discounts the informational advantages which banks have with respect to their customers. It seems, however, that Williamson draws his distinctions too sharply. As previously stated, we do not know to what degree vertical integration and vertical interlocks alleviate coordinational and transactional difficulties, nor do we know the extent of their influence on organizational effectiveness.

Horizontally interdependent firms do not only have the trade-off between greater market power, intelligence and possible increased coordination costs, but also the threat of antitrust suits. In the case of horizontal mergers the coordination costs are rather insignificant, as the merged components in the resulting larger firm maintain a pooled or parallel interdependence. Pooled interdependent units require little coordination and can be organized as a multi-divisional firm. The intelligence advantage, however, is limited to the firms which participate in the merger. In contrast, interlocks may perform information gathering functions that can extend beyond the two firms involved. Any interlocking directorate has the potential of being a hub in a network of organizations and of generating market information from sources that extend beyond his organiational dyad.

Whereas the research on horizontal merger correlations has been substantial, the research to date has not shed any light on the informational advantages of horizontal interlocks in general, or on specific implications in regard to effectiveness in particular. This dearth of empirical research findings is critical, as both policy makers and many political scientists continue to espouse the position that interlocking directorates reduce competition, foster corporate conspiracy, and harm the public interest. They see invisible interorganizational structures as spheres of corporate influence which should be eradicated, since they might disproportionately benefit the interlocked organizations at the cost of public interest (e.g. Levine, 1972; Gogel et al., 1976; and Bearden et al., 1975).

8. Discussion

This chapter has attempted to discuss some vertical and horizontal aspects of mergers and interlocking directorates. It concludes that *there is weak evidence that transactionally interdependent organizations are more prone to merge than to form interlocks. There is virtually no evidence on the relationship between horizontal interdependence and mergers and interlocks.*

Ideally, future work should be based on research designs that jointly consider information on interorganizational interdependence, mergers, and interlocking directorates, and organizational and interorganizational outcomes such as effectiveness. These designs will vary according to the mode of interdependence (horizontal or vertical). It is also apparent that the unit of analysis will be different. Vertical interdependence is primarily pertinent to dyads of organizations which exchange resources. Such an exchange capability suggests that other organizations can replace actors in the focal organization's environment, and should therefore be considered for the measurement of vertical interdependence (the primary focus, however, is on actors such as suppliers and buyers vis-à-vis the focal organization). In contrast, horizontally interdependent organizations are typically composed of organizations such as a community chest or a two-digit industry. The antecedents of mergers and interlocking directorates in the first case are to be attributed to dyad characteristics, while in the latter case, aspects of the organization as well as the horizontal action set to which it belongs must be considered.

Interdependence between competing organizations may be measured following the suggestions of Pfeffer (1972) and Pfeffer and Nowak (1976), who computed the deviation of an industry's four-firm concentration ratio from the mean concentration ratio of all industries. However, Pfeffer's research did not examine the asymmetrical relationship between the deviation index, merger propensity, and the frequency of interlocking directorates with competitors, and future studies should consider these aspects. More than likely the relationship would vary according to whether one deals with mergers or with interlocking directorates. It is clear that antitrust threats represent a negative incentive for mergers, especially in the United States. In countries with less severe antitrust legislation, the relationship between interdependence and merger is undoubtedly stronger. Since interlocking directorates are less likely to be subject of regulation, it is possible that when compared with horizontal mergers, the horizontal interlocks are strongly related to competitive interdependence. However, it is reasonable to hypothesize that the propensity toward interlocking decreases at a much faster rate for firms in industries whose concentration ratio is more than average, and at a slower rate for firms in industries which are less concentrated. This hypothesis is based on the assumption that in highly concentrated industries there is comparatively little need for interlocking directorates since the number of firms allows for simpler decoding of their behavior. The decoding of a firm's behavior is more problematic in industries with less than average concentration ratios, and therefore an asymmetrical relationship between concentration deviation and frequency of interlocking directorates can be hypothesized.

In comparison with mergers, the inter-firm structures that compose interlocking directorates are rather thin and superficial, and as Williamson (1975) and Stigler (1968) have asserted, rather ineffectual in managing interorganizational interdependence. On the other hand, interlocking directorates are relatively more flexible, and their utilization as coordination devices often circumvents regulatory interference (cf. U.S. Congress, 1978). In spite of legislation to curtail interfirm organization, the U.S. agencies concerned have been rather passive in instituting measures to meet these requirements. Part of their reluctance might stem from the many ways in which interlocking manifests itself.

Organizations are not only linked directly but also indirectly. Furthermore, interlocks may be strong or weak, and clumps of firms can be detected based on the relative strength of their linkages. According to Granovetter (1973), we can define such clumps as sets of organizations which are strongly tied; the strength of the ties can be measured by amount of time or other resources intimacy and reciprocity of the interlocking directors. This implies that the stronger the tie between two organizations, the larger the overlap among the two sets of organizations that are inter-connected with each of them. In other words, if A has a subset S_1 with which it is tied, and B has another subset S_2 with which it is tied, then the stronger the linkage between A and B, the greater is the proportion of organizations in in S_1 and S_2 with which both A and B will be linked. Possible results of this strong linkage include superior intelligence and parochialism. An interesting study would be a comparison of strongly tied firms with weakly tied firms. Is the notion of »shared monopoly« more appropriate in those oligopolies that consist of strongly tied firms, e.g., do such firms display more conformity and/or uniformity of behavior? The concept of strong linkage may be useful in assessing the role of intermediate forms of interfirm organization. Weak ties are also of significance, and in the long run firms which enjoy both strong and weak ties may outperform firms with only a few or no weak ties, in that they have better access into remote domains. For instance, they may be more successful in their diffusion of information because the weak linkages allow them to reach into such remote domains and protect them against parochialism (Pennings, 1978).

117

This issue also illustrates a potential advantage of interlocking directorates over mergers. Mergers are typically limited to two organizations, whereas interlocks can extend to a multitude of organizations.

Since vertical interdependence is more salient for dyads of organizations, mergers are more crucial than are interlocks. The vertical interlocking directorates are undoubtedly not effective enough to overcome the transactional difficulties that may exist, particularly between banks and manufacturing organizations. However, a merger is often not feasible, not only because of legal constraints, but also because the policy and charter of organizations precludes vertical integrations. As a result, a great deal of interest is being generated to examine other modes of interorganizational structure and process which, in addition to interlocking directorates, include joint ventures, flows of executive personnel and self-regulation. This research may then eventually accumulate into a body of knowledge that will result in a more general and more elaborate theory of organizations. The recent contribution by Williamson (1975) suggests that organizational theory should deal with both intra and interorganizational aspects. Research on mergers and interlocking directorates can contribute to the foundations of a more encompassing theory of organizations.

9. References

Aldrich, Howard, 1981
»Organization sets, action sets, and networks: making the most of simplicity». In Paul C. Nystrom and William H. Starbuck (eds.). *Handbook of Organizational Design,* Oxford and New York: Oxford University Press.

Allen, Michael Patrick, 1974
»The structure of interorganizational elite cooptation: interlocking corporate directorates». *American Sociological Review,* 39: 393-405.

Bearden, J., Atwood, W., Freitag, P.J., Hendricks, C., Mintz, B., and Schwartz, M., 1975
»The Nature and Extent of Bank Centrality in Corporate Networks». Working paper. State University of New York at Stony Brooks: Department of Sociology.

Bell, Frederick W., and Murphy, Neil B., 1969
»Impact of market structure on the price of a commercial banking service». *Review of Economics and Statistics,* 51: 210-213.

Berle, A.A., and Means, G.C., 1932
The Modern Corporation and Private Property, New York: McGraw Hill.

Blankenship, L. Vaughn, and Elling, Ray H., 1962
»Organizational support and community power structure: the hospital». *Journal of Health and Human Behavior,* 3: 257-269.

Bunting, D and Liu, Tsung-Hua, 1977
»Economic and Social Dimensions of Interlocking». Paper presented at the Annual Meeting of the American Sociological Association, Chicago, Ill.

Comanor, William S., 1967
»Vertical mergers, market power, and the antitrust laws». *American Economic Review,* Papers and Proceedings, 57: 254-265.

Dill, William R., 1958
»Environment as an influence on managerial autonomy», *Administrative Science Quarterly,* 2: 409-443.

Domhoff, G. William, 1967
Who Rules America, Englewood Cliffs, N.J.: Prentice-Hall.

Dooely, Peter, 1969
»The interlocking directorate». *American Economic Review,* 59: 314-323.

Esposito, Louis, and Esposito, Frances Ferguson, 1971
»Foreign competition and domestic industry profitability». *Review of Economics and Statistics,* 53: 343-353.

Evan, William M., 1973
»An organization set model of inter-organizational relations». In R. Chisholm, M Tuite, and M. Radnor (eds.) *Inter-organizational Decision Making.* p. 181-199. Chicago: Aldine.

Gogel, M., Koenig, T., and Sonquist, J.A., 1976
Corporate Control Re-examined. Mimeo. Santa Barbara: University of California.

Granovetter, Mark S., 1973
»The strength of weak ties». *American Journal of Sociology,* 78, 6: 1360-1380.

Hannan, Michael, and Freeman, John, 1977
»The population ecology of organizations». *American Journal of Sociology,* 82: 929-966.

Hawkins, Kevin H., and Radcliffe, Rosemary, 1972
»Competition in the brewing industry». *Journal of Industrial Economics,* 20: 20-41.

Helmich, Donald L., 1977
»Administrative Succession and Organization - Environment Linkage Behavior». Paper presented to the Western Academy of Management Meeting, Sun Valley, Idaho.

Hirsch, Paul M., 1975
»Organizational analysis and industrial sociology: An instance of cultural lag». *American Sociologist,* 10: 3-12.

Ijiri, Yuji, and Simon, Herbert A., 1974
»Interpretations of departures from the Pareto curve firm-size distributions«, *Journal of Political Economy,* 82: 315-331.

Katz, Daniel, and Kahn Robert L., 1978
The Social Psychology of Organizations New York: Wiley.

Levine, Joel H., 1972
»The sphere of influence«. *American Sociological Review,* 37: 14-27.

Lieberson, Stanley E., and O'Connor James F., 1972
»Leadership and organizational performance: A study of large corporations«. *American Sociological Review,* 37: 117-130.

Mandelker, Gershon, 1974
»Risk and return: The case of merging firms«. *Journal of Financial Economics,* 1: 303-335.

Mann, H. Michael, 1966
»Seller concentration, barriers to entry, and rates of return in thirty industries, 1950-1960«. *Review of Economics and Statistics,* 48: 296-307.

Mintzberg, Henry, 1973
The Nature of Managerial Work, New York: Harper & Row.

Pennings, Johannes M., 1981
»Strategically Interdependent Organizations«. In Paul C. Nystrom, and William H. Starbuck (eds.) *Handbook of Organizational Design,* Vol. 1. Oxford and New York: Oxford University Press.

Pennings, Johannes M., 1978
»Interlocking Directorates: A Selective Review and Proposal«. Working paper No. 20-77-78. Pittsburgh: Carnegie-Mellon University.

Pennings, Johannes M., and Goodman, Paul S., 1977
»Towards a workable framework«. In Paul S. Goodman and Johannes M. Pennings (eds.) *New Perspectives of Organizational Effectiveness* San Francisco: Jossey Bass.

Perrucci, Robert, and Pilisuk, Mark, 1972
»Leaders and ruling elites: The interorganizational bases of community power«. *American Sociological Review,* 35: 1040-1057.

Pfeffer, Jeffrey, 1972
»Size and composition of corporate boards of directors: The organization and its environment«, *Administrative Science Quarterly,* 17: 218-228.

Pfeffer, Jeffrey, and Nowak, Philip, 1976
Organizational Context and Interorganizational Linkages among Corporations. Mimeo. Berkeley: University of California.

Rumelt, Richard, 1974
Strategy, Structure and Economic Performance Cambridge: Harvard University Press.

Scherer, F. M., 1970
Industrial Market Structure and Economic Performance, Chicago: Rand McNally.

Selznick, Philip, 1949
TVA and the Grass Roots, Berkeley: University of California Press.

Stern, Fritz, 1976
Gold and Iron: Bismarck, Bleichroder and the Building of the German Empire, New York: Alfred A. Knopf.

Stern, Louis W., and Morgenroth, William M., 1968
»Concentration, mutually recognized interdependence and the allocation of marketing resources», *Journal of Business,* 41: 56-57.

Stigler, George C., 1968
The Organization of Industry, Homewood, Ill.: Irwin.

Terreberry, Shirley, 1968
The Organization of Environments. Unpublished Doctoral Dissertation. Ann Arbor: The University of Michigan.

U.S. Congress, House of Representatives, 1978
»Interlocking Directorates among Major U.S. Corporations», No. 052-070-04984-5. Washington D.C.: Government Printing Office.

Weiss, Leonard W., 1965
»An evaluation of mergers in six industries», *Review of Economics and Statistics,* 47: 172-181.

Williamson, Oliver E., 1975
Markets and Hierarchies, New York: Free Press.

6. INTEGRATION FORMS OF INDUSTRIAL ENTERPRISES IN POLAND

Jerzy Kortan
Institute of Organization and Management
University of Łodz, Poland

1. Introduction

Concentration and integration processes of production in countries with planned economies have been intensified in the last couple of years because of the tendency to establish their positions on foreign markets and to satisfy the constantly growing demands posed by society. This trend is also prompted by requirements of a very rapid process of technical progress. These pursuits and demands can be realized only through the employment of large-scale production. Economic integration among industries of COMECON countries is especially important. It is a great step forward towards further improvement of the international devision of labour, and through proper specialization policy it promotes considerable growth of mass production due to enormous enlargement of the consumer's market. This developing production-concentration in socialist countries is connected with the perfection of specialization of enterprises and the creation of large economic organizations, including merging enterprises into combines, and creation of integration links.

The formation of large economic organizations is thus the expression of a process of production-concentration and may be achieved by means of investments or integration activity. Quite frequently both methods are used simultaneously.

Investment forms of concentration consist of:

a.   The establishment of new large enterprises,

b.   The growth of the existing enterprises by gradual, even or stepwise extension.

Integration forms of concentration consist of:

a.   Permanent joining of smaller, independent, enterprises into one of a consolidated economic organism which receives new functions and new possibilities of activity.

b. The creation of looser groups of independent economic units, often belonging to different lines of industry which decide or are compelled to enter a conventional agreement concerning long-term co-operation.

In this paper we deal with the integration-type concentration.

2. Integration Consisting of Close Consolidation of Economic Units

In the new economic and financial system which is currently being introduced in Poland and in the formation of new enterprise-groupings within the framework of the so-called initiating units, the tendency to base economic management on large economic organizations manifests itself more and more explicitly. All the documents formulating the fundamentals of changes in the field of organization of economic management recognize large economic organizations such as industrial associations, multiplant enterprises and combines, as the fundamental link or units of management system, and thus, as the fundamental economic unit. Therefore, when we speak of a large economic organization we mean a grouping of enterprises and plants. These groupings integrated in the above-mentioned way have the characteristics of enterprises and must act on a self-financing basis. Since the enterprises grouped within large economic organizations may retain their legal and economic independence, we may treat the entire economic organization as an enterprise of a higher level[1] whereas the integrated enterprises can be regarded as subordinated, internal enterprises (as is the case with concerns or trusts).

The integration process in Poland is diversified but assumes mainly the following forms:

1. Emergence of a large, integrated economic organization by means of merging a few enterprises in the same line of industry into one enterprise. At the moment, this form is most frequently used, although usually it is not a new enterprise that is formed as a result. What takes place instead is that the integrated units are incorporated into the enterprise which most often plays the leading role (German: Leitunternehmen). The merged enterprises frequently become subordinated plants. In cases where a clear division of labour exists they may retain their status of enterprises, but of a subordinate type only. Here the process of integration usually runs in a horizontal direction.

---

[1] Gliński and Kołysz, 1973, p. 1

124

2. Enlargement of enterprises by means of incorporation of enterprises belonging to local industry, or in some instances by incorporation of co-operative factories into key industries, provided that they produce on a large scale and have at their disposal a sufficiently powerful technical potential. This kind of process occurred first in the furniture industry, and was then followed by a large scale incorporation of local industry enterprises into key industry enterprises in the years 1975-76. This second form most often integrates horizontally, although vertical merging is not infrequent.

3. Creation of large integrated economic organizations through the merging of enterprises under the control of different associations of industrial producers or even ministries provided that these enterprises participate in consecutive stages of manufacturing in the same end product. The integration most often assumes a vertical or mixed form. This type of integration usually leads to combines, but as departmental barriers must first be overcome, it is not used very often.

4.. Integration of industrial associations through merger of two or three independently operating associations. This type of merger takes place when extensive co-operation between the organizations is required, and especially so in the area of joint forecasting, expansion of production in definite product groups or co-operation in manufacturing semi-related products.

These processes of integration into large economic organizations must take into account organizational and economic consolidation of the production and the pre-production (research and development, preparation) as well as the postproduction (marketing) spheres.

Thus there can be distinguished two basic types of large economic organizations:

1. Industrial associations

2. Multiplant enterprises

However, this division can be still further differentiated by taking into account the functions and the rights of management of large organizations and their subordinate units. Jakubowicz[1] used this approach in identifying organizations as enterprises or having enterprise character. He distinguishes the following types and forms:

---

[1]   1974, p. 5 ff.

Type A.   Industrial Association

Type B.   Enterprise Association

Type C.   Multiplant Enterprise, with the following forms of factory groupings: - multiplant enterprise - vertical combine - horizontal combine

2.1 Type A. Industrial Associations

An industrial association integrates enterprises turning out capital or consumer goods. Because it is often the case that such organizations are the sole producer of a particular article, they frequently monopolize the domestic market with the only alternative being the import of such articles. Industrial associations are horizontally integrated with considerable centralization of functions, rights and means. The dominating role is played by the central board of the association, which remains isolated from the enterprises. The enterprises, in spite of the fact that they retain their legal status and finance themselves, are seriously limited in their economic independence.

2.2 Type B. Enterprise Associations

An enterprise association is usually a horizontally integrated economic organization, applying a considerable degree of decentralization of functions, rights and means. Its incorporated enterprises are also legally as well as financially independent. Their action space and independence are much larger when compared to enterprises organized under Type A (Industrial Associations). Enterprises belonging to a Type B Associations usually act on their own, under their own name or brand, rather than as units of an enterprise association. As was the case with the industrial association, the central board of an enterprise association remains separated from the enterprises. It fulfils fewer functions than that of an industrial association. For example, the production programme and its structuring are not determined by the board, but by the enterprise itself.

The integrated enterprises in this decentralization type of association are mainly those which produce articles geared to meet the mass demands of consumers, i.e., consumer goods. It is in this respect that the decentralization of the central board and the internal enterprises help the enterprise association to remain flexible with regard to market demands. This decentralization even enables competition between the enterprises of the same association. The internal relations of such an association are based on running mid-term, negotiable contracts.

2.3 Type C. Multiplant Enterprises

A multiplant enterprise is an integrated economic organization with highly centralized functions, rights and means. The subordinated units have no legal status of their own, but are factories of one enterprise, managed by a board of directors, or by a board of directors of the leading factory which plays the dominant role. In the multiplant enterprise a horizontal as well as a vertical (or mixed) form of integration may exist. If the vertical form dominates, we speak of a vertical combine, which has the highest degree of centralization. The lowest degree of centralization exists in the simple form of horizontally integrated multiplant enterprises. The single factories are devoid of legal status, but are internally self-financing. However, it is difficult to produce evidence of explicit differences between the simple form of multiplant enterprises and the horizontal combine. The difference between a horizontally integrated multiplant firm and a horizontal combine lies in the fact that a combine, as opposed to the simple multiplant firms, caters for a substantial flow of internal deliveries of suppliers between the plants. Simultaneously, functions, rights and means are highly centralized within a combine while the plants operate along self-financing principles.[1]

Since the combine, as a socialist prototype of inter-firm co-operation is of considerable interest to readers unfamiliar with the concept, it will be described in some detail below.

2.4 A Combine

Classically defined, an industrial combine is a merger of various production stages which are connected by the flow of raw materials within one territorially consolidated plant (for example, the successive stages of a particular technological process resulting in semi-finished products or subassemblies within an integrated flow of production). A combine is thus primarily a form of vertical integration.

The combining of production in industrial enterprises may exist in a variety of versions, among which the primary ones are:

☐ Combination of two or more production stages which are linked by a flow of materials (for example, pig iron output, steel melting and a rolling mill in a metallurgical combine);

☐ Combination of a few production stages in order to utilize the by-products and waste materials of the enterprise;

☐ Combination of some of the stages of production in sequential or parallel order in order to concatenate the fundamental production processes towards the manufacture of an end product;

☐ Combination of a few production stages in an enterprise (plant) for a complex utilization of one or more raw materials, simultaneously developed products, or a chemical compound (for example in order to utilize all derivates of a compound substance such as petroleum, natural gas or coal);

---

[1] As this chapter is concerned with interfirm co-operation and merger, the traditionally most common independent one-factory firm is not treated here.

☐ Combination of a few production stages towards the manufacture of complex end-products, sometimes even belonging to different lines of industry (such as in the engineering industry or in the construction industry).

The combination of production stages connected by the flow of materials within one enterprise can be planned when investment decisions are in process. If these stages fulfil certain conditions, concatenation may render considerable savings and advantageous economic effects, both on micro- and macro-economic scales.

With regard to this classical definition of combines,[1] that is, as being territorially consolidated objects (i.e., located in one place), a considerable reduction in social input of labour may be achieved by combining production stages in the direct production process. For example, if a semi-product is to be further processed in another factory or enterprise, it must be prepared by means of certain technical operations to make it suitable for transport and storage. But in the following stages, the result of these operations must very often be reversed, so as to make the semi-product suitable for further processing. For example, in order to be transported, a certain semi-product must be cooled. At the site of further treatment it must be melted or heated again to allow its further processing. Similar reverse procedures must be followed with various other semi-products (for example, condensing and subsequent attenuating of gases, concentrating and then diluting of some substances, drying and moisturizing).

If these successive stages are combined in one factory or enterprise, such auxiliary operations become technologically superfluous and the unnecessary investment outlays, costs of labour, auxiliary materials, and interfactory transports can be eliminated.

Thanks to the shortening of technological process, elimination of transports and reduction of indispensable semi-product reserves, combining production stages inside one enterprise also produces savings of fixed assets. Additionally, because the amount of inventories in this system may be considerably lower than when the production stages are not combined in one factory, the need for building big warehouses diminishes. Similarly, there can be reduced general economic costs of goods turnover (transport and trade costs).

However, the classical definition of the term »combine» has been considerably widened. A combine no longer only means territorial consolidation in one factory. In many cases, an integrated enterprise based on the horizontal division of labour is now considered to be a combine.

---

[1] Combine, in Polish »Kombinat», is a multiplant enterprise with the preponderance of vertical internal links.

128

Three basic types of combine-enterprises exist in our economy:

1. Combines of the classical definition type; that is large enterprises which carry out the production stages of a particular product in one territorially consolidated factory or enterprise.

2. Combines with some territorially separated factories whose division of labour is vertical or horizontal. Because the flow of raw materials is interconnected, a closed co-operation circuit is formed, which requires inter-factory transports.

3. Economic units with some territorially separated factories of the combine type, between which there is no division of labour. If there is any at all, it is a horizontal division only, so that there is no linkage of the flow of materials.

The last variant of a combine is, in fact, a multiplant enterprise. However, due to its high degree of centralization of functions, rights, and means, and in its general economic significance, it is treated as a combine.

In order to fully utilize the production potential built up as a result of joining enterprises into combines, management seeks to systematically improve and strengthen vertical and diagonal production and organizational links, i.e., the material co-operation between factories of a combine. In this way the advantages of combining production stages can be exploited.

Management structures must be precisely adjusted to the character of a combine along with the degree of centralization of the enterprise's decision-making system. Although combined enterprises work on the basis of self-financing systems, assignments for them are prepared by the combine management. Combine management (be it a leading factory, a parent factory, or a separate one) is appointed to ensure a uniform concept of development of the combine as a whole, and to provide all necessary scientific, technical, and economic conditions for improved labour productivity and effectiveness of production in the enterprises of the combine. This uniform management of the whole industrial cycle ought to be skilfully linked with the self-financing system of the combine-type enterprises and with their material interests. Therefore, combine enterprises work out their own plans based on assignments received from their central board. In order to fulfil these assignments they are equipped with their own means.

The formation of combines in socialist economies is a result of specific conditions. As a socialist society develops, it is possible to observe increases in demands for the improvement of enterprise productivity, flexibility, and adaptability to changes in the environment. The most effective method of meeting these demands is to form combines, which, at the same time, can be considered both as a result of and condition for the intensification of social production processes. Thus, the process of forming enterprises of the combine-type has been carried out very intensively in socialist countries. In the German Democratic Republic (GDR), for example, there were 120 combines at the end of 1972, 37 of which were subordinated to appropriate ministries, and 83 to industrial associations. At that time, enterprises integrated in the combines produced 20% of the entired commodity production[1] of the key industry. In the Soviet Union this process is being realized by means of creating production and scientific associations[2] of varying types. This large scale formation of combines in socialist countries is not simply a result of fashion or fascination by their large size. Combines which concentrate the individual phases of fundamental and auxiliary production within one economic organization and integrate them both with initial processes (research and development, processes of constructional and technological preparations) and after-production processes (organization of sales, customer-services) have a much better chance to concentrate particular stages of the social production process and optimize their fixed assets and material reserves, and then to efficaciously use these assets and reserves towards a resolution of general economic problems.

Since in a territorially dispersed combine goods are produced in one process mutually agreed upon and based on inter-factory labour division there exist favourable conditions for establishment of co-operative links. This in turn paves the way for planning and balancing of the co-operation in economic plan assignments. Improving the inside-factory division of labour combines may optimize production, and they are then better able to recognize demand for their products and arrange this with trade organizations.

Vertical connecting of individual stages of the entire industrial cycle in the combine, beginning with research and development, through the preparation and production processes, and ending with the organization of marketing, facilitates the mastery of science and production. Introduction of the results of research-development studies into production is also made possible through such connecting arrangements.

Vertically integrated combines enjoy favourable conditions for concentration of production of the same or similar products within one or very few factories. This facilitates creation of central units in special factories or departments producing components or sub-assemblies being typical for a given combine or even line of industry. On the other hand, this solution promotes specialization of individual factories and the improvement of intra-combine co-operation of production. Additionally, those combines producing particular systems of machines and appliances have a much better chance of becoming the leading enterprise in the production of these product lines. Although managing the combine activities is far more difficult than managing a horizontally integrated economic organization (such as a simple multiplant enterprise or industrial association), the potential possibilities of such a vertically integrated system, and the development of production relations and of

---

[1]   Commodity production: joint value of end-products sold outside an enterprise and of semi-products and subsidiary production sold outside and not used for further processing in the same enterprise.

[2]   The Scientific and Production Associations created in the USSR are special kinds of combines which include, e.g. research institutes, engineering offices, technological-development offices, and industrial enterprises. Managed principally as research institutes, they work upon the task of reducing to a minimum the time-period of introducing the results of research into production. The managing staff of research centres directs at the same time the basic sectors of production.

130

productive labour in such a system render advantages not present in a horizontally integrated organization.

3. Creation of Looser (Co-operational) Associations of Independent Economic Units

Many economic units participate in the social process of production in national economies. Their activities are co-ordinated by means of co-operational links (vertical) or horizontal links (through similarities of the goods manufactured, technologies used, joint exploitation of certain facilities etc.). Those links are not always strong enough to justify permanent binding of the units into one, new and coherent organism of the multiplant-enterprise type. Because such links comprise only certain functions, stages of production, or certain groups of goods constituting but a part of the entire production, they do not have an integrated character. These ties can also find expression in a mere pursuit of co-ordination or joint organization of activities in delineated areas, or in a desire to benefit from technical and personnel experience of the leading producer in this particular product range. Such inter-connections can occur between enterprises of varying character such as key industry enterprises, local and co-operative ones. In these cases the creation of a more flexible, loose form of integration of a co-operative type is more advantageous than the stricter, more permanent ties within the multiplant enterprise. The factories remain independent, often belonging to different lines of industry or ministries as well as sectors. In such linkages, enterprises retain their legal independence, and without changing their affiliation, they enter into agreements on long-term co-operation in certain fields.

In this way, new forms of co-operation between enterprises are developed, which last for longer periods of time. The result is the formation of diversified, but stable co-operational links between enterprises (combines), which, being subordinated to different managing bodies, co-operate with one another in resolving common tasks on a long-term basis and in a planned way. This co-operational integration of enterprises aims at increasing the economic effectiveness of the activities of the involved units. Research and development, production, and marketing of goods as well as other spheres, can be better organized through such co-operation. Co-operational links can arise both on the initiative of partners themselves and as a result of governmental decisions. Although such links are very diverse in nature, they are all based on agreements defining the object, type, and mode of co-operation. These agreements mirror the mutual interests of the partners and stipulate their rights and obligations.

Co-operational links are usually formed between the producers of end-products and the bigger suppliers of components, assemblies, and semi-processed products. Usually the participants in such an arrangement are those whose services exert a substantial influence on the quality, the cost, and the price of an end-product, and whose supplies largely determine the volume of production over a longer period of time. Accordingly, such links are normally vertically integrated, since their co-operation must be oriented towards manufacturing end-products. Apart from this co-operation in the sphere of supplying materials, components, assemblies, and semi-processed products etc., the co-operation may also encompass such provinces as: forecasting of market trends, forecasting the development of products, research and development of new products or technologies and their introduction into production, together with the development of technology and the improvement of the organization of production, consumer-service etc. In such areas, however, horizontal links are also common.

One type of co-operative integration is the territorial co-operative association, composed of enterprises of the same or different lines of industry with varying ministry or industry affiliation. The advantages arising from such a system are as follows:

☐ Spatial co-ordination and effective co-operation in particular phases of the manufacturing of product lines. Harmonization of reciprocal deliveries of materials and technologies and joint organization of supplies.

☐ Joint exploitation of free production capacities through planned assignment of mutual industrial services. This is an important source of utilization of reserves in the national economy.

☐ Possibility of joint investments into projects which would otherwise be unaffordable for the individual partners, and joint exploitation of these projects (e.g. warehouses, factory sidings, loading devices, power plants, water reservoirs etc.).

☐ Possibilities for joint organization and exploitation of rolling stock and repair shops.

☐ Possibilities for the organization of joint social and cultural facilities and joint centres of professional training.

Even though integration of this type brings considerable advantages both to the units participating in it and to the national economy as a whole, the development of such territorial co-operational associations is often inhibited due to existing loyalties and ties. Another substantial factor impeding the development of these associations is the inability to successfully carry out bigger undertakings and to clearly regulate the distribution of duties, responsibilities, and profits resulting from co-operation.

Co-operative links may be established for the purpose of realizing particular goals only. In such cases the co-operation is limited to a specific section, particularly when it comes to jointly solving of scientific and technical problems which call for large expenditures and efficient co-operation of partners (e.g. for the purpose of the proper utilization of expensive research apparatus, development of data-processing systems etc.).

Co-operative ties also exist in the field of sales and export organization etc. Due to joint centres of research, repair and transport facilities, the partners are able to accomplish their respective tasks at lower expenses than would be the case if these tasks were carried out individually by each enterprise.

Yet another form of co-operative integration is that of an association of producers. This is a group of independent enterprises, producing similar articles or using similar technologies, which co-operate on the basis of a voluntary agreement in order to solve technical, economic and organizational problems, thus increasing the effectiveness of their activities. In contrast to links in which a vertical form of integration predominates, an association of producers is a form of integration which horizontally unites the producers of the same or similar products. Such an association is most advantageous to small and medium-sized enterprises.

Co-operation within an association of producers usually occurs within the following domains:

☐ Current and future research on the development of products and technological processes used in the given field of production; pursuance of a co-ordinated and uniform policy in all enterprises within the association; procurement of jointly needed research and development studies,

☐ co-ordination of the preparation and realization of investments,

☐ systematic improvement of organization within the association, and especially comprehensive specialization of enterprises, formation of common devices, for example, in the sphere of production and instrumentation; organization of centralized manufacturing plants (e.g. centralized preparation of production); improvement of technical operation within enterprises,

☐ joint marketing research and co-ordination of activities in the field of marketing on the domestic market as well as in the export market, and also in the field of customer-service,

☐ extensive exchange of experience concerning the whole sphere of preparation, production, and marketing, and organization of management, planning, recording, analysis, and control.

The industrial association should establish the principles of the organization of management, planning accounting, and control, as both a well-functioning co-operation and an exchange of experience between the enterprises integrated in the association helps to improve their activities.

If an industrial association manages a line of industry within which several associations have been formed, then it may be furnished with rights and duties of the leading association in relation to other associations, dealing with similar production activities and whose enterprises participate in associations of producers.

Associations of producers aim at providing mutual assistance and mutual profits resulting from the integrated activities, basing their co-operation on collective co-ordination of activities of mutual interest. This allows the elimination of supremacy or the subordination of individual enterprises. The main instrument employed by such associations are plans of partner-enterprises, and the success of a given association is determined by consistent consideration of material interests of the integrated units.

Organization of such associations and steering their activities is the duty of leading factories, which are appointed by industrial associations, or in some cases, by ministries. These leaders ought to be carefully chosen, as the result of activities in the whole association depends on their work. For this reason, enterprises playing the role of the leading factories usually maintain a high technical level with a high standard of modernity and quality of goods. Their organization of production and marketing is also generally very effective.

The so-called councils of the producers-association are the organs which make decisions on behalf of all integrated enterprises as far as problems of co-ordination and co-operation are concerned. The trend to strengthen the inter-enterprise co-operation by means of a vertical division of labour has recently become more pronounced due to successes scored by many associations of producers. A similar trend can be observed in other socialist states, which employ the same form of co-operation (e.g. in the German Democratic Republic). Specialization of individual enterprises in production of definite components or assembly of end-products is applied more and more frequently, especially in those associations whose enterprises manufacture products from assemblies and components. This specialization usually begins with the formation of central factories producing components or assemblies typical for the whole association. This paves the way for a vertical division of labour and for commodity-financial asset relations between the enterprises integrated in the association, which replace horizontal relations of the information-transmission type being typical for this form of integration. Benefits of concentration are further enhanced by increased purchases and utilization of joint equipment.

This tendency, however, is still in the process of development. It is thus difficult to determine whether the trend will continue or if associations of producers should rather be regarded as a preliminary stage of integration of a higher level.

4. References

Gliński, B., and Kołysz, J., 1973
»Evolution of Industrial Associations Against the Background of Experiences of Other Socialist States». Scientific Conference on *Functioning of Large Economic Organizations,* p. 1. U.L. Łodz.

Jakubowicz, Sz., 1974
»Theses Concerning Organization of Industry under the Conditions of New Financial-Economic Systems». Scientific Session on Financial-Economic System of Initiating Units, p. 5 ff. Warsaw: Institute of Planning.

7. INTERORGANIZATIONAL STRATEGIES AND STRUCTURES OF HOSPITALS: A COMPARATIVE STUDY OF A CONSORTIUM, A JOINT VENTURE, A MERGER AND A CORPORATE MANAGEMENT SYSTEM*

William M. Evan and R. Christopher Klemm [1]
University of Pennsylvania
Philadelphia, Pa., U.S.A.

* *The authors would like to express their gratitude to the National Health Care Management Centre at the Leonard Davis Institute of Health Economics of the University of Pennsylvania for supporting this study. Although the hospital administrators and physicians we interviewed must remain anonymous, the authors would nevertheless like to thank them for their generous cooperation The authors would also like to express their indebtedness to Janet Bly, William F. Hamilton, Jane Murphy, and Gordon Walker for invaluable comments on the first draft of this paper. They would, in addition, like to express their appreciation to Dr. Samuel P. Martin, III, and his colleagues for expert advice in the course of processing the data. It should be evident that any views expressed in this paper are the sole responsibility of the authors and should not be attributed to the National Health Care Management Centre.*

1. Introduction

In the burgeoning field of interorganizational relations (Evan, 1976a,b), two different ideal-typical or archetypal perspectives recur in an effort to throw light on the relationship between organizations and their environments. These contrasting perspectives recall the old philosophical dichotomy between free will and determinism. The first pair of models is the natural selection or environmental determinism vs. resource dependence (Aldrich and Pfeffer, 1976). According to environmental determinists, the structural

---
[1] Also occupied at Stevens Institute of Technology, Hoboken, N.J.

attributes of a population of organizations (not a single organization) are a function of the constellation of environmental or ecological characteristics. At face value, this conception is congenial to a sociological view of organizations, in comparison with, for example, a psychological view. In contrast, the resource dependence perspective suggests that organizational decision-makers hold the key to an organiation's fate by choices and actions affecting the acquisition of essential resources. An analogous pair of models was proposed in a well-known paper by Gouldner (1959), in which he contrasts a rational model of organizations with a natural-system model. A similar distinction was developed by Simon (1969), who analyses the difference between knowledge of natural systems vs. knowledge of artificial systems (1969: 1-22).

Understandably, students of business administration, organizational behavior, management science, and decision science, while acknowledging environmental constraints, focus on organizational design problems (Galbraith, 1973, 1977) or decisional strategies (Ansoff, 1965). This is also true of Chandler's influential study (1962) of the structural histories of four large corporations, in which he proposes the thesis that by instituting innovative changes in strategy, viz., product diversification, these corporations transformed their functional structure to a multi-divisional structure. The recent studies by Channon (1973) and Rumelt (1974), both inspired by Chandler's work, tend to support the proposition linking strategy with structure. As with any ideal type, archetype, or model, applying it to a body of empirical phenomena entails the use of an »auxiliary theory» (Blalock, 1968) so that the type may be adapted to observed data. Regarding the antimony between environmental determinism and resource dependency, it is reasonable to assume that a dialectical interplay occurs in real world organizations. From this vantage point, contingency theory may be interpreted as an effort to explain the interaction between the organizational design decisions of managers and a variety of environmental constraints (Evan, 1976b: 262). For example, the American automobile industry, because of its oligopolistic market structure and its extensive capital investment, requires a managerial strategy of producing automobiles differing in models, styles, and price categories such that consumers will be motivated to purchase a new car every 3-4 years. Given this strategy, a multi-divisional structure has been adopted in the automobile industry (Chandler, 1962). Contingency theory points that there is a »fit» between an organization's environment and its strategy and structure. The »goodness of fit» is reflected in the performance level of the organization.

The purpose of this chapter is to explore some of these organization-environment relations with reference to the hospital industry in the U.S. In particular, the emergence of four distinct inter-hospital structures has been examined - a consortium, a joint venture, a merger, and a corporate management system. How do these structures differ in strategy? In view of the contingency theory prediction, do they differ in performance? Before dealing with these questions, several salient features of the American hospital industry will first be considered and then the theoretical relationships among the concepts of strategy, structure, and performance will be articulated.

2. Some Observations on Inter-Hospital Relations in the U.S.

Unlike other countries such as Great Britain and Sweden, hospitals in the United States operate as »free standing» or autonomous organizations. As of 1975 there were over 7.000 hospitals with a capacity of about one and a half million beds (AHA, 1976: 6). There is a substantial amount of heterogeneity among these hospitals, not only in size, but also in the nature of organizational auspices and in the type of functions. Among the major distinctions that have been made among hospitals are the following: government-owned hospitals (federal, state or local); short-term, acute disease hospitals vs. long-term chronic-illness hospitals; general vs. specialized hospitals; church-affiliated vs. secular hospitals; voluntary non-profit community hospitals vs. proprietary, profit oriented hospitals; and teaching vs. non-teaching hospitals (Heydebrand, 1974: 110-120).

The relatively fragmented nature of the American hospital industry is not unrelated to the mode of organization of the medical profession, the overwhelming proportion of whose members are accustomed to practicing as free entrepreneurs on a fee-for-service basis rather than as salaried employees. Thus, with the exception of pathologists, anaesthesiologists, and radiologists, (who may be employed by a hospital on a contract or on a salary), and interns and residents, most physicians are not employees of hospitals; instead they have admitting privileges and bill the patients they admit for their services. Under such circumstances, individual hospitals tend to compete with one another for physicians who will admit patients and thus assure maximum utilization of the bed capacity of the hospital.

Lest one conclude from these facts that American hospitals operate in a competitive market such that prices for health services are a function of the relationship between supply and demand, and thus beneficial to the consumers, it should be noted that hospitals constitute a substantially regulated industry. Many federal, state, and local laws have been passed which specifically affect the operation of hospitals, be it in regard to building and safety codes, capital improvements, utilization of hospital facilities, or reimbursement for services rendered to elderly and indigent patients. An additional infra-structure of the American health care system is the existence of a variety of private health insurance companies that serve as fiscal intermediaries or »third party payers» between hospital and patients. The launching of federally-supported health programmes for the elderly (Medicare) and for the indigent (Medicaid) has increased government involvement in the financing of medical care. With the passage of Medicare and Medicaid legislation in 1965, the U.S. took one large step toward establishing a national health insurance system, but a variety of legislative proposals for extending health service to the entire population has been pending for years. In the meantime, the cost of health care, particularly hospital-based health care, has been rising at a rate significantly higher than the cost of living. To contain hospital costs and upgrade quality, Congress passed the Professional Standard Review Organization Law in 1972 in order to regulate the utilization of hospital services. In 1974, the National Health Planning and Resources Development Act was passed in a further effort to contain costs by regulating capital expansion and renovation programmes and by promoting the regionalization of health care.

Because of several persistent problems, including the unevenness in the quality of health care, and the inflationary spiral in health costs, it is very likely that the regulatory efforts will continue, possibly in the direction of a comprehensive national insurance system for the entire population. Ironically, not all federal legislation serves to check the costs of health care. For example, the 1974 amendment to the Taft-Hartley Labour Law extending the right of collective bargaining to hospital employees has already had the effect of increasing by threefold - from 6% to 18% - the proportion of hospital employees who are unionized, thereby resulting in a substantial increase in hospital labour costs (Fottler, 1977).

To cope with an unstable environment due to competition, uncertainty about future government legislation, and rapidly advancing medical technology, hospitals have in the past tended to joint trade associations at a local, state and national level to obtain specific services: e.g. collective bargaining representation with private hospital insurance companies, such as Blue Cross, and political representation in state and federal legislatures to protect member hospitals from adverse forms of government regulation. Additionally, hospitals have increasingly begun to experiment with new interorganizational cooperative arrangements, possibly as a result of an intensification in the level of environmental uncertainty and threat in the past decade or so. These interorganizational innovations have taken a variety of forms and have come to be known as »multi-hospital systems» (Brown and Lewis, 1976; Portnoy, 1977). In a survey conducted in 1975 by the American Hospital Association it was found that 307 multi-hospital systems were in existence, not counting those operating within a framework of a local, state or federal government agency. These systems had collectively over 289.000 beds - approximately 20% of the bed capacity in the US.

Although no data are currently available on the distribution of different types of interorganizational structures among the population of 307 multi-hospital systems, it is not unreasonable to expect that the four types which are here investigated are prominent among them, viz., a consortium, a joint venture, a merger, and a corporate management system.

In a *consortium,* two or more hospitals join in a legal compact in order to accomplish one or more objectives while preserving their respective organizational identities. An example of a consortium outside the hospital field is the Midwest Consortium of Universities, designed to make the library and curricular resources of ten large universities available to all the students of the individual universities, thus effecting substantial savings for all the universities concerned.

In a *joint venture,* two or more hospitals enter into a legal agreement whereby they jointly establish, operate, and control a separate health care facility while maintaining their own individual organizational identities. This form of interorganizational structure has in recent years been commonly used by the multinational corporation which, in order to establish a subsidiary in a host country, enters into a joint venture with the host government.

138

Unlike a consortium and a joint venture, a *merger* entails the legal fusion of two or more hospitals into a new organizational identity. The pre-merger organizations are christened as subunits within the new organization; in the case of corporate mergers, a previous organization is typically reborn as a new division.

The fourth type of interorganizational structure is that which is designated here as a *corporate management system.* It consists of two or more hospitals organized and operated for profit, a purpose which distinguishes this mode of organization from the other three types of multi-hospital systems. A recent survey established that there are 1.060 investor-owned hospitals that are managed by »hospital chains», which is about 14% of the population of hospitals in the U.S. (Springate and McNeil, 1977). These hospitals tend to be considerably smaller in bed size than voluntary hospitals, the mean for the proprietary being 79.3 and for the voluntary, 178.7 (Rafferty and Schweitzer, 1974: 305).

To repeat, we are not asserting that these four models of interorganizational structure exhaust the variety of multi-hospital systems that are emerging as a means of coping with mounting environmental uncertainties. One hospital system from each of the four types has been selected on the assumption that they constitute progressive stages of functional coordination and integration. In other words, a consortium is more functionally specific and makes fewer demands on interorganizational integration than a joint venture; a merger represents a significantly higher level of functional integration than either a consortium or a joint venture; and a corporate management system, because of its profit orientation, requires a still higher level of functional integration. To test this assumption we undertook four case studies of multi-hospital systems for the purpose of studying the interrelationship between strategy, structure, and performance.

3. Strategy, Structure, and Performance

In his well-known study of the historical transformation of four large corportation - GM, duPont, Sears-Roebuck, and Standard Oil of New Jersey - Chandler (1962) formulates his pivotal concepts of strategy and structure. Although he does not link these concepts explicitly with performance, it is clear throughout his study that as these hugh corporations resorted to the strategy of diversification and subsequently introduced a multi-divisional structure, they succeeded in making more efficient and profitable use of their resources. At least one organizational researcher (Rumelt, 1974), who has used Chandler's work as a point of departure, has explicitly investigated the interrelationship between strategy, structure and performance.

Notwithstanding Chandler's arresting thesis that

>»structure follows strategy and that the most complex type of structure is the result of the concatenation of several basic strategies» (Chandler, 1962: 16)

the meaning of this pair of concepts warrants attention. Some clarification is essential if the concepts, developed in the context of industrial organizations, are to be extended to non-industrial organizations such as hospitals.

Of the two above concepts, structure is relatively free of ambiguity. It is, according to Chandler,

> »The design of organization through which the enterprise is administered. This design, whether formally or informally defined, has two aspects. It includes, first, the lines of authority and communication between the different administrative offices and officers and, second, the information and data that flow through these lines of communication and authority.» (Chandler, 1962: 16).

This definition is reasonably clear and resonates with the Weberian conceptualization of structure as reflected in the researches of Pugh et al. (1963: 1969), Blau and Schoenherr (1971) and others. By contrast, Chandler's definition of strategy is problematic.

> »Strategy can be defined as the determination of the basic long-term goals and objectives of an enterprise, and the adoption of courses of action and the allocation of resources necessary for carrying out these goals.» (Chandler, 1962: 16)

From this definition it is evident that strategy is not a unitary concept. In effect, it includes three concepts: determination of goals, adoption of means, and allocation of resources. If the goal of a corporation is expansion or growth, the means chosen to achieve this goal may include vertical integration, product diversification, geographical expansion, etc. Whatever means are chosen, it will be necessary to allocate appropriate resources to achieve the desired goal.

It is also reasonable to expect that the selection of a given strategy by decision-makers is a function of a set of environmental forces. As Chandler puts it,

> »Changes in strategy ... appear to have been in response to the opportunities and needs created by changing population and changing national income and by technological innovation.» (Chandler, 1962: 18).

In this formulation, Chandler, in effect, achieves a dialectical resolution of the two contrasting models of organizations and environments mentioned earlier in the paper: the natural selection model and the resource dependence model.

We may summarize Chandler's general thesis in the schematic diagram presented in Figure 7.1.

In his in-depth case studies of these four large corporations in which he finds a one-to-one correspondence between strategy and structure, Chandler did not concern himself with the quantitative relationships among the variables in his model. The attempt to operationalize Chandler's conceptual recursive model and to translate it into the context of the health care system in the U.S. is by no means a simple undertaking, as will be seen shortly.

140

| Changes in Environmental Conditions ("opportunities and needs") | ➡️ | Changes in Corporate Strategy | ➡️ | Changes in Corporate Structure |

Figure 7.1 Chandler's model of strategy and structure.

The changing environment of American hospitals is a blend of opportunities, needs and threats. The demand for health care is rising as the level of awareness of health care among consumers increases. Along with the rising demand for hospital services has come the growing threat of malpractice suits, the occurrence of which contributes to increasing hospital costs and increases in physicians' insurance premiums that are, in turn, passed on to patients in higher fees. At the same time, ongoing medical research results in rapidly advancing medical technology that further adds to the rising costs of hospital services; however, it also creates opportunities for changing the strategy and structure of hospitals.

A new diagnostic machine known as CAT - an acronym for computerized axial tomography - or a radiation therapy unit is very expensive and entails a substantial investment in capital equipment; its use, however, can potentially raise the quality of patient care of a hospital. To avail themselves of such costly medical technology it may be necessary for hospitals to form a »shared service organization» or a »multi-hospital system» so that they can share the use of such equipment. It may also be necessary to recruit physicians with appropriate specialities, on salary or on contract, to operate the new technology. Can the average general hospital, especially if it is not a teaching hospital - viz., one that is affiliated with a medical school - cope with the challenging new medico-technological innovations? Similar questions can be raised about the tendency for general hospitals to enlarge their number of clinical services, including such sophisticated services as open heart surgery. If the frequency of use of such services is relatively low in a given hospital compared to a neighbouring hospital, it results in higher costs per operation as well as a higher risk of inferior quality of care (i.e., a higher post-operative complications rate and a higher post-operative death rate) (Graham and Paloucek, 1963). To rationalize scarce resources and to upgrade the quality of health care, there is a need for a consolidation of medical services among a group of hospitals, a function performed by some multi-hospital systems.

While creating opportunities for hospitals, advances in medical technology also generate threats by steadily raising hospital costs and leaving hospitals potentially vulnerable to another source of environmental disruption. In pursuing malpractice suits against hospitals and physicians, lawyers have successfully argued that a hospital, to avoid legal repercussions, must do everything in its power to provide the best medical care possible, a concept that includes diagnosis through state-of-the art medical technology. Thus, a hospital that does not own or have access to advanced medical technology units such as CAT scanners, can be held potentially liable in a malpractice suit. In addition to raising costs of insurance to cover malpractice, the recent increase of malpractice suits against hospitals and physicians in the U.S. has also served to increase demand and therefore costs incurred in keeping abreast of medical technology developments. These costs have, in turn, added to the federal government's health budget for the elderly, the indigent, manpower training, etc., hence, the mounting pressures for further government regulation of hospitals.

Given the opportunities, needs, and threats comprising the environments of American hospitals, the emergence of various forms of multi-hospital systems may be viewed as an adaptive response by hospitals to rationalize their resources and operations in the interest of extending the scope of *self-regulation* so as to ward off the spectre of further *government regulation.* Implied in the willingness to join a multi-hospital system is the acknowledgement that the traditional strategy of organizational autonomy is dysfunctional and needs to be replaced with a strategy of inter-hospital coordination. Since inter-hospital coordination is a matter of degree, adopting such a new strategy does not bring in its train a single inter-hospital structure, as witnessed by the four different types - a consortium, a joint venture, a merger, and a corporate management system - we are investigating in this study. Nor is there reason to suppose that combining different types of inter-hospital strategies with various types of inter-hospital structures will result in similar levels of performance.

Given this adaptation of Chandler's thesis regarding strategy and structure to the American hospital system, a recursive model is presented in Figure 7.2.

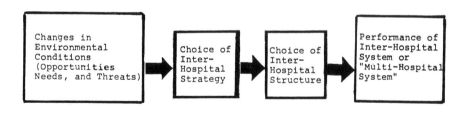

Figure 7.2 A model of the strategy, structure, and performance of multi-hospital systems.

Operationalizing the concepts of inter-hospital strategy, inter-hospital structure, and performance in the model entails various factual and methodological complexities, some of which will be dealt with in the course of describing the source of the data and setting forth an account of the formation of our four multi-hospital systems. However, some clarification regarding the conceptualization of performance used here is in order.

142

Evan's model of organizational effectiveness, which rests on a systems perspective (Evan, 1976c), is here applied. In its interaction with the environment, an organization activates at least four systematic processes:

1. Inputs (I);

2. Transformations of input resources (T);

3. Outputs (0); and

4. Feedback effects.

These systemic processes suggest a multidimensional conceptualization of organizational effectiveness, viz., »the capacity of an organization to cope with all four systemic processes relative to its goal-seeking behaviour - however explicit or implicit this may be» (Evan 1976c: 21). Operationalizing these four processes in terms of systemic interrelations yields three static ratios of organizational effectiveness (O/I, T/I, and T/O) and six dynamic ratios ($\Delta I/I$, $\Delta T/T$, $\Delta O/O$, $\Delta O/I$, $\Delta T/I$ and $\Delta T/O$). In principle, these organizational effectiveness ratios are applicable to all types of organizations.

4. Sources of Data

We began our collection of data with unstructured interviews of key informants such as hospital administrators, chiefs of medical staff, controllers, etc. A second source of data is organizational documents including organizational charts, annual reports, articles of incorporation, by-laws, information releases, etc. Because of the difficulty hospital administrative personnel have in retrieving statistical information which hospitals do not traditionally collect, we have resorted to a secondary analysis of data originally gathered for administrative purposes by the American Hospital Association in their annual surveys (AHA 1954, 1960, 1965-1977).

In short, while our qualitative data are adequate for our purpose of studying the strategy, structure and performance of multi-hospital systems, our quantitative data are not. To measure the strategies and structures of the multi-hospital systems, we have used perceptions based on our interviews, organizational documents, and administratively collected data. To measure performance, we have relied primarily on administratively collected data. The quality of hospital performance has been conceptualized as including »structure quality», »process quality», and »outcome quality» dimensions. (Donabedian, 1966, 1968, 1978a,b). At present, there is no agreement as to which of the three dimensions is a more appropriate measure of quality, as each has supporters and detractors. Since a number of social scientists (Scott, Forrest, and Brown, 1976; Shortell, Becker, and Neuhauser, 1976; Heydebrand, 1973; Neuhauser and Anderson, 1972) and the accreditation agencies have based assessments of hospital performance on structure quality indicators, we have chosen to follow in the same tradition, while acknowledging that this is not the only conceptualization of hospital performance available.

Unfortunately, this problem of indicator validity recurs with all of our measures of strategy, structure, and performance. Clearly, the more indirect and unrefined the indicators of the concepts we are seeking to measure, the greater the uncertainty about the relationships amount the variables. This is an unavoidable limitation of our present data set.

5. Results

Emergence of the Four Multi-Hospital Systems. The hospitals examined in this study enjoyed an independent existence ranging from less than one to nearly fifteen decades prior to making the decision to join a multi-hospital system. In each case, their decision to relinquish a measure of their organizational autonomy by joining a multi-hospital system can be related to a significant change in the environment.

5.1 The Consortium

For the consortium, the triggering mechanism was a shift in the regional hospital balance of power, stimulated by state planning and legislative decision. In the early 1960's the state in which the consortium is located decided to establish a medical school near the state capital. Although the most rational location for the medical school was adjacent to the largest and most prestigious hospital in the selected area, a compromise location outside of town was eventually chosen due to pressure from this hospital's competitors. This decision left the medical school and its newly established hospital in a competitive position with the region's leading hospital as well as with the other hospitals.

Having broken the link between the prestigious hospital and the new state hospital and medical school, and in the process, having neutralized the former to some extent, the other hospitals in the region felt a need to protect their autonomy from the state-owned medical centre. In seeking teaching affiliations, the medical school sought hospitals where it could control the appointments of the chiefs of services positions as part of the affiliation agreement. Individually, hospitals that desired a teaching affiliation were powerless to counter this demand; however, since the medical school needed affiliated hospitals for its residents and interns, the local hospitals collectively enjoyed a considerable degree of influence. The only factor structurally missing in this pattern of hospital relations was a mechanism that would formalize the *de facto* balance of power.

An additional impetus for collective action by the hospitals was another act of the state legislature which established a commission to regulate hospital costs. Empowered to review and approve all hospital budgets, the commission was viewed as a potential threat by individual hospital decision-makers, and they therefore accelerated the hospital's collective response to the situation created by the presence of the medical school. In short, the emergence of the consortium of nine hospitals may be viewed as a political response to threats emanating from the establishment of a new medical school and a state hospital cost commission.

The formal relationship among the nine hospitals comprising the consortium is analogous to an all-channel network with each member able to communicate with each of the other hospitals. To facilitate communication, three channels were created: a board of directors drawn from boards of each of the member hospitals, a committee of all nine hospital administrators, and a committee of the nine medical chiefs of staffs. Informally, however, communications flows tend to be centralized in the office of the director of the consortium (see Figure 7.3).

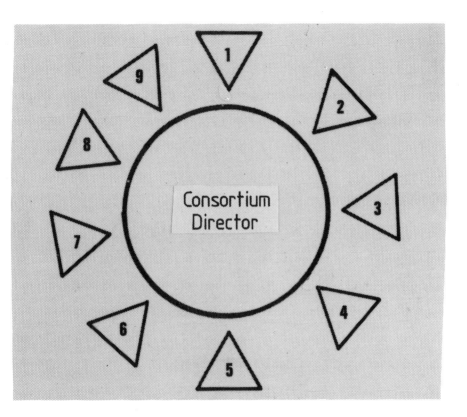

Figure 7.3 Informal structure of the consortium.

Some have criticized the consortium as being »all talk and no action», with few direct and concrete cost-reducing measures to its credit - a criticism that ignores the essential basis of the consortium as a regional approach to health care. Within this regional system, there are constraints on the flexibility of the nine member institutions to make capital expansions beyond a specified

145

level without unanimous consent of the other institutions. Since the 22 committees of the consortium represent board members, administrators, and physicians, any individual change in service receives a wide hearing before it is adopted. In this sense, the consortium has acted to rationalize resource allocation, usually at the expense of past competitive habits. Thus, for a time the consortium supported an open heart surgery team shared between two hospitals and owned only one CAT scanner, whereas other regions across the country with the same number of beds boasted of having four or more scanners. In addition, attending physicians at all nine hospitals in the consortium have been granted the right to apply for admitting privileges in any of the consortium hospitals, subject to approval by the credentials committees of the various hospitals.

Politically, the consortium's record is impressive. It has succeeded in creating a regional health care unit from a group of hospitals once dominated by competition. According to those involved, several of the teaching relationships that have evolved between the medical school and other consortium members owe their successful existence to the consortium. In the summer of 1977, one of the consortium hospitals won a law suit in which it challenged the state cost commission's method of reviewing hospital budgets.

5.2 The Joint Venture

The joint venture developed in the middle 1960's out of a need for three community hospitals to expand and modernize in response to growing community health care requirements. At the suggestion of local industrialists, who sat on the boards of the three hospitals, the decision was made to sponsor a regional hospital fund-raising campaign. While one of the hospitals, an osteopathic institution, decided to use its share of the fund-raising proceeds independently, the other two hospitals, one church affiliated, the other nondenominational, decided to merge their facilities in a new structure. As originally planned, this new hospital would house each member hospital in a separate wing and pool the administrative and ancillary functions in a central tower. The hospital planners therefore initiated the fund-raising drive on the assumption that the proceeds would fund the establishment of the joint hospital (the actual wording on the pledge cards was »joint facility«). At the dinner launching the fund drive, the clergyman whose church owned one of the hospitals involved delivered the invocation. As someone wryly commented, it seemed a certain success, because the clergyman »almost always gets what he prays for«. In this case, the prayers went unanswered.

Within six months of the initiation of the fund-raising drive, a suit was filed charging the board of the church-affiliated hospital with dereliction of duty and enjoining the establishment of the joint facility. Those individuals directly involved are unwilling to discuss the matter, but it appears that the clergyman had been approached by several of the physicians at his hospital who believed that the joint facility irrevocably threatened the religious and neighbourhood-oriented nature of the hospital. Possibly in response to these apprenhensions, a member of the clergyman's staff sponsered a full-page advertisement in the local newspaper voicing opposition to the joint facility hospital plan. To protect the integrity of the religious hospital, four private individuals, all of whom were church members, then filed a law suit against the hospital's board.

146

The case was resolved through a consent decree enjoining the construction of the hospital until its economic feasibility could be reviewed. Charges of bad faith followed hard on the heels of the consent decree and the issue was eventually settled by a compromise: the joint facility would be built as a *joint venture* rather than as a merger. This left the »offspring» organization with legal and financial independence but its policies were controlled by the two »parent» hospitals.

The structure of the joint venture reflects the compromise between the regional health care goal of the original plans and the local attitude favoured by the religious hospital. As presented in Figure 7.4, the joint venture hospital, C, is tied to the original hospitals, A and B, through the board directors, half of whom also sit on the board of hospital A, the other half of whom represent hospital B.

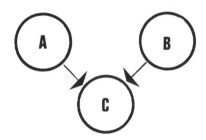

Figure 7.4 Structure of the joint venture.

Each board bloc votes as a separate unit, and a majority of the board requires a majority of each of the board blocs. Thus while coalition formations are possible in this triadic relationship, the potential is minimized by the veto of the dessenting board bloc. Nevertheless, officials of the member hospitals in the joint venture appear to be uneasy about the compromise structure they have created. Some of them are of the opinion that the »parent» hospitals will eventually »divorce», leaving the »offspring» hospital free to »marry» the secular hospital, which it would then be able to dominate.

The joint venture as implemented, while not expressing the regionalization objectives of the hospital planners over a decade ago, has permitted a moderate-sized community ready access to an impressive array of medical services, including open heart surgery and a burn care centre. Economically, the cost has been high, for the same number of beds is now divided among three hospitals rather than two, necessitating additional facility, administrative and overhead costs. In addition, whatever economies of scale might have resulted from a merged hospital have been lost.

5.3 The Merger

The merger evolved when the goals of three hospitals and the local business community converged. The respective interest of each party in establishing a teaching medical centre and in rationalizing hospital services by eliminating duplication and triplication were brought together as a result of a variety of cost pressures. In the late 1950's, the city in which the merger is located began feeling the impact of post-war migration and a changing population profile. These population changes resulted in increased indigent and emergency service visits and, in turn, in the need for expansion of hospital facilities. The hospitals' response to these pressures led them to intensify their searches for funding, searches that more often than not led to the local corporate coffers. In an area where the business community is dominated by a small number of corporations, this meant repeatedly approaching the same people.

Concomitantly, an opportunity arose for a medical school to be established in the state. The hospital officials drew the conclusion that by combining their resources they would be selected as the teaching hospital of the hoped-for medical programme. Such an arrangement would enable the state, and these dominant hospitals within the state, to train their own medical students out-of-state and subsequently import physicians.

The impetus uniting these convergent interests came from several family relatives who represented local industry and sat on the boards of the three non-denominational voluntary hospitals in the city. Together these individuals mapped out a plan to merge the hospitals which, after presentation to the full boards and extensive review, was instituted as the merger in 1965.

Structurally, the merger, as illustrated in Figure 7.5, replaced three autonomous hospitals with one merged hospital operating with three divisions.

To date, the three facilities which house the three original hospitals have been maintained, but common services have been consolidated rather than offered in each of the separate divisions.

Since the establishment of the merger, a number of its promises have been fulfilled and it has proceeded further than the other non-profit hospital systems under consideration in rationalizing its structure. As originally intended, most of the duplicated and triplicated services, such as emergency care services, have been combined. One factor allowing the merger to achieve many of its goals is time; unlike the consortium and joint venture which thus far have eight years of experience of multi-hospital life behind them, the merger has seventeen. A second factor contributing to the merger's success is the intensive and careful planning with preceded its formation. Had the joint venture followed a comparably detailed and intricate planning process, the results might have been different.

In its dream of becoming the hospital seat of a state-sponsored medical school, the merger has not fared as well. As time passed and the likelihood of a state-supported medical school waned, the merger has affiliated itself with

148

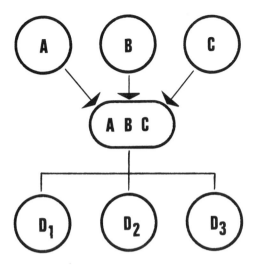

D_1 D_2 and D_3 are divisions within the merger

Figure 7.5 Formal structure of the merger.

a medical school in a neighbouring state. Under this arrangement, the home state legislature annually sponsors thirty medical students in this medical programme, and they fulfil their residency requirements at the merged hospital.

As a further means of rationalizing its services, the merger has sought to vacate its downtown sites in favour of a suburban location more central to the region's population locus. Land has been donated to the hospital by one of the principal corporations in the area, the same one that was instrumental in the formation of the merger. For the time being, however, the merger has not been able to proceed with its relocation plans because of pressures from the city, which does not want to lose the wage tax paid by the hospital's employees, and from a coalition of neighbourhood groups that is seeking to keep the health care facilities close at hand. By filing a lawsuit against the merger, the neighbourhood coalition has to date effectively halted the merger's efforts to relocate. In the meantime, it is rumoured that an investor-owned hospital chain is considering building a hospital near the merger's new suburban location unless the latter's plan for a new and expanded facility is soon realized.

5.4 The Corporate Management System

Of the multi-hospital system responses considered in this chapter, the investor-owned hospital chain, or what we refer to as the »corporate management system», is unique in responding to opportunities rather than threats in its environment. Since its founding in 1968, the history of the system is one of meteoric growth. In its first year of operation, the corporation bought nine hospitals; in its second year, an additional sixteen hospitals and a construction company were acquired. Within three years, operating revenues exceeded 100 million. Not surprisingly, within five years of its establishment the corporation suffered from massive indigestion and the entrepreneurial founders were replaced with professionally-oriented managers.

The corporate system as a national corporation operates with a larger hierarchy and a different mode of control than the other multi-hospital systems. Unlike the other systems where hospital professionals are employed throughout, the upper echelons of the corporate system hierarchy are staffed with functional professionals whose background is not in health care administration. This business-like approach to the management of hospitals creates conflicting responses at the local level of the hierarchy. One hospital administrator proudly told us that he could »cost out a sneeze in the hall» if it were required by corporate headquarters. Another administrator, one with a few more years experience in the corporation, feels that the corporation's control procedures are becoming excessive, to the point of impeding individual hospital performance. Preferring a more independent role, »As a captain of a ship, but still an integral part of the navy», this hospital administrator finds that the corporate headquarters is much too involved in his day-to-day activities.

Structurally, the corporate management system follows a traditional hierarchical organization profile, as shown in Figure 7.6. Functional (F) and regional (R) vice presidents report to the president (P); individual hospitals in the system, indicated by the letters A,B,C, report to the regional officers.

Performance in the corporate system is carefully planned, structured, and monitored with an eye to meeting the planned goals. It is alleged that, in planning the scope of their activities, investor-owned multi-hospital systems have tended to include a profitable case-mix range and exclude those areas which, because of frequency of use or cost of medical equipment, do not yield a favourable entrepreneurial return on investment (Ruchlin, Pointer, and Cannedy, 1973, 1974; Rafferty and Schweitzer, 1974). Our data are not presently in a form that permits us to examine this aspect of the performance of the corporate system, although some results which suggest »skimming» (operating in the profitable case-mix area and excluding those unprofitable services) are presented below.

Another performance feature related to the nature of the corporate management system is the difficulty experienced by its hospitals in developing positive public images in their local communities. The hospitals in the corporate management system tend to be viewed as profit-making enterprises and hence lacking in local community legitimacy. In contrast, the community-based voluntary hospital, with the influential community elite serving on its board, is better equipped to negotiate with local regulators such as the officials of a Health Systems Agency than the investor-owned hospital that lacks access to local channels of influence.

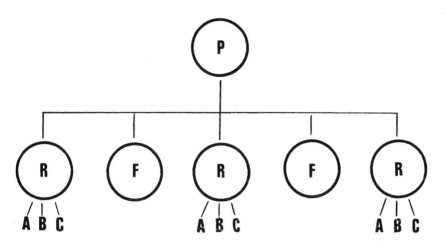

P is for president
R is for regional vice president
F is for functional vice president
A,B,C are individual hospitals in
        the corporate management system

Figure 7.6 Formal structure of the corporate management system.

5.5 Strategy of Multi-Hospital Systems

Assessing the strategy of multi-hospital systems in terms of Chandler's model of strategy and structure is problematic because his conception of environmental »opportunities and needs» as generating new strategies is not as applicable to the three non-profit hospital systems under consideration as it is to the corporate management system. For the consortium, the joint venture, and the merger, threats were important features of the environment that stimulated the multi-hospital system response. It is also evident that Chandler's concept of strategy, which presupposes organizational growth, is not as crucial to the three non-profit systems as it is to the corporate management system. If hospitals are not primarily pursuing a strategy of growth and are not primarily responding to »opportunities and needs,» they are, we suggest, following a course of service and facility improvement within a framework of organizational autonomy as their primary strategy. In other words, hospitals strive to become more effective by changing the scope of their facilities and by upgrading the level of expertise of their personnel. Presumably, the ideal hospital is one that can handle any and all health care problems that are referred to it. Multi-hospital systems need to balance this conception of the ideal hospital with the availability of resources within their environment. It makes little sense for each individual hospital to approach the ideal hospital as long as the objectives of the ideal hospital can be more rationally pursued by the multi-hospital system. Hospital strategy within a multi-hospital system thus involves creating the optimal blend of facilities and personnel within the

151

constraints defined by the organization's available resources and environment.

Strategy was measured here by means of two types of indicators: availability of complex medical technology in the multi-hospital system (Mahajan & Schoeman, 1977) and an assessment of the system goals of patient care, education, and research with the aid of a content analysis based on a word frequency count of each system's articles of incorporation and by-laws (Holsti, 1969). These two types of indicators reflect, respectively, the »operative» and »official» goals of the multi-hospital system (Perrow, 1963).

On the surface, one would expect the official goals of the multi-hospital systems (those goals and purposes espoused in the articles of incorporation and by-laws of the systems) to reflect differences in strategy. However, since lawyers draft such documents, there is a tendency for the draftsmen to impose a homogeneous structure, regardless of individual nuances distinguishing the strategies of the systems involved. As shown in Table 7.1, we have found this to be the case to some degree. However, despite the relative similarity between the goal-formulation documents, some clear differences do emerge. The joint venture is the system most concerned with patient care, and the merger appears to be the system most concerned with education. These results are consonant with our qualitative assessments, although the relative »distance» between the rankings for patient care, mentioned four times in the merger's documents (ranked third) and twelve times in the joint venture's documents (ranked fourth), is not indicative of the service actually offered. Similarly, the distance between the consortium, ranked third in education with a word count frequency of four, and the merger, with a word count frequency of ten and ranked fourth, is not an accurate reflection of the actual education programmes in existence. Thus the rankings appear appropriate for patient care and education, but the actual scores are somewhat distorted by the nature of the legal documents.

The system goal of research is more difficult to interpret. The corporate management system appropriately omits any reference to research in its documents. Among the other systems, the word research has varying meanings. Clinical and laboratory research are being conducted only in the consortium, while some drug testing research is being conducted in the joint venture and merger. Thus, judging from our interview data, the frequency scores for research in Table 7.1 and the rankings of the systems are partially distorted. In the case of the merger, which calls itself a »medical centre», its high ranking on research more accurately reflects its aspirations than its accomplishments.

As suggested by Perrow (1963), the »official» goals of the hospital systems are not necessarily congruent with the »operative» goals. In fact, one may be pursued at the expense of the other. In measuring the operative goals we have used availability of complex medical technology to indicate the extent to which the systems are realizing their medical care potential. While mere possessions of complex medical technology is no indication of its frequency of use, it does show the relative commitment of the systems to invest in service-related equipment. Not surprisingly, the corporate system, as seen in Table 7.2, has the lowest percentage of complex medical technology available, a finding that lends credence to the notion that investor-owned hospitals oper-

Table 7.1   Frequency of mention and rank order of strategy-related terms in the articles of incorporation and by-laws of the multi-hospital systems.

System	Patient care	Rank order	Education	Content Analysis Categories Rank order	Research	Rank Order
Consortium	3	2	4	3	2	2
Joint venture	12	4	2	1	2	2
Merger	4	3	10	4	3	4
Corporate management system	2	1	3	2	0	1

Kendall W = .55, not significant at .05

ate with a more restricted case-mix and leave complicated health care problems requiring more costly equipment and personnel to other hospitals. Rather surprisingly, the merger, the second largest of the non-profit systems, has the next lowest percentage of complex medical technology. The high standing of the joint venture had not been anticipated because of its location in a small city, approximately 70 miles from a large complex of medical facilities.

Several of the operative goals are better explained when they are compared to the official goals. Assuming that none of the systems has unilimited resources, it follows that those highly ranked in one area are not likely to be highly ranked in all areas. Thus, the merger with its high commitment to education, may to some degree compromise its investment in complex medical technology, i.e., in patient care. The joint venture which its interests and resources devoted to medical technology consequently invests fewer resources in education. According to this interpretation, the consortium comes closest to being the »ideal» system with a relatively high resource commitment to both education and medical technology (patient care), a position built in part upon its greater size. The corporate system is in effect operating on a different plane. Its commitment to education is low; yet its resources are not being applied to sophisticated patient care. Comparisons based on the system goal of research are confounded by the variety of meanings attachd to the word.

Table 7.2   Percentage and rank order of complex technology indicators of the multi-hospital systems in 1976.

System	Per cent	Rank order
Consortium	87.5	3
Joint venture	87.5*	4
Merger	62.5	2
Corporate management system	25.0	1

* The complex medical technology indicators as rated in descending order of complexity by ten knowledgeable physicians are:

Rank order	Indicator
1	Burn care
2	Open heart surgery
3	Organ bank
4	Hemodialysis outpatient
5	Hemodialysis inpatient
6	Therapeutic radio isotope
7	Diagnostic radio isotope
8	EEG

The tie between the consortium (missing the burn care unit) and the joint venture (missing the organ bank) was resolved on the basis of this rating of 10 experts.

5.6 Structure of Multi-Hospital Systems

In contrast to the difficulties of conceptualizing and measuring the strategy of the hospital systems, the analysis of structure is relatively straightforward. We have defined structure as formal linkages, among the hospitals comprising a multi-hospital system, and have identified six relevant indicators:

1. Degree of centralization of budgetary process

154

2. degree of standardization of the management information system

3. number of decision-making centres

4. degree of integration of administrative services

5. degree of integration of medical services

6. degree of integration of medical personnel

Whereas the parameters of *organizational structure* have been extensively studied, those of *interorganizational structure* have been relatively neglected. The formal interorganizational linkages, upon which our definition of multi-hospital system structure is based, were selected after analyzing organizational documents and reviewing our interview data. Table 7.3 is based on our subjective ratings.

It is noteworthy that the corporate system does not rank highest on two of the variables: the degree of integration of medical services and the degree of integration of medical personnel. Because of its prõtective attitude toward the entrepreneurial prerogatives of physicians, the corporate system does not structurally integrate its medical services of medical personnel. Medical services might be shared, but in the hospitals we have studied in the corporate system, several of which are situated physically close to one another, this is the exception to the rule, and is not a matter of policy. Similarly, medical personnel might refer patients to more than one of the corporate system's hospitals, but this decision is left to the discretion of the physicians. Instead of using physicians as integrating agents within the hospital system, the corporate management system prefers to rely on the other four structural mechanisms for integrating its hospitals. If any policy exists with respect to medical services and personnel, it is an informal one that the hospitals should compete for physicians and patients.

Otherwise, the rank orderings of the structural indicators are not surprising. The corporate management system and the merger have more centralized, standardized, and integrated structures than the joint venture of the consortium.

5.7 Performance of Multi-Hospital Systems

The performance or effectiveness of multi-hospital systems poses a new set of measurement challenges. Ultimately, hospitals treat patients, and the performance of hospitals is thus related to the success with which a hospital can provide health care and cure patients. The difficulties involved in developing such outcome measures (Brook et al., 1976), have recently been observed by Shortell et al., (1976: 7):

>»Unlike cost and productivity data, which can usually be obtained from existing data sources, objective measures of quality must usually be collected first-

155

hand by the researcher in each organization. This, of course, raises problems of gaining access to medical records, which contributes to the more general problem of obtaining the participation of hospitals and other health service delivery organizations in the proposed search.»

Table 7.3   Rank order of the multi-hospital systems on structure.

System	Degree of centralization of budgetary process	Degree of standardization of management information system	Number of decision-making centers	Degree of integration of administrative services	Degree of integration of medical services	Degree integration o medica person
Consortium	1	1	1	1	2	2
Joint venture	2	2	2	2	3	3
Merger	3	3	3	3	4	4
Corporate management system	4	4	4	4	1	1

Kendall W = .47, significant at .05

Quality of health care has been conceptualized as including structure, process, and outcome dimensions (Donabedian, 1966, 1968, 1978). »Structure quality» is defined by Donabedian (1966: 170)

»as the adequacy of facilities and equipment; the qualifications of medical staff and their organization; the administrative structure and operations of programmes and institutions providing care; fiscal organization and the like».

In other words, structure quality refers to the instrumentalities regarding the operation of the health care organization, both medically and organizationally. »Process quality» is concerned with the manner in which medicine has been practiced. In turn, outcome quality examines the results of the medical intervention. Currently, the dispute regarding the relative advantages and disadvantages of each of three quality dimensions is being resolved in favour of the outcome quality approach.

We have, however, selected the structure quality perspective for two reasons. Some have argued that the formation of multi-hospital systems is ulitmately not the result of a concern for improving quality; rather »multi-unit organizational arrangements (of hospitals) essentially are systems of organization and management» (Stull, 1977: 45). In other words, multi-hospital systems are systems for redesigning structure quality and only tangentially affect pro-

156

cess and outcome quality, these effects are likely to be manifested only after some period of time. Since two of the multi-hospital systems under consideration, the consortium and the joint venture, were only seven years old when examined, and both are still experimenting with their organizational structures, it seemed that any interorganizational impact on process or outcome quality is likely to lie in the future. Consequently, we have concentrated on measuring structure quality effects in developing our performance indicators. The reader is therefore reminded that our performance measures at this stage in our multi-hospital system research represent the *administrative* functions of the multi-hospital systems.

Using a systems model, Evan (1976c) has proposed that organizational effectiveness can be conceptualized with the aid of a series of ratios between inputs, transformations, and outputs, and their changes over time resulting in feedback effects. This model can also be used to compare static and dynamic relationships between inputs, transformations, and output. Initially, we attempted to compare the multi-hospital systems over time, before and after the constituent hospitals entered the hospital systems, using the Evan model of organizational effectiveness. The resulting values and rank orderings of this application of the model are shown in Table 7.4. The values presented here are the percentage of change in the average annual value of the effectiveness ratio before and after the formation of the various multi-hospital systems.

Regarding the change in the total expenses to admissions indicator ($\Delta O/I$), total expenses are increasing faster than admissions in each of the hospital systems, although the rates of increase vary widely. Surprisingly, the rate of increase is the largest in the corporate management system with its presumed superior ability to control costs. It is conceivable that the higher rate of increase of total expenses to admissions in the corporate management system is a function of its case-mix, which yields a higher net revenue per patient than is true of the other systems. An expected finding is the change of physicians to admissions indicator ($\Delta T/I$), namely, in the non-profit systems the numbers of physicians are increasing faster than admissions. In the corporate management system, however, relatively fewer physicians are admitting more patients, a finding consistent with the structural characteristics of the corporate system in regard to its physicians.

The change in numbers of nurses to payroll, the $\Delta T/O$ indicator, illustrates the fact that in the merger and in the joint venture, payroll is rising faster than the number of nurses, a possible consequence of the educational thrust in the merger but of undetermined origin in the joint venture. In the corporate system and in the consortium there is no apparent reason why the numbers of nurses are rising faster than the payroll increases. Change in admissions over admissions, the $\Delta I/I$ indicator, suggests that admissions are relatively sluggish in the merger, stable in the consortium, and growing fastest in the joint venture. In three of the four systems, the numbers of nurses are rising faster than the numbers of physicians ($\Delta T/T$), and indication of probable increase in the quality of health care, but for reasons not at all clear, this is not true of the joint venture. Finally, the consortium and merger appear most successful in linking the rate of payroll increase to the total expense level ($\Delta O/O$).

Table 7.4   Rank order of values of multi-hospital system performance, using the Evan dynamic* organizational effectiveness indicators**.

System	Total expenses Admissions (Δ0/I)	Rank order	Physicians Admissions (ΔT/I)	Rank order	Nurses Payroll (ΔT/0)	Rank order
Consortium	59.48	1	52.82	3	74.96	3
Joint venture	309.00	3	80.22	4	-92.61	1
Merger	158.48	2	42.55	2	-39.12	2
Corporate management system	327.00	4	-82.65	1	164.27	4

System	Admissions Admissions (ΔI/I)	Rank order	Nurses Physicians (ΔT/T)	Rank order	Payroll Total expenses (Δ0/0)	Rank order
Consortium	3.48	2	113.67	4	5.84	2
Joint venture	53.84	4	-93.76	1	212.32	4
Merger	-92.29	1	32.90	2	1.33	1
Corporate management system	30.34	3	60.30	3	129.48	3

Kendall W = .21, not significant at .05

*   See page 143 for definition

** I = inputs
    T = transformation
    0 = outputs

Effectiveness ratios are based on the following time intervals:

Time	Before system formation	After system formation
Consortium	1970-1974	1974-1976
Joint venture	1970-1974	1974-1976
Merger	1954-1965	1965-1976
Corporate management system	1966-1969	1969-1977

158

As compared with the degree of concordance in the rankings of the measures of strategy (see Table 7.1) and in the measures of structure (see Table 7.3), the relatively low Kendall W coefficient in Table 7.4 is somewhat puzzling. We initially attributed the low degree of concordance in the rankings of the performance measures to the potential unreliability of comparing the static measures of strategy and structure with the dynamic measures of performance. Consequently, we examined the rank order of the four systems using the three Evan static measures of effectiveness (see Table 7.5). While the use of the static performance measures does increase the level of Kendall W somewhat, the degree of concordance in the rankings of the performance measures continues to fall well below those of strategy and structure. It is very likely that the nature of our performance measures not only accounts for the low values of Kendall W, but also accounts for the fact that they are lower than the Kendall W values we obtained with our measures of strategy and structure.

Table 7.5   Rank order of values of multi-hospital system performance, using the Evan static organizational effectiveness indicators*.

System	Nurses Payroll (T/O)	Rank order	Nurses Admissions (T/I)	Rank order	Expenses Admissions (O/I)	Rank order
Consortium	.000028	1	.032	3	1123.0	4
Joint venture	.000037	2	.027	1	721.0	2
Merger	.000050	3	.041	4	810.0	3
Corporate management system	.000078	4	.031	2	389.0	1

Kendall W = .29, not significant at .05

* All values are for 1976;
  I = inputs
  T = transactions
  O = outputs

159

5.8 Interrelationship of Strategy and Structure.

On the basis of our model presented in Figure 7.2, we would expect inter-hospital strategy to determine inter-hospital structure, as has been shown in a variety of industrial enterprises (Chandler, 1952; Channon, 1973; Rumelt, 1974). Using our official measures of hospital strategy based on a content analysis of systems goals, the Kendall W for the strategy and structure relationship equals .31, a value which is significant at .05. When the operative measures of hospital strategy based on availability of complex medical technology are used, the strategy-structure relationship yields a Kendall W of .27, a value which is not significant at .05. Thus the strategy-structure link noted in industrial enterprises cannot be unambiguously generalized to multi-hospital systems.

Since strategy formation in multi-hospital systems is a complicated process whereby three interest groups - board members, administrators, and physicians - negotiate from their relative positions of self-interest, whatever decisions emerge »favour ... short-term planning and parochial gains» (Perrow, 1963: 142). From this perspective, the structure of the joint venture, as we have observed, can scarcely be said to have followed from strategy; as a compromise, it was presumably distasteful to all participants, and evolved from a would-be merger because of a lack of agreement on a set of hospital expansion and co-operation plans. In short, the joint venture we have observed, as a type of inter-hospital structure, occurred despite strategy, not as a result of it. Presumably, then, the rank order correlation between strategy and structure in all four systems as measured by the Kendall W coefficient of concordance would be higher were it not for the peculiar history of the joint venture.

5.9 Interrelationship of Strategy, Structure, and Performance

We had not hypothesized a relationship between strategy, structure, and performance in the four multi-hospital systems, and there is no clear indication that such a relationship should be obtained. Chandler (1962) relates performance to strategy and structure only by implication; and Channon (1973) assesses only strategy and structure. Rumelt (1974), while linking performance with strategy and structure, finds little relationship between the three variables across or within industries. In other words, it is difficult to relate performance to strategy and structure between, for example, the oil and automobile industries. Within an industry, performance appears to be more related to market share and other external factors than to strategy and structure.

Exploring the relationship between strategy, structure, and performance in the multi-hospital systems by using the various combinations of measures, yields mixed results. Strategy, it will be recalled, has been operationalized as official goals (based on a content analysis) and operative goals (based on the extent of availability of complex medical technology); structure was measured with the aid of subjective ratings on six dimensions; the performance

160

measures were based on Evan's static and dynamic indicators. Using the dynamic indicators of performance with the official measures of strategy, we obtain a negligible Kendall W value of .07 for strategy, structure, and performance and substituting the operative measures of strategy yields a Kendall W value of .08, which is also not statistically significant. However, when the Evan static indicators are used in addition to the official measures of strategy, the Kendall W for strategy, structure, and performance equals .26, which is significant at .05. On the other hand, when the operative measures of strategy are used, the Kendall W equals .12, which is not significant at .05.

This finding, based on the static performance and the official strategy measures is consistent with the statistically significant relationship we have observed between strategy and structure. Moreover, the partial relationships, i.e. the relationships between strategy and performance (Kendall W equals .34 and .03 for official and operative measures of strategy, respectively) and structure and performance (Kendall W equals .29) support our inference that our findings concerning the interrelationship of official strategy, structure and static performance are statistically significant. Thus, the multi-hospital systems under consideration appear to have achieved performance levels that are to some extent consistent with their strategies and structures.

6. Summary and Conclusions

Extending Chandler's concept of strategy to non-profit organizations such as multi-hospital systems is fraught with ambiguity. In our effort to apply this concept we have had to differentiate official or stated goals from operative goals. Unlike the strategy of growth in the case of industrial organizations, the operative goals of multi-hospital systems do not lend themselves as readily to measurement. Nevertheless, given our interview data supplemented by a secondary analysis of administrative data, we have observed some appreciable differences in the strategies of the four multi-hospital systems.

The consortium which was formed with a political strategy in mind - namely, to achieve a balance of power among the member hospitals and to increase their collective bargaining power vis-à-vis the state hospital cost commission - has, additionally, a high commitment to regional patient care as evidenced by its investment in complex medical technology. Moreover, because the consortium includes a state hospital associated with the new state medical school, it is also conducting research (clinical and laboratory) and operating an extensive medical education programme for medical students, interns, and residents.

In the joint venture, which sought to modernize as well as to regionalize health care, the highest level of commitment to patient care was observed, as indicated by the availability of complex medical technology and by its articulation of stated patient care goals in its articles of incorporation and by-laws.

In the formation of the merger, two strategies appeared to be of uppermost significance to the decision-makers: rationalization of hospital costs by eliminating duplication and triplication of services and the creation of a critical mass, in regard to the number of hospital beds and level of medical expertise. This dual strategy is reflected in the importance the merger attaches to education, as evidenced by its high ranking in the content analysis of the articles of incorporation and by-laws. This emphasis may be partially at the expense of patient care, since it has a relatively low investment in complex medical technology.

The strategy of the corporate management system revolves principally around maximizing the rate of return to its investors through a carefully planned and monitored budgetary and management information system. Compared with other multi-hospital systems, it has the lowest level of investment in complex medical technology, is relatively low in education, and conducts no research at all.

Clearly, the strategies of the four hospital systems differ. Their structures, though differing along many dimensions (such as degree of centralization, standardization, and functional integration), do not, however, seem to be associated with their different strategies in as unique a manner as in the case of the industrial organizations studied by Chandler (1962), Channon (1973), and Rumelt (1974).

The relationship between strategy and structure in multi-hospital systems does not approach the one to one correspondence noted in the case of industrial enterprises. This difference may be a function of the absence of a competitive market structure in which health services are offered to consumers. Operating in a quasi-regulated industry, the services of multi-hospital systems are not put to a test, nor is the goodness of fit between their strategies and structures tested to the same degree that the products, strategies, and structures of industrial organizations are. Under these circumstances, the level of our strategy-structure fit may be understandable.

Our finding that strategy, structure, and performance (using the Evan static indicators and the official measures of strategy) are significantly interrelated indicates that the multi-hospital systems have, to some extent, linked performance to strategy and structure. To increase our understanding of the interrelationship of strategy, structure and performance, and to discover the scope of its generalizability, our finding suggests the need to reexamine our research strategy for studying multi-hospital systems. It may prove necessary to select a sample of hospital consortia or a sample of corporate management systems that are functional equivalents of an industry type in order to ascertain the conditions under which strategy, structure, and performance are consistently and strongly interrelated in multi-hospital systems. Obviously, a sample of multi-hospital systems rather than our four case studies, or Chandler's case studies for that matter, would permit a proper statistical test of the interrelationship of the three categories of variables.

The tentative nature of these research findings highlights the variety of problematic issues of a theoretical as well as of an applied nature associated with the interrelationships of strategy, structure, and performance. For one thing, there is a ready presumption on the part of organizational researchers that these interrelationships are hard constructs that are objectively measurable. In addition, there is a widespread rationalistic assumption that organizations deliberately make strategic decisions, consciously design their organizational structures, and carefully measure their performance. In the four multi-hospital systems under consideration, one can seriously doubt that such activities are being carried out. Of the four, only the corporate management system came close to meeting such expectations and given the current uncertainties in the U.S. hospital environment discussed above, it is doubtful that even this system is able to make very deliberate strategic decisions. The other systems have been less rationalistic in their behaviour.

Central to future considerations of the U.S. hospital environment is whether hospitals as members of multi-hospital systems, will need to become more rationalistic in order to survive. Those organizations that are not rationalistic either have environments that are benign or munificent or they are sufficiently large and prosperous that they have no compelling incentive to act like rational, maximizing decison-makers. On the other hand, some environments may be so complex and dynamic as to make strategic decision-making highly problematic, given the state of the art of management, science, and technology, especially in health care settings. Indeed, researchers and health care administrators generally agree that health care environments are moving from benign to complex and dynamic. There is considerable disagreement concerning appropriate responses to this shift, especially considering the uncertain future role of the federal government in cost containment, national health care insurance, etc.

A final problematic issue is the culturally patterned differences in styles of management decision-making. Is strategy, for example, a concept that has the same meaning in a variety of cultural settings? Is it reasonable to assume that top executives of large corporations in, say, West Germany and Japan more closely approximate the rationale of the maximizing decision-maker (carefully mapping strategies, designing structures, and measuring performance) than their counterparts in the U.S.? If such a difference were observed, it might well be a function of the differential impact of higher education on the industry of these countries. In West Germany and Japan, top executives of corporations probably have more advanced education than those in the U.S. What is more, they may value advanced education more highly and have a more intellectual orientation toward management than American executives do.

By systematically exploring the interrelationship of strategy, structure, and performance in a variety of organizational contexts, organizational researchers will very likely increase their understanding of how organizations are interrelated with their environments.

7. References

Aldrich, Howard E., and Pfeffer, Jeffrey, 1976
    Environments of Organizations, *Annual Review of Sociology,* 2: 79-105.

Ansoff, H. Igor, 1965
Corporate Strategy. New York: McGraw-Hill.

Blalock Jr., Hubert M., 1968
The Measurement Problem: A Gap Between the Languages of Theory and Research. In Hubert M. Blalock and Ann B. Blalock (eds.) *Methodology in Social Research.* New York: McGraw-Hill.

Brook, R.H., Avery, A.D., Greenfield, S., Lelah, T., Solomon, N., and Ware Jr., J.E., 1976
Quality of Medical Care Assessment Using Outcome Measures: An Overview of the Method. Santa Monica, California: The Rand Corporation.

Brown, Montague, and Lewis, Howard L., 1976
Hospital Management Systems. Germantown, Md.: Aspen Systems Corporation.

Chandler Jr., A.D., 1962
Strategy and Structure Cambridge, Mass.: MIT Press

Channon, Derek F.,
The Strategy and Structure of British Enterprise. Boston Mass.: Division of Research, Graduate School of Business Administration of Harvard University.

Donabedian, A., 1978a
»The Quality of Medical Care.» *Science,* 200, May 26: 856-864.

Donabedian, A., 1978b
»Needed Research in the Assessment and Monitoring of the Quality of Medical Care.» NCHSR Research Report Series, U.S. Department of Health, Education, and Welfare.

Donabedian, A., 1968
»Promoting Quality through Evaluating the Process of Patient Care.» *Medical Care,* 6, May, June: 181-202.

Donabedian, A., 1966
»Evaluating the Quality of Medical Care.» *The Milbank Memorial Fund Quarterly,* July (Part 2), 44: 166-203.

Evan, William M. (ed.), 1976a
Interorganizational Relations. Harmondsworth: Penguin Books.

Evan, William M. (ed.), 1976b
Organization Theory: Structures, Systems and Environments. New York: Wiley-Interscience.

Evan, William M., 1976c
Organization Theory and Organizational Effectiveness: An Exploratory Analysis, *Organization and Administrative Science.* 7 (Spring-Summer): 15-28.

164

Fottler, Myron D., 1977
   The Union Impact on Hospital Wages, *Industrial and Labor Relations* April, 30: 342-555.

Galbraith, Jay, 1973
   Designing Complex Organizations Reading, Mass.: Addison-Wesley Publishing Co.

Galbraith, Jay, 1973
   Organization Design Reading, Mass.: Addison-Wesley Publishing Co.

Gouldner, Alvin W., 1959
   Organizational Analysis. In Robert K. Merton, Leonard Broom and Leonard S. Cottrell, Jr. *Sociology Today.* New York: Basic Books, 400-428.

Graham, J.B., and Paloucek, F.P., 1963
   Where Should Cancer of the Cervix be Treated? *American Journal of Obstetrics and Gynecology* October, 87V: 405-409

Guide to the Health Care Field, 1977,
   Hospitals, 45. Chicago

Guide to the Health Care Field, 1976
   Hospitals, 47-49, 141, 143, Chicago

Guide to th Health Care Field, 1975
   Hospitals, 57, 59, 150, 153, 190. Chicago

Guide to the Health Care Field, 1974
   Hospitals, 56, 57, 59, 187. Chicago

Guide to the Health Care Field, 1973
   Hospitals, 49-51, 179. Chicago

Guide to the Health Care Field, 1972
   Hospitals, 47, 49, 184. Chicago

Heydebrand, Wolf V., 1973
   Hospital Bureaucracy. New York: Dunellen

Holsti, Ole R., 1969
   Content Analysis for the Social Science and Humanities. Reading, Mass.: Addison-Wesley Publishing Co.

Hospitals, 1971
   Journal of the American Hospital Association, 45: 47,49,179

Hospitals, 1970
   Journal of the American Hospital Association, August, 44: 48-50,181

Hospitals, 1969
Journal of the American Hospital Association, August, 43: 143

Hospitals, 1968
Journal of the American Hospital Association, August, 42: 144

Hospitals, 1967
Journal of the American Hospital Association, August, 41: 168

Hospitals, 1966
Journal of the American Hospital Association, August, 40: 146

Hospitals, 1965
Journal of the American Hospital Association, August, 39: 56

Hospitals, 1960
Journal of the American Hospital Association, August, 34: 48-49

Hospitals, 1954
Journal of the American Hospital Association, June, 28: 85

Mahajan, Vijay, and Schoeman, Milton E.F., 1977
The Use of Computers in Hospitals: An Analysis of Adopters and Nonadopters. *Interfaces,* May, 7: 95-107

Neuhauser, D., and Anderson, R., 1972
»Structural-Comparative Studies of Hospitals.» In B. Georgopolous, ed., *Organization Research on Hospitals.* Ann Arbor: Institute of Social Research, University of Michigan.

Perrow, Charles, 1963
Goals and Power Structures: A Historical Case Study». In Eliot Freidson (ed.), *The Hospital in Modern Society.* New York: The Free Press of Glencoe. 112-146

Portnoy, Steven, 1977
The Swelling Tide: Services and Management in Systems, *Hospitals, Journal of the American Hospital Association. 51 (April): 63-67* April, 51: 63-67

Rafferty, John and Schweitzer, Stuart O., 1974
Comparison of For-Profit and Nonprofit Hospitals: A Re-evaluation. *Inquiry,* December, XI: 304-309

Ruchlin, Hirsch S., Pointer, Dennis D., and Cannedy, Lloyd L., 1973
A Comparison of For-Profit Investor-Owned Chain and Nonprofit Hospitals. *Inquiry,* December, X: 13-23

Ruchlin, Hirsch S., Pointer, Dennis D., and Cannedy, Lloyd L., 1973
Reply. *Inquiry,* December, XI: 310-311

Rumelt, Richard P., 1974
   Strategy, Structure, and Economic Performance. Boston, Mass.: Division of Research, Graduate School of Business Administration, Harvard University.

Scott, W. Richard, Forrest Jr., William H., and Brown Jr., Bryan W., 1976
   Hospital Structure and Post-Operative Mortality and Morbidity. In Stephen M. Shortell and Montague Brown (eds.), *Organizational Research in Hospitals.* Chicago: Blue Cross Association. An Inquiry Book. 72-89

Shortell, Stephen M., 1976
   Organization Theory and Health Services Delivery. In Stephen M. Shortell and Montague Brown (eds.) *Organizational Research in Hospitals.* Chicago: Blue Cross Association. An Inquiry Book. 1-12

Shortell, Stephen M., Becker, Selwyn W., and Neuhauser, Duncan, 1976
   The Effects of Management Practices on Hospital Efficiency and Quality of Care. In Stephen M. Shortell and Montague Brown (eds.), *Organizational Research in Hospitals.* Chicago: Blue Cross Association. An Inquiry Book.

Simon, Herbert A., 1969
   The Sciences of the Artificial. Cambridge, Mass.: MIT Press

Springate, d D. and McNeil, Melissa Craig, 1977
   Management Policies in Investor-Owned Hospitals, *HCM Review,* Summer: 57-67

Stull, Richard J., 1977
   Many Concepts Mold Multi-institutional Systems, *Hospitals, Journal of the American Hospital Association,* March, 51: 43-45

8. THE DETERMINANTS OF THE HIERARCHICAL ORGANIZATION OF INDUSTRY*

Herman Daems
European Institute for Advanced Studies in Management, EIASM,
Brussels, Belgium

* *Research for this paper was supported by a grant from the German Marshall Fund in Washington. The author is also grateful to Marc Van Heukelsen for valuable assistance in collecting the data and to Peter Cuypers for the computing help.*

1. Large Size Hierarchical Firms

In several industries the coordination of activities, the allocation of resources and the monitoring of performance is administered by managerial hierarchies. These managerial hierarchies are operated by a central administrative office that, first, consolidates ownership over factories, laboratories, warehouses and sales offices and second, supervises the functioning of the establishments under its legal control. The large, diversified and integrated multi-unit establishment firms that dominate certain industries reflect the operation of these central administrative offices. The size, diversification and integration of, and the managerial control over these multi-establishment firms has worried many economists, and numerous studies were undertaken to assess the impact of these centrally administered organizations on the economy and society.[1] The question why these managerial hierarchies came to dominate certain industries has only recently received more attention. From the viewpoint of public policy, however, knowing why giant hierarchies developed is certainly as important as knowing their impact on society. This chapter attempts to explain why such managerial hierarchies developed in certain industries.

---

[1]   The literature on this subject is so extensive and also so well known that I have decided not to attempt to give a bibliographic reference.

2. The Facts

The extent of hierarchical organization of modern industry is illustrated by the following statistics. In 1972, the non-communist world had 256 giant industrial corporations, each employing over 30,000 persons. The share of non-communist world employment of these companies in various manufacturing industries is estimated in Table 8.1. The data show that considerable differences exist among industries. Large scale hierarchical organizations are most important in petroleum and electrical machinery, whereas in textiles and apparel, wood, furniture, printing and leather, large hierarchies are of no significance for organizing industrial activities.

A similar trend can be identified in the United States. According to the *1972 Enterprise Statistics* (published by the *Bureau of the U.S. Census,* 447), 170,000 establishments such as factories, laboratories, warehouses and sales offices were operated by firms in the manufacturing industry. Approximately half of these establishments were independent firms, the others were administered by a central office that coordinated activities, allocated resources and monitored performance of several establishments. One-fourth of the total number of establishments was operated by 305 companies. On the average each of these 305 companies employed 31,269 persons, and none had less than 10,000 persons. The managerial hierarchies of these companies administered 352 establishments on the average. All the companies were functioning in more than one industry. As was the case in the non-communist world, large managerial hierarchies in the U.S. became the dominant mode of organizing coordination, allocation and monitoring only in a limited number of industries (see Table 8.2). In petroleum, transportation equipment, tobacco and chemicals, coordination, allocation and monitoring was administered by managerial hierarchies. In such industries as apparel, wood, furniture and metal products, such managerial hierarchies were less prominent.

The picture obtained from the statistical data is supported by the historical findings of Professor Alfred D. Chandler, Jr. His recent work shows that large managerial hierarchies came to administer strategies of vertical integration from the 1880s onwards. These giant hierarchies also operated successfully in only a few industries. Until the World War I, these industries were food and tobacco, milk, soup, cereals, (meat, beer, distilled liquors and cigarettes), various standardized and assembled non-electrical machinery and equipment for private, industrial, administrative and agricultural uses (typewriters, sewing machines, harvesters, cash registers), chemicals (soap, paints, dynamite, soda), electrical machinery, equipment and supplies (cables, telephones, light and power generators), petroleum and also primary metals (steel). After the World War I, managerial hierarchies came to operate in the fields of transportation equipment (cars first and airplanes later) and household appliances (refrigerators). From the 1920s on, mangerial hierarchies not only administered coordination of vertically interrelated activities, but they came also to manage strategies of product and geographical diversification. After the World War II the managerial hierarchies continued to grow in size in the forementioned industries, but as the statistical data showed, the trend

Table 8.1. Number of companies with over 30,000 people employed and their share in non-communist world employment for various manufacturing industries for 1973.

	Number	Share
Food & Beverages	31	20.5
Tobacco	5	38.1
Textiles & Apparel	8	2.6
Wood	1	1.4
Furniture	-	0.-
Paper	8	15.9
Printing	-	0.-
Chemicals	33	39.5
Petroleum	14	72.1
Rubber	7	50.1
Leather	1	3.0
Glass, Stone, Clay	4	11.9
Primary Metals	34	41.7
Metal Products	10	8.8
Non Electric Machinery	16	10.9
Electrical Machinery	42	70.3
Transportation Equipment	40	62.0
Measuring Optical, Photographic	4	19.5
	256	

Sources: Calculated from Fortune 500 U.S.
and Fortune 500 outside U.S.
and various United Nations Statistical Yearbook.

Non-communist countries

Developing countries are included.

171

Table 8.2. Share of +10,000 employees companies in total United States employment in various manufacturing industries for 1972.

	in %
20 Food	25
21 Tobacco	71.1
22 Textiles	32.9
23 Apparel	9.6
24 Wood	4.8
25 Furniture	7.1
26 Pulp and paper	49.9
27 Printing and publishing	13.8
28 Chemicals	60.4
29 Petroleum	84.7
30 Rubber	41.6
31 Leather	42.1
32 Glass	33.9
33 Primary metals	59.9
34 Metal products	13.5
35 Machinery	37
36 Electrical machinery	64.4
37 Transportation equipment	80.3
38 Measuring and optical	33.5
39 Miscellaneous	12.4

Source: 1972 Enterprise Statistics, U.S. Bureau of the Census.

did not spread to other industries such as clothing and furniture. There the typical enterprises tend to remain single product, single function, single region firms. These historical findings further document the fact that managerial hierarchies only developed and survived in certain industries.[1]

---

[1] Ongoing historical research suggests that such was also the case in the U.K., Germany and France. See also Chandler, Jr. and Daems, 1980

As illustrated by the data in the *1972 Enterprise Statistics,* a considerable amount of resources is being used to administer these multi-establishment organizations. In the United States, 422,766 persons were employed to staff the central administration of these large companies, at an annual cost of U.S. Dollars 6.2 billion (approximately 6 per cent of the total payroll of these companies). In other words, for every 21 employees in a large company there is at least one employee to administer coordination, allocation and monitoring. Although it is impossible to estimate the amount of capital used for administrative purposes correctly from the census data, it is likely that it is not negligible.

Two conclusions can be drawn from these statistics and historical findings. First, hierarchies are used to administer such fundamental economic functions as coordination, allocation and monitoring in certain industries but not in others. Second, the cost of administration is not negligible. In turn, these conclusions raise two closely related questions. Why are scarce resources utilized to administer the functioning of establishments at all? What determines the development of hierarchy in certain industries?

3. Previous Literature

The extensive literature on the economies of multi-plant operations, of diversification and of integration is relevant for answering the questions raised above. However, this literature should be expanded in two directions. Firstly, in order to explain interindustry differences in the degree of multi-plant operation, diversification, and integration, the technological and market conditions causing such differences should be more thoroughly explored. Secondly, and more importantly, those conditions necessary to creating a successful centralized administration of managerial hierarchies must be identified. The existing literature deals mainly with this second topic: Managerial hierarchies are necessary to handle the economies of multi-establishment operations, of diversification, and of integration. But are such hierarchies also necessary for reaping the benefits of diversification and integration? By focusing on the various institutional arrangements that establishments use to organize coordination allocation and monitoring, this paper develops the conditions that favor hierarchical organizations of industry. This focus was inspired by the pathbreaking work of Alfred D. Chandler, Jr., Ronald E. Coase and Oliver E. Williamson.

4. A Choice of Institutional Arrangements

Coordination of activities, allocation of resources and monitoring of performance require communication of information concerning opportunities and actions. In order to ensure effective coordination it is also necessary that compliance with contracts is enforced. It is possible to distinguish three alternative institutional arrangements which help to communicate information and to enforce compliance: markets, federations and hierarchies.[1] As shown in Figure 8.1, markets, federations and hierarchies differ in three ways: in the way they structure ownership, in the way they distribute returns, and in the way they organize supervision to deal with the communication of information and the enforcement of compliance.

Production and distribution establishments that are independently owned, that do not share returns, and that do not mutually supervise one another, rely on contingent prices to exchange information and to enforce compliance. In such industries with predominantly single products, single function, single establishment firms, activities are coordinated, resources allocated and performance monitored by prices and markets.

In other cases, the establishments, while remaining independent, may try to pool returns in order to stimulate communication of information and compliance with contracts. Returns can be pooled in various ways: by sharing profits, by dividing markets or by centrally allocating orders. Such arrangements are called federations. Firms that are federated in this way rely on joint decision making for coordination, allocation and monitoring. Cartels are federations but no all federations are cartels. In some industries, particularly in Europe and Japan, firms are linked through extensive interlocking stockholdings. Such financial constructs are often called *industrial groups*. [2] These groups, however, do not rely on central administrative offices to supervise the group members. *Industrial groups* are therefore not fundamentally different from profit pooling arrangements, because the interlocking stockholdings ensure that the group members share, in a complex manner, the total returns to the group. For this reason, *industrial groups* are federations. Another way for independent establishments to form a federation is to agree on mutual supervision. Franchising by hotels, fast food restaurants and soft-drink bottlers are examples of this second type of federation without pooling of returns.

The last institutional arrangement to deal with information and compliance is the managerial hierarchy. Managerial hierarchies consolidate legal control over production and distribution establishments. Consequently, they also pool rewards and, most importantly, they supervise the functioning of the establishments. Vertically integrated and product and geographically diversified firms are hierarchical arrangements for coordination, allocation, and monitoring.

These three alternative institutions are observable in modern industrialized economies. In some industries hierarchies are used to coordinate interrelated activities, to allocate resources and to monitor performance. In other industries federations dominate. Finally, there are many industries where markets are used for coordination, allocating and monitoring. The transition from one institutional arrangement to another is observable in mergers and divestitures. In this way, studies of industrial organization, concentration and mergers can be viewed as studies of why hierarchies or federations or markets are relied upon to organize coordination, allocation and monitoring. A

---

[1]   Richardson, 1972.
[2]   Daems, 1978.

174

Type of institution	Ownership	Returns	Supervision	Examples
Markets	Independent	No-pooling	No	Exchanges Contingent contracts
Federations	Independent	Pooling	No	Cartels
	Consolidated ->	Pooling	No	Industrial Groups
	Independent	No-pooling	Yes	Franchising Interlocking Directorship
Hierarchies	Consolidated ->	Pooling	Yes	Integrated and diversified companies

Figure 8.1 Basic characteristics of markets, federations, and hierarchies.

theory dealing with the conditions under which consolidated ownership and supervision (hierarchies) replace independent ownership without pooling and supervision (markets) would be extremely helpful in explaining the organization of industry in these terms. Recent theoretical work in institutional economics provides extremely useful insights for the development of such a theory.[1]

In a profit-oriented economic system, it only makes sense for a group of production and distribution units to coordinate activities, to allocate resources and to monitor performance when such measures lead to concerted actions among establishments that increase joint returns without lowering the return of one of the individual establishments. If no benefits can be obtained from concerted actions there is no point in using scarce resources to organize an institutional arrangement, be it a market, a federation or a hierarchy, for the exchange of information and the enforcement of contracts. It is well known from existing economic theory that in cases of production and/or demand externalities or interdependencies, concerted actions lead to higher returns. Such is also the case when production establishments collude to monopolize supply. However, there is little in traditional theory to explain which institutional arrangement will be used to organize the concerted action. Production units could just as well earn monopoly rents by means of tacit collusion among independent non-profit pooling sellers, such as cartels and holding companies, or by consolidating ownership and supervising the rate of production.

---

[1] Davis & North, 1971; Williamson, 1975; Stiglitz, 1975; Coase, 1937; Alchian & Demsetz, 1972.

Concerted action in the case of externalities and interdependencies could just as well be organized by contingent contracting between independent units, for example by pooling returns, by supervising actions, or by consolidating ownership. Why, then, is it that under certain conditions concerted action is organized by means of hierarchies, and under other conditions, federations and markets are used? Formulated differently, what are the conditions that lead administrative offices to provide managerial services in exchange for legal consolidation and supervision instead of market contracting between independent establishments? If no answer exists to these questions, then the forementioned institutional arrangements are irrelevant for economic activity. Such would also imply that all the commonly used statistical measures of sellers concentration based on the degree of legal independence of the suppliers are irrelevant for measuring monopolizing power, and that the statistical measures of integration and diversification cannot tell us anything about the benefits of integration and diversification. Indeed, both measures implicitly assume that consolidated ownership makes a difference. Since most economists are not ready to accept the conclusion that institutional arrangements are irrelevant (why else would institutions exist?), a need exists to find the determinants that affect such institutional choices.

5. The Determinants of Hierarchy

It is easier to discuss the determinants of hierarchy if the argument is developed in three successive steps. In the first it is assumed that the three institutional arrangements have the same installation and operating costs, and that the difference between the various institutions results in differing effects on the joint return. More accurately, we begin by assuming that the pay-off to the joint activity is a function only of the contractual relations existing between the cooperating units. In the second step, the assumption of step 1 is dropped and attention is focused on the differences in installation and operating costs of the three alternative institutional arrangements. In the final step, the two previous steps are combined in order to discuss the net advantage of a particular institution.

The first step implies that the institutional arrangement leading to the highest joint pay-off be adopted by the participating units. The following example illustrates this reasoning. If the total joint return to monopolizing supply is higher through consolidated ownership and supervision (hierarchy) than through independent units and profit-pooling (federation), we expect multi-unit hierarchies to be used for monopolizing supply, provided, as we assumed above, that the costs of installation and operation of a hierarchy and federation are equal and not higher than the cost of tacit collusion. Similarly, if the joint return to concerted action in the case of an externality is higher under hierarchy than under any other institutional arrangement, we expect hierarchy to be the only institution to deal with externalities and interdependencies.

However, the argument as yet fails to explain why it is that joint returns are influenced by the particular institutional arrangement governing the cooperation between units. Upon reflection, it is clear that the explanation lies in the superiority of a particular institution to handle the exchange of information and the enforcement of compliance needed for the coordination, allocation and monitoring processes in the joint activity. A particular institutional arrangement can only achieve higher joint returns on concerted actions if it communicates information better and/or enforces compliance more effectively than other institutional arrangements with equal installation and operation costs.

The superiority of a particular institutional arrangement is not absolute, but is dependent on the *specific* needs for information and compliance. In some cases a concerted action of interdependent units requires a considerable exchange of complex information and a tight enforcement of compliance. In other cases the full pay-off to the joint action can be achieved with a limited amount of simple information and without policing compliance. It thus remains to be clarified why different concerted actions lead to different needs for information and compliance.

Concerted actions are the results of explicit or implicit transactions between cooperating units. These transactions are responsible for differences in the need for information and compliance. Professor Oliver Williamson has recently identified the three critical dimensions of every transaction as being: the degree of uncertainty involved in fully completing the transaction, the size of transaction-specific investments, and the frequency of recurrence of the transaction.[1] The third dimension is less relevant at this point, but will be of critical importance in the second step of the argument when operation costs of institutions are discussed. The first two dimensions of a transaction have important implications, however. The greater the uncertainty is about successfully completing transactions and concerted actions in a particular industry, the greater are the specific needs for information and compliance in that industry. Transaction-specific investments are easier to describe with reference to some examples. The marketing of some perishable products, for instance, requires highly specialized equipment. In such cases, transactions between processing and distributing units require investments designated for unique and highly specific uses. Another example might be the selling of complex products, which often requires special knowledge about specifications and special servicing.

Once again, transactions between manufacturing and distributing units are only possible when transaction-specific investments are made. The greater the amount of resources that is irreversibly committed for specific or transaction-specific purposes, the more the need exists for tight compliance. Since hierarchies, for a variety of reasons, have superior enforcement mechanisms and information networks, it seems plausible to postulate that consolidated ownership and supervision will be used more frequently in industries where the coordination, allocation and monitoring processes of concerted actions are subject to considerable uncertainty, or which require resources for highly specialized and unique uses.

---

[1] Williamson, 1979.

177

It is unreasonable to assume, as was done in the first step of the argument, that the costs of organizing concerted action are independent of the particular institutional arrangement used. This brings us to the second step of the argument. In reality, the costs of installation and operation of an institutional arrangement are a function of the type of institution chosen. Coordinating activities, allocating resources and monitoring performance through market contracting is costly because resources are needed to collect information and to enforce contract provisions. The costs of hierarchy are associated with two factors: first, the consolidation of ownership stimulates shirking, and second, the supervision consumes resources.[1] Because of profit-pooling, federations are also subject to shirking costs, and the recurrent negotiating process is likely to consume a considerable amount of resources.

The frequency with which transactions must recur to sustain a concerted action between cooperating units over a longer period of time is important for comparing the cost advantages of the various institutional arrangements. The total costs of the installation and operation of a hierarchy are probably constant or slightly increasing with the frequency of recurrence. Federations face lower fixed costs than hierarchies, but have some variable costs for every transaction that is negotiated. This implies that federations face increasing total cost with respect to frequency of recurrence. Market contracting has the lowest fixed cost but the highest variable cost. In this case, total information and compliance cost for organizing concerted actions is nearly proportional to the frequency with which such actions need to be negotiated. These cost conditions suggest that economies exist in organizing the concerted actions of units with hierarchies when the frequency of transactions between these units is high.

In many cases, the costs of installation and operation of an institutional arrangement are also affected by government regulations and taxes. The costs of forming a new hierarchical arrangement by merger, for instance, is influenced by corporation taxes and by anti-trust legislation. The costs of organizing a federation in the form of a cartel are also prohibitively high in the U.S., and in some cases in Europe, because governments have outlawed cartel arrangements. As for market mechanisms, the costs associated with the coordination of vertical interdependencies are sometimes affected by sales taxes.

Both previous steps can be combined to discuss the net gain in organizing coordination, allocation and monitoring by a particular institution. Similar to technologies, institutional arrangements compete with one another. In a competitive world with free institutional choices, only those institutions that promise the highest net return to the cooperating units will survive in the long run. This leads to an important conclusion: hierarchies rival with federations and markets to provide coordination, allocation and monitoring. This rivalry is termed as *institutional competition*. It is only when hierarchies promise a higher net return in the long run than other institutional arrangements that they can hope to survive over an extended period of time.

---

[1] See the statistics in the beginning of the chapter for an estimate of this second source of costs.

It was shown that the superiority of a hierarchical arrangement is not absolute, but depends on specific conditions. These conditions vary among industries and they are influenced by the needs for information and compliance. Hence, hierarchies will be more successful in certain industries than in others. They will tend to operate in industries where exchange of information and enforcement of compliance is important, due to large uncertainty about successful completion of transactions, transaction-specific investments, and high frequency of recurrence of these transactions. This argument also implies that when multi-unit hierarchies are used as a dominant institutional mode in a particular industry, it must be because such hierarchical arrangements lead to higher returns than what would be reaped under non-hierarchical arrangements.

6. Hypotheses

The concept of institutional competition enables us to formulate two hypotheses.

First, multi-establishment enterprises that consolidate ownership and organize supervision will only be successful in a limited number of industries. Also, multi-establishment enterprises will be operating in the same industries in different nations, provided governments do not impose legal and fiscal obstacles to the choice of institutional arrangements. The characteristics of these industries are discussed below.

Second, in these industries large-scale enterprises will be more profitable than non-consolidated and single establishment firms. It is very important to stress that this hypothesis does not imply that multi-establishment enterprises will necessarily earn higher returns in comparison with all enterprises in the economy. It is only *within* certain industries that integrated and diversified enterprises outperform single product, single establishment, single function firms in the long run. In those industries the stability over time of integrated and/or diversified enterprises should also be larger than the stability of non-integrated and/or non-diversified firms. Such firms will be attracted to these industries during the upturn of the industry's business cycle, when the cost of expanding the hierarchy of the existing firms further is larger than the benefits of such expansion. During a downturn the non-integrated, non-diversified firms will be forced out of the industry. Thus, over the course of an industry's business cycle, differences in stability of integrated and diversified firms and non-integrated and non-diversified firms will be observable.

In order to test these hypotheses the precise characteristics of the hierarchically organized industries must be derived from the arguments developed in previous sections of this chapter. Three characteristics will be important:

1. the research intensity of the industry,

2. the extent to which demand in the industry is dependent on supplier provided information, and

3. the size of the industry's material input requirements.

Research intensity stimulates consolidation of ownership and supervision by hierarchies for several reasons. One is that research and development activities must build on production and marketing experiences for improving processes and products. This exchange of experience and knowledge makes production and marketing activities interdependent with research and development activities,[1] and such interdependence makes concerted actions advantageous. The transactions needed to organize the concerted actions are subject to large uncertainties and require some transaction-specific investments. One source of uncertainty, for instance, is the presence of information impactedness, which occurs when the parties involved have unequal access to knowledge and information. Another source is the public goods nature of knowledge. Under such circumstances and without proper institutional management, the cooperating units will most likely exploit the information impactedness to their own advantage. In turn, such opportunistic behaviour makes joint action difficult to sustain in the long run.

Another reason (why research intensity stimulates supervision by hierarchies) is that when new processes, products, or applications are invented, transfer of this knowledge involves highly uncertain transactions. Again the sources for this uncertainty are information impactedness and the public goods nature of knowledge. In most cases transaction-specific investments are also needed. Consolidation of ownership and supervision will often be the most efficient arrangement to make sure that the return on the invention is fully appropriated and to learn about new opportunities for further improvements. Consequently, it is to be expected that research intensive industries will tend to be organized by hierarchies, and multi-establishment firms will dominate under such circumstances.

In some industries, market demand is a function of supplier provided information and services. Indeed, in markets for consumer durables, processed foods, and *standardized equipment* for business uses the potential customer is confronted with a choice problem characterized by uncertainty. The customer has imperfect information about possible uses of the product, reliability, quality and after sales servicing. The manufacturer attempts to widen the market by reducing the customer's uncertainty. One way for the manufacturer to achieve this is to rely on branding. Brand names allow the supplier to communicate information about the product to the customer. However, once a brand name has gained customer acceptance it must be protected from free riders and distortions. In this case, free riders are competitors who try to profit from the specific investments in the brand by copying the product as closely as possible. For the protection of their brands most manufacturers need to rely on close cooperation with the distributors of their products.[2]

Distortions in the brand image with respect to quality are likely to arise when the product has to move through successive stages of processing and distribution before it reaches the customer. Often different units in different locations are responsible for the successive stages, and close cooperation between these units is needed to sustain product quality and brand image.

---

[1] For an interesting analysis of this interdependence see Freeman, 1974, especially Chapter 5.
[2] Porter, 1976

Another likely source of brand image distortions, this time not only with respect to quality but also with respect to servicing, arises when several independent manufacturing establishments try to jointly exploit the economies of scale in branding. Again a very tight cooperation is necessary to prevent brand image distortions. Both protection against free riders and against brand distortions therefore require joint action. Transactions are needed to organize such joint actions. Not only is uncertainty about successful competition of the transactions large, but transaction-specific investment are also often involved. In most cases, consolidated ownership and supervision will be most efficient in handling the specific information and compliance needs. In some cases, however, federations will be used. Because of the costs involved in writing and enforcing complex contingent contracts, market contracting is unlikely to survive for very long in these circumstances. In general, then, we expect multi-unit hierarchies to be used in industries where demand is dependent on branding. It is not possible to obtain a perfect measure of branding. Advertising expenditures measured as percentages of sales are used as close enough proxies of the extent of branding industry by industry.

Industries that require a large volume of specific intermediate products for their activities tend to carry out their transactions with specialized suppliers on a recurrent basis. Very often quality and timely delivery are critically important for a least cost operation, and thus close cooperation between users and suppliers is necessary. It was earlier suggested that the specific information and compliance needs of recurrent transactions make it profitable to economize on transactions by consolidated ownership and supervision. Thus, industries that consume a high volume of special intermediate products will rely on hierarchies for organizing the vertical interdependence. It is proposed that the dependence of an industry on intermediate inputs be measured by the ratio of value of intermediate products and services to total sales. The larger this ratio, the more the industry will be hierarchically organized.

7. Empirical Evidence

Several empirical studies, although some written with a different perspective in mind, lend support to the basic hypotheses of this chapter. Papers by Mahityahu Marcus, Richard C. Osborn, Harold Demsetz, Michael E. Porter, and Robert J. Stonebraker found that returns are positively influenced by firm size in certain industries but not in others. Since the size of firms is in most cases an accurate estimate of the extent of multi-establishment operations and of the use of managerial hierarchies, their research findings come as no surprise. Marcus observed that the dependence of the rate of return on firm size varied from industry to industry, but he failed to indicate whether the industries in which size had a positive effect, shared common characteristics. Osborn first, and Demsetz later, showed that performance differences between the largest firms and the smallest firms in an industry depend on the concentration ratio. In most cases, industries with large managerial hierarchies are also the most concentrated ones. Demsetz' findings, then, lend support to the hypothesis.

The empirical findings of Porter are of particular relevance. He found that the rate of return for the largest firms in an industry was positively and significantly influenced by advertising intensity, which was measured as the share of advertising expenditures in sales, thus suggesting that when advertising was not used extensively, it was more difficult for the large firms to outperform small firms. Finally, Stonebraker attempted to explain the profit risk of small firms. He found that profit risk and failure rate of small firms was directly related to advertising intensity and, most importantly, to R and D expenditures. These findings suggest that research and advertising intensive industries will be less successfully organized by small firms, presumably single establishment firms.

The hypotheses was recently further tested. Data for these tests were obtained from the *U.S. Census of Manufacturers* in 1972 and *IRS Source Book of Corporation Income 1972*. The dependent variable is the extent to which managerial hierarchies are used to administer coordination, allocation and monitoring of establishments in particular industries. The spread of such hierarchies is reflected in the appearance of multi-establishment firms. Therefore, it was decided to measure the extent of the hierarchical organization of an industry by the share of multi-establishment firms in total employment of that industry. This variable was labelled HIER.

Multiestablishment firms tend to operate in several industries at the same time. In order to minimize the risk of measurement biases resulting from multi-industry operations industries were defined at the two-digit level. This broad definition of industry makes overlapping between industries less likely. Two other dependent variables were constructed. One measures the share of employment in companies with over 10,000 people and is called TEN. The other measures the share of industry employment in multi industry companies and is indicated by MULTI. The correlation between these three dependent variables is extremely high, as can be seen from the correlation matrix in Table 8.3.

Table 8.3.   Correlation matrix of dependent variables.

	TEN	MULTI	HIER	Average	Standard deviation
TEN	1			0.39	0.25
MULTI	0.93	1		0.69	0.20
HIER	0.92	0.99	1	0.76	0.16

According to the hypotheses interindustry differences in HIER, TEN and MULTI, should be explainable by research intensity, advertising intensity, and by the size of the input requirements. Research intensity (RND) was measured by the ratio of expenditures on applied research by product *(not* by industries) to sales for the product. The data was obtained from publications by the *National Science Foundation.* The advertising-to-sales ratio (ADV) was computed from IRS Source Book on Corporation Income. Sales minus value added over sales based on Census establishment data was labelled INP and was taken as an estimate of the need for material inputs.

The regression results are reported in Table 8.4. They support the hypotheses advanced in this paper. It is only in industries where the need for communication of information and enforcement of compliance are large because of research and development activities, advertising and large input requirements, that hierarchies will be used to administer coordination, allocation and monitoring of establishments.

Table 8.4.   Regression results of dependent variables.

Dependent variable	Constant	ADV	RND	INP	$R^{2\,1)}$ only	F-stat
TEN	-0.441 (1.824)*	5.337 (1.312)	6.887 (3.148)**	1.294 (3.129)**	0.403	5.279*
MULTI	0.082 (0.435)	6.020 (1.887)*	5.668 (3.304)**	0.887 (2.705)**	0.419	5.570**
HIER	0.242 (1.518)	5.232 (1.952)*	4.497 (3.121)**	9.745 (2.736)**	0.406	5.337**

Number of observations

* 5% sign. level
** 1% sign. level

1) Adjusted for degrees of freedom

This brings up the second hypothesis. It was argued that in those particular industries where multi-establishment firms have a competitive advantage because of their particular way of organization, such firms must outperform single establishment firms. A direct test of this hypothesis is not possible. But since multi-unit firms tend to be much larger than single unit firms, an indirect test (exploiting this size difference) can be devised. The technique employed was inspired by Demsetz' work.

The IRS industries for 1972 were regrouped in four size classes: Class 1 for firms with assets under U.S. Dollars 500,000, Class 2 for firms between U.S. Dollars 500,000 and U.S. Dollars 5,000,000, Class 3 for firms in between U.S. Dollars 5,000,000 and U.S. Dollars 50,000,000 and finally Class 4 for firms beyond U.S. Dollars 50,000,000. For every size class, accounting rates of return (profits before taxes plus interest over total assets) were calculated. These rates of return are called R_1, R_2, R_3 and R_4. Several authors have argued that the profit data in the bottom IRS size class are unreliable because of the under-reporting of profits by small corporations. Hence, we constructed Class 1-2, which includes all firms in Class 1 and Class 2. The rates of return for that class is labelled R_{12}. Next the following differences are defined: $R4MR1 = R_4 - R_1$, $R4MR2 = R_4 - R_2$, $R4MR3 = R_4 - R_3$, $R4MR12 = R_4 - R_{12}$. If research activities and advertising necessitate consolidated ownership and supervision for efficient handling of information and compliance, we expect the performance difference between large firms and small firms to be positively associated with research intensity and advertising-to-sales ratio.

Because of the under-reporting in Class 1 it was decided not to limit tests of the positive association to R4MR1, but also to consider R4MR2 and R4MR12. The IRS data allowed for a study of 41 industries. Since research and development data were not available for all these industries, a dummy variable was constructed to capture research intensity. RNDO1 equals 1 only when, on the basis of NFS data, we had reason to believe that the research expenditures in that industry were more than 0.1 per cent of total business receipts. RNDO1 was put equal to zero in the remaining industries. An alternative and more strict measure was used by raising the cut off point to 0.2 per cent. This variable was named RNDO2.

Table 8.5 reports the results of the regression analysis. The hypothesis is supported quite well by the data. Industries characterized by large research and development activities and by large outlays for advertising are more profitably organized by large firms; presumably such firms are also multi-establishment firms. As could be expected, equations 1 and 2 perform less well in the regression analysis. Indeed, in Class 1 the under reporting makes stochastic noise on profits so large that it lowers the coefficient of determination. In equations 3 and 4 the stochastic noise is reduced and the positive effect of advertising and research intensity are clearly observable. The similarities of these results with equations 7 and 8 are worth noting. Equations 5 and 6 show that the positive effect of research intensity tapers off when the size class is increased. This suggest that once a certain size is reached, organization of research and development does not require further expansion of firm sizes. However, this is not the case for advertising.

The tests reported here, thus support the view that large hierarchies develop in some modern industries in response to specific needs for communication of information and enforcement of compliance. The results also suggest that such hierarchies, because of consolidated ownership and supervision, are a more efficient arrangement for organizing certain industries than other non-hierarchical arrangements.

184

Table 8.5.   Regression analysis results. Equation results.

Dependent variable	Constant	ADV	RND01	RND02	$R^{2\underline{1}}$	F
1. R4MR1	-0.0067 (-0.4249)	0.9417 (1.6362)	0.0332 (1.7744)*		0.08	2.82
2.	-0.0015 (-0.1127)	0.8012 (1.3970)		0.0377 (1.9511)*	0.09	3.17
3. R4MR2	-0.0282 (-2.1347)*	1.3425 (2.7730)**	0.0334 (2.7730)**		0.19	5.92**
4.	-0.0247 (-2.2049)*	1.1857 (2.5213)**		0.0432 (2.7273)**	0.24	7.64**
5. R4MR3	-0.0309 (-2.9314)	0.9917 (2.5673)**	0.0049 (0.3950)		0.10	3.34*
6.	-0.0284 (-3.0631)**	0.9858 (2.5350)**		0.0004 (0.0325)	0.10	3.25*
7. R4MR12	-0.0177 (-1.3678)	1.2159 (2.5506)**	0.0277 (1.7918)*		0.15	4.723
8.	-0.0153 (-1.3793)	1.0821 (2.3248)*		0.0371 (2.3673)*	0.20	6.10**

*   5% sign. level

**   1% sign. level

1) Adjusted for degrees of freedom.

8. Conclusion

By focusing on the various institutional arrangements that production and distribution units use to organize concerted action, this study has suggested a new perspective for studying the organization of industry. The search for an efficient organization of information and compliance was central to our analysis. Institutional competition assures that the most efficient arrangement will be used for the coordination of activities, the allocation of resources and the monitoring of performance. In some industries the organizational advantages of consolidated ownership and supervision provide diversified and integrated multi-establishment firms with a competitive superiority for administering concerted action. The result is concentration, which is a product of a search for efficient organization in a competitive economy.

9. References

Alchian, Armen A., and Demsetz, Harold, 1972
  Production, Information Costs and Economic Organization, *American Economic Review,* Vol. 62: 777-793.

Chandler, Jr. Alfred D., 1977
  The Visible Hand. The Managerial Revolution in American Business. Cambridge, Ma.: Harvard University Press.

Chandler, Jr. Alfred D., Daems, Herman, 1980
  Managerial Hierarchies, Cambridge, Ma.: Harvard University Press.

Coase, Ronald E., 1937
  The Nature of the Firm, *Economica* Vol. 4: 386-405.

Daems, Herman, 1978
  Holding Company and Corporate Control. Leiden, Boston.

Davis, Lance E., and North, Douglas C., 1971
  Institutional Change and American Economic Growth, Cambridge, U.K.: Cambridge University Press.

Demsetz, Harold, 1973
  Industry Structure, Market Rivalry and Public Policy, *Journal of Law and Economics* April, Vol. 16: 1-9.

Freeman, Christopher, 1974
  The Economics of Industrial Innovation, Harmondsworth: Penguin Books.

Marcus, Mahityahu, 1969
  Profitability and Size of Firm, *Review of Economics and Statistics,* February, Vol. 51: 104-107.

Osborn, Richard C., 1970
  Concentration and the Profitability of Small Manufacturing Corporations. *Quarterly Review of Economics and Business.* Summer, Vol. 56: 15-26.

Porter, Michael E., 1979
  The Structure within Industries and Companies' Performance, *Review of Economics and Statistics,* July, Vol. 61: 214-227.

Porter, Michael E., 1976
   Interbrand Choice; Strategy and Bilateral Market Power. Cambridge, Ma.

Richardson, G.B., 1972
   The Organization of Industry, *The Economic Journal,* Vol. 82, 883-896.

Stiglitz, Joseph E., 1975
   Incentives, Risk and Information: Notes Towards a Theory of Hierarchy, *The Bell Journal of Economics,* Vol. 6, 552-579.

Stonebraker, Robert J., 1979
   Corporate Profits and the Risks of Entry, *Review of Economics and Statistics,* February, Vol. 58: 33-39.

Williamson, Oliver E., 1979
   Transaction-Cost Economics: The Governance of Contractual Relations, *The Journal of Law and Economics,* Oct., Vol. 22: 233-262.

Williamson, Oliver E., 1975
   Markets and Hierarchies: Analysis and Antitrust Implications New York: The Free Press.

9. DESIGN OF SUPPLY SYSTEMS FOR TECHNOLOGY TRANSFERS - AN ANALYSIS FROM THE EQUIPMENT SUPPLIER'S POINT OF VIEW

Lars-Gunnar Mattsson,
Stockholm School of Economics,
Stockholm, Sweden

1. Introduction

Transfer of technology (TT) is an area of increasing interest in both developed and developing nations, and can be witnessed in many activities at inter-governmental, governmental, business, and academic levels. Research, professional, and educational publications are increasingly viewing transfer of technology as a more encompassing and valid means of international resource transfer than that of direct investment - the latter being only one of several vehicles for transfer of technology.[1]

While direct investment and international trade in goods and services are topics that are rather well documented and have certainly been the subjects of much theoretical and empirical research, the other vehicles for technology transfers - including joint ventures, licensing, turn-key projects, management contracts, production sharing, technology sharing, service contracts, etc. - are much less known. The relative lack of knowledge is particularly pronounced in the areas of industrial organization characteristics of the markets and organizational and strategical problems for the firms involved in these types of resource transfers.

The chapter is concerned with some of the strategic considerations involved in technology transfers from the supplying firm's point of view. The technology-supplying organization must act within a system in which the stakes of the host government, the home government, and the recipient organization are often high and somewhat in conflict with each other, and in which it often must acquire additional resources through co-operation with other organizations.

In dealing with the interorganizational nature of the supply system in technology transfer projects (below referred to as TT-projects) and with the equipment supplying firm's need to link itself to resources outside of its own organization in order to be successful in selling to TT-projects, this chapter

---

[1]   See e.g. J.H. Dunning, 1979, or M. Casson, 1979.

will characterize a few typical transfer modes and the role of the equipment supplier in each of these projects. With reference to two case studies, the relations between organizations in the supply network for TT-projects will then be analysed. Finally, problems of the design of such networks for the equipment supplying firm will be discussed in relation to the above analysis. The design problem is regarded as a major dimension in the equipment selling firm's marketing and purchasing strategy and in its corporate development strategy. It also has industrial policy implications for the export-promoting home government.

2. Some Typical Transfer Modes

The technology package can be transferred in relatively integrated form, and can be defined as consisting of those processes and products requiring »know-how» *(technical know-how),* design of the physical plant, *supply of equipment* needed for the plant, *construction* of the plant, *management* of the plant, *financing* of the TT, establishment and development of links to suppliers of inputs needed for production in the completed plant *(purchasing)* and establishment and development of links to customers buying the output from the production process *(marketing).* Technical know-how, design, supply of equipment, construction, management, financing, purchasing and marketing are rarely under the complete control of one single organization. The supplying organization has the most control in the case of *direct investment.* Yet even then, outside sources are usually needed, e.g. for supply of equipment, construction and financing. The host country government can impose certain restrictions on the selection between different alternatives regarding the elements in the TT.

The other extreme is the control by the buyer of the selection mechanism for a *very debundled package.* A consultant firm might, for instance, be used for the technical know-how and the design; a construction firm for the construction and selection of equipment suppliers according to the design specifications; financing might be obtained on the international capital market; management could be awarded to a local entrepreneur who also is responsible for purchasing; marketing, finally, can be done through independent agents located on export markets.

Several institutional forms lie between these two extremes, for example, joint ventures, management contracts, licensing, production sharing, turn-key projects, and service contracts. These modes often overlap or complement to some extent, and they are all used by the supplier and buyer as a means of control over the different elements in the TT-package. The equipment supplier's responsibilities and the resources needed to fulfill an agreement on each side vary in different cases. Table 9.1 systematizes these differences in responsibilities. With the exception of »supply of equipment», the *direct investment* form of Technology Transfer gives all the major responsibilities to the foreign firm that makes the investment. Such a company can be designated a »product company» because it manufactures the *products* rather than the equipment to manufacture the products. For instance, firms manufacturing steel or pulp are »product companies», and firms manufacturing production equipment for steel works or pulp factories are »equipment suppliers» in TT-projects through which steel or pulp plants are established. It is typically a multinational corporation which makes the investment, perhaps in joint ownership with a local firm. The role of the equipment supplier is restricted to the domain of the equipment he manufactures himself, and within this domain he may be responsible for design, technical know-how, construction, and training.

The major difference in a *turn-key* project situation (given that the contractor is an equipment supplier and not a contracting/consulting organization or a »product company») is that the equipment supplier has responsibility for the entire TT-project until the plant is ready and the personnel is trained to manage it. In a *turn-key-plus* situation a management contract is added and often also a responsibility to market some of the output. Some financial participation might also be required. If this is the case, the equipment supplier has in fact become a joint venture partner in a »product company», and has thus entered the same industry as his customers in the direct investment case.

Table 9.1   The equipment supplier's responsibilities in three forms of TT projects.

	Direct investment	Turn-key project	Turn key plus (including management contract)
Technical know-how	(S)	S	S
Design	(S)	S	S
Supply of equipment	S	S	S
Construction	(S)	S	S
Management	((S))	(S)	S
Financing			((S))
Purchasing			(S)
Marketing			(S)

S   = Equipment supplier plays a major role in decision and execution

(S)   = Limited role

((S)) = Very limited role

Generally, the equipment supplier cannot rely only on his own resources in order to be able to construct the production plant, but rather, he must work with other suppliers. Some of these suppliers might also assume the contractor's role in a turn-key project. Since the mode of transfer is not necessarily given in advance and since the contractor might belong to any of several equipment supplying industries (depending on the circumstances and on the type of project, he might belong to the »product company» industry or to a consulting or construction firm), the equipment supplier is faced with a rather complex competitive and co-operative situation vis-à-vis other firms, both in the individual project situation and in the international project market in the short and the long run (see Table 9.2).

Table 9.2   The equipment supplier's relations to »product companies» and to other equipment suppliers.

	Direct investment by "product company" P	Turn-key project with A as main contractor	Turn-key project with B as main contractor
A's relation to P	P is a customer	No relation or P might be a supplier of technical know-how and/or A can become a competitor because A might enter P's industry	No relation
A's relation to B	No relation	B is a supplier to A	A is a supplier to B
A's relation to other suppliers of A	Competitors for sales to P	Competitors if also other A-suppliers bid for turn-key contract	Competitors in selling to B

A = Equipment supplier of subsystem A

B = Equipment supplier of subsystem B

P = "Product company", i.e., user of equipment

As in Table 9.2, let us assume that the transfer mode and the type of major TT-contractor is given. Thus, if there is to be a direct investment (or a highly debundled TT-package), the equipment supplier A will be a supplier to P and compete only with other suppliers of A. However, if it is not given in advance which of the three columns in Table 9.2 will be selected, competitive relations might exist among all the organizations involved. If the firms are involved in several projects, they might experience all three situations. Since a typical characteristic of these TT-projects is the *changing* capacity of the individual organizations to perform the different tasks in the TT-package, as more experience is accumulated and new resources are added, long term competitive relations between firms in different industries might develop. There might be reversals in the hierarchical ordering of the organizations (suppliers becoming customers); in the horizontal relations (non-related firms becoming competitors); and in the type of relations (horizontal relations becoming vertical, non-related or competitive relations becoming co-operative).

Depending on the circumstances, these shifts may usher in a long-term trend or they might switch back and forth between projects. The inherent instability in the position of a specific company in the TT-supply network obviously has effects on how the individual equipment supplier relates to its neighbouring organizations. How dependent are two organizations on each other in a specific project? How dependent are they over time, over several projects? Is the interdependency symmetrical or asymmetrical?

The design of the relations in the supplier network, the extent to which the network is stable or not over a number of projects, which organizations are co-operating and competing with each other in a specific project or over time - these matters are influenced both by individual firms within the supplier network and by organizations without the supply system. Among the latter are the recipient organization and its government, and the organizations or agencies in the supplying countries trying to design co-operating systems (export consortia, etc.).

Two case studies analysed below refer to two different types of supplier networks. In the first one, two firms, A and B, cover two major subsystems of the total system. For some customers and market segments, A is a more natural choice as a main turn-key contractor, for others A might be a supplier to B, with B being the contractor (cf. Table 9.2). In the second case, firm C is clearly the turn-key contractor; the focus of this study is on the relations between C and its many complementary suppliers. While in the first case, the hierarchical ordering of the suppliers varies from market segment to market segment, the second case illustrates a situation in which one firm clearly dominates the others in terms of system customers' supplier contacts. In both cases we are interested in the conditions which promote or hinder the co-operation of suppliers to TT-projects over time, i.e. in several projects and not only in single projects. If the promoting factors are strong, then it is to be expected that firms design rather stable supplier structures of co-operating firms. If the hindering factors are strong, supplier network relations will tend to change from project to project and from period to period.

3. Cases

3.1 Case 1: Two Co-operating Suppliers of Complementary Subsystems

The first case has been described in some detail elsewhere.[1] The following is a summary of that analysis.

---

[1]   L.G. Mattsson, 1979.

A and B are relatively large, successful, market-oriented firms which have a high proportion of their sales in foreign markets, and which belong to different engineering industries. Minor product groups in each firm are complementary to each other as major components in a sub-process, the Z-process of the production process in several industries. In the mid-60's firms A and B began to co-operate with each other.

Firm A manufactured a-components that are used in the α-function of the Z-process. B manufactured b-components that are used the β-function of Z. A's know-how was concentrated on the α-function and B's on the β-function. Whereas B had more experience of project oriented operations, A's marketing organization, responsible for a rather wide assortment of engineering type products, was larger and more geographically dispersed than B's. B concentrated on large organizations and engineering projects, while A's sales organization reached out to a large number of small and medium sized firms. In terms of product range, process know-how, and market coverage, A and B matched each other well in relation to what seemed to be a growing market for system sales of the Z-process.

As stated, a co-operative agreement between A and B was reached in the mid-60's. This included a specific licensing agreement which permitted A to use a patent for a b-component that was important for development of a complete Z-system for small and medium sized operations. B also agreed to do some product development to help standardize system solutions concerning the β-function. Furthermore, A and B were to help each other in the acquisition and realization of Z-systems selling projects in general and were to promote each other's products in system specification, etc. Which of the two firms should be »market responsible« was to be decided in each separate case, depending on earlier customer relations, size of the project, the relative importance of the α- & β-functions, etc. Generally speaking, this meant that A usually took care of the smaller projects, where the α-function's share of the project value is higher than in the larger projects. Because of the β-function's and the b-components' dominant share of the project value it was natural for B to be the systems seller in the larger projects.

Even if the complementary nature of A's and B's resources, when applied to the customer's system needs, seems very strong on the surface, the co-operative efforts have not been successful. The following sections will try to provide an explanation for this. Studies of inter-organizational relations have been approached from many directions and have used many conceptual frameworks. At this point, the following topics will be analysed:

a.   The influence of attributes of the wider inter-organizational network on the A-B relation,

b.   the organization and content of the exchange process between A and B, and

c.   the inter-dependency between A and B.

3.1.1 Inter-Organizational Context

A and B are not the only suppliers of components and sub-systems to the Z-process. There exist A^1- and B^1-type suppliers who are heterogeneously distributed over different markets and are thus available as alternatives. In some instances customer firms have clear preference for A or A^1, for B or B^1. These firms have to a varying, but increasing, degree preferences for systems buying of the Z-process. However, strong co-operative links between A^1 and B^1 type firms do not exist. Indeed, even firms from other industries than A or B can sometimes act as system sellers of the Z-process. Thus, integration between organizations for systems selling purposes in the wider network is not important. Alternative suppliers do exist. These alternatives vary on the different markets and customer preferences for alternative suppliers are heterogeneous. These factors diminish the necessity for close co-operation between A and B. If A^1 and B^1 were more integrated, for example, A and B would tend to match this integration for competitive reasons. Or if the customers had more homogeneous preferences for particular markets or weaker preferences for specific suppliers, A and B would also tend to become more integrated in systems selling. As already stated, this is, however, not the case. Thus, the characteristics of the wider inter-organizational network tend to de-emphasize a strong integration between A and B.

3.1.2 Exchange Between A and B

The exchange between A and B can be classified as *strategic* (dealing with objectives of and forms for the co-operation), *operative* (dealing with the actual exchange of goods, commercial, and technical information related to the on-going business), *economic* (having to do with financial flows emanating from the A-B co-operation), and finally, non-task related *social* exchange between persons in both organizations. These exchanges take place in an organizational context and are influenced by changes in the environment.

The formulation of *strategic* exchange initially took place between a few middle management executives, whose visions about the business opportunities had been influenced by a few business transactions in which they had taken part shortly before the idea was first discussed. Some of these experiences were shared by members of both firms. Neither top management in the two concerns nor the sales subsidiaries on the foreign markets played an active role at this point. The objectives were very generally formulated in the written agreement, with the exception of the licensing agreement, which was specific. Firm A built an organization for Z-projects. Its organizational counterpart unit in B, however, was more diffuse and was given other major goals by top management in the concern, i.e. goals related to projects with little or no »Z-process business» involved. Follow-up and further discussions on the strategic level were not formally organized until a few years ago, when meetings involving several persons on both sides were arranged to discuss if future co-operation would be warranted. Development of objectives for co-operation between A and B was not supported by the firms' organizational structures either at the outset or later in the exchange. Nor does the formulation of mutually rewarding objectives seem to have been facilitated by exchange of experience on the operative level.

The environmental change during recent years means that the market is increasing, though mainly on the β-function side; it has inspired increased exchange on the strategic level, the outcome of which is not yet known.

Operative exchange has been rather asymmetric. A has bought, or specified, much larger volumes of B's b-components than B has bought or specified of A's components. It seems that initially A sought technical information about the β-process from B more frequently than later, and also more often than B inquired about the α-function. A was generally disappointed about the way in which B handled these inquiries and also in B's lack of interest in A's requests for standardization development by B. Only a few of the customers' inquiries to one of the firms have been referred to the other.

The *economic* exchange, that is payments going between the firms for goods and services rendered, has been of a small volume. The license fees over a 10-year period are insignificant, and the payment from A to B was even forgotten for a number of years. A purchases more from B than vice versa, and seems to have had relatively favourable terms for the b-components they bought.

The *social* exchange was more dominant at the outset of their relations than later in the process. Re-organizations changed that, and many of the recent strategic exchanges took place between individuals who were not involved in the beginning years. In the intermediate period some co-operational problems of a personal kind did arise. Thus, the strategic exchange was insufficient and dit not develop mutually rewarding objectives that could be understood in both organizations. The operating exchange existed mostly through the initiative of only one of the parties, and did not receive enough attention by the other. The economic exchange was at a low level, and the social exchange seemed to deteriorate as the years passed.

3.1.3 Interdependence

The major reason for interdependence between A and B is that the α- and β-functions are both part of the Z-process, which is being purchased more and more as an integrated system. Since A and B had access to and were concerned with different market segments, the two firms did not initially look upon each other as competitors, but rather as having complementary resources for the exploitation of a business idea. At the outset, A was more dependent on B than vice versa. First, A's strategy was more linked with systems selling of the Z-process than was B's. Second, B's customers often had preferences for a-components sold by competitors to A, and they preferred not to buy complete Z-systems. Third, the α-function was a small part of the projects to which B sold β-functions. However, A cannot be regarded as very dependent, since it had acquired its own resources for the β-function (including the license). Indeed, on the corporate level the degree of interdependence resulting from the co-operation on the Z-market was close to zero.

It seems that too little and too asymmetrical interdependence existed, or was created, to make the co-operative efforts more substantive. During recent years, however, the interdependence seems to have increased due to the rising market demand.

196

A and B are competing for an important segment of this market - the position as a systems seller. The systems seller has the initiative, direct customer contacts, and recontrols component specifications. It is not a competition between sellers of substitutable hardware, where the firms are complementary. As software sellers, they are partly competitive, partly complementary. It is therefore possible that the increased interdependence brought about by the growing market demand can help to create new co-operative agreements with more substantive effects.

3.2 Case 2: The Turn-Key Contractor and its Suppliers

Over the last decades company C has developed its ability to take responsibility for turn-key-projects in the food processing industry. The equipment that it manufactures itself generally amounts to only 25% of the total contract sum. Another 10% is supplied by companies within the same ownership group, while roughly 2/3 is bought from 30-40 external suppliers. Some 10 suppliers account for 80% of this externally supplied volume. Because the supplier-network-design point of view interests us in this chapter, a typical project was studied in order to understand how company C related to its complementary suppliers.

Nine suppliers have been selected to illustrate several different types of relations. One of these, company D, sold directly to the customer in the studied project. Thus, that subsystem was not included in the turn-key contract as such. The other 8 suppliers accounted for approximately 30% of the total project value. Information about the characteristics of the relations between C and the suppliers is summarized in Table 9.3.

The relationships have generally been developed over many years and in several projects. Note that company C started to bid on turn-key projects some ten years ago. There is usually a high frequency of re-selection of the same supplier when a specific technical solution is chosen. The factors influencing this re-selection seem to be institutional links and technological and commercial interdependencies. These determinants will now be discussed.

The creation of *institutional links* such as ownership and contractual agreements is, of course, likely to depend on perceived advantages of integration. The following reasons are suggested by the information in the case.

First of all, if a subsystem is closely linked to company C's »core knowledge and core processes», ownership of this adjacent system is preferred because of the better control and development of technological know-how that it provides. Ownership of supplier E is an example of this.

Second, if there is a lack of »independent» suppliers or a perceived possibility of such a lack in the future, competing blocks tend to make acquisitions of such suppliers. Thus, in order to preserve capacity and independence in relation to a competitor, C might also buy an external supplier. Supplier I is an example of that.

Other such institutional links are co-operative agreements. In our case there are two such instances. One of the motivating forces behind such an agreement was to ensure capacity in a situation of scarce supply (earlier agreement with K). Another instance was to ensure a continuous supply of important components and to make these products unavailable to competitors (as with firm L).

Institutional links to competing blocks existed for supplier G, but they were used only when no good alternative suppliers existed for that specific technology. Competitors bought supplier K after the studied project was completed, and that caused the transactions to be much less frequent and terminated the co-operative agreement.

Technological interdependence is another factor influencing re-selection of a certain supplier. Whereas technological interdependence between subsystems of the total system can be of different kinds, it must be compatible if the subsystems are linked to each other. Such compatibility might be predesigned through standardization across the supplier/turn-key contractor network, or standardized in relation to specific supplier/turn-key contractor dyads. The more the compatibility is standardized at the supplier specific level, and the more the project specific compatibility is dependent on previous experience of working together in designing compatible subsystems, the higher the interdependence will be between a turn-key contractor and a supplier of a subsystem. For these reasons, the higher the interdependence, the higher the frequency will be with which that specific supplier is selected in a set of projects. The relations with company D are an example of a high degree of compatibility between subsystems.

Technical interdependence can also be related to subsystems which are *linked through several interfaces.* (It is not only a question of linking the output end of one system to the input end of another.) In such a case, the interdependence might become more complicated and difficult to standardize. Joint efforts in product development and system design might be necessary. The experience gained by working together on several projects is then important and favours frequent selection of that specific supplier. The relation to supplier J is an example of such a situation. If the subsystem delivered by J had been closer to the »core technology» of company C, J would probably have been financially integrated into C.

Another aspect of technological interdependence is caused by the *preferences expressed by the customer,* the TT-recipient. If the customer has preferences for a specific solution, the frequency with which a specific supplier is selected depends not only on the frequency with which that solution is selected, but also on the number of suppliers available who can provide it. In a monopoly situation, of course, that specific supplier will be selected every time the customer selects that solution. Supplier D is in such a position, while supplier F has competitors. If the customer has no specific preferences, then the turn-key contractor has more freedom to choose between available suppliers. However, that does not necessarily mean that there will be less stability in the latter case. The heterogeneity in customer preferences may be quite high; thus the supplier selected will vary from project to project and the frequency with which a specific supplier is selected for a project goes down.

Customer preferences are not only important for selection of a specific supplier for a specific subsystem, but also for the total design of the systems

198

Table 9.3   Characteristics of some supplier relations for a turn-key project between the main contractor C and the suppliers of subsystems.

Sup-plier	Commercial contact with C	Institutional relation to C	Type of subsystem	Preselection by C (before contract awarded)	Technical interdependence	Commercial interdependence
D	> 10 yrs.	None	Major, end of process. Monopoly position for specific technology	D sells directly to customer	Highly compatible systems. Little need for project specific integration	Customer preferences. No "customer protection.* Partly conflicting expansion ambitions
E	> 10 yrs.	Ownership links. Same type of contract as with external suppliers	Major, of critical technical importance. Tailor-made with standard components	Yes, co-operation in designing the offer. Joint contact with customer	C designs interface with E system. E designs own system.	Joint negotiation with customer. Internal pricing" influences income allocation between C and E
F	5 yrs.	None	Important, end of process, specific technical solution, rapid development in industry	Yes, customer asked for this technology	Some exchange of technical information about future development	Customer preferences. "Customer protection" for the project. F views C as a "reseller of F's systems
G	7 yrs.	Owned by competitor	Important, highly complext equipment. Dynamic industry. End of process	No, customer had preference for type of technology	C can only formulate functional requirements	Competing bloc status. Order won by G in competition
H	5-10 yrs.	None	Side function to main process consisting of a rather loosely connected "package". Small volume	No	Very little. Easy for C to specify equipment needed	No customer preferences. H rather dependent on C's volume
I	> 10 yrs.	Ownership	Rather complicated equipment in major process	Formally no, in reality yes	C has high competence, helps somewhat in I's product development	Sometimes customer preferences. Alternative suppliers are members of competing "blocs". "High internal transfer price as compared to market price".
J	> 10 yrs.	None	Important. Subsystem that integrates other subsystems. Standard components for project tailored solutions	Formally no, in reality yes	Rather high because of integrating nature but not important for the "core" process technology. Important co-operation in product/systems development	No customer preferences. J very dependent on C's volume. Exchange of planning information
K	5 yrs.	Contractual subsupplier. Recently included in competing bloc	Important equipment. Secret design but production technology simple	No, but agreement to use certain capacity	C has developed the design. K manufactures according to this	K sells also to competitors. No customer preferences. C has also supply capacity in own "bloc"
L	5 yrs.	A has a sales contract on Nordic market with L who is an agent	Rather complicated process equipment which has to be linked to main process	No	Exchange of information needed for the design of subsystems. A installs the equipment. A has good knowledge.	No customer preferences. L does not sell to competitors. Sales contract

* "Customer protection" means that the supplier does not sell to competitors or directly to the customer in a specific project.

Table 9.3 (cont'd)

Supplier	Selection frequency in C's projects	Major problems in development of the relations	Major benefits to the parties from development of the relation
D	Always when this solution is selected by the customer since D's solution is unique	D wants to lease the equipment and to make the profit from sales of packaging material. Somewhat overlapping system coverage. D does not give customer protection	Easy to make the systems compatible. Manages to keep its independence of the turn-key contractor by not entering any specific long-term agreement
E	Always when subsystem is included. Difficult to get bids from other suppliers because of close link C-E		Open exchange of information. Highly competent supplier who gives customer protection
F	Very high when that technology is chosen by customer	Organizational and personnel changes in F. Complicated machinery and too little service capacity at F. F small and sometimes lacks expert capacity when needed	C introduced F to, for F new, national markets. C can get better service if a supplier is involved also in future projects. Also when the guarantee period is over
G	Infrequent but big transactions	G belongs to a competing bloc	C is sometimes supplier to projects where G is the contractor. G provides needed supply capacity for specific technology
H	Earlier high, lately somewhat lower	C was highly dependent because of lack of suppliers, H charged too high prices, now more competition introduced by C supplier search	H seems now to give C preferential treatment. Some exchange of market and capacity requirement information
I	Always, corporate policy because of competitive "bloc" situation (since 5 years)	Alternative suppliers belong to competing blocs. Could buy from them at less price. Earlier the alternative suppliers were considered to have higher quality	C is assured of supply. Would otherwise be at the mercy of suppliers belonging to competitors. C helps in marketing of I products
J	Very frequently when this type of technology is selected	C afraid to make J too dependent on C. Earlier fear of lack of competitive pricing. Small size of J in relation to instability of project order volume from C	Joint efforts in product development. C sells J product through C subsidiaries abroad. J sells to competitors only after consultation with C. J has a unique competence for this kind of project
K	Earlier main supplier. After the studied project, very low because of membership in the competing bloc	Capacity was scarce in peak demand situations and K was not co-operative. K later demanded and got special co-operative agreement with C to be able to reserve capacity for C	K provides capacity for manufacturing according to C's desi of a subsystem with low degree manufacturing complexity
L	Very high, has a co-operative agreement (has later been cancelled)	L is an agent for manufacturer. C decided later to buy a manufacturer of this equipment	Supply of special type of equip ment. Need to assure continuous source. Exchange of technical information important. L does not sell to competitors

(which subsystems will be included and which will not). That is, the decisions about the input and output assortments have an influence on the selection frequency. This variability in the formation of the entire plant (what it should include and what it should exclude), is also important for the hierarchical structure of the TT-supply system. If a subsystem X is added to plant Y, this might change the identity of the turn-key contractor from a Y-process contractor to an X-process contractor. If that is the case, the whole TT-supplier network might change, since company Y might have supplier contacts that only partially overlap those of supplier X.

A third type of interdependence relation between a turn-key contractor and his suppliers can be labelled *commercial interdependence*. The more that the behaviour of one of the parties has an influence on the commercial outcome (sales volume, profit etc.) for the other party, the higher the interdependence. This interdependence can be more or less asymmetrical, i.e., one party can be more dependent on the other. Factors influencing the degree of interdependence are the existence of alternative partners, the economic significance of a partner's contribution to a project (or set of projects), and the technological significance of the partner's contribution. The commercial interdependence can be defined on the project level and on the firm level. On the project level, the interdependence is greatly influenced by the TT-recipient's technological and commercial preferences, and by the capacity available in the supplier network. It is also influenced by the interdependence on the firm level. The latter is a result of the overall strategies of the two firms, of the structure of the supply and demand markets, and of the earlier experiences of conflict and co-operation between the firms. Examples of strategies that influence the commercial interdependence are creation of institutional links, diversification of markets, and size of operations. Examples of structural characteristics of the supply markets are number and location of alternative suppliers, technological diversification, development of institutional links between suppliers, and degree of »coverage» by individual suppliers of a specific project market's hardware and software needs (»coverage» is the extent to which an individual supplier, including his closely linked co-operative suppliers, covers the know-how and the hardware needed to carry out a turn-key contract). In this case, firm C covers 25-35% of the hardware, and much more of the software, needed for the project through its own closely linked operations. Both the hardware and the software coverage of the technological »core process» were much higher.

Supplier D, enjoying a unique position for a specific technology for which customer preferences exist, wants to stay commercially independent of C and be able to sell directly to the TT-recipient, or to any turn-key contractor who wins the bid. Customer preferences, strong market position, and low complexity in linking the subsystem to the total system make this possible. Even if C would like to increase D's dependence on C, that would clearly not be in D's interest. Differences between projects and customer preferences regarding technology for the subsystem that D sells also make higher integration less favourable.

Company E, on the other hand, is preselected by C before the contract is signed and does not sell to C's competitors. The commercial interdependence is high. The customer does not have preferences for supplier specific technology. Even if there were no institutional links between C and E, their long term common experience and the lack of good alternative suppliers outside of the competing blocs would make for a high degree of interdependency, both on a project and on a firm level.

Company F was also preselected in the studied project, because the customer initially expressed preferences for a specific technology. Thus C and F worked together in the sales process. Alternative suppliers exist; the specific technology is not chosen very frequently and seems also to be losing ground in this very dynamic industry.

The commercial interdependence with company G is interesting, as G belongs to a competing bloc. G was selected in competition with other bidders on the subsystem after C had won the contract. G could obviously not be preselected since it could have then used its position as a member of a competing bloc. C and G linked this project agreement to another project going on at the same time in another country where C was dependent on G's resources. Thus, the commercial interdependence in one project was linked to another project. On the firm level, C's and G's commercial interdependence is of a competitive nature. Supplier H is commercially dependent on C (volume-wise), but C is not very dependent on H, since alternative suppliers exist and the subsystem delivered is rather peripheral to the core process. With I, however, the commercial interdependence is high, because there is a lack of alternative suppliers (as a result of the bloc formation) and of a corporate policy to protect this supplier within C's own bloc.

F is commercially very dependent on C because of the relative size of F's capacity that C takes. The technological interdependence resulting from the integrative nature of F's subsystem makes C also dependent on F, even if alternative suppliers exist and even if the customer has no preferences for any specific supplier. In most cases, the capacity requirements have made C somewhat dependent on K, and at times, much more dependent on K than vice versa. Since C controls the technology and since the K-type manufacturing is relatively simple, the commercial interdependence should be low during »normal» supply-demand conditions. The commercial interdependence with supplier L has been relatively high, as indicated by the institutional link and the acquisition by C of an L-type manufacturer.

4. Analysis and Conclusions

The design problems and opportunities for the equipment supplier will be treated in this section on three levels, partly with reference to the analysis of the two cases: The possible influence on the mode of transfer will first be discussed; then, given the mode of transfer, the influence on the position of the supplier in the supplier network will be examined; finally, given the mode and position, the question of what influences the nature of the links to individual suppliers will be dealt with.

4.1 Mode of Transfer

Obviously the recipient organization and the government in the recipient country has a major influence on the choice between direct investment, licensing, turn-key, management contract, etc., and combinations thereof. But this choice is also determined by the supply alternatives available to the recipient and by communication from suppliers and other sources about these alternatives. The supply alternatives have probably demonstrated their viability in other similar projects in the same or other countries. The risks involved for the recipients are often so high that they are reluctant to try radically new designs of the supply alternatives. The recipients are also influenced by the availability of inputs to the project within their own country (e.g. management and technical knowledge, suppliers of hardware subsystems) and their goals as to control of the project over time.

The equipment supplier can influence the selection of the mode of transfer by communication with the recipient. (This is sometimes done on a »trade mission» level in which government representatives and several suppliers participate.) To make such communication credible, the supplier needs to show his capability to help carry out the TT-project within the context of the transfer mode he prefers. One important aspect of this capability is to be able to relate to complementary suppliers, especially if the equipment supplier himself has a relatively small »coverage» of the system that the potential project refers to. The greater the coverage is of the technologically significant parts of the system by own or closely linked supply resources, the greater the ability of the equipment supplier to influence the mode of transfer. Increasing the coverage through internal development, through co-operation with other firms, and through mergers/acquisitions takes time and can involve significant investments. Another problem is the differences between different recipient situations that might call for different technologies, different modes and different partners from one project to another. Such market heterogeneity calls for a more flexible supplier network design than that which is created in the development of closely linked organizations with high coverage.

However, if the network suggested to the recipient is very loosely connected, as is true in some of the export consortia on a national basis that some industrial countries have tried to develop during recent years, then the credibility and the ability to influence the mode of transfer are probably lower. Efforts to form export consortia with a TT-capability for relatively large scale projects only on a national basis also suffer from the small set of eligible members of the group and also sometimes from competition or otherwise incompatible goals among the organizations. (Cf. the co-operation problems between A and B in case 1.)

If the mode of transfer alternatives also includes production sharing and buy-back agreements, the »supply» network must also include marketing resources and potential markets for the output from the TT-project. This adds an important dimension to the equipment suppliers' design problems.

Suppose that the equipment supplier wants to influence the selection of the mode in a more debundled direction. The supplier does not want to take responsibilities outside his own hardware competence and wants to deal directly with the TT-recipient. His ability to do so is probably positively related to the customer preferences for his supplier-specific technology and to the separability of his subsystem from the total system. (Cf. firm B in case 1 and D in case 2.)

4.2 Position in the Network

The next important topic in our analysis deals with the position of the supplier in the network. Given the mode of transfer, how can the equipment supplier influence this position? More specifically, given that it is a turn-key project, what determines his ability to become the major contractor (if for economic and/or other reasons he prefers that position) instead of just a supplier of a subsystem?

The major contractor probably has a greater coverage of the technically crucial parts of the system, more experience and resources for project work, and longer experience in selling products and subsystems to that specific industry. The latter is important because it implies greater know-how about the market conditions for the recipient and better initial customer contacts. In the first case, we saw how the hierarchical positions of firms A and B were different, depending on the relative importance of their inputs to the project and their earlier market connections. We also saw that there was an increasingly important market in between the small and the large projects (between A's and B's respective »natural» markets), where it was unclear who was going to get the major contractor role in the majority of cases. There are two types of activities used by suppliers to influence the recipient and obtain the desired position:

a.   Traditional marketing communication activities, and

b.   Network- and resource-building activities.

One important factor is that potential or actual firms to be included in the network may also have ambitions to assume major contracting responsibility, thus creating competition for hierarchically superior positions (as in case 1). Another problem is that there are differences between projects in the same time period, current projects and projects in the future as far as technology and system delimitation are concerned. Thus, the coverage by a specific supplier varies from project to project and also over time. This means that the network and resource building must also be flexible and dynamic if the firm wants to maintain a network position as the major contractor in a substantial part of the total market.

Many equipment suppliers do not aspire to achieve the necessary coverage in order to assume this position. Indeed, they may find it less risky and more profitable to stay in a narrower field and to be suppliers of subsystems. A major decision for these firms is if and to what extent they should relate to one turn-key contractor, or if they should try to remain open to sell to any or several such firms. Being linked to one firm obviously increases the probability of selling to a particular project if that firm gets the contract, but reduces the probability if another firm wins the bid. Being linked to one firm may create a situation of asymmetrical commercial interdependence that can have a negative effect on profit margins. A supplier might want to preserve an independent position in relation to all turn-key contractors by going directly to the TT-recipient. The real or potential customer preferences for the supplier's technology and independence of the turn-key contractor's marketing organization are obviously important factors for the feasibility of such a strategy.

204

4.3 Nature of the Turn-Key Contractor's Link to Suppliers

Given the mode of TT that a particular company is the turn-key contractor, how should that company design the supplier network system? Should it build a closely linked network of co-operating firms or should it instead try to stay as flexible as possible? (The following discussion expands the analysis of case 2.)

It was previously argued that in order to reach the position as a turn-key operating equipment supplier, one must cover a major part of the technologically crucial system through a network of one's own and closely linked resources. But given the heterogeneity of situations on the project level, one would probably want more flexibility in the choice between different suppliers.

This flexibility itself is limited not only by the firm's own closely linked suppliers but also by those of competing turn-key contractors. Thus, the set of suppliers that are independent of the »competing blocs» is severely limited. The need for flexibility from project to project is related to the following factors:

a. The turn-key contractor perceives that competition between alternative suppliers can bring the price down.

b. The recipient has supplier-specific preferences depending on technology, nationality, etc.

c. Regardless of customer preference, the projects might differ as to size, scope, technology, etc. The frequency of a specific technology might be low across several projects.

d. The turn-key contractor does not want to commit financial resources to achieve a close link.

e. The technological development is rapid and might come from »new» suppliers.

It is here hypothesized that the turn-key contractor will more often develop closely linked suppliers (institutionally linked or with a very high selection frequency):

1. If the supplier's subsystem is close to the »core» technology of the turn-key contractor. (The close link is needed to increase coverage, protect the know-how, and to improve technological development.)

2. If customer preferences that are supplier-specific and heterogeneous across projects are few in number.

3. If it is difficult to delimit and to standardize the interfaces between the supplier's subsystem and the total system.

205

4. If suppliers not closely (or potentially closely) linked to competitors are few in number.

5. If the technologies are similar across projects for the supplier's subsystem.

6. If the need is great, given the supply and demand conditions, for the turn-key contractor to ensure a stable supply.

5. References

Casson, M., 1979
    Alternatives to the Multinational Enterprise. London.

Dunning, J.H., 1979
    Recent Developments in Research on Multinational Enterprises: An Economist's Viewpoint. In L.G. Mattsson & F. Wiedersheim-Paul (eds.). Recent Research on the Internationalization of Business. Uppsala.

Mattsson, L.G., 1979
    Cooperation between Firms in International Systems Selling. In L.G. Mattsson & F. Wiedersheim-Paul (eds.). Recent Research on the Internationalization of Business. Uppsala.

SECTION III: PROCESSES

1. Section Contents: An Overview

The Seven-Countries Study (and the majority of earlier studies) reports that mergers have only modest, or even negligible, effects:

- Higher profitability is not necessarily a result of merger.

- Shareholders of acquiring firms tend to lose from mergers, whereas those of acquired firms may occasionally gain.

- Merging firms experience a negligible increase in market power.

- Economic efficiencies increase as little as sales do expand or as costs of production and, eventually, prices to customers decline.

- Anticipated benefits of mergers are generally overestimated in the pre-merger phase.

- There seems to be no difference in effects (as of yet, no reliable long term studies are available, so it is difficult to draw final conclusions) of vertical, horizontal, or conglomerate mergers. Enterprises grow in size through merger, but do not »improve».

- Mergers have only in the long run a modest effect, if any, on company performance.

- Management does not improve; surviving top management may gain higher income.

- No effects are reported in spreading of risks, resistance to disturbance, or increased bargaining power, and leverage.

- No effects are reported in spreading of risks, resistance to disturbance, or increased bargaining power, and leverage.

After differentiated analysis of merger causes, Pfeffer and Salancik (1978) conclude that *resource interdependence* renders the only significant explanation of vertical mergers. They find moderate correlations between merger activities and a) *purchase* interdependence, and b) *concentration* of the organizations' economic environment. *Sales dependence as well as a low concentration* of the economic environment render a low correlation with merger activity. Following a suggestion by Stern and Morgenroth (1968) that sales uncertainty is greatest when the concentration of economic environment is intermediate in strength, Pfeffer-Salancik find a significantly higher proportion of *sales* dependence induced mergers under such market conditions.

According to their analysis, the presence of large firms in an industry predicts a higher degree of vertical merger, independently of resource exchange patterns.

In summary, Pfeffer and Salancik conclude (with support from their data) that mergers are undertaken to control *symbiotic interdependence*. Industrial concentration has a little explanatory power as profitability. They see rather a tendency to merge with less profitable industries.

The failing *firm/industry* hypothesis in *conglomerate* mergers[1] is refuted by Conn (1976). He used pre-merger data from 56 mergers in U.S. manufacturing and mining industries, and determined that firms of similar profitability and profitability trends tend to merge. Acquiring firms seem to perform on approximately the same level as their industry. Industries of acquired firms show significant growth in the five-year pre-merger period, and are as profitable as the acquiring firms' industries by the time of merger.

Furthermore, Pfeffer and Salancik (1978) assert that for *horizontal* mergers *(competitive* interdependence), uncertainty is curvilinearly related to industrial concentration in an inverted U-shape relationship. Their analyses support the hypothesis that the proportion of mergers within the same industry is highest when concentration is intermediate, and lowest when concentration is low (powerless firms) or high (only a few of the firms competing are capable of co-ordinating interfirm activity).

The difference in concentration measure is not correlated with the measures of resource exchange, but with the number of larger firms in the given industry. The measures of resource dependence and difference in concentration are not correlated with each other.

The conclusions of the Seven Countries Study on conglomerate merger (as cited above in summary) are supported by many researchers, albeit never in the comprehensive manner shown there:

- No effects on profits: Gort (1962), Mueller (1969), Reid (1968), Meeks (1977), Mandelker (1974), and Lev and Mandelker (1972);

- Negligible increase in market power: Penrose (1959)

- Shareholders of acquiring firms tend to lose, and those of acquired firms tend to gain: Firth (1969, 1976, 1980), Meeks (1977), Utton (1974), Dodd (1976), Dodd and Ruback (1977);

- Earnings of firms engaging in mergers decline after consolidation: Dewing (1921), Firth (1975), Meeks (1977), Utton (1974), Kelley (1967);

- Anticipated benefits of mergers are overestimated in the pre-merger phase: Dewing (1921), Firth (1976), Livermore (1935), Reid (1962);

---

[1]   Cf. Gort, 1969; Marcus, 1966; Mueller, 1969; Scherer, 1970; Weston-Mansinghka, 1971.

208

- Acquiring firms are *less:* Reid (1962); or *equally:* Kelley (1967), Firth (1979) profitable as compared to non-acquiring firms;

- Management of acquiring firms is the only winner: Firth (1980);

- Stock prices of merger active firms do not differ significantly from those of non-active firms: Hogarty (1970).

Not investigated in the Seven Countries Study, but corroborated elsewhere, are the following hypotheses:

- Acquisitions for the purpose of horizontal expansion or vertical integration are less profitable than acquisitions for diversification purposes: Pfeffer-Salancik (1978);

- The correlation between technological intensity and diversification found by Gort (1962) is thought to be spurious, as both may be related to selling to dominant customers, e.g. to government: Pfeffer-Salancik (1978), Aharoni (1971).

Thus, the results of these competently designed and conducted studies seemingly indicate that mergers produce few, if any, positive effects. Why, then, do firms continue to initiate and participate in the merger process? Is it generally poor design of research, lack of economic rationality, or failure in merging processes which account for the merger results?

If the answers to these questions were available, further research would not be necessary. Indeed, the »answers» which come to mind are speculative ones at best.

Perhaps the approach taken by economic merger researchers is too simplistic. It is possible that the wrong questions were asked, or that valuable information was discarded in the process of averaging, and therefore incomplete conclusions were developed as a result. It seems possible that many mergers are undertaken to salvage equity or jobs. Throwing such »defensive» mergers together with »offensive» ones may account for at least some of the levelling of results (analysis shows rather that this is unlikely to be true).

In any case, the outcomes of the bulk of merger studies suggest at least two complementary research strategies:

a. observation of *merger cases,* which facilitates the analysis of causes of outcomes;

b. *longitudinal* case studies of *merger processes, which facilitate an understanding of* their effects.

These two strategies may well be combined, although the second strategy will require much more time, as well as a different design, than the first one.

The research reported in this volume deals with merger processes for two main reasons. Firstly, process research is obviously better established in the field of organizational research compared to economic research, both as far as need and methodology for it is concerned. Secondly, in the light of the present findings resulting from traditional merger research, process research of mergers seems to be particularly in demand as a complement to the traditional approach.

Again, it must be stressed that due to the scarcity of resources available for this research programme, systematic attempts at depth were impossible. It should also be emphasized once again that the research in the three sections of this volume is characterized by overlap, insofar as some of the chapters in the »Motives» and »Modes» sections are relevant to the »Processes» section as well. In particular, it seems that unclear, conflicting, open or hidden, conscious or unconscious motives play an important role as causes of later conflicts during the merger process. Such motives thus account at least in part for poor outcomes of mergers.

Process research tends to deal with the actors in the merger process: their motives, behaviour, the outcomes of their behaviour, and when relevant, the contextual conditions and contingencies.

Andersson investigates the birth, or rather the stillbirth, of a joint venture. Basically, he studies the objectives and expectations at different points of the time of »pregnancy» of the main actors, i.e. the participating entrepreneurs. He also describes the dynamics of the context in which the »pregnancy» takes place. In his investigations, Andersson applies a dual approach by intertwining a temporal approach (he breaks up the process into an idea phase, an internal evaluation phase, and an external evaluation phase) with a hierarchical process analysis (ranging from low to high involvement of participants' individual objectives) in a both pragmatically and theoretically useful way.

The *task development* process is visionary, if not euphoric, in character. The business idea is developed during this phase. The participants look to the future, disregarding the petty cash of daily business. Ideas are outlined, and cost-profit estimates projected. Contacts with the market and other relevant systems are established. Optimism dominates.

The *strategy development* process is much more realistic and conflict laden. It is concerned with the necessary modes and means to accomplish the tasks to be undertaken, and with the implementation of the venture.

The *distribution* process is concerned with development of norms for the distribution of outcomes of the results achieved. Contributions made during the venture by various participants are considered in the development of these norms.

In reality, the processes are not sequentially arranged, but to a considerable extent, run parallel to each other. This study proposes not only a useful paradigm for merger management, but also demonstrates the crucial influence of individual goals and of emerging conflicts on the merger process.

It should be stressed here that conflict avoidance per se is neither a panacea nor a condition sine qua non for merger (as little as it is for organizational processes in general). Tension brought about by the dissatisfaction stemming from lack of congruence of desired and real states is a most powerful phenomenon leading to progress and innovation. A very simple model may explain the principal relations.

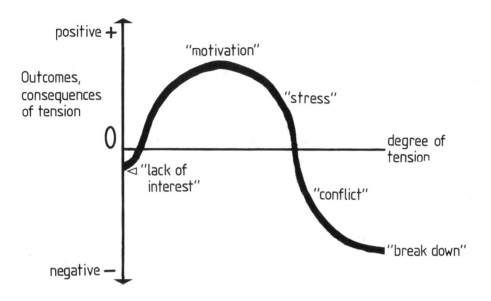

Figure III.1 Tension - conflict: A schematic representation (non-reversible).

The *Edström-Alarik* chapter, a longitudinal study and analysis of a merger in the textile industry as a means of capacity reduction would lend itself readily to an application of the Andersson model, as its conclusions (not its design) are rather similar to those reached by Andersson. Edström-Alarik develop some hypotheses about conflict management during merger implementation against the background of conflict antedecent identification and conflict resolution process analysis.

The chapter by *Goldberg* on merger as a means of achieving capacity reduction in the steel industry also demonstrates similarities to Andersson's birth process, although it stresses different aspects. In the case of the Swedish steel industry, employment maintenance in mono-structured regions played a dominant role, in particular given the fact that not only the steel processing industry faced trouble at that point in time. In fact, the entire economy was (and still is) in severe trouble. At the same time, the populace had been told for a long time that the Swedish system, more so than any other, would protect the individual against disasters of the type the economy is now facing. This prevailing myth (cf. Nyström-Utterström's socio-political context) required a process model compatible with such expectations. It also had to demonstrate that, despite the fact that the country at the time of the occurrance of the disaster was ruled by a non-labour government, the individual (rather than capital) would still (indeed, even more so) be the focus of political and economic concern.

211

The steel industry merger case demonstrates how complex motives (capacity reduction, re-establishment of competitiveness, maintenance of regional employment, job protection, political acceptance of the chosen mode etc.) lead to complex processes. Conflict resolution plays a crucial role. The author concludes the case with a thorough analysis of the techno-economic and socio-political factors influencing and controlling the merger process.

The *Aldrich-Sproule* study of the impact of merger upon personnel functions in a very small segment of U.S. enterprises is in sharp contrast to the Swedish case, but is very much in line with the techno-economic socio-political factor paradigm of Nyström-Utterström. The authors conclude that functions and processes labelled as industrial and labour relations are hardly, if at all, affected by merger. They also assert that there are »fashion waves» of the socio-political type (of Nyström-Utterström) which have little relation to real problems, in this case, with respect to industrial and labour relations.

The editor of this volume claims that »proper» involvement of those parties primarily concerned by the merger into the pre-merger and post-merger process, on task development, strategy development, and distributive decisions processes seem to be[1] a fairly efficient approach to initiate and implement in particular mergers for the purpose of capacity reduction. In such cases, all parties are losers. If negative consequences are to be minimized, then »proper» participation is a must; it cannot be confined to the distribution phase alone.

In a theoretical treatment of interorganizational co-operation processes in a pluralistic economy, *Metcalfe* underlines this conclusion at a societal level by using a different terminology. His evidence stems from macro management of decline in Great Britain. The main difference between his macro approach and the above micro level »problem solving» approach is that in the micro organization (for example, the enterprise) a »strong» change agent may be taking care of the process. In Metcalfe's macro system at the regional, sectoral, or national levels committees will have to act. Are they able to?

2. Conclusions

The consequences for policy at various levels can be rather simply deduced: »The proof of the pudding is in the eating».

The well corroborated fact that pre-merger expectations have not been met after the merger has been implemented (cf. the opening paragraphs of the introduction to this section) may, at least to some extent, be explained by the following hypothetical conjectural conclusions: Due to the internal problems (i.e., those of the merging enterprises), and the conflicts that evolve during the merger process, the attention of the participants is diverted from coping with the environment (i.e. acting on markets, taking advantage of opportunities, etc.), instead focusing on internal conflict resolution. Indeed, many of

---

[1]   The unscientific phrasing indicates that the conjecture has not been derived by strict scientifical procedure. Rather it is based on empirical observations from a number of cases only.

the participants must fight for their continued existence. Thus, the new enterprise is severely handicapped during the implementation of the merger, and therefore loses much of its previous contact with the environment (for example, customers, market shares, and suppliers are lost). The temporary weakness of the firm is observed and exploited by competitors, who experience a unique chance to enlarge their domains at the expense of the merging enterprises. Even when it finally overcomes its re-organizational trauma, the new enterprise must mobilize its resources to cope with an environment which is quite different from the pre-merger environment.

The above situation is well known, and has been documented from micro behaviour studies, where it has been labelled the *Psychological Pit*.

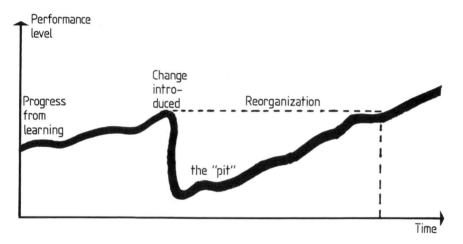

Figure III.2 The psychological pit as consequence of change in behaviour.

This pit implies losses in performance level following a change. The depth and the duration of the pit is determined by behavioural reorientation due to the change, and is subject to certain influences. Volitional action may thus affect its depth and duration.

The character, progress, management, etc. of the merger process is crucial for the outcome of the merger. In the complex organizations of today, very deliberate planning and efforts are required. The chapters in this volume and their conclusions will hopefully be of value in this respect both to practitioners and to theorists.

3. References

Aharoni, Y., 1971
   The Israeli Manager. Israeli Institute of Business Research, Tel Aviv University, Tel Aviv.

Conn, R.L., 1976
   »The Failing Firm/Industry Doctrines in Conglomerate Mergers», *Journal of Industrial Economics, XXIV: 181-187.*

Dewing, A.S., 1921
   »A Statistical Test of the Success of Consolidations», *Quarterly Journal of Economics,* 36: 231-258.

Dodd, P.R., 1976
   »Company Takeovers and the Australian Equity Market», *Australian Journal of Management,* I: 13-35.

Dodd, P.R., and Ruback, R., 1977
   »Tender Offers and Stockholder Returns», *Journal of Financial Economics,* V (Dec.): 351-73.

Firth, M.A., 1980
   »Takeovers, Shareholders Returns and the Theory of the Firm», *Quarterly Journal of Economics,* XCIV (March) 2: 235-60.

Firth, M.A., 1979
   »The Profitability of Takeovers and Mergers», unpublished paper.

Firth, M.A., 1977
   The Valuation of Shares and the Efficient Market Theory. London: MacMillan.

Firth, M.A., 1976
   Share Prices and Mergers. Westmead, Farnborough: Saxon House.

Gort, M., 1969
   »An Economic Disturbance Theory of Mergers», *Quarterly Journal of Economics,* LXXXIII (Nov.): 624-42.

Gort, M., 1963
   »Analysis of Stability and Change in Market Shares», *Journal of Political Economy,* 71: 51-63.

Gort, M., 1962
   Diversification and Integration in American Industry. Princeton: Princeton University Press.

Hogarty, T.F., 1970
»The Profitability of Corporate Mergers», *Journal of Business,* 43: 317-327.

Kelley, E.M., 1967
The Profitability of Growth Through Mergers, Pennsylvania State University Press.

Lev, B., and Mandelker, G., 1972
»The Microeconomic Consequences of Corporate Mergers», *Journal of Business,* XLV (Jan.): 85-104.

Livermore, S., 1935
»The Success of Industrial Mergers», *Quarterly Journal of Economics, L: 68-96.*

Mandelker, G., 1974
»Risk and Return: The Case of Merging Firms», *Jornal of Financial Economics,* I (Dec.): 303-35.

Marcus, P., 1966
»The Failing Industry and Failing Management Doctrines in Antitrust», *Antitrust Bulletin,* XL: 833-56.

Meeks, G., 1977
Disappointing Marriage: A Study of the Gains from Merger. London: Cambridge University Press.

Mueller, D.C., 1980
The Determinants and Effects of Mergers: An International Comparison. Cambridge, Mass.: Oelgeschlager, Gunn & Hain.

Mueller, D.C., 1969
»A Theory of Conglomerate Mergers», *Quarterly Journal of Economics,* LXXXIII: 643-659.

Penrose, E.T., 1959
The Theory of the Growth of the Firm. Oxford: Basil Blackwell.

Pfeffer, J., and Salancik, G.R., 1978
The External Control of Organizations, New York.

Reid, S.R., 1968
Mergers, Managers, and the Economy. New York: McGraw-Hill.

Reid, S.R., 1962
Corporate Mergers and Acquisitions Involving Firms in Missouri, 1950-1959. Ann Arbor: University Microfilms.

Scherer, F.M., 1970
Industrial Market Structure and Economic Performance. Chicago: Rand McNally.

Stern. L.W., and Morgenroth, W.M., 1968
»Concentration, Mutually Recognized Interdependence, and the Allocation of Marketing Resources», *Journal of Business,* 41: 56-67.

Utton, M.A., 1974
»On Measuring the Effects of Industrial Mergers», *Scottish Journal of Political Economy,* XXI (Feb.): 13-28.

Weston, J.F., and Mansinghka, S.K., 1971
»Tests of the Efficiency Performance of Conglomerate Firms», *Journal of Finance,* XXVI: 919-36.

10. POST-MERGER INTEGRATION AS A PROCESS OF CONFLICT RESOLUTION

Björn Alarik
University of Gothenburg

Anders Edström
Stockholm School of Economics

We gratefully acknowledge financial support for the project from the Scientific Fund of the Stockholm Savings Bank.

1. Background and Purpose

The present chapter is focused on reorganization of productive resources through horizontal mergers between firms of approximately equal size. In particular our interest is concentrated on the process of post-merger integration which follows after a decision to merge has been taken. Then is the time to realize anticipated cost reductions, advantages of a stronger market position, and complementary product lines.

From a managerial perspective one can distinguish management of post-merger integration from pre-merger planning. Both activities are obviously important and interconnected. Careful planning of the merger will facilitate the implementation of organizational changes during the post-merger period. The importance of planning for the success of a merger has also been demonstrated empirically by Ansoff et al. (1971) and Kitching (1973). It has been more difficult to study the consequences of managerial action during post-merger integration or what Kitching has termed »the post-merger battle». The difficulties have been access to firms, availability of research resources, and methodologies.

Some form of longitudinal study seems to be most appropriate, but this would require ample resources and good access. Therefore it is no wonder that research on post-merger integration is scarce. To the extent that it exists, it is in the form of case studies which are not widely distributed. One such case study has been performed by a research group at Ashridge Management Center (1975). They have analysed the acquisition and integration of a small printing firm into a larger group of printing companies. One of their observations was the key importance of a co-ordinator role to handle conflicts which arose during post-merger integration. In a study of a merger in the Swedish manual glass industry, Johannisson (1980) observes that decision-making is seriously delayed or even avoided because of conflicts between different ownership groups. Unclear responsibility and a fear that others would intrude on ones own sphere of influence prevent concerted actions. Again there seems to be problems of integration.

217

Goldberg provides in this book a synthesis of a number of studies of a large steel merger. In this very complicated merger one is on the whole successful in making difficult decisions during the merger negotiations. Possible explanations for this are generous financial support from the government and strong, capable leaders on both the union and management side. Conflicts tended to occur more among local unions than between union and management.

From previous case studies and from our own observations we are able to conclude that one of the key tasks during post-merger integration is to establish effective mechanisms for handling conflicts. It is predictable that conflicts, whether they depend upon differences of interest, perception or orientation, will be frequent in a newly merged company. We would argue that failing to achieve effective conflict resolution leads to sub-optimization, increased costs, and in serious instances to chaos. The success of a merger is the result of a large number of interacting factors (Edgren and Rydén, 1978). It is argued here that effective conflict resolution is one such factor but by no means the only one. For instance, it may be that a merger is an inappropriate solution to the problem at hand or that management in perfect harmony makes bad judgements or takes inappropriate decisions.

The purpose of the present study is to identify antecedents of conflicts, analyze processes of conflict resolution, and how they are managed in order to develop some hypotheses about conflict management in post-merger integration.

The study is based on detailed observations of two horizontal mergers; one in the textile industry (Textile Products) and one in the leisure goods industry (Leisure Goods). Both mergers involved Swedish companies. In the textile case three firms (A, B, and C) of the same size formed Textile Products (TP). Textile Products then subsequently bought two additional companies (D and E). Leisure Goods (LG) was also created by a merger of three firms of approximately the same size (X, Y, and Z). Management and unions in the companies concerned have kindly co-operated and made it possible to follow the emergence of events in the two situations approximately as they have unfolded. Data collection instruments have been personal interviews, surveys, and analysis of documents of such kinds as minutes of board meetings and internal memoranda. The period of detailed observation was one year in the case of Textile Products and a year and a half in Leisure Goods. Persons on several organizational levels have been interviewed as well as representatives of both management and unions. Textile Products and Leisure Goods have been chosen for this study because of their similarity in size, number of companies, and motive for a merger in both instances. The main difference between them is that in Leisure Goods two of the merging companies are subsidiaries of larger firms while in Textile Products all three firms are small family-owned businesses. As a consequence of this fact, differences in conflict resolution were expected.

2. Effective Conflict Resolution

A large number of both strategic and tactical decisions about the goals, policies, structure, and operations of the new company were not taken until the post-merger period. By strategic decisions we mean those which concern the long-term viability of the company, such as directions for product-market development, the overall organizational design, and allocation of resources. Tactical decisions are taken within given strategic guidelines. At the same time as the organization has to take decisions on strategy and tactics, it has to cope with day-to-day operations. This implies that the work-load on employees in general, and on key managers in particular, will be extremely high at the beginning of the post-merger period.

In deciding on strategy and tactics one tries to achieve the benefits of integration. Such benefits can be formed by several functions; administration, finance, marketing, production, and purchasing. In taking these decisions it is necessary to balance different interests, to consider different points of view, and to build on different types of knowledge and competence. Since most people in a newly merged organization have lived their lives in different organizations they have identified with different organizational goals and have different experiences and perceptions of how things are best done. Thus, conflicts are quite likely to emerge.

We need to develop a more precise understanding of the antecedents of conflict. Broadly following the treatment of March and Simon (1958) we find it convenient to start with a dyadic (two party) situation. The conflict appears when each party arrives at a different preferred alternative in a decision-making situation which they are engaged in and which they share the definition of. They can arrive at different conclusions for basically two reasons. Either they value the consequences of an alternative differently or they have different perceptions of the consequences of an alternative or both. The first is a motivational and the second a cognitive base for the conflict. In an organizational context, where we find a multitude of such dyadic relationships, conflicts can arise because of differences in goals and differences in perceptions of reality. Individuals acquire goals through some form of identification process and perceptions of reality through work and experience. The internal realities of different organizations or sub-units of organizations can be quite different. To describe such differences we use the term organizational climate. Following Schneider (1975), organizational climate is defined as perceptions which people can agree characterize a system's practices and procedures. Such differences are important since in a merger one has to design practices and procedures for a new organization.

Conflicts can be resolved in different ways. Following previous research (e.g. Lawrence and Lorsch, 1967) we will distinguish between three modes of conflict resolution: confrontation, forcing and smoothing. Confrontation implies that the parties openly confront the conflict and work on a problem until a solution which meets organizational goals is found. If one of the parties has sanctionary power over the other, a conflict can be resolved by forcing. Such power can be based on formal position or on control of scarce resources. When it is not mandatory to reach a decision, which is very often the case, a conflict can be resolved by smoothing, i.e. the parties agree to disagree. Lawrence and Lorsch (1967) found in their classic study of the effectiveness of organizations in different enviroments, that the management of inter-group conflict was an important determinant of the quality of integration. They specifically identified that effective organizations tended to confront conflicts openly.

The effectiveness of conflict resolution is not only dependent upon the mode of conflict resolution but also on the existence and the quality of the integrating devices. If we go back to a dyadic situation where there is a marked power difference between the parties, what is there to prevent the stronger party from forcing its preferred alternative as the joint solution? In this, and also in other situations, there is a need for a third-party or integrator. The role of the integrator will vary according to two conditions: whether the decision is mandatory or optional and also, the difference in conceptual frameworks between the two parties (de Brabander and Edström, 1977). If we make the simplifying assumption that if a decision is mandatory or optional it applies equally to both parties we can distinguish the following four situations (Figure 10.1).

Perceptional differences are:	Decision	
	Mandatory	Optional
large	A	B
small	C	D

Figure 10.1 Different conditions for an integration.

In A we need an integrator who has such high power that any existing asymmetries between the original two parties can be overcome. In this way an integrator can prevent the stronger party from forcing a decision. In addition, however, the integrator should have an encompassing conceptual framework and be able to provide a form of semantic bridge between the two parties.

In B we need an integrator with an encompassing conceptual framework to be able to facilitate communication and problem-solving between the two parties. Since the decision is optional, there is no real basis for forcing a decision. One of the parties can always choose not to participate.

In C the integrator need not interfere in the decision-making. He has only to prevent forcing.

In D an integrator is not strictly needed.

Whether a decision is mandatory or not may in itself be a matter of controversy between the parties. A decision may seem mandatory to one party and optional to the other. An integrator in this case may be needed to establish the proper conditions. Failing to do this would infer that conflicts would be resolved too often by smoothing.

The need for an integrator to provide a semantic bridge is consistent with the findings of Lawrence and Lorsch (1967). They found that individuals who managed conflicts had their influence based on competence and knowledge. Further, they observed that integrators had orientations balanced between those of the groups whose efforts they were integrating. Orientation is defined in terms of both cognitive and emotional dimensions, e.g. time orientation and inter-personal orientation.

In this section we have argued that confrontation is the preferred mode of conflict resolution. An important explanation for deviations from this mode is a lack of integrators with the appropriate qualities.

3. The Emergence of Textile Products and Leisure Goods

Textile Products is a new company which is formed to manage and develop the operations of three family-owned, independent firms A, B, and C. The new company was formed on the 1st January 1976. The shares of C were bought by Textile Products and the owners of A and B hold the shares of TP. The previous managing director/owner of A holds 45% of the shares of TP and the managing director of B and his close relatives hold 55%. Firm A had showed low profitability since the early sixties. A low profit level forced the firm to reduce its investments, and its reinvestments were kept to a minimum for many years. In 1967 firm A acquired another small firm with a complementary product line, which was rather smoothly integrated into the existing organization. However, the new acquisition did not contribute to a better profitability. The beginning of the seventies showed essentially break-even results. The managing director of A was over seventy and wanted to get out of the business but had no suitable internal succession candidate. Firms B and C showed similar patterns of profitability as A (Table 10.1).

The low solvency of B is, however, notable. Long periods of insufficient profitability and unsuccessful attempts to increase volume through acquisition of competitors have induced the companies to start merger negotiations. Suggestions for co-operation had been made several times by the managing directors/owners of the Swedish Industrial Board. The latest initiative was taken by the managing director of B, who suggested that the three companies should meet to explore in more detail the possibilities for co-operation. Following this suggestion three meetings were held in the spring of 1974. At the third meeting one company concluded that economic calcula-

221

Table 10.1   Economic Performance of the merging firms in Textile Products based on annual reports. SKR (Swedish Kronor) 1.000.

Turnover	1971	1972	1973	1974	1975
A	9.600	9.600	9.500	10.500	15.000
B	7.800	7.600	6.900	8.400	8.000
C	5.400	8.500	8.300	9.300	10.000
D	5.200	4.700	5.000	5.700	5.900
Net profit					
A	70	29	18	61	41
B	0	1	0	0	- 218
C	24	21	27	2	-
D	20	18	21	19	746
Liquidity					
A	0.18	0.26	0.35	0.37	0.57
B	0.71	0.83	0.77	0.92	0.21
C	0.70	0.63	0.46	0.27	-
D	0.87	0.51	0.52	0.54	1.82
Working capital					
A	- 400	- 559	- 470	- 332	1.281
B	1.143	1.929	2.070	2.172	349
C	1.148	1.259	1.017	1.196	-
D	373	326	469	482	1.524
Dept paying capacity					
A	0.09	0.08	0.08	0.08	0.06
B	0.46	0.46	0.44	0.45	0.40
C	0.34	0.24	0.22	0.20	-
D	0.12	0.14	0.15	0.14	0.35

Liquidity $= \dfrac{\text{Current Assets - Inventories}}{\text{Current Liabilities}}$

Working capital $=$ Current Assets - Current

Debt paying capacity $= \dfrac{\text{Stockholders' Equity}}{\text{Stockholders' Equity - Liabilities}}$

tions should be made in order to be able to decide whether to go for a closer co-ordination or not. The advantages which were anticipated were reduced costs and increased market power.

The preliminary calculations showed a reduction of personnel costs of 1.3 million SKR to be possible. The companies estimated a joint turnover of 28 million SKR. The three companies applied for economic support for consulting services during the pre-merger phase from the Swedish Industry board. The application was treated positively and a number of consultants were called upon to look at the marketing, administrative and technical aspects of the integration of the three companies. The consultants began their work at the beginning of 1975 and the majority of all studies were completed in the Summer of 1975. Decisions on the financial reconstruction of the company delayed the merger until January 1976. The research on the reorganization started in September 1976.

Leisure Goods was formed at the beginning of 1977 on the basis of a preliminary agreement. The final merger took place on 1st October 1977. At the time a number of large Swedish companies diversified into different segments of the leisure goods industry. Company X was acquired in 1974 by an investment company as part of a larger merger. Company X, as well as other companies in the industry, was in the process of building a new factory in response to expectations of a growing market. A new managing director for X was recruited from outside the group and started work in the middle of 1976. Company Y was bought out by a large transportation company as of 1st January 1975. The transportation company had very good profits in 1974 and had decided to diversify its interests. It was informed by its bank that company Y was for sale. Leisure goods were popular at the time and the particular segment where company Y operated was considered to have a very bright future. Company Y was bought without any careful analyses of its economic situation and future possibilities. When the figures for 1974 became available it became apparent that the acquisition was a mistake. A new managing director was recruited from outside to run the company as of September 1975. His firm major conclusion was that it was impossible to make the company profitable with its present volume of business. The company could not expand in its present facilities. Also, there was already an over-capacity in the industry; hence a further acquisition or some form of co-operation was considered.

Company Z was started in 1968 but went bankrupt in 1973. Later that year the company was acquired by a private individual. In 1974 a decision was taken to build a new factory which was ready towards the end of 1975. In 1974 the company also acquired two additional production facilities. Both of these were sold, however, during the latter half of 1975. The sale of these facilities meant substantial losses for the company. Z showed a loss for the period ending December 1976 of 2 million SKR. The financial data for X, Y, and Z are presented in Table 10.2.

At the beginning of 1976 the managing director of company Y approached a number of competitors, among them X and Z, in order to explore their interest for some form of co-operation. They were all willing to discuss the matter but since 1976 looked as if it was going to be a good year there was no real interest for concrete action. In the summer of 1976 the chairman of Y

223

Table 10.2   Economic performance of the merging firms in Leisure Goods based on annual reports. SKR (Swedish Kronor) 1.000.

Turnover	1971	1972	1973	1974	1975	1976
Y	42.000	46.900	71.200	64.900 (9 months)	81.300	88.500
X	13.900	14.400	17.300	26.000	24.300	41.800
Z	-	-	-	3.600	35.100 (18 months)	31.200 (15 month
Net profit after tax						
Y	1.000	1.000	3.000	4.000 (9 months)	- 4.000	- 12.000
X	-	+ 42	+ 32	- 1.818	- 2.921	- 555
Z	-	-	-	0	- 900	- 1.900
Liquidity						
Y	0.46	0.58	0.52	0.52	0.38	0.57
X	0.73	0.59	0.73	0.48	0.64	0.68
Z	-	-	-	0.38	0.66	0.70
Working capital						
Y	9.184	12.369	6.832	7.265	3.112	24.292
X	3.129	3.617	4.278	2.604	9.410	12.174
Z	-	-	-	480	1.149	1.745
Debt paying capacity						
Y	0.02	0.03	0.07	0.22	0.17	0.14
X	0.12	0.10	0.08	0.02	0.01	0.01
Z	-	-	-	0.10	0.02	0.05

$$\text{Liquidity} = \frac{\text{Current Assets - Inventories}}{\text{Current Liabilities}}$$

$$\text{Working capital} = \text{Current Assets - Current Liabilities}$$

$$\text{Debt paying capacity} = \frac{\text{Stockholders' Equity}}{\text{Stockholders' Equity - Liabilities}}$$

approached the owner of Z to find out if he was willing to sell. The contact indicated that there was an interest to sell the company and within Z figures were prepared to show the position of the company. At the beginning of the fall 1976 company X was discussing a sale of the company to its largest competitor. The price which was offered for X was, however, unacceptable to its board and negotiations were terminated later that year. At this point contacts were renewed between X and Y and preliminary discussions were held between the managing directors of both of these companies. Both of them saw it as an advantage to include Z in a potential merger. Z had modern products, a contract with a well-known designer, and modern production facilities. One company was, however, not willing to buy Z. The real negotiations were held between the chairman of X, Y, and Z and the managing directors of X and Y. An agreement to merge was concluded and accepted by the boards of the companies in the beginning of 1977. The formal merger was to take place at the end of that year.

The background of the two mergers were similar. In the case of Textile Products there had been an intensive competition from imported products which made it very difficult for companies to increase their prices enough to cover automatic increases in costs. In addition, the possibilities to increase volume were small. This lead to a process of concentration among producers. For rather a long time there had also been a process of concentration in the distribution system which was an additional incentive for producer co-operation. In the case of Leisure Goods, a crisis was generated within the country through an over-optimistic forecast of demand. Several large producers increased their capacity and in the summer of 1976 there was 50% over-capacity in the industry. Under such conditions it was difficult to increase prices to cover increases in costs.

For practically all the companies involved, the decision to merge was a last resort. They had tried to cope with the situation by themselves up to a point where their financial position was very weak. The alternative to a merger was bankruptcy, either immediately or in the relatively near future, or in some instances a sale of the company. Since reorganization costs money, the companies were dependent upon financing. For Textile Products some form of state support and financing was a pre-condition for the merger. Even though the owners of X and Y had substantial financial resources it was important for them that the financial positions of the mother companies was not weakened too much by the subsidaries. This was also the reason why none of the companies wanted to own 50% of LG. Leisure Goods obtained a substantial loan from the State Investment Bank.

4. Antecedents of Conflict

We have previously distinguished between motivational and cognitive bases of conflict. Obviously these are interrelated, since people tend to perceive what they like and like what they see. Goals, as an expression of motivation, are acquired through socialization and identification with goals and norms of an organization, family group, professional group, etc. Since the key factors in both Textile Products and Leisure Goods are the previous managing directors, this group should be analyzed more closely.

The managing directors of companies A, B, and C which formed Textile Products have worked in their respective companies for almost all of their lives. In A and B the managing directors had complete ownership control while in C the managing director was the single largest stockholder. All of them strongly identified with their own firm. Since their private wealth was so dependent upon the success of the business, they regarded their firms as their own in a very real sense. This implied not only that they would work very hard for the company but also that they did not consider that anyone else had the right to influence major decisions. This strong link between personal wealth and the success of the business is obviously typical of family-owned firms. Through the merger the previous managing director of B became managing director of Textile Products, and with the help of his family he controlled 55% of the shares. The previous MD of A retired but got a seat on the board of TP. Even though he had retired, he was by no means willing to let the new MD run the company as he liked for two main reasons: First, he owned 45% of the shares which constituted his personal capital. Second, he had his son still working in the company. The shares of C were bought by Textile Products and the MD of C became the head of purchasing in the new company. Since he was not a board member, and since his position in Textile Products was relatively insignificant, his power position was weak.

The managing directors of both X and Y had been hired in order to turn their respective company into a profitable position. They felt a responsibility primarily to their respective chairmen, who in both cases were the people who hired them. Commitment is partly a function of time (Whyte, 1956; Kaufmann, 1960) and since none of them had worked more than a year and a half in their respective subsidiary they had not had any time to develop a strong local commitment. In company Z the owner was not the managing director from the beginning, but he was clearly the most influential person in Z. At the time of the merger the managing director was a person who had been borrowed from another firm which was owned by the same person. During the major portion of the reorganization process, however, Z was run by a four-man team: the owner, the marketing manager, the production manager, and the controller. Since the MD's of X and Y were primarily dependent upon their respective chairmen, and the owner of Z was clearly the dominating man in that company, we must analyse the motives of the owners. The chairmen of Z and Y were important executives within the investment and transportation company respectively. Their main objective was to try to make X and Y profitable. The alternative for Y would have been to liquidate the company. Its plant was old-fashioned and unsuited for a rational material flow. The most likely alternative for X would have been sale of the company. In any case there would have been substantial losses. Since the owner of Z was a private individual he was much more restricted in his possibilities to withstand losses or to contribute more capital. His prime interest was to sell his company and he never wanted a merger. The other parties, however, did not want to buy him out. They felt he should contribute to the reorganization of the companies. As the owner of Z expressed it: »They wanted me to share the losses with them.» Through the force of circumstances he still chose to participate in the merger but with the aim of getting out as soon as possible.

The cognitive bases of conflict are generally a function of differences in the environment and technology among the companies. Company A in Textile Products produces textiles with rather complicated patterns. The complex patterns make for substantial set-up costs which also require more complex machines. Skilled machine operators are a key factor in getting high productivity. B's production is concentrated on products without patterns or with only simple patterns. The production is in long series and requires less skilled labour than in A. Companies A and B use different distribution channels for their products. Company A is primarily selling through large retail chains while B is selling through small independent dealers. Company B is selling under their own brand-name while company A does not have an established brand-name. Company C is more heterogeneous than that of both A and B in terms of products, technology, and distribution channels. In other words, C lacks a unique competence. The above differences will condition know-how, perceptions, and patterns of behaviour in the companies concerned.

Differences in products, technology, and distribution channels also exist within Leisure Goods. Companies X and Y were living on products, the majority of which were old in design. Company X was strong in products with motors while Y was strong in the manual end of the range. Z was also strong in the manual range and had modern designed products. The factory in Y was rather old and the production was more oriented towards crafts-manship. Both X and Z had very modern production facilities.

Plastic is an important ingredient in the final products. Y and Z had made their own plastic components for quite some time while X had just started manufacturing of its own plastic components at the time of the merger. X and Z had their own points of sale, while Y was selling through a network of agents. As an example of differences in know-how and perceptions, one may contrast salesmen of motor and manual products. They use a different language when they describe their different products to their respective customers and they are also representatives of different life styles. This has the effect that customers need or desire to talk to one of their own type.

5. Processes of Conflict Resolution

5.1 Textile Products

Processes of conflict resolution can only be observed in relation to particular issues or decisions. There was a fundamental difference in views between the former managing director of A (MDA) and the former MD of B who was now managing director of TP. Their differences in views tended to focus upon the organization design and the future location of production. MDB's visions of the future organization of TP were built upon centralization. He wanted all administration to be concentrated in one place and also that the production should ideally be concentrated geographically. In the preliminary analysis before the actual merger MDB made a calculation of the benefits in terms of cost savings, if all three companies moved »under the same roof». MDA's vision of the new organization was built upon decentralization. He proposed that the organization should be built up around very independent product groups. The product line could naturally be divided into products for men, women, and children. Company A had a strong position in products for men and to some extent for children. Company B had their strength in products for women and finally C was more of a mixed bag. The production facilities at C were also the worst of the three. Directly after the merger TP bought a new company D which was strong in men's products. In the longer run MDA could envisage production at A, B, and D being specialized according to product group.

There are both personal interests and more technical economic reasons for these different points of view. There is consistent evidence in our interviews which indicate that MDB has kept all major decisions to himself regarding the running of B. He has been able to do it in B through an informal system of communication and through a pronounced skill in human relations. MDB visited the factory daily to talk to the people and to get a first-hand view of the situation. He was considered in the office to be a good and charming listener. As a custom he would keep his office door open so that people could feel free to just pop in and talk about a problem. His style seemed open and he was pleasant to talk with. The actual decisions, however, he would always keep to himself. No one was prepared to challenge his position. MDB's brother was the head of marketing and sales and was not interested in confronting his brother. The head of accounting was a long time employee of the company and had learnt to accept his position as a trusted employee, and he was always loyal to the MDB. MDB's style of decision-making was one of manipulation. In the case of a conflict, he would never come out and openly act as the arbitrator and final decision-maker. Instead, he would do nothing at all, hoping that the conflict would go away or be resolved by the parties directly involved. Also, he would act informally and talk to people until it was clear that there was a large majority sharing his opinion.

In summary MDB wanted not only to be in control but also to exercise his control very informally and often indirectly. The basis for his control was an informal personal information system through which he would be the best informed person, not only of facts but also of opinions of people within the company. He wanted as MDTP to run the company himself in the style to which he was accustomed. There were also some economic and business reasons for his view. The over-riding purpose of the merger was to achieve a better balance between turnover and fixed costs. This could be achieved by cutting administrative and production costs, by increasing sales through a better product line, better market coverage, and finally through increased size and market power. This would enable better terms in negotiations with suppliers, banks, and other stakeholders. Administrative resources need to be pooled in order to cut administrative costs. MDTP considered productivity to be low at A and C. In the longer run these production units would need to be cut. To arrive at a better market position there was a need for co-ordination of marketing. This function should be at B, the new headquarters of TP.

MDA had a personal interest in arguing for a decentralized organization and for preservation of production at A. He felt a strong responsibility, primarily to his son but also to his employees, to preserve employment at A. Responsibility for a product line and close connection with production would be a reasonable managerial platform for the future. Such an arrangement would enable MDA to provide some continued support for A.

MDA also had some other reasons for his position. For instance, he knew from previous experience that the removal of machines and production which would be necessary in the case of closedown of A would be very costly.

In addition, if production would be moved he knew that the skilled operators, who were so essential for the production of A's products, would not move. In addition he argued that MDTP did not understand the complexity of the products at A and considering this, productivity was not unreasonably low.

Prior to the merger it had been agreed that centralization of administrative functions would be at B and that any reduction of production would primarily come from C. At the time of the merger there was also a preliminary organization plan which, however, needed finalization and more detailed specification of responsibilites.

After the formal decision of a merger was made in January 1976, accounting and invoicing was rapidly transferred to B. The management of B became the management of Textile Products. The marketing manager of B became product manager for women's products and also marketing manager of TP. The son of MDA became product manager of children's products and was stationed at A. MDD became the product manager of men's products and was stationed at D.

A number of strategic decisions were made during 1976. The following deserve mentioning:

☐ Introduction of a new computer system

☐ The purchase of a new factory

☐ The purchase of company F

The introduction of a centralized computer system is significant for at least two reasons. First, it symbolizes a centralization of administrative functions at B, which is clearly in line with what was decided before the merger took place. Secondly, by centralizing the information flow at B, MDB had a monopoly on basic operational information. The centralization of information turned out to be a major problem for Textile Products. Insufficient preparation for the changeover and problems with the new computer system made the basic reporting system a mess for more than six months. In addition to the formal information system, MDB established good personal contacts both at A and C. The people he relied upon for information were not part of the previous power structure at either place. In this way MDB was able to extend his informal information system to A and C.

There was general disappointment particularly from MDA about the way information was flowing and of the methods of consultation for decision-making. In particular MDA was concerned with the uncertainty about the future organization. He talked repeatedly to MDB about it, but the latter was stalling. In March 1976 Textile Products had the opportunity to acquire a very modern factory close to the site of C at a very favourable price. Everyone was convinced that this was a good opportunity and the factory was bought in April the same year. Later that year Textile Products bought the inventory, orderstock, etc. of a bankrupt company E with a related product. The motive for this acquisition seems to have been the possibility to sell the factory at B and move into a new factory with a favourable rent. This new factory was owned by the local community. TP also received considerable subsidies in order to take over personnel from the other company. In this matter considerable doubt was expressed by MDA, but a formal decision was taken at a board meeting two weeks after the deal was concluded. In both of these matters which were of extreme importance for Textile Products, MDB worked and consulted with two members of the board who had no ownership share.

From the beginning the board consisted of five members and one substitute. The members were MDA, MDB, the brother of MDB, and two consultants. The consultants had been working with studies during the pre-merger phase One of the consultants had been project leader. In this constellation it was clear that MDB had a substantial information advantage. The two consultants were also dependent upon MDB for any future consultancy. Also the personalities of the consultants were such that they preferred to be diplomatic rather than to take a strong personal position. They were still acting as consultants who were dependent upon their client. Only MDA could voice any real opposition. However, he was still careful for two reasons. First, since MDB controlled the board he realized that he would lose in almost any conflict situation. Second, too strong an opposition would perhaps have repercussions on the position of his son in the firm. Thus, a lot of the basic differences in views and conflicts would be suppressed. Further, MDB's working style was to work individually with the board members and avoid meetings with the whole board. During the crucial first year of the merger there were only three meetings of the board. These board meetings were primarily to confirm decisions which had already been taken.

The basic conflicts which were suppressed concerned the closing-down of operations at A and moving machines to C. These were discussed during the second board meeting of 1976. The following excerpt is taken from the minutes of that meeting:

»When the possibility to acquire the new factory at C arose and the deal was concluded according to the terms in §6; the goals of the company were changed. A concentration of production to C would take place. Production would be gradually reduced at A and in the longer term closed-down. It had been declared at a meeting with the joint labour-management committee that the reduction would take place in phase with the natural reduction in personnel, and that a transfer to C would not start until the transfer of production from the old plant at C to the newly acquired one was completed.«

Related to the localization of production was the organization plan. Later at the same board meeting it was recorded that:

»MDA and MDD emphasized the importance of a detailed organizational plan and said that many employees today were doubtful of whom they should ask in many matters. MDA also wanted better information to be given to the personnel at A about the future.«

This is really the first time that a possible coalition against MDB is noticeable. MDD had been included as a member of the board during the summer of 1976. This coalition emerged more clearly towards the end of 1976. It was, however, too late. A number of factors drove the company into a liquidity crisis and later to bankruptcy. Among these were high costs for consultants, transfer of production, drop in demand, poor production planning and cost control, as well as an overload on top management.

On the operational level a number of problems occurred during the post-merger integration. During the spring of 1976 Textile Products received a very large number of orders. In the integration and modification of the organization, which occurred simultaneously, the productions was not closely in tune with the orderstock. This meant that products were produced which at the same time went to inventory and tied-up capital. Substantial delivery problems were thus encountered. In the scramble for products which occurred, the salesmen favoured their old established contacts. Since the sales-force came primarily from B, it meant that the large customers of A were not very well treated. Further, the move of production from A to C required substantial efforts. Nobody from A chose to start working att C and the personnel had to be trained from scratch. This meant lower productivity during a critical phase in the life of Textile Products.

Also production was moved from B to the factory of E within the same community. Since it was within the same town the personnel chose to stay with the company. Even in this case substantial problems were connected with the move. The personnel at E felt that they were trodden-on by the people from A. Several spontaneous comments from our interviews show the differences in organizational climate between the two groups of personnel:

»All what they (people from B) say must be done immediately. If it isn't, they run down to MDTP and then he comes and tells us that we must do it.»
(Employee at E)

»They have had it arranged so that daddy (MDTP) looks after everything. He pulls all the strings. We have had more of a division of labour.»
(Employee at E)

»The people from E come from a large company where you sell your labour for money for a restricted period of time. If jobs in the meantime pile up on your desk, this creates problems in other parts of the company but they don't give a damn. The climate of B was quite the opposite. One worked until the job was finished and then went home.»
(Consultant)

»They (E) have much more paper work. Everything must be photocopied. I have never photocopied so much in my entire life. You must send papers everywhere.»
(Employee at B)

»We have not worked hard but we have worked according to the rules which exist. It has been a bit sloppy out there (B). There will be problems for us. We have had much clearer rules.»
(Employee at E)

»There are big differences between the personnel at E and B. They don't work collectively at all. We have always done that. This is your job and this my job and then there is nothing in between.»
(Employee at B)

The modes of conflict resolution at Textile Products can, at the strategic level, be characterized as smoothing. In the beginning MDTP was stalling and avoided joint decision-making even when it would have been appropriate (the purchase of E). MDA was consulted before the decision was formally made but not until all others were in favour. There was a constant complaint from MDA of lack of information and lack of involvement. Both major parties were suspicious of each other's motives. Towards the end of 1976 a coalition between MDA and MDD was emerging and signs of more active politics could be noticed. No real confrontation took place because the company came into a serious economic crisis at the beginning of 1977 and this finally led to bankruptcy in the summer of the same year.

On the operational level, especially in conflicts over deliveries and in relation to people at E, forcing was used. In the case of deliveries, the co-ordinator, i.e., the marketing manager of TP, did not use his capacities. In the case of E, MDTP always seemed to favour his old employees.

5.2 Leisure Goods

The major issue on a strategic level in Leisure Goods was the contribution of the different parties to the work of integrating the companies. On the tactical level, the major issue was the integration of the marketing organizations.

The agreement about a merger was concluded in January 1977. At this point the owner of Z felt forced to participate although his desire was to sell the company. In the agreement there was a special paragraph about the economic responsibility of each partner. Since the decision to merge was made without any thorough analysis of the financial position of each company, it was concluded that each company should cover its own losses during the year 1977 and a formal merger would be effective as of January 1st, 1978. Any inventory at the end of 1977 would be taken over by Leisure Goods at production cost. There was a clear interest on the part of each company to sell a product as long as it would get more than the production cost. This became a substantial problem, since sales were at a very low level during the first half of 1977 and the companies each had substantial inventories. Under these conditions there was intensive competition between the companies and it is clear that this created worsening conditions for a closer integration of the sales organizations.

Directly after the agreement in January 1977, a project organization to study different aspects of integration between the companies involved was created. Project groups were initiated in the areas of accounting and control, administration, marketing, purchasing, and new product development. The previous MDY became vice-president of Leisure Goods and head of the project organization. The former MDX became president of Leisure Goods and primarily responsible for the running of the company. Since each company was economically independent the new MD of Leisure Goods had limited power.

By the beginning of July 1977 the project groups were supposed to be ready with reports and recommendations. However, the owner of Z would only allow his closest collaborators to participate marginally in the project groups. There were two major reasons for this. Firstly, since he was responsible economically for the company he wanted his employees to concentrate fully on company matters. Secondly, he used participation in the integration work as a weapon to force his partners to buy him out. MDY who was responsible for the project organization also said in an interview regarding the project work:

>»We have had most difficulties on the marketing side. Since any action may affect the economic result of the unit and since each owner is responsible for his results it has been difficult to get anything done.»

The owner of Z had a personal interest to get out of the merger. He had invested a substantial amount of money in his business and was afraid that he might lose everything. In addition, during his years in the business he had become very sceptical of the potentials of large enterprises. He considered that there were no real advantages of scale. On the contrary, small business would adapt much easier to the strong variations in demand.

The conflict of interest was finally resolved in September 1977 when the owner of Z sold the machinery, inventory, etc. of his company but kept the factory building which was rented by Leisure Goods.

The agreement to merge was greeted positively both by X and Z while the employee representatives from Y were against it. The opposition from employees at Y was based on the reduction in employment, particularly among administrative personnel, and the fear that the factory at E would be closed completely. Since Y had the oldest and least productive factory it was clear that any drastic reduction in capacity would hit Y hard. This was exactly what happened towards the end of 1977. Sales had been at a very low level for each of the companies and the large overhead costs were a tremendous burden on the company. A decision was reached by the board to close down operations at Y. This created strong opposition among employees at Y but it was a unanimous management decision. After intense discussions this was the preferred decision.

In Leisure Goods, the integration of the companies proceeded stepwise. Care was taken not to touch the marketing organization during the first year. In order not to lose volume nothing should be noticed from the outside. In addition, it was the desire from top management to keep the marketing managers of both X and Z. Success was achieved in designing two jobs with equal status and work load and which also fitted each individual's particular interest. However, a number of problems appeared later, when it became necessary to have more contacts between the different sales forces. The old controversy between motor and manual products was extremely hard to overcome.

Contrary to Textile Products, the board of Leisure Goods was heavily involved in making strategic decisions. During the first year, board meetings were held every month and there were also frequent informal contacts inbetween. The board consisted of a key executive from the investment and transportation company respectively, the owner of Z and the managing directors of X and Y. All important decisions had the approval of the board.

Both forcing and open confrontation can be characterized as the modes of conflict resolution. In the negotiations with Z, a merger was forced on the owner since he did not see any better alternative. This created problems until the owner of Z was bought out. Also in closing down Y a decision was forced upon the union representative. It was not done, however, until quite thorough investigations had been made. In other instances problems could be handled openly in the project organization and important decisions were openly debated by the board.

6. Management of Conflicts

6.1 Textile Products

Three bases of conflicts have been identified in both Leisure Goods and Textile Products: different personal interests and perspectives of key people, differences in technology and distribution channels, and differences in company cultures. In Textile Products the conflict of interest between key people was apparent primarily in two issues: the re-location of production from A to C and the lack of a detailed organizational plan for the company. The conflict of interest was primarily between the former MDA and the present MD of Textile Products (former MDB). The strategy of the managing director of Textile Products was to avoid or suppress conflicts for the former MDA. There were three tactics which were used: monopolization of the information flow, maintenance of the present loyal management group of B as management group of Textile Products, and individual consultation with board members and use of the board's approval for decisions already made.

The information flow was controlled through centralization of information flow to headquarters, building-up of an informal person-to-person network for data collection, and monopolizing the contacts with consultants. An employee of B stated in an interview:

»I have heard rumours that there exists an organizational plan. As far as I know only MDB has seen it. It was some consultant who made a proposal which just didn't lead to anything. I don't know why and I don't think anyone else does either.»

By keeping the management team of B as management of Textile Products, MDTP was assured of a loyal group and few conflicts.

As was previously mentioned, the board was only reassembled three times during the first critical year of the merger. Only when the company was facing an acure liquidity crisis did the board start to meet more regularly. At the first three board meetings not even an agenda was distributed beforehand. Informal contacts took place before a board meeting but no information was distributed. Minutes of the board meetings would be circulated, but with long delays.

The conflict of interests among the owners and the local emphasis of the management of TP escalated conflicts on the operational level. For example, when the orderstock was substantial and there was a shortage of products, salesmen and even the marketing manager would give priority to the old customers of B. In order to make an overall optimal allocation, product impartiality would be needed and a special effort exerted to encounter the inherent bias of the salesforce.

Another example is the tendency of MDTP to favour the personnel of B when they moved into the same facilities as E. A new union was going to be formed for the common workplace. However, its board consisted of only personnel from B.

The avoidance of conflicts and the unwillingness to let others share in decision-making had a number of negative consequences. A number of things were unsettled and this left many employees with uncertainty. This was part of the problem when allocation of products to customers had to be made. The role of the marketing manager was not clearly defined. A number of similar problem appeared in other areas as well. Any new competence deriving from experience with a different technology and different distribution channels was not allowed to influence the decision-making. The warnings of consultants were not forwarded to others and the questions and worries of a few board members were not taken seriously - at least they did not lead to any action being taken.

There was no integrating force in Textile Products which could enforce more joint decision-making and which could have led the parties to open confrontation in the important issues which the company faced. No integrating force could neutralize the powerful position of MDTP. The board, which theoretically could have played this role, was in the hands of MDTP. It seems that an integrator is particularly important when large enterprises act as if they were family businesses, i.e., when personal interests and biases are intertwined with business considerations.

6.2 Leisure Goods

To some extent there is a similarity between Textile Products and Leisure Goods. In Leisure Goods there is also a fundamental conflict of interests between the owners. These conflicts escalated to operational decisions when demand went down in the spring of 1977. The management of conflict is, however, quite different in each company. While in Textile Products the tendency is to avoid conflict, the tendency in Leisure Goods is much more towards open confrontation. The strength of X and Y together could, for a time, force Z to go along too. Since the tactics used by the owner of Z were efficient, and the negative consequences of the conflict of interests became apparent, an agreement was made to buy him out. This was really a basis for the further integration of the companies. The managers on the operational level were very positive towards this solution.

Leisure Goods experienced much fewer problems of integration than Textile Products. One reason for this is that there has not been any particular company orientation. Also the Board of Directors did control managerial performance quite closely. Its members stayed in close and frequent contact with Leisure Goods' top management, e.g. by means of a well developed reporting system. Board meetings were held once a month on the average. In particular the Chairman of the Board exercised substantial personal influence on the reorganization of Leisure Goods. Any conflicts on strategy between managers have been resolved at the board level by open arguments.

Many of the integration issues have been resolved through the project organization, which was instituted once a decision to merge had been made. Reports from project groups were generated and discussed. The whole approach was one of open confrontation and problem-solving.

Particularly the chairman and the deputy chairman of the board served as an important integrative force. They were both key executives in the parent companies and had had previous experience with mergers. They could therefore base their influence both on competence and on the fact that they represented the owners.

7. Conclusion and Discussion

In terms of conflict resolution and management of conflict, Leisure Goods showed a much better performance. We would agree that this depends on an integrating force which has the ability to balance between different local interests because it is based on a solid power base, competence, and ownership control. An additional important factor is that the MD's of two of the companies are professional managers who have not developed a strong local commitment. We have assumed that the most effective mode of conflict resolution is primarily open confrontation.

What could have been done in Textile Products? Nobody within the company seems to have been in a strong enough position to change the course of events. Primarily, the Swedish Industrial Board which helped in negotiations by financial support for consulting services and by a loan remains. Later the Department of Industry came in and granted a substantial loan to the company. As a condition for its loan, the Industrial Board required the Board of Textile Products to be extended to include external members with competence in certain areas. Later developments showed that this was not enough. Another possibility would have been for the Industrial Board to work towards another structural model. Instead of having the companies sort out their problems one might have created a holding company where the original companies had become subsidiaries. The holding company should have a very small separate management and be separate from its subsidiaries. In this way one could have created the necessary integrating force. To make such a solution worthwhile one may have to try to include some more companies within the industry. As it transpired, Textile Products bought a viable company D and the substance of another E. If such a solution had been envisaged from the beginning, a holding company solution could have been viable. This structural model would at least have a good chance to meet the requirements for effective conflict resolution. However, it obviously needs to be evaluated from other aspects as well.

8. References

Ansoff, I., Brandenburg, R.G., Portner, F.E., and Radosevich, H.R., 1971
Acquisition Behavior of U.S. Manufacturing Firms, 1946-1965. Nashville, Tenn.: Vanderbilt University Press.

Ashridge Management Research Unit, 1975
Danbury Limited. A Case Study on the Acquisition and Integration of Small Company into a Larger Group of Printing Companies.

de Brabander, B., and Edström, A., 1977
»Successful Information System Development Projects», *Management Science,* Vol. 24, No. 2:191-199.

Edgren, J.-O., and Rydén, B., 1978
»Large Mergers in Sweden, 1962-1976 - Determinants and economic effects», in: D.C. Mueller (ed.) (1980), *The Determinants and Effects of Mergers. An International Comparison.* Cambridge, Mass.: Oelgeschlager, Gunn & Hain.

Johannisson, B., 1980
Den organisatoriska smältdegeln. Stockholm: Liber.

Kaufmann, H., 1960
The Forest Ranger. Baltimore, Md.: John Hopkins Press.

Kitching, J. (1973)
Acquisitions in Europe: Causes of Corporate Success and Failures, Business International.

Lawrence, P., and Lorsch, J., 1967
Organization and Environment, Harvard University, Boston, Mass.

March, J.G., and Simon, H.A., 1958
Organizations. New York: Wiley.

Schneider, B., 1975
»Organizational Climates: An Essay.» *Personnel Psychology,* Vol. 28, No. 4:447-479.

Whyte, W.H., 1956
The Organization Man. New York: Simon & Schuster.

11. CODETERMINED MERGER

A Case of Capacity Reduction [1]

Walter H. Goldberg
University of Gothenburg
Gothenburg

1. Introduction

The aim of this chapter is to describe and analyse the decision-making processes in quite a unique merger case aiming at drastic reduction of capacity in steel production, modernization/rationalization of plants and processes and, hopefully, reestablishment of a capability to compete in the market, for the merged enterprises. The decision processes in context to the merger take place under full participation from the unions. Union claims regarding job protection, in particular job security for surplus personnel, but also quests regarding structure, goals and policies of the new firm and codetermination procedures in managing it, are fully integrated in the new organization.

The analysis of the case attempts to lay open the influence of techno-economic as well as socio-political contingencies, conflict resolution processes, in particular on problems of close downs, and the co-operation between unions and their consultants. To begin with, a, as far as possible, comprehensive and objective description of the merging firms and the merger process is provided. The analysis concludes in an application of Nyström-Utterström's [2] techno-economic plus socio-political model for merger analysis.

1.1 Steel-Making

Steel-making [3] was a growth industry during the post World War II period. There have always been ups and downs in the steel-making industry, however. Britain was the outstanding steel producer during the 19th century. Around the turn of the century, U.S. and continental European firms quickly grew large. Immediately before World War I, Western Europe produced half of the world's output, the U.S. and Russia about 43% and 6% respectively

---

[1] The empirical section of the chapter is based upon reports produced by researchers at the Department of Business Administration, University of Gothenburg, undertaken on behalf of the Swedish Centre for Working Life Studies, and by members of this centre (see bibliography).

[2] See the Nyström-Utterström chapter in this volume.

[3] The study is not concerned with production of special purpose steel or steel alloys, but only with production of standard bulk steel.

of an approximate total of 75 million tons. Immediately before World War II Europe's output was about 38%, that of the United States 40%, whereas the Soviet Union produced about 15% of a total of approximately 140 million tons. In 1973 Western Europe's and the United States' share had shrunk to 26% and 22%. Eastern Europe had advanced to 25%, Japan to 17%, and the developing countries to 8% of a total approximating 700 million tons. As viewed by many experts, the outlook was altogether (and even overly) optimistic. The International Iron and Steel Institute for example foresaw a dramatic growth laying ahead, as late as in 1973, to about 1120 million tons by 1985.[1] Only five years later, however, the total world demand would be 150 million tons below the forecast figure for 1978 (for comparison purposes, 150 million tons approximately equals Japan's total production in 1978). As predicted, the growth had been most dramatic in Japan, whose capacity had grown by 1500% over the last 20 years, and in the developing world (with an output increase by about 14% and an increase of the market share by approximately 100%). The optimistic forecasts and the super year 1974, the world's best for ever, as far as output of steel is concerned, triggered heavy investment in many countries and regions.

The years to come would be extremely gloomy. To concentrate now on the Swedish situation, the annual capacity of Sweden's steel mills in the mid 1970's was approximately 5 millions tons per year, 80% of which in standard bulk steel qualities. At that time, decisions had been taken to expand the annual capacity by not less than 40%. They were, however, never realized. A national commission appointed in early 1976 (see below) estimated that the capacity of Swedish steel mills in standard steel production would have to be cut by approximately one half by 1980 and by about two thirds by 1985. An annual growth of between 2% to 4% was foreseeable for the following ten years. Productivity as measured in tons of steel produced per employee was 212 tons per employee in 1975. According to the committee's optimistic/pessimistic forecast, it should grow to a maximum of 311, minimum of 267 tons per employee by 1985. The market for ordinary steel products would be in Sweden only. The share of Swedish non-speciality products on the Swedish market had been declining from 64% in 1968 to only 47% in 1977, mainly because prices were not competitive. At the same time, consumption on the Swedish market started to decline, due to a drastic decline in ship-building industry, stagnation in construction industry, and a levelling-off of the economy in general.

1.2 Enterprises to Merge

»Swedish Steel», a synonym for highest quality alloy steel, has a tradition of several centuries. It was originally based upon the availability of high quality ore and charcoal in the inland, south of the geographical centre of the country (the D factory, see below, is located there). In the course of industrialization, the demand for standard steel (of lower, i.e., standard quality) grew in the world. Because of bulk shipments of Swedish iron ore during this century, it seemed to be logical to establish furnaces and rolling mills at seaside (bulk coal in, bulk ore out) (Factory N, see below, is located at the very nothern end of the Baltic Sea; Factory 0 at an ice-free harbour southwest of

---

[1]   Although clear signs of stagnation were discernible, but neglected, cf. Goldberg, W., (1980).

Stockholm).

D Steel works had existed for exactly 100 years when it merged in 1978. It is part of the world's oldest (600 years) still existing corporation which, at the turn of the century, was Scandinavia's largest industrial enterprise. It grew out of the high quality steel tradition, which still is held in high esteem in this region. D is progressive and leading in R&D, both in metallurgy and in process development. As Scandinavia's largest integrated steel producer, it has a reputation of being very well managed. Until the crisis of 1975 it made profits above the industry average. A high degree of loyalty and co-operation between management, supervision, and personnel is matched by an appreciation of management's competence from the union's and personnel's side. D's annual standard steel capacity is 1.1 million tons. Employment is approximately 5,300. Its final products are more profitable and more in customers' demand than any of O and N's together. D owns mines at reasonable distance from its furnaces.

After heavy losses incurred in 1975 and following years, D's management decided to cut down the steel sector and, instead, to further develop the forest division (lumber, pulp and paper, etc.) and the power sector. The enterprise was reorganized (divisionalized) in 1977.

Enterprise O grew out of a little plant located at the year round ice-free terminal of an iron ore bulk transport oriented railway (the mine end of which is in the D factory and mine region). The railway, as well as a sizeable ore-bulk fleet, is owned by Gränges. When Gränges sold its majority holding in the huge iron ore mines in the north of Sweden (factory N Region) to the Swedish State in 1955, it invested part of the funds received in exchange into the establishment of a »latest technology factory» at O. (Another part of the funds was used for the joint investment of Gränges and Bethlehem Steel into LAMCO, a mine/steel combine in Liberia).

O's new high technology, integrated steel factory became operational in 1957. It was quite profitable until 1974. Two thirds of O's output were regularly sold to the ship-building industry.

Gränges enjoyed world-wide reputation for its progressive personnel policy. Until struck by crisis, it was an exemplary enterprise in this respect. Earlier than any other corporation, it had involved personnel in formal and informal codetermination at all levels and on all matters, from operations to strategic levels of decision making. It invited blue and white collar representatives to become adjunct members of the board at corporate as well as enterprise levels. This policy payed off well to both sides: The O factory should keep its plants in operation on a five shift around the clock around the year continual production scheme. In 1973 blue collar workers were put on salary.

Lacking the tradition of factory D, the owner-management-employee relations at O (as well as at Gränges in general) provided for an open, co-operative problem solving attitude. As a matter of fact, when Gränges was struck by crisis even in the railway and in the ship-owning division, Gränges was found to be almost incapable of taking strong central decisions (as D factory could do). The principal cause of this stalemate in decision making was the very loose, highly decentralized management style. After decades of prosperity, the Gränges corporation was very close to bankruptcy at the time of the merger in 1978.

O's capacity in 1978 was comparable to D's, namely 1.2 million tons per year, employment 3,850. Gränges' railway division, which also serves passengers, employed slightly under 1.000 workers.

In 1978, D's and O's *mines* in the D region had a capacity equivalent to 4 million tons steel per year. They together employed approximately 2,100.

The mines are limited in size. Some of them are almost exhausted. Profitability is on the decline. Even if the steel mills had not run into difficulties, the mines would have been closed one after the other because of low productivity and poor competitiveness. Gränges, however, invested about 150 million SKR[1] into the mines during the early 70's, whereas D adopted quite early a restrictive attitude towards its mining sector.

N factory was a political project from the very beginning. During its entire lifetime it came out of the red figures only occasionally. N factory was intended to help alleviate the notorious unemployment problems in northern Sweden. Government decided in 1937 to investigate the feasibility of a steel plant in the troubled region. Operations at N factory started in 1943. N was from the start up a 100% state-owned enterprise. As intended, it did help to reduce the severity of the unemployment problem in northern Sweden. However, during the 1950's N factory was forced to lay off heavily because of running at deficit year after year.

The local unions very actively took stance for the maintenance and development of employment opportunities. The union leader developed strong relations to labour (= social democrat) government. (It should be mentioned that communism had a stronghold in this troubled region. Political controversies between social democracy and communism essentially and traditionally overtly take place on the union scene. A labour government, or any non-communist government, always wants social democrats to hold union leadership positions, rather than communists.)

In 1970 N was made part of the new state enterprise holding corporation. This immediately brought new investment of approximately 250 million SKR to N, plus plans to further invest 1.5 billion SKR.

The Swedish labour party gradually lost voters during the 70's (It lost governmental power to non-labour parties in 1976). The weakening support to the labour party certainly contributed to the planning and, (in 1974) decisions to establish an entirely new 4 million ton per year capacity integrated steel plant within N. It was supposed to provide 2,300 new jobs in the region. Strong opposition, however, was launched against this project from many sides, including the chairman and the president of the state enterprises' holding corporation. Government's plan was modified under strong union influence.

---

[1]   SKR = Swedish Kronor

242

The metalworkers' union had for some time been requesting the cooordina-
tion of standard steel production in Sweden. The unions (despite the cool or
even negative attitude of their members at O, and in particular at D, against
the giant plant, as well as against changes in ownership) raised a strong plea
in favour of nationalization of the entire steel industry. Joint ventures
between N and D, and later between N, D, and O, were discussed and even
developed to a concrete planning document stage. A totally new physical
investment of approximately 12 billion SKR plus some additional billions
into working capital, aiming at an annual capacity of 4 million tons per year
of raw steel, to be processed and finished within the N-O-D combine (»Steel
Works 80/85») was planned for and submitted to government for decision.

In February 1976, the decision process suddenly stalled. However, a national
commission appointed in April 1976 to look into the market, capacity and
structure/organization problems of Swedish steel industry, was asked to
regard »Steel Works 80/85» as a reality. It was only in November 1976, after
general elections had brought a non-labour government to office, that »Steel
Works 80/85» was taken off the agenda.

A new and dynamic CEO was hired for N from private industry and took
office in September 1976. He immediately began to reorganize, divisionalize,
and, as one of a range of measures, to reduce the heavy and growing deficits
of N. At the takeover date (January 1978), N hade a capacity of 1.7 million
tons per year, and employment of over 5,100 (of which, according to the
reorganization study of the new CEO, approximately 1,000 were superfluous).

The unions' situation at N was quite different from that at O and D. The
metalworkers' union at N was highly political and influential. Both the old
management and the management of the merged firm (as described below)
were quite constrained by and dependent upon this contingency. White collar
unions felt let down and uninfluential, even under the new management.

N's metalworkers' union was also quite active on external issues and certainly had a strong influence upon the nationalization and co-ordination
issues for the steel industry during the 70's. Thus, of all the local unions, the
N-metalworker union was the most active one internally as well as externally,
and is also the most politically dominant and experienced union. The unions
at D and O were active mainly on local and internal matters. White and blue
collar unions co-operated well at O only. At D, a similar co-operation
atmosphere developed only around 1975. Within D a more militant leftist
fraction within the metalworkers' union played a certain role during the
merger negotiations. This group claimed that the union representatives were
too permissive in their requests.

2. The Merger Process

2.1 Prehistory

Sweden's standard steel producing industry has faced a series of business cycle induced crises. Its problems emanate from the small size of plants and high cost of labour. Merger alternatives between O and D were contemplated in 1968/69, and again in 1972, at corporate level. The interest waned each time the business cycle improved. 1974 was the best year ever for the industry. The downswing of 1975-76 was thought to be of business cycle character, but when it continued throughout 1977 as well, it became evident that a new structure must be developed, implying a drastic reduction in capacity. As mentioned above, the metalworker union explicitly and repetitively had requested government to become active and to intervene into steel industry's structure and ownership. The metalworkers' union knew about the occasional, but never fulfilled merger talks between O and D and referred to them as a motive for a »grand solution». Labour government did not react to these requests until it involved itself in »Steel Works 80» (later Steel Works 80/85) in 1974.

2.2 The National Committee

As a result of the repeated union request and, in particular, of the uncertainty about »Steel Works 80/85», the labour Secretary of Industry in February 1976 appointed a national committee to study the future (approximately towards 1985) markets, the problems and the structure of the standard steel producing industry of Sweden. »Steel Works 80/85» was at that time still to begin operations, at two distinct levels of production, in 1980 and 1985. The Secretary of Industry's letter of instruction to the national committee explicitly referred to this fact.

The committee consisted of representatives from industry, unions, and the Department of Industry. The chief economist of the steel-making industries' research organization (he was soon to be appointed to the presidency of the Association of Swedish Industries) was to chair the committee.

However, this man never gained the full support of the union representatives, as they regarded him to be an employers' man. Furthermore, in their opinion he lacked experience in dealing with unions. Because of his old and new positions, he had very good contacts with the leaders in the industry, and had therefore also good access to whatever information he wanted. The union representatives felt they were not properly informed and thus lacked influence in the formation of the committee's conclusions. The (blue and white collar) unions requested societal consequences and costs of restructuring the industry to be considered. These requests were turned down in the committee, which correctly claimed that such considerations were beyond the scope of the tasks assigned to the committee by the Secretary of Industry. This refusal to comply with the union requests triggered a »closing of the ranks» among the unions representatives. This was reflected in a separate statement of joint opinion and partial dissent from the majority of the committee regarding employment consequences of the proposal submitted to government.

The committee proposed a merger essentially of the type which later took place, calling for a reduction of a minimum of 3,800, a maximum of 4,500 jobs. Raw steel production at D was to be dropped. As a consequence, many of the mines in the D region would be closed. New investment between a minimum of 800 and a maximum of 1,800 million SKR would be necessary.

2.3 Merger Negotiation Committee

As a consequence of the proposal, the (now non-labour-) Secretary of Industry appointed a merger negotiation committee under the same chairmanship as the recently dissolved national committee. Members were to be representatives of the potentially merging organizations (including the new CEO of N, who was the designated CEO of the new enterprise, Swedish Steel Inc., in brief SSAB).

Union representatives would normally not be appointed to such a committee. Gränges, however, in accordance with its established routine and tradition, requested to have its unions participate. Following their lead, D and N also wanted to have their union leaders as observer participants.

Because of the subject matter to be dealt with, the union representatives jointly requested to be permitted to have a consultant admitted. They chose a very strong man from the top ranks of the metalworker's union, who also had been under-secretary of labour affairs in the last labour government. He (AL) played a very important role both during the negotiations and later.

The committee of 18 members decided to form subcommittees for:

personnel
(on personnel policies, personnel statistics, and principles for personnel transition during the merger and the years to come)

forecasting
(essentially to prepare the estimates for the necessary capital support to be applied for), and

organization
(at the request of the unions, in order to commit the top-management of the new enterprise. The unions wanted to test the new top-management during this task).

The negotiations were nearly jeopardized when, upon a proposal to proceed along the basis of the National Committee's recommendations (which would cause the closure of steel production at D), the union representatives from D requested to be dismissed from the Committee. (The union representatives from N and O, however, strongly supported the closure proposal.) AL »settled» the conflict by proposing new technical and economic information should be made available. Similar »conflict management» was also applied later, either by postponing decisions, not making decisions, or by looking for solutions at »higher levels» (e.g. at »societal» rather than »business economic» levels).

245

Two surprising conclusions from this information search had some influence on further negotiations:

a. The calculations showed that maintaining or even concentrating steel furnaces at/to D rather than O, would make little difference. As the majority (approximately twelve members) supported the original proposal anyway, different assumptions about the cost of ore were introduced, underlining the superiority of the National Committee's proposal to close down D's steel production.

b. A British and a French consulting firm each came up with surprisingly divergent assessments/valuations of the property of the merging firms.

	N	D	O
French proposal	40	30	30 % of total
British proposal	30	40	30
adopted values	33	33	33

i.e. despite drastic differences in book and going concern values on one side and assessed values by the French and British consultants on the other, equal values were assumed for the three firms, mainly because Gränges would go bankrupt if less than approximately 1.2 billion SKR were invested.

The »solution» was to be:

• 700 million for each of N, O and D

• additional 480 million for Gränges Railway (which had been running at deficit for a long time)

• government would grant the State Enterprise Holding Corporation an additional 700 million by issuing new shares

• government would compensate SSAB by 530 million SKR for the undervalue assigned to N's property.

Thus Gränges (its shareholders) was salvaged from bankruptcy at the taxpayers' expense. Even D, the big loser, fared quite well, as its deficit mines were taken over.

Despite requests from the unions, from Gränges as well as from D, to let SSAB be 100% state-owned, or at least to let the state be the holder of a good majority, ownership was distributed with 50% going to the state, 25% to Gränges, and 25% to K (the holders of D). The Secretary of Industry had requested a 40/30/30% solution.

The negotiations were concluded by the end of November 1977, an agreement to the above extent signed on the 1st of January, 1978.

2.4 Codetermination Negotiations

The unions, in recognizing that some further improvements on the agreement might be made, used their legal right (Codetermination Law of 1976) to request local negotiations on certain issues. They succeeded in securing some additional property of both personnel and non-personnel character for the transfer (e.g. houses, lots, some premises, and, most strikingly, huge underground fuel stores at O, with no or at best little functional relationship to the O factory). AL played an important background role as mediator in this case.

The unions were also successful in persuading K and Gränges to establish local investment funds to further the creation of new jobs in the D and O regions. However, they did not succeed in securing the very profitable power stations of both K and Gränges for the arrangement.

The total gain of the codetermination negotiations has been estimated at the value of approximately 200 million SKR.

2.5 Principal Content of the Merger Agreement

In brief, the financial agreements for SSAB are the following:

> The share capital of SSAB was to be 2 billion SKR plus a reserve fund of 0.8 billion. For reconstruction purposes and structural improvement, SSAB will be granted two state loans on different, very liberal conditions, together amounting to 3.1 billion SKR.

It should be mentioned that the negotiations were extremely difficult. The Secretary of Industry refused the deal twice, maintaining that it would be too expensive for the State. Furthermore, the labour party opposition also strongly objected to the agreement, which, in their opinion, was very favourable (at the taxpayers' expense) for the holders of the private corporations Gränges and K. The social democrat opposition announced that if it was re-elected to government in the general election of 1979, it would re-open the negotiations, thus assuring a new deal less favourable to the capital holders and a rearrangement of the power structure in SSAB. (However, labour was not re-elected in September 1979.)

Noteworthy is the unions' strategy with respect to securing future jobs, as it turned out to be in favour of the holders of Gränges and K, by having the non-profitable mines included in the deal. The representatives of N as well as of the State Enterprise Holding Corporation strongly objected the inclusion of the non-profitable mines in the takeover. Similar objections were raised against the unusually favourable deal about the Gränges Railroad.

The board of SSAB was to consist of nine members plus four substitutes, to be appointed by the shareholders: The State Enterprise Holding Corporation will nominate five members, including the chairman, plus three substitutes; K and Gränges will nominate two members each, including the deputy chairman, plus one substitute.

The union will have three seats plus three substitutes. This is one member and one substitute more than provided for by the Board Representation Law of 1976.

The agreement stipulates explicitly that SSAB is to be managed and run as an efficiently competing enterprise. If SSAB should be requested to undertake non-business tasks, separate agreements on these and compensation for costs incurred thereby must first be concluded.

In order to maintain proper liason and feedback with the local member organizations, the union representatives participating in the merger agreement negotiations were supported by a union reference group of approximately 40 persons. This group also served as a sounding board. Its members kept the local members up to date with the process of the negotiations.

2.6 Swedish Centre for Working Life Studies

The Swedish Centre for Working Life Studies played a certain role during the merger process. The Centre was established on the initiative of the Swedish TUC[1] by the last labour government, in order to, via pragmatically oriented research, further the improvement and the democratization of working life in Sweden. The Centre had just begun activities when AL proposed and induced its participation in the forthcoming negotiations to organize the merger implementation. The researchers of the Centre and those working under contract with the Centre were to adopt an employee's perspective, i.e. to act as analysts and consultants on behalf of personnel. The principal study undertaken by the Centre was labelled »Structural Studies - Codetermination». The project aimed to record the role of the unions in the merger of SSAB. In particular, it was to study the organization and personnel policy of SSAB and, in general, to provide advice to the employee representatives so that they might improve their position in the negotiations.

The Centre's task force group began operations in November 1977, i.e. when the principal agreement on the merger was reached, but before the contract was concluded. Their work lasted until the summer of 1978. The group was organized into a number of sub-groups on personnel, structural studies, and central project co-ordination. During the spring, the Department of Business Administration at the University of Gothenburg was asked to undertake a study into the societal consequences for the D region of the very drastic reduction of operations at D factory.

Further studies undertaken at SSAB dealt with the pre-history of the merger case, in particular with the union activities during the 20th century in the steel industry and at the enterprises which later would merge into SSAB.

---

[1] Trade Union Council = The roof organization of nearly all blue collar unions.

A doctoral student at the Department of Business Administration, under contract with the Centre, recorded the merger activities of 1977 and '78.

The Centre's participation was arranged in agreement with the designated CEO of SSAB. The major contributions of the Centre during the merger organization negotiations (November 1977 through July 1978) were assessed quite positively by the metalworker union representatives, who felt that they had received many good inputs. The white collar union representatives were more modest in their estimation. The contribution to personnel policies and in particular to the (matrix type) project organization for merger implementation were positively assessed. Top-management of SSAB inclines to share this latter opinion.

3. Organizing for Merger Implementation

3.1 CEO-Proposal.

In October 1977, i.e. even before the negotiations were concluded, the designated CEO of SSAB submitted a proposal for the organization of SSAB. It foresaw a divisonalized organization of the same type he had introduced at N (after having applied it successfully in a private forestry based operation). He also submitted a program for the new enterprise, which had been developed by a consultant of utmost reputation on corporate crisis resolutions.

The union representatives essentially accepted the new CEO:s proposal, as they not only had high confidence in him but also knew that this type of organizational structure had been succcessfully introduced at N. O had traditionally been operating in a divisonalized environment, and D had also recently divisionalized. Thus, the starting conditions were unusually favourable. At this point, it should be noted that the positive experience reported by employee representatives on both organizational form and on the capacity and behaviour of the designated CEO provided inputs of high leverage to the merger process.

The designated CEO's principal motivation for the proposed organizational strategy may be summarized as follows. The merging organizations would have to overcome problems of internal bureaucratization and centralization (in particular N and D). Thinking and acting in performance and achievement was poorly-developed at all of the units. In order to become competitive, the organization would need to overcome the handicaps imposed by their environment of highly monostructured regions (which are highly dependent upon employment in the merging enterprise) as soon as possible. Furthermore, the organization would also need to overcome the consequences of the hitherto fairly outspoken competition between the three merging units.

CEO's proposal stressed organizational, technical, and business rationality as cornerstones for the viability of SSAB. Consequently, a number of decision rules and instruments were outlined. Decentralization, grassroot decision making, improvement of the working environment, job security, physical and psychical well-being, influence, responsibility, involvement, and initiative were key-words often used during the preparatory phase from October until December 1977.

It may be claimed ex post facto that it is very difficult, in the course of an extremely difficult and constrained reorganization for merger, to live up to visions hammered out during the »task and blueprint phase» of the merger. Certainly the co-ordination and organization processes necessary when merging three enterprises into a new one, make quasi political, visionary, programmatic statements indispensable. When later compared to achievement and reality, the gap between vision and fact may seem to be quite large.

3.2 Project Organization for Merger

It was a mutually expressed desire to continue the close co-operation developed during the pre-merger negotiations even when preparing the de facto merger. As no clear concept had been made available for the transitional phase, one of the consultants under contract with the Working Life Center was asked to outline a proposal for merger organization. The consultant, a senior lecturer from the Department of Business Administration at the University of Gothenburg, brought with him not only many years experience as a consultant in difficult organization cases, but also his experience with a recent merger of larger wholesaling organizations. In mid-November he proposed a temporary project organization aiming at merger implementation. The proposal was accepted with minor amendments. The task of the project group and its sub-groups was to develop principal guidelines for the effective and efficient implementation of the merger. The deadline was set to be 1st June 1978 (later to be overrun by six weeks by the central project management group and by four months by the sub-group on personnel).

The basic objectives of the »Merger Organization Project» were the following:

☐ to design SSAB's central objectives, functions, and principal procedures

☐ to involve the participation of as many personnel representatives as possible in the decision making on all essential issues, including future business orientation as well as principal strategies.

☐ To avoid undue bureaucratic problems during the pursuance of the project.

Approximately 300 employee representatives participated in the project.

As indicated above, the implementation project was broken down into a number of sub-groups.

The *central project management group,* CPM, was not only to be the principal co-ordinator for the merger project, but in reality to be the essential management of SSAB under formation, as well as acting principal co-ordinator of the sub-groups at central, division, and local levels. All decision proposals elaborated by different sub-groups would have to be corroborated by CPM.

CPM was manned by SSAB's top management plus one blue collar and one white collar representative from each of the five principal unions of SSAB: N, O, D, the railway unit, and the mine unit. Similar principles of representation were adopted for all sub-groups of the »Merger Organization Project».

CPM's principal tasks were to develop, amend and determine areas of competence and guidelines for central project groups, division groups, and local project groups. Further responsibilities were to co-ordinate sub-groups, to assume responsibility for information issues arising out of the merger and, last but not least, to take final decisions on principal issues of future SSAB.

Central project group organization, CPO, (identical with CPM in composition and staffing) was to carry responsibility for the organization design of SSAB in principle and the realization of the decentralization philosophy. The group was not only supposed to draw up organizational charts and guidelines, thus delineating divisions and other principal units. It was also asked to develop principal guidelines for economic performance and enterprise development, defining the action space for the divisions, to develop codetermination procedures at all levels and finally to issue principles for internal and transfer pricing within SSAB.

The *central project group personnel,* CPP, was given the task to develop the personnel policy for SSAB, to outline the missions and the organization for SSAB personnel management, to organize an internal (re-)placement pool for SSAB, to co-ordinate/modify the different programmes, services rendered, payment schemes offered, as well as the assets of so-called personnel foundations, stemming from the different merging enterprises.

As indicated, CPP needed considerable time to fulfil its tasks. Whenever it presented its proposals to CPM it experienced a considerable degree of frustration, as the proposals were very often rejected or returned for further elaboration. In contrast, SSAB's CEO usually accepted proposals submitted by the representatives of »heavy» unions. This should not, however, be interpreted as an indication of opportunism with the CEO. Rather it reflects differing degrees of competence of the union representatives.

The *central project group finance and administration,* CPF, was regarded as a »technical» committee of little interest to the unions and with minor influence to exercise upon.

CPF's tasks were to establish principles and systems for the financial and administrative functions of SSAB, to define central economic and non-economic parameters and criteria to be applied in the enterprise, to develop principles for continued development of administrative systems and to formulate organizational, economic and human/social objectives for SSAB's administrative development.

The *central project group information,* CPI, was asked to develop the information policy for SSAB, to assume responsibility for internal as well as external information during the merger phase, and to develop a permanent organization responsible for the information function of SSAB.

CPI was also regarded to be a »technical» committee. CPI met only twice, whereas CPO and CPP met up to approximately twenty times.

The *central project group for research and development,* CPRD, was regarded to be a »technical» committee in the meaning of having little interest to the employee representatives and consequently little influence to exercise. Its tasks were to develop goals for SSAB's R&D and to propose an R&D organization, thereby assuring proper relations between divisions, technological product and process development at central and division levels; coordination with external laboratories and research organizations should be paid proper attention to.

It was also asked not only to make up a mid-term budget for R&D but also to link SSAB's R&D to its principal strategic objectives.

The *central project group structure,* CPS, was asked to develop proposals for the restructuring and long-term strategy of SSAB in accordance with the following assumptions:

> Sweden and Scandinavia would be the main markets for SSAB's products. In order to exploit possible economies of scale, certain product groups would have to be exported as well. Since the Swedish and Scandinavian markets should be served by a product range well covering their needs, this also would imply that certain products would have to be purchased abroad, if they could not be produced profitably by SSAB.

One of the principle guidelines was that SSAB's productive units should, even in the long run, be competitive with comparable western European steel works, in regard to prices, quality, and efficiency.

The *central project group working conditions,* CPW, was to review ongoing as well as implemented projects undertaken to improve the working environment and conditions in steel and mine production, as well as in railroad, sea, and other transportation. CPW was also to develop guidelines for issues concerning the working environment, to be observed and applied to physical investment decisions. CPW was instructed to review internal and external resources as well as relevant research and development, at home and elsewhere, which might have bearing on the working environment within the SSAB enterprises. Finally, CPW was asked to submit proposals for the future organization of the working environment management function within SSAB, as well as for guiding principles and basic procedures to the betterment of the working environment.

3.3 Groups and Committees at Division and Local Levels

Groups and Committees at Division and Local Levels were established to serve both as sounding boards and as advisors regarding the practicability of proposals developed by the central groups. They were also used for information purposes in both directions. By means of those committees and groups as many »grassroot members» of SSAB as possible should become involved into the process of change.

3.4 Observations on the Functioning and Processes of the Merger Organization

The merger organization was generally assessed to have contributed in a positive way to the making and implementation of difficult capacity reduction decisions. The quite deep involvement of many members of the organization through many groups and committees established was appreciated as one of the main factors accounting for a smooth transition from the old to the new organization. The general agreement on principal goals and issues connected with the drastic reduction of capacity was regarded as a sine qua non for the change.

As fas as the employee representatives are concerned, it should be emphasized that not only there were differences between white collar and blue collar, but also, that much severer differences existed between the different units represented. After the experience during the pre-merger negotiations and again during the initial phase of the merger organization, the employee representatives decided to meet in advance of each session, in order to co-ordinate issues and differing viewpoints. All groups supported the attitude »united we stand, divided the CEO will decide». Perhaps the most striking features, which characterized the entire decision process were

a. that a very high level of ability to compromise was developed, not only between the different personnel representatives, but from all sides, and

b. that management never by itself decided on issues without proper attention being paid to the »other sides'» points of view.

Despite the central and strategic position of CPM, it, rather than deciding unilaterally on controversial issues, brought the matters back to the sub-groups for renegotiation. This created an atmosphere of confidence indispensible for the resolution of many conflicts on principal issues.

As stressed before and by no means unexpectedly, CPP and CPS turned out to be the most important sub-groups, attracting high participation from the concerned parties. Issues to be solved in those groups by their very nature often were of controversial character. In contrast, and because of their technical character, the work in CPW, CPRD, and CPI was practically free from conflict and controversy.

CPP was given the most difficult task to take care of personnel made superfluous by capacity reduction. In the deliberations of this group the conflicting corporate policy, to be a competitive enterprise on one side and to be a leader in industry on personnel and employment issue were laid open and had to be settled.

The principles developed within CPP regarding surplus personnel will be highlighted in brief, as they will have consequences for several decades to come.

Surplus personnel would be taken out of the productive organization and transferred to special purpose units. Voluntary transfer is the preferred mode. Voluntary movers would be given priority to new openings at the same site. If voluntarism cannot solve the problems within a reasonable period, e.g. of four months, SSAB and the unions would then negotiate on numbers of surplus personnel, on positions available, and on steps to be taken to solve the issues. Problems of surplus personnel should be solved within two years. Temporary job assignments in special units should last not longer than two years. Assignments to special units would also imply further training. The personnel improvement policy adopted by SSAB means that improvement of professional capacity of personnel of all categories was to be employed as much as possible. It should here be remembered that, through codetermination negotiations, the union representatives had succeeded in having personnel improvement funds to be established in practically all divisions of SSAB, aiming at the creation of new, good jobs at various sites.

One major subject of controversy between the merging organization and the Secretary of Industry during the autumn of 1977 was the size of capital needed to solve personnel surplus and unemployment problems. Although the numbers of surplus personnel were not exactly known, they were estimated to range between 3,800 and 4,500. Very likely they will grow to approximately 5,000 or even higher. Notwithstanding which the correct figure will be, it has not been possible to calculate how much cost will be incurred to support individuals and their families affected by the changes.

In this regard, a differentiated program and consequent cost coverage has been proposed from a variety of sources.

75% of the total cost of employment per individual may be covered from the regional employment administration during the time in which the individual is kept occupied in the enterprise which wants to dismiss her or him.

By general agreement between the principal partners on the Swedish labour market, several job security funds have been established on the basis of contributions from the employers. These funds may be used as resources for unemployment relief, if both parties are in agreement that eligibility has been established.

The local or regional employment administration office may grant (a) (geographical) mobility subsidies and/or (b) subsidies to promote the starting of new businesses, to persons and families wishing to move out of the region or out of their present jobs.

Beyond those means available within the regular labour market policy programs, some part of the special loans granted to SSAB for reconstruction purposes may be used towards the solution of pertinent problems.

According to the participants' own viewpoints, employee participation in the principal pre-merger negotiations, as well as in the CP Personnel, helped to call proper attention to the issues, not only within the merging enterprises but, most importantly, vis-a-vis government. The employee participation accounted also for the establishment of a special program aiming at a minimization of the individuals' as well as the concerned families' sufferings from the change.

The agreement asserts that nobody may be dismissed within two years after the surplus character of a certain job has been established and agreed upon. In effect, however, all this means that society, i.e. the taxpayer, is carrying the financial burden of this most drastic capacity reduction. The logic is simple: the economic as well as mental sacrifices experienced by individuals losing their jobs, should be minimized and distributed over a majority of taxpayers, meaning a marginal reduction of their disposable incomes only.

One of the most difficult problems in the long run, is the change of the function and status of the SSAB personnel function, as well as that of SSAB middle-management in general. Given the extremely influential position of the employee representatives, i.e. the strong and »untouchable» position of the union clerks, as a consequence of the extremely high union participation in Sweden, the position of the personnel manager but also that of managers in general has become very weak. On any issue to be resolved, the personnel manager, as well as the manager in general must enjoy the support of the union, if the issue is to be successfully settled. The (personnel) manager is thus in essence becoming more dependent on the unions than on the enterprise or its management.

A conflict arose between the unions and corporate management on the matter of the organization of the personnel department. The unions requested the local personnel units to be subordinated to the central personnel office. Management, however, requested that the personnel officers should be subordinated to the division heads, in view of the division heads' cost responsibility. In this case, as in many others, the unions' view was adopted.

3.5 Controversies about Structure

The controversies about structure came early to concentrate on the employment consequences of structural change. Whereas the National Committee's forecast of 1977 estimated the number of jobs lost because of capacity reduction to approximately 4,000, the negotiations by the end of summer 1978 resulted in an agreement on only 1,015 specified jobs to be dropped.

The aim of structural planning was to specify the structural changes in detail, given the superordinate objective of SSAB to become a competitive, profitable and stable steel combine. The unions, however, made the agreement on any structural plan for future SSAB dependent on certain strongly advocated conditions, the most important one being that local employment at the SSAB sites would be maintained. In reality, this would imply that no lay-offs could be decided upon without a comparable number of »good and safe» jobs having been established at the same place or within the region. Further, such replacement jobs should be made available immediately after the lay-offs or after a transitional period, during which special jobs as well as training for the new position would be offered.

Whereas the management of SSAB based its reasoning merely on economic grounds, the unions pointed to the fact, that the Secretary of Industry, in his proposition of 1977 to government, had explicitly stated that other than strictly economic reasons very likely had to be taken into consideration when restructuring SSAB. The Secretary at that time also had claimed that society should carry the cost for the employment consequences of capacity reduction within SSAB. Thus, the unions in all phases of the merger strove to fully exploit the opportunities contained in the Secretary's proposition to government.

In order to end the stalemate in negotiations on structural planning occurring early in spring 1978, a new forecasting exercise was undertaken under the auspices of the CPS. This exercise comprised the investigation of several alternatives beyond the ones which already had been scrutinized by the National Committee. However, their resultant estimates were very similar to those of the national committee.

It should be mentioned that the development of the structural plan created as many severe tensions between the different groupings of employees as between the unions and management. In particular, the unions at D, in a desperate attempt to turn the tide which was moving aginst them, took a number of political initiatives which, however, were very much disliked by most of the other union representatives. In the end they lost, to some extent because of their minority position.

It is, of course, much too early to determine if the proposed structural changes will be thorough enough to guarantee the further existence of SSAB, or if further drastic changes eventually become necessary. Most likely, e.g. the number of jobs lost will be closer or above the National Committee's forecast than to the CPS estimate. At the time present, it is only possible to speculate about what would have happened if the SSAB project had not survived the negotiation rounds of 1977 and 1978:

• Already during 1977, O would have been closed due to Gränges' unavoidable bankruptcy;

• K would have fulfilled its structural plans by closing a major part of the standard steel production sections at D;

• N would most likely have continued its deficit operations at about the same level as earlier;

• The employment consequences would very likely have been much beyond the 4,500 maximum estimation of the National Committee. The losses of jobs, physical capital and equity would have been much more severe than even the very high cost resulting from the SSAB merger.

3.6 Management-Union Relations

As indicated above, the unions wanted to test management during the merger organization phase. Indeed, management passed the test. The unions had already been pro-management during the pre-merger phase and, although there were many conflicts which occurred and had to be settled during the merger organization phase, they did not essentially change the unions' positive attitude towards management. The toughness of management certainly seems to have impressed the unions. They were clever enough to understand that tough management is good management, and that only good management can navigate SSAB to safe shores. Certainly, the total openness of management contributed to the atmosphere of confidence. And given an obvious disaster situation, whatever could have prevented management from laying all its cards open?

One should not forget that SSAB is and will remain a political construct. In the end, the most reasonable strategy for all concerned parties was to lay open and deal with all the conflicts during the very early phases of the merger so that one could secure a maximum commitment from the government. At the same time, to start with a minimum burden of expectations was to be met. (In contrast, the »visionary phase» was a necessary part of the pre-merger exercises.)

The proof of the pudding will be the eating. The enterprise must overcome tremendous difficulties because of the local interests vested in the old domiciles. Both management and the unions will have much to do to establish a loyalty towards SSAB rather than to the local units only. In this regard, the pre-merger conflicts produced only a tiny, if any, basis for the development of a loyalty towards SSAB.[1]

4. Analysis

The comprehensive description of SSAB formation is rich of interpretations and partial analysis. The following analysis will, against the background of the SSAB merger, also deal with properties of merger processes in general.

4.1 The Process

Both during and after the process all the participants claim that the process had been an extremely speedy one. However, if one measures speed by progress made and by milestones established, one can clearly see different »speed phases».

When government appointed the national Committee in early 1976, it was in the belief that the steel industry was still a growth industry. At that time, »Steel Works 80/85» was still regarded to be a realistic project. The National Committee, however, had not only been called to life because of the union's request (given the labour government's particular sensibility to union proposals, during the months immediately preceding the 1976 election). The establishment of the committee simply could not be avoided because of the many expert opinions opposing »Steel Works 80/85».

During the life time of approximately ten months of the National Committee (which is very short according to Swedish standards), two drastic changes occurred in the context:

---

[1] Cf. also Leffler (1982).

a.   labour government was not re-elected

b.   the steel crisis, then world-wide, was recognized as a fact.

It is indicative of the competence of the National Committee, that it quickly interpreted its task to be the development of a proposal for a viable Swedish standard steel industry. It is particularly astonishing, how well the Committee perceived the available options, how quickly it developed »the» solution, and how well that solution met all later challenges.

The structural alternative proposed by the National Committee was both challenged and reconfirmed twice during the SSAB merger negotiations. At both times, needless to say, the information base on the steel industry, as developed by the National Committee, had to be used again. The two »iterations» (one having to do with the survival of D or not, the other with the regional employment consequences and their management) were part of conflict resolution processes. In both conflict situations, resort was taken to periods of non-decision-making, by pushing the issues not only to further investigation but also to higher levels of problem perception.

This »regressive» behaviour of non-decision-making, in terms of social and industrial psychology, as a reaction to crises during problem solving processes, is a phenomenon which obviously occurs with some frequency, in particular in political decision-making (cf. Maier, Solem, Maier, *Problem Solving,* New York, London, 1969).

A similar process may be observed in the development of the organization issue.

An organization proposal was developed and submitted by a »hat-trick» by the CEO as early as October 1977, at which time the principal agreement and the base for the merger contract were near to finalization. CEO's proposal and the »guiding principles» for SSAB, which had been developed by the CEO's superconsultant also triggered a loop in the decision-making process, during which essentially no progress was made. At the end of this loop, however, the proposal was accepted at the end of October 1977. The »guiding principles», however, had been put back to the drawer but will most certainly be considered in the years to come.

Essentially no participant in the process experienced those periods of non-decision-making as slow-downs in the decision process. Indeed, the opposite may have been sensed, viz. the conflict situations causing the loop were experienced as a severe stress by all parties.

Brunsson (1979) sub-titles his interpretation of the merger process as »A Case Study of a Decision Process without Decions-Making». He does not only claim that no new decisions were taken, but also maintains that although the unions considered themselves winners, no progress was made over and above the initial proposal. This interpretation, however, cannot be subscribed to as in fact important decisions were made during it and earlier decisions were corroborated. The unions also gained considerable strength, internally as well as externally during the period.

Brunsson's interpretation is based on the fact that indeed no proposals exceeding the conclusions of the National Committee's report of the spring of 1977 were submitted or decided upon. It must be emphasized, however, that the National Committee was not a decision-making body. Its report was a descriptive instrument, not a decision document. As may be remembered, important decision makers from industry participated in the study as well as union representatives. The unions, however, felt outside of the decision process, although they had been given formal power to influence the National Committee's proposal. The conclusions from the National Committee's report were that a merger should take place. Merger negotiations, thus, were called for. The National Committee's report was perhaps the most important information input for the entire merger process. Nevertheless, it was not designed and could not be employed as a merger decision document. In consequence, the stalemate, which in Brunsson's opinion existed between April 1977 and summer 1978, definitely was not a stalemate in the decision process as claimed by him.

Indeed, the three major phases between spring 1976 and summer 1978 cannot be regarded as a single decision process. A single decision-making body capable of making decisions did not even exist. Rather, it was an information seeking process and a decision stream, during which problems were identified, contingencies assessed, decision-making bodies instituted, and even decisions made. The process was essentially characterized by the fact that most of the time no single decision body was available. Thus, decisions had to be taken by committees representing diverse and often conflicting interests. Three power centres developed during the process:

1. The *Department of Industry,* as a political bureaucracy, which in the mid 1970's was faced by a range of structural crises in the steel industry, in ship-building, in the textile industry, in mining, and a range of other industries. Many of those industries and their corresponding industrial regions of Sweden had until quite recently been prospering. The Department of Industry was thus suddenly confronted with techno-economical as well as with socio-political problems which, in quantity, size, and quality were unprecedented. In the midst of these crises, governmental power shifted from labour to non-labour in October 1976. The expectations about the new non-labour government's conflict and crises handling capacity were very high. At the same time, the new labour opposition was extremely eager to advocate, that the new bourgeois rulers were incapable of coping with crises and employment problems. In retrospect, one might criticize the behaviour of and some of the decisions taken by the Department.

    However, given the particular crisis situation in Sweden, and the structural crises in the entire western economy, the Department's ability to develop a decision-making capacity out of practically nothing was remarkable. As a bureaucracy, the Department of Industry was extremely young, having been established only in 1971. Many of its central decision makers were quite young academicians, often with a labour party membership or corresponding inclination. The new Secretary of Industry was an active farmer and academically trained social worker, with seven years experience as an M.P.

259

2. The second decision centre which developed was the *SSAB Management Group*. Although being quite experienced in management and business matters, it had no mandate for about twelve most critical months. It, however, enjoyed the support of the State Enterprise Holding Corporation's top management. It produced an action plan quite early. The plan was quite well funded, so it was later adopted practically unchanged. Only the principal rules and guidelines were not accepted. As may be remembered, this group was formalized only at the beginning of 1978 in the shape of the CPM. It was, however, not given a legal decision-making mandate. Parliament took the decision on the formation of SSAB as a government enterprise and on the financial restructuring of SSAB as late as in May 1978 (let be »retroactively» as of January 1, 1978). Again, the behaviour of this group is remarkable insofar as it took the lead, without having been entrusted with formal decision-making capacity. Despite its lacking legal status, it earned acceptance and support, in particular from the unions, but also from other concerned parties.

There is no doubt about the fact that the power entrusted to the unions on the formation of SSAB, must have not only been a surprise but indeed a shock to the management group, which, however, accomodated swiftly.

3. The third power group, *employee representation,* was the most remarkable one. It was originally composed only of local representatives, which by the mere problem of drastic capacity reduction, entered the process with highly conflicting interests and mandates. They also represented, in particular on the white collar side, a wide range of diverse unions and member interests. The group was clearly dominated by the metalworker union, which was the only union that had paid attention to the techno-economical development of the steel industry, and which had taken a number of political steps to induce its restructuring. The group developed a conflict-handling capacity which can be considered quite unique. It had to settle its internal conflicts, e.g. those stemming from the problem that D factory would be heavily affected; O would gain most from the merger, being salvaged from bankruptcy, whereas the situation of N was ambiguous: »Steel Works 80/85» was their pet project. It was lost during the process. Still, N was offered a second-best solution.

Despite those internal conflicts the employee representatives developed a strong negotiation capacity vis-a-vis the other partners, i.e. SSAB management and, in particular, the Department of Industry.

No doubt, AL played an important role in both processes. His expertise, his political experience (not only as a member of the internal government circle but also as a political journalist), and in particular, his neutrality and integrety, were characteristics which qualified him as the natural informal leader of the employee representation.

4.2 Merger Process Models

Andersson[1] presents two merger models. The first comprises five *stages* (a) idea generation, (b) establishment, (c) systems development, (d) internal evaluation, and (e) external evaluation.

His second model divides the merger into three *processes,* viz.: (a) the task process, (b) the strategy process, and (c) the distributive process.

Brunsson (op.cit.) characterizes a merger as a decision process which is composed of three elements, viz., *will, expectation,* and *commitment.*

Will is the emotional aspect of decision. A decision is an expression of what the decision maker wants.

Expectation is the cognitive aspect of decision. Since decisions concern actions in the future, the formation of expectation is an important part of the cognitive subset of the decision-making process. The decision in itself is an expression of the expectation that the action involved in the decision will take place.

Commitment is the social aspect of the decision. Commitment arises when, in the eyes of others, the individuals become tied to a planned action. Commitment involves responsibility for an action. Declaring one's intent or one's participation in or support of an intent or to act in a certain way, is one way of committing oneself. Expressions of wishes, perceptions, and expectations during the decision-making process are other ways. (Cf. Brunsson, 1976).

Brunsson applies this model to the SSAB case (Brunsson, 1979) and concludes that no decisions were taken between April 1977 (when the national Committee's structural proposal was made available) and May 1978 (when the temporary merger organization of SSAB took some major decisions on strategical and organizational issues for SSAB, and when parliament decided upon the formation of SSAB). Brunsson obviously disregards the character of the decision-making body. The National Committee was not a decision-making body. Its function was to produce a valid and reliable forecast for the steel industry until 1985, and to submit structural options, based on this forecast. Indeed, the Committee submitted a structural proposal, which withstood all further challenge. This speaks more for the quality of its recommendations and conclusions than for the absence of decision-making in Brunsson's terms.

In regard to *will,* the formation of will and its expression is not a single and simple process. Even at top levels there was the will to salvage jobs in the steel industry, as a common least denominator for all parties concerned. What followed dealt with how the will would, should, or could be implemented. At lower levels, i.e. in the single participating bodies (which above have been characterized as committees or groups rather than as decision entities), the

---

[1]   Andersson, J.G.A., »The Birth Process of a New Organization: The Case of a Joint Venture», in this volume.

varying »wills» diverged, because the expectations were so different. A substantive proportion of the decision process dealt with the adjustment of these differing expectations. Indeed, even coalitions were formed to influence expectations, as, for example, between the SSAB management group and the unions, in relation to the Department of Industry. Their joint ideas about needed resources and the Department's preparedness to contribute financially to the solution of the crisis at taxpayers' expense could, of course, not be compatible in such a situation.

Another example is that the expectations at D had to be different from those at O. O was in drastic need of a quick decision, whereas D wanted to extend the search for alternatives less disasterous to D than those proposed by the national Committee. In this respect, D was successful in triggering a new search phase. However, the National Committee's recommendation withstood all challenge. D lost on the issue.

Expectation and *commitment* are related. Whereas expectations are »broader», commitments are easier to achieve at »higher levels of problem solving» (cf. Maier, N.R.C.F., *Industrial Psychology,* Boston, 1958; Maier, Solem, Maier, *Problem Solving,* New York, London, 1969). Brunsson claims that the National Committee did not involve and commit the unions enough, i.e. the unions did not feel involved and committed. However, the task of a National Committee is to make an investigation and to propose alternative solutions. It is not a decision-making body. The National Committee's composition reflects the parties concerned. In this case, the unions were represented. Differing opinions about the way in which the investigation should be undertaken occurred. The metalworker union's representatives wanted the Committee to take up the agenda, on which the metalworkers union had been acting during the 1970's, i.e. to nationalize and co-ordinate the entire steel industry. The Committee, however, decided to stick to the letter of instructions issued for the Committee by the then labour party Secretary of Industry in spring 1976. He had requested the Committee to confine its deliberations to the competitive and market situation of the steel industry and the consequences for the industry's structure. This refusal to follow the unions' opinion then caused a negative attitude from the union's side towards the Committee's proposal.

As a consequence, the Secretary of Industry appointed a successor to the National Committee after it had delivered its report and recommendations, this in order to respond to the unions' request for information and influence on the structural change in the steel industry. Several governmental departments (industry, labour, and treasure), all major unions (AL representing the metalworkers' union), as well as pertinent industrial organizations participated in this new Committee. Given the fact that merger negotiations progressed well in the standard steel sector, the Committee, however, came to concentrate its deliberations to the special steel sector. The Committee was dissolved at the end of December 1977, i.e. when the merger agreement for the standard steel sector was reached. It should be mentioned in this context, that the labour party opposition frequently claimed that the non-labour government was unable to co-operate with the unions. In reality, however, this certainly was not the case, as the instructions to SSAB, with an unprecedented power attached to the unions to influence important decisions, have demonstrated.

Brunsson's model of political decision-making thus seems to have limited applicability to such a complex merger case.

In contrast, Andersson's dual model seems to fit even a complex merger situation quite well. Andersson stresses the fact that the decision process is never straightforward, but that there are many loops and recursions.

The *idea development phase* is, even in the SSAB case, loaded with visions and perhaps dreams. SSAB would be the first fully codetermined enterprise (a) to be established and (b) to be run (Volvo's experiment with an assembly-line-free car manufacturing plant at Kalmar and similar experimental attempts undertaken by SAAB-Scania are predecessors which come to mind). The visionary character of the idea phase is necessary in order to stimulate involvement. This may have been particularly important in a case where a stagnation-struck industry fights for its own survival as an industry, and, within the industry, also the single enterprises and factories. Reality then very often must be different from vision.

Andersson's *establishment* and *system development* phases are clearly discernable in the SSAB case. The establishment phase was dominant in the pre-merger negotiations of summer and autumn 1977; the systems' development phase was dominant during the merger organization of spring and summer 1978. Both, however, included *internal* as well as *external evaluation* elements, again at different decision levels. For example, the internal evaluation triggered the new forecasting exercise during autumn 1977 as well as the »societal consequence investigation» of May 1978. The latter is considered as internal evaluation because it essentially served, like the forecasting exercise of autumn 1977, to test the validity and reliability of the National Committee's structural proposal. Because the »internal» calculation failed to support the future viability of D factory, an »external» estimate of the societal consequences and cost was later undertaken, and once again it concentrated on the problems of the D factory region.

In terms of the Andersson phase model what followed after the system development phase was its subset of system's *implementation*. The internal evaluation had been present during the preceding phase, and was to continue during the systems' implementation phase.

Until this point, the external evaluation has mainly been of socio-political character. From 1982, i.e. when SSAB becomes fully operational, it will converge into the acid test of market evaluation.

Andersson's process model (task process, strategy process, distribution process) can essentially be regarded as a subset, or perhaps »diagonal», of his first model. The *task process* is dominant in the idea and establishment phases, but is also present during the following ones, although perhaps with less emphasis. The *strategy process* is clearly visible during the merger organization phase of spring and summer 1978.

Because of its special character as a job preservation task, the *distributive processes* are always present: How many jobs can be preserved within SSAB? How many jobs can be created outside of SSAB? Who carries the burden? Who covers the costs?

In summary, the Andersson model seems to me a suitable one for *descriptive,* and very likely also for *normative* purposes in merger cases.

4.2.1 Techno-Economic and Socio-Political Contingencies

The context in which a merger takes place obviously plays a very important role. In the merger studies undertaken by many economists, as reported upon, for example, in the Seven Countries Study,[1] the context must by necessity be suppressed or even neglected. At best, business cycle conditions or industrial cycle conditions are accounted for, and are perhaps even included in the regressions. However, the context is never static, and there are differences as to speed and quality of contextual change.

The following brief characterization intends to highlight the most important contextual conditions and trends. It is not claimed that this short examination is by any means complete or exhaustive, nor does a strict delineation exist between the different factors.

4.2.2 Techno-Economic Contingencies

TE I: The situation of the steel industry of the world is a manifestation of stagnation conditions, which essentially have been caused by governmentally decided or induced investment acitivtes. The decisions, in particular in the very large-scale industries, often were based on the same forecasts. When, under such conditions, production-supply suddenly and drastically exceeds demand, a crisis is caused.[2] The steel crisis is world-wide and has particularly struck older, outmoded steel industries, and those whose cost of labour is high (United States, Sweden), or, at the other extreme, highly modern, high technology mills just starting up, which must accomodate high costs of test production at the same time as they have not yet established market segments (Italy). The disaster on the shipbuilding market greatly accentuated the problems.

TE II: Within this world-wide steel production crisis, the Swedish situation has its individual peculiarities. The problems associated with the high cost of labour, small scale of market and production character of the Swedish standard steel works were well understood, in particular by the metalworker union. The plan to establish »Steel Works 80/85» was originally considered as response to these problems, as only the most modern type of production facility would give Swedish steel production a chance. It was then realized that the Swedish bulk steel industry would never again be internationally competive on the standard steel market, and thus, that a drastic reduction in capacity was necessary.

TE III: »Sweden in crisis» was a relatively new experience confronting the country's industry and, in particular, the political decision makers. A country which had the reputation of being one of the world's richest, suddenly found its economy in danger, as it was based on a range of industries which faced crises (iron ore, steel, shipbuilding, car manufacturing, and also paper and pulp were in trouble at this time). Strength was suddenly transformed

---

[1] Mueller, D.C. (ed.) 1980.
[2] Cf. Goldberg, W.H., (1980).

into weakness. The Departments of Industry, Labour, and Treasury were challenged by many simultaneously occurring crises and by demands to live up to the expectations and to given political promises (that the standard of living of Sweden's population would be maintained). Clearly, Sweden was living beyond the level of its capacity. However, no one was willing to cut back.

TE IV: Raw material changes and, in particular, price changes played an important role. The Swedish steel industry developed as a result of Sweden's access to iron ore. Towards the end of the 1960's and beginning of the 1970's, however, Sweden's »gold» lost its value due to several factors: the exploitation of good mines in less developed countries, the availability of cheap, large-scale cargo for ore transportation, a loss of the high reliability of Swedish supplies as a result of the long strike in the big iron ore mines at the end of the 1960's which forced many continental European steel works to search for new sources of supply.

An important role was also played by the oil price crisis, which pushed many industries in the world into structural crises. Another contributing factor is a trend towards lighter constructions in many industries, thus lowering the amount of steel used.

4.2.3 Socio-Political Contingencies

SP I: Northern Sweden has a long-standing tradition as a crisis region. Because of its political implications, job creation in northern Sweden has been a central governmental issue for many decades during the era of industrialization. N factory was established during World War II. Employment maintenance in northern Sweden was a must for the labour government, and would have been it for any other government as well. At any point in time, northern Sweden failed to be a good industrial region. There are, for example, no ice-free harbours on the Swedish side. On the Norwegian side there is Narvik, which is ice-free. It, however, implies high costs for logistics.

SP II: Democratization of industry: Co-operation and openness are cornerstones of the traditional »Swedish model». However, given the declining voter constituency of the Swedish labour party, the frontiers had to be pushed forward towards widening societal as well as industrial democracy. In view of this, codetermination laws were promulgated. In essence, however, these framework laws only codified the traditional co-operative behaviour which had been established in Sweden over the decades.

In principle, no action which has any bearing on employment situations can be taken without formal consensus. In that regard, the State Enterprises Holding Corporation formalized an agreement on codetermination with the unions stating that its enterprises are to be business-oriented, but at the same time, to behave as leaders in good personnel practices, including codetermination.

The unions are entitled to request the support of »employee consultants», i.e. consultants (of any type) who act and counsel in the interest of the employed. This right has been given to the unions in order to virtually and effectively strengthen the competence of the employed to participate in decision-making on economic and business issues.

The democratization also extends into a wider participation in decision-making processes by regional and local authorities, in particular regarding the exchange of information with industry on plans for employment, investment, research and development, marketing, production etc.

The strong, formal and informal, position wielded by the unions and employee representatives has forced the personnel management function in enterprises into an »in between» situation. Never before, the personnel management function has been as important and central in enterprises of practically any type as since the mid 1970's. At the same time, however, the position of the personnel manager is characterized by high or even extreme ambiguity.

SP III: The politization of the economy and of decision-making processes implies a changing role for the enterprises. The role, the action space available for independent decision-making of enterprises, has been drastically reduced, in particular since the non-labour government took office in 1976. The enterprises' obligation to society rank on top of the goal expectations held by society on business. Job maintenance and job creation is objective number 1. General measures have been replaced by direct interaction between the public sector and the individual enterprise. The financial deficit of the country has increased drastically at the same time as the country is meeting harder competition and as the capacity of industry to cater for the necessary foreign currency is faltering.

Political science issues are becoming more relevant to business and industry than business administration topics. The political decision makers act as representatives of their constituencies, with mandates and re-election concerns on their minds, rather than considering what may be good for the economy or for industry in particular. Negotiations are more important than analyses, compromise is superior to decision-making.

SP IV: The »Åsling doctrine», named after the first non-labour Secretary of Industry, implies that local industry is responsible for local employment. It is an example of the present trend away from a general economic welfare policy to a range of selective policies and regulations. The enterprise is the new »agent of the state». Even on issues other than employment, both the quickly growing national administration and regional and local offices have recently gained strong influence. Consequently, consensus seeking activities in mixed interest committees are growing in importance. Negotiations take more and more time at the expense of business activities.

SP V: Consensus seeking gains importance, not only between different interest groups as between enterprises, the public sector, and unions, but also, as demonstrated in the SSAB case, between different unions. (The union at D deviates on structural matters, but at the same time acts as a very loyal participant in supporting strategies towards e.g. government. During the SSAB merger the D unions have irritated the other unions more than any other party. However, it must be understood that the D unions were in the most difficult position as losers. At home, they were facing a militant radical group, which simply refused to accept or even recognize the realities of the situation).

The efficiency of the consensus seeking methods and procedures is a very important contextual constraint.

SP VI: Once decisions are reached at the end of such complex processes, they are quite stable. Indeed, when new conditions emerge, it is quite difficult to reopen the discussions in order to readjust the decisions reached. The entire SSAB decision process provides ample evidence of the tendency to stick to an agreement, once it has been reached. This quite new phenomenon obviously must lead to increased inflexibility.

SP VII: The Secretary of Industry claims (end of 1980) that state owned firms in which the state holds majorities, cannot go bankrupt. Such a policy, if actually adhered to, will basically change the economic system of Sweden. To mention only a few of the many consequences, it would imply that bankruptcy is confined to the (diminishing) private sector of the economy as a means of weeding out incompetent management. The efficiency criteria for state owned enterprises would become similar to those of public administration in general.

Certainly many of the TEs and SBs mentioned are particular to the Swedish situation. However, they also represent a general tendency. The SSAB case is thus of general interest as it may provide a scenario valid for other situations, industries, and even countries as well.

5. Concluding Remarks

Merger motives differ. They constitute major contingencies to merger processes. Their impact on merger results seems to be well established. Merger studies in which mergers induced by differing motives and implemented by different processes are treated as if they were uniform, can only render averaged and thus inconclusive results. If mergers for growth are thrown together with mergers for capacity reduction, »neutral», inconclusive evidence will result. Merger students thus should refine their research methodology consequently.

6. References

Brunsson, N., 1976
   Propensity to Change: An Empirical Study of Decisions on Reorientation. Gothenburg: BAS.

Brunsson, N., 1979,
   »Adaptability and Influence in State-Owned Enterprises: A Case Study of a Decision Process without Decision Making», *FE Rapport 1979,* 135, Dept of Business Administration, University of Gothenburg.

Goldberg, W., 1980
»Innovation and Stagnation, Relevant Policy Questions», to appear in a report from IIASA, Vienna.

Hammarström, O., and Hörte, S.A., 1978
Facket inför handelsstålkrisen», Arbetslivscentrum, 1978:13, Stockholm.

Hedberg, B., 1978
»SSAB-Fusionen: Erfarenheter kring förändringsstrategier och löntagarkonsultroll», Arbetslivscentrum, 1978:14, Stockholm.

Leffler, J., 1982
Fackliga informationssystem (Decision support systems for the unions) with a summary in English. Gothenburg: BAS.

Maier, N.R.C.F., 1958
Industrial Psychology, Boston.

Maier, N.R.C.F., Solem, R., and Maier, A., 1969
Problem Solving, New York, London.

Mueller, D.C. (ed.), 1980
The Determinants and Effects of Merger. An International Comparison, Cambridge, Mass.: Oelgeschlager, Gunn & Hain.

Samhällsekonomisk utredning av strukturförändringar inom Svenskt Stål AB, Arbetslivscentrum, 1978:4, Stockholm.

Sternhufvud, U., 1978
»En beskrivande studie av en fusionsprocess - Tillkomsten av SSAB: Svenskt Stål AB», Arbetslivscentrum, 1978:12, Stockholm.

12. THE BIRTH PROCESS OF A NEW ORGANIZATION, THE CASE OF A JOINT VENTURE

R. Göran A. Andersson
Högskolan i Växjö
Företagsekonomiska institutionen
Växjö, Sweden

1. Introduction

1.1 The Birth Process

The birth process of a new organization is a very critical period in its life. The primary focal point of this study is the birth process of a joint venture. This is an area of increasing importance, since the number of joint venture agreements have risen rapidly in recent years (Edström & Gullander, 1975; Friedman & Beguin, 1971, p. VI; Gullander, 1975, pp. 46 ff; Rydén, 1971, pp. 65 ff).

Earlier studies in this field have mainly dealt with two decisions necessary for the birth and continued existence of a new organization: the selection of a comparative strategy and the selection of partners (Berg & Friedman, 1977; Gullander, 1975; Ibielski, 1974; Stopford & Wells, 1972; Tomlinson, 1970). Another question which has interested many researchers concerns the legal arrangements of a co-operative system (Ballon, 1967; Bivens & Lovell, 1966; CEPES, 1968; Friedman & Beguin, 1971; Gullander, 1975).

This study concentrates on the dynamic aspects of the birth process, i.e. the flow of activities, decisions and events, from the time when the joint venture idea is proposed to the point at which a working system is established. The main purpose is to describe and explain this introductory part of a joint venture process. This study is one of the first ones dealing with this phenomenon.

A few studies of birth processes of other organizations have been made. Researchers have, for instance, taken an interest in the creation of new small businesses and the concept of entrepreneurship. Many studies have dealt with the psychological and socio-economic background of entrepreneurs (Boswell, 1972; Litvak & Maule, 1973; Shapero, 1975; Stanworth & Curran, 1976; Wainer & Rubin, 1969).

Some studies have also been made of the birth process for new small firms. Susbauer (1975) has described the birth process in twelve sequential steps, and Watkins (1976) has developed an iterative model of six decision steps. The birth process of mergers has been similarly described in sequential steps (Rydén, 1971, p. 38; Starkweather, 1971, pp. 44 ff).

However, neither new small firms nor mergers can directly be compared to a joint venture, since both these kinds of organizations have a clear hierarchy and a decision making capability, which is not the case in a joint venture. Additionally, the models developed in these areas are usually based on the idea of rational decision making, which may be too simplified for the study of the birth process of a joint venture. Furthermore, the models of the birth of a new firm are in many cases normative. Many of them are not even based on studies of real processes. This means that it is not possible to draw concrete analogies to earlier studies of other birth processes.

1.2 Joint Venture between Small and Medium-Sized Firms

Joint Venture, JV, or joint organization is a kind of co-operation where the partners have joint ownership of resources (Aiken & Hage, 1968, pp. 913 ff). In a JV the agreement is formalized, and the partners are more or less bound by financial and legal commitments.

A JV can be regarded as a means for specific firms to implement a joint strategy. In a JV system there is no superior hierarchial level which controls the co-operating partners. This means that the formerly independent firms have to make certain decisions together and even have to carry out certain joint activities (Schermerhorn, 1975, p. 849). A JV is, therefore, a combination of independence in some functions, and joint decision making and action in other functions.

The JV process studied in this investigation involves small and mediumsized firms. One of the conclusions drawn from previous research is that small firms often need complementary resources (Neilsen, 1974; Small Firms, 1972). A JV means that the co-operating firms together acquire larger resources in the co-operation function. Therefore, a JV seems to be a particularly good strategy for small firms (Said, 1976), but the performance of co-operation activities can be very complicated and costly for these firms (Slipsager, 1967). A simple and common way of defining small and medium-sized firms is to give a limit on a size scale: those firms with less than 500 employees will be identified as such.

1.3 Research Methods

The lack of earlier studies of the birth process has largely been due to problems with methods. An investigation of such a process requires a longitudinal approach and preferably a real time data collection (Pettigrew, 1977; Schermerhorn , 1975, p. 855). The cross-sectional approach normally used has limited earlier investigations to studies of a small number of variables at one point in time.

In this study a combination of different methods has been used. Most resources have been spent on a longitudinal case study, in which four firms co-operated in the development and marketing of prefabricated Swedish wooden houses for export markets. Data collection in the case study consists of direct observations, interviews and document analysis.

In this case, the JV process began with the first meeting in July 1975, and it was closely observed from October 1975 until November 1978. Nearly all the meetings of the board have been attended. Many informal talks and interviews with all decision makers who were involved in this JV process were carried out.

The document analysis material consists of the annual reports of the firms, minutes of the proceedings, correspondence of the joint organization, etc. Much information has been recorded on tape - for example, interviews, and summaries from the meetings made by the researcher. The data recorded refers to facts, actions, atmosphere, attitudes and so on. It was thus possible later on in the research process to reproduce and re-analyse the collected data.

In this case study the researcher has acted mostly as a participant observer. Definitions of the problem, collections of data, and analysis and feedback of the results have been joint processes going on during the whole investigation. The method used can be regarded as theoretical sampling (Glaser & Strauss, 1967).

It has been very useful to follow an ongoing birth process of a JV in detail. This made it possible to understand and interpret decisions and activities in their historical context and to concentrate on the dynamic aspects of a JV process. The lack of earlier studies on ongoing birth processes means that the concepts and models presented are generated from the empirical data and the interpretation of this data (Glaser & Strauss, 1967, p. 12).

2. Background of the Joint Venture

2.1 The Market Situation for Swedish Firms in the Prefabricated Small Wooden House Industry

The construction of apartments in Sweden decreased from 1970 to 1976 by 75%. (All the data in part 2, unless otherwise stated, stem from official Swedish statistics). During the same time period the construction of prefabricated small wooden houses has increased by 10%. Since that time, competition in the Swedish small house market has increased even more, because some contractors of apartments have started to build small houses.

Many producers of prefabricated small houses have from time to time used just 50% or less of their production capacity. Their profitability has fluctuated tremendously during the 1970's. According to a governmental study of the long-term economic outlook, annual housing construction will either diminish or remain unchanged up to the year 1985 (SOU 1975:89).

As late as 1968, export were quite unimportant and constituted only 3% of all production in the industry. The export share of production rose to 11% during 1973, which meant an export value of 33 million (All amounts are given in US dollars). In 1974 and 1975 export decreased, but increased again in 1976.

Until 1973 the export markets were primarily Denmark and West Germany. New export markets arose in the Middle East when these countries' purchasing power increased with higher oil prices. Housing exports to the Middle East only amounted to 0,1% in 1973 but rose in 1975 to nearly 17% of the total export value. The 16 largest companies accounted for 81% of the total exports in 1973. Their share of the Swedish market was 61%. This indicates that it is chiefly the largest Swedish prefab firms which concentrate their marketing on exports (Starell & Lundell, 1975, p. 6).

Most of the prefab firms in Sweden are very small. Only 13 of the 129 firms in the industry have more than 200 employees. In 1975, the average number of employees per firm was 75.

It is thus apparent that conditions have changed rapidly for the prefab firms (Brodén, 1976, p. 13). The increased competition in the Swedish market and the decreased profitability have forced the firms to develop a greater interest in export activities. Some firms have also seen exports as a means to stabilize the fluctuating demand for production capacity.

2.2 Some Earlier Attempts to Co-operate in the Industry

The costs for marketing are very high for the prefab firms. Many of the small producers can work only in a local market. Export markets normally demand higher introduction costs than small firms can invest on their own. Some customers, for instance in the Middle East market, ask for tenders for big projects, thus excluding the single small firm from the competition because it cannot produce the quantity demanded. These are some of the reasons behind the attempts at co-operation in the industry (Andersson, 1978).

The most successful earlier JV was AB Svenska Trähus, which functioned from 1930 to 1968. This JV sold houses for the co-operating partners only on the Swedish market. In a few years it reached a market share of over 50%. The JV was dissolved when the market conditions changed during the 1960's.

The Swedish Timber House Export Association, STEX, was established in 1941 and aimed at co-ordinating exports to disaster areas. Exports were organized under a joint name for all the ten participating partners. STEX was closely connected to AB Svenska Trähus. During and after the war STEX sold a lot of basic houses mainly to European countries. The company was dissolved in 1965 because of administrative, economic and technical problems. The main reasons for breaking up the joint contract were:

1. that each participating firm had its own constructions and designs (lack of standardization) and

2. that it was very difficult to assign incoming orders to individual firms on an equitable basis.

An ambitious attempt was SWEBEX AB, which was initiated by the national Housing Department in November, 1970. 29 firms became members, 13 of which produced prefabricated houses, 7 were contractors, and 9 were component suppliers. SWEBEX was to provide marketing analyses, information, and public relations in the North European market. It was financed by an annual contribution of 2.000 per member. After three years it ceased operations because great differences of opinion had arisen between house producers and contractors.

MFT, a JV consisting of three firms, was another effort at co-operation in the field of exports. However, they failed to get enough orders. After three years the group was dissolved in 1964. Norrlandshus was yet another group of three firms with the same aims and development as MFT.

Thus, none of the earlier co-operative attempts in the industry were operative in 1975. The main motives for these early attempts at co-operation were to reduce costs and reach new markets by joint marketing. The failures were caused mainly by changed market conditions and internal control problems. Due to these failures, many people in the industry were rather disappointed and became suspicious of new JV proposals (Andersson, 1978).

2.3 AB Scandinavian FAST Building Systems (FAST)

Under these circumstances, AB Scandinavian FAST Building Systems (FAST) was established in 1975. FAST was set up by four legally and financially independent firms (Aneby Industrier AB, Fribohus AB, Smålands-Hus AB and Toringe-Hus AB), each of which received 25% of the shares. The size and profile of the firms are shown in figure 12.1. The presentation of the partners in this section deals with the situation from the establishment of the JV in 1975.

The aim of FAST was to develop and market small wooden houses in the Middle East. The four owner planned to produce the jointly developed house in their separate factories in Sweden, thereby employing their unutilized capacities. At a later stage the owners also discussed markets outside the Middle East.

Aneby-Hys AB is a company which produces and markets prefab houses in the Aneby Industrier AB Corporation, which also owns a company in Norway producing about 500 houses per year for the Norwegian market. The corporation also runs sawmills, transport facilities and some forest areas. AB Aneby Industrier is the only member of the JV in which the manager, Mr. Erik Engström (EE), is not also the owner. EE is 43 years old and has worked in the industry for 20 years in different positions and with different companies. He also has previous experience in exporting wooden houses.

Firm	Turnover 1975 Million $		Average number of employees in 1975		Number of delivered houses in 1975
	Total	Export	Total	Production	Total
Aneby Industrier AB	23	1.1	410	163	875
Fribohus	7	0.05	126	42	350
Smålands-Hus AB	4	0.1	60	42	250
Toringe-Hus	3	1.9	51	36	425

Figure 12.1 The four partners in FAST.

Fribohus AB had economic problems in the early part of 1975, when the present owner, Kurt Thorsson (KT), took over. When FAST was established, KT owned 40% of the shares in Fribohus. He is 43 years old and had earlier worked with sawmills and exports of wooden products.

Smålands-Hus AB belongs to a bigger enterprise group named Storcks Industrier AB, which is fully owned and managed by Jan Storck (JS). The turnover of the group was about $ 9 million in 1975, and the export share was about 10%. The group also owns forest areas. Jan Storck is 36 years old an belongs to the third generation of owner-managers in the group. He took over in July 1974 and bought AB Smålands-hus in May 1975.

In contrast to the others, Toringe-Hus AB produces only houses for non-permanent residence, used mainly in vacation areas. Production methods, however, differ very little between permanent and non-permanent houses. Toringe-Hus, with its export share of 65%, has the biggest export market of the members. The main recipient countries are Denmark and Japan. Export to Japan comprised about 20% of production in 1975. The owner-manager, Per-Inge Johansson (PIJ), is 45 years old. He started Toringe-Hus together with his father in 1959.

All four firms are either small or medium-sized producers of prefab wooden houses, whose market aims at the private, individual house owner. Production lines and machinery are similar. Not one of the four firms was utilizing its full production capacity when FAST was established.

All the managers had some experience in exports, but only Toringe-Hus had an export market of any significant size. The profits and the debt-equity ratio differed a great deal among the firms during 1970-76. Fribohus and Toringe-Hus had lower profits and a higher debt-equity ratio than the industry average, while the other two had better values than the average.

2.4 Brief Diary of the Joint Venture Process under Study

May 1975	A government official suggested that Aneby Industrier and Fribohus should co-operate in export for the Middle East area.
July 1975	Smålands-Hus and Toringe-Hus were invited to participate, and they accepted.
Dec. 1975	A market investigation of Iran was finished.
Jan.-Sept. 1976	Product development. A test house was erected in Sweden.
April 1976	The Swedish government granted 112,000, 50% of the estimated costs for the product development.
Nov. 1976	Storcks Industrier, owner of Smålands-Hus, bought all the shares in Toringe-Hus.
Dec. 1976	Fribohus left the JV. In February 1977 Fribohus had great economic problems and stopped all payments.
Jan.-April 1977	A second test house was erected in Sweden.
April-Dec. 1977	Mainly preparation for marketing. Agreement with a local contractor in Saudi Arabia.
Febr. 1978	An exhibit house was erected in Riyadh, Saudi Arabia.
March-Sept. 1978	Marketing activities. The demand in Saudi Arabia decreased dramatically during 1978.
Oct. 1978	The partners decided not to commit any more resources to the JV, FAST, until the market conditions would improve.

3. The Birth of a Joint Venture

3.1 Sequential Phases in the Introduction of a Joint Venture Process

The birth process can be analysed in many ways. The normal method of analysing developments over time is to try to find a sequence of phases in the

275

given process. Most investigations and analyses of longer processes normally result in a description of parts sequential in time, which form phases in the whole process. This confirms the fact that time is of central importance in understanding processes. This type of division into phases is used here as one method of analysis.

Such a division is made by selecting important changes which have taken place in the JV process, for example, an important decision made by the JV system, or an important result achieved. These changes delineate phases in which decisions and activities in the phase are as homogeneous and as distinct as possible. In spite of this, some of the phases partly overlap, which is necessary for getting a homogeneous content in each phase. *The JV process* begins when the idea of co-operation is conceived, and it continues until a working JV system has been established. In other words, feedback has been received and adaptation has been made in response to the first main activity in the co-operation process.

In the case study the main activity was to export small houses. This point has not yet been reached by FAST, and thus the JV process is still in its introductory period.

The duration of the introductory period can vary extensively from case to case (Rydén, 1971, p. 37). While a period of one to two years seems common (CEPES, 1968, pp. 55 ff; Gullander, 1975, p. 199), there are cases in which a much longer time period is necessary. The total introductory period has been divided here into five different and sequential phases:

1.   The idea phase

2.   The establishing phase

3.   The system development phase

4.   The internal evaluation phase

5.   The external evaluation phase

The first phase in the introduction is *the idea phase,* which extends from the time when the idea is conceived until an agreement has been reached to establish a JV system. This phase involves the first contacts, judgements of the business idea, selection of partners, and negotiations between the presumtive partners - all of which leads to the decision whether or not to enter into a co-operation agreement. In this phase it is rather usual that a »marriage broker» plays an important role (Benson, 1975, p. 248).

In the case study the idea was presented at an export seminar in May 1975 by an external government official, who also indicated the possibilities for governmental support. The idea appealed to the participants from Fribohus and Aneby Industrier. They gathered together for further discussions in Aneby after the seminar.

An informal meeting was held at Fribohus two weeks later. At this meeting the participants discussed, among other things, 7 criteria for choice of partners. It was decided to invite representatives from Smålands-Hus and Toringe-Hus to negotiations. These negotiations led to an agreement to start a JV project in July 1975. Because of some practical difficulties, however, the formal official company was not established until January 1976. In any case, this phase can be said to have ended in July 1975 after one and a half month, when the agreement was reached to proceed with plans.

As a principle of co-operation it was agreed that contributions and actual orders should be divided according to the stated production capacities. This meant that Aneby Industrier and Fribohus should get one third each, and that Smålands-Hus and Toringe-Hus should get one sixth each of the expected orders.

The second, *establishing phase* is characterised by the search for information, both externally and internally. During this phase the business idea is defined and delineated, but the members do not make very many other important decisions.

The activities in this phase create a commitment of identification among the partners. The commitment increases in the following phases. This commitment is necessary for the survival of the JV (Thompson and McEwen, 1958, p. 28. For a discussion of the commitment concept see Buchanan, 1974; Sheldon, 1971, and Steers, 1977). At the same time the identy of the JV system is built up. The roles and »rules of the game» gradually develop both within the co-operating system and between the system and its environment (Butler et al., 1974).

It is the »social» activities of this phase which most often overlap with the other phases of the process. They appear most frequently from the time of the original agreement until the concrete system begins to develop. When the business idea is quite clear and when the partners know each other very well, the establishing phase can be very short.

In the case of FAST, this phase began with some rather informal board meetings where the people involved met and got acquainted. During the latter part of this phase, the meetings became more formalized. At the same time, members of the board made policy decisions for FAST and some practical actions were performed, such as writing down partnership by-laws, establish bank contacts, contributing the share capital, and so on. In contrast to the earlier agreement concerning orders, the share capital was divided into four equal parts. The total share capital was 12,000.

It was during this phase that a market investigation of Iran was made, partly financed by a grant of U.S. dollar 10,000 from STU (Swedish Board for Technical Development, a government agency). This and the following grants from STU must be paid back if and when the project makes a profit. The market investigation advised against activities in Iran because of the particularly competitive market there, and recommended Saudi Arabia as a possible alternative.

Some members of the board also gained experience of their own through travel in the Middle East area, and later in the process Saudi Arabia was treated as a prime market for FAST. The establishing phase ended after six months, when the market investigation was presented in December, 1977.

The system development phase marks the concrete development of a system which can realize the business goals. This phase involves a »gearing up» of the process, and leads the partners to a much stronger commitment than earlier phases. The exploratory process of the earlier phases is now transformed into more systematic goal-oriented activities, which demand considerable investments.

A management organization can now be identified, which uses some rules and norms, and which controls the system. The economic and technical contributions from the partners become more clearly defined in terms of goals and time-schedules.

In our case, FAST started the technical development of a house adapted to the Middle East market. An architect was engaged as product developer, and a technical reference group was created. This group was made up of one member from each firm and it met approximately once a week during the first half of 1976.

A very noticeable change in the process occurred when the first blueprints of the test house were presented. Because there was now a concrete project to discuss, activities and involvement of the members increased considerably. During the phase there were many discussions, decisions, and activities dealing with technical and practical questions. An application was made to STU, and FAST received 112,000 for product development. This was 50% of the estimated costs for the project.

In March, 1976, Storcks Industrier, owner of Smålands-Hus, sold 25 houses to an old customer in Saudi Arabia. The partners had decided at the outset that tenders which had been carried over should be finished by the individual firms. This deal did upset at least one board member. As a consequence the problems of drawing boundaries between the JV and its individual partners were discussed.

The board also decided to progress very cautiously on any business projects proposed through international business agents. They felt that many of these projects were not serious, and that it demanded too many resources to investigate all of them. The main strategy for the board at this time was to develop and market their own house. The first system development phase continued for nine months. During this time a test house was erected in Sweden in September, 1976.

In the fourth phase, *the internal evaluation phase,* an internal evaluation of the existing system takes place. Adjustments are made, and the subsequent development is planned. This sometimes rather short period of evaluation is treated as a separate phase because it seems to be a particularly critical element in the birth process. Indeed, this evaluation may question the practicability of the joint business venture.

The system development phase and the internal evaluation phase are interconnected in a trial and error process. The feedback from the evaluation directs the ensuing work on the system development. This loop can make several turns before the system development at last is accepted internally.

In FAST's case, the first real internal evaluation took place when the first test house was built. Several board members were disappointed in the quality of the test house and initiated a discussion of long and short term goals of FAST. In spite of this undercurrent of dissatisfaction, it was decided to formalize the organization and engage S. Richtér of Aneby-Hus, as half-time director for FAST.

An external event important to the JV process during this phase was that Storcks Industrier, owner of Smålands-Hus, bought all the shares in Toringe-Hus. This meant that Storcks Industrier now owned 50% of the shares of FAST and had one third of the delivery rights. After some highly emotional board meetings, Fribohus decided to leave FAST. Their shares were bought by Aneby Industrier. The outcome was, that from this point on FAST consisted of two partners equal in both ownership and delivery rights.

These problems took some time and effort to solve. A new system development phase started shortly after the solution was reached in December, 1976. The first internal evaluation phase continued for three months.

The second system development phase proceeded without any complications. It involved development and erection of a new test house in Sweden and the establishment of some marketing activities, such as contacts with potential customers and development of a sales catalogue and other sales material. This phase ended after four months, when the new test house was finished.

The second internal evaluation phase involved an approval of the system development in the preceding phase. The two remaining partners decided to offer S. Richtér a full-time position from the first of June 1977. He accepted the offer. This can be regarded as the end of this phase, which lasted for just one month.

The third system development phase in our case study comprised the erection of an exhibit house in Riyadh, Saudi-Arabia, and the development of a local marketing system for FAST. An agreement was reached with »Saudico», a contractor in Saudi Arabia, making him the local partner of FAST in the future. He will sell and assemble their houses in Saudi Arabia. After some difficulties, the test house was erected in February, 1978. This marked the end of this phase of altogether nine months.

FAST had financial problems during this phase and the two following ones. The total expended costs for the project up to the end of 1977 was 350,000. STU had granted 122,000 of this amount. One of the partners, Storcks Industrier, also had internal difficulties. In October 1977 this firm submitted a bankruptcy petition to their new daughter company, Toringe-Hus. These problems were said to be caused by a reduction in demand from customers in foreign countries. The financial problems consequentlyly emerging for FAST were considered at several special crisis meetings during these phases.

The third internal evaluation phase was just a check point in the case study. The new house in Riyadh was approved, and the partners decided to continue the project in stages.

In the following *external evaluation phase* the project proposal and the developed system are tested against the business environment. When the product has been selected, feedbacks received, and adaptations made, the introductory segment of the JV process is considered to be finished. A working JV system has been developed. Just as for the internal evaluation, this external evaluation phase can involve a trial and error process with many loops. This phase can also be the input for a new internal evaluation, and thereafter input for further work on system development.

In our study this phase began when the house in Riyadh was completed. During the spring and summer of 1978, FAST had continuing difficulties in meeting its payments. So did Storcks Industrier, and they delayed their payments to FAST from time to time. The financial problems in Storcks Industrier led to an engagement of a new part-owner in that group. The earlier sole owner, J. Storck, sold 50% of his shares to R. Ottosson in September, 1978.

FAST applied for additional grants from STU and received 33,000 in April, 1978. From that time FAST followed an extremely low-cost budget. For example, the office was closed and the managing director, S. Richtér, returned to working part-time for Aneby-Hus. The marketing in Saudi Arabia was carried out by agents of the local partner, Saudico. However, they did not succeed in selling one single house during 1978. Indeed, the demand for prefab houses in Saudi Arabia had decreased dramatically during this year. The total Swedish export in 1978 of prefab houses to this contry was less than 20% of the exports to Saudi Arabia during 1977. Foreign competitors on the Saudi market made similar experience.

The reason for this drastic drop in demand seemed to be a decrease in the economic activity in Saudi Arabia. This decrease was a result of a lower export of oil than expected and of inflation. It implied reduced construction activities. The decrease also meant that many foreign firms took personnel out of Saudi Arabia, and many existing small wooden houses were offered on the market. Yet another challenge was a drastic increase of the market share of small concrete prefab houses, at the expense of wooden prefabs.

When the JV did not succeed a *fourth internal evaluation phase* took place. In November 1978 the partners decided to let the JV be idle until market conditions improved in Saudi Arabia. They also decided to market the jointly developed house separately in markets outside the Middle East. The manager of the JV, S. Richtér, returned to his earlier full-time occupation in Aneby-Hus. This phase also ended the intensive real-time data collection of this case study. The entire sequence of phases is illustrated in figure 12.2.

In this brief structured presentation of the case, it has only been possible to include a small number of all observations and data. A total of 19 formal board meetings took place. The time for each meeting varied between 2 and 6 hours. They have mainly been held in a friendly and relaxed atmosphere. Additionally, decisions have been made at shareholders' meetings, at more informal meetings, and at meetings of the technical reference group.

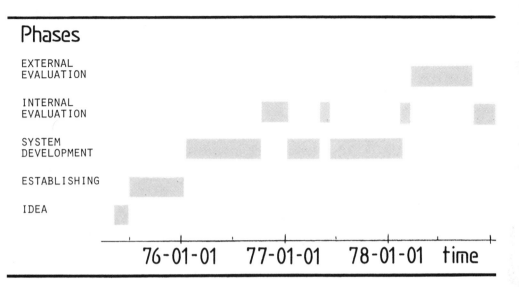

Phases

EXTERNAL
EVALUATION

INTERNAL
EVALUATION

SYSTEM
DEVELOPMENT

ESTABLISHING

IDEA

76-01-01   77-01-01   78-01-01   time

Figure 12.2 The sequential phases in the birth process of FAST.

The case study does not comprise a number of »Side activities» as many discussions of temporary business projects, particularly outside the Middle East area; technical product development problems; practical administrative questions; and several trips, both inside Europe and to the Middle East.

3.2 Parallel Processes in the Introduction of a Joint Venture

In interviews with decision maker involved in co-operation cases, many researchers have noticed that such a process has many facets. Within the same process there will be conflicting as well as joint interests (Butler et al., 1974, p. 5; Guetzkow, 1966, p. 38; Litwak & Hylton, 1962, p. 399).

Because the method employed made detailed observations possible, we were able to study this characteristic in depth. During many of the board meetings and other activities, the work proceeded in such a harmonious way that neither the participants nor an outside observer would notice that the group consisted of participants from four independent firms. Nearly all the activities in the work on product development and technical solutions proceeded in this manner.

281

In contrast, those activities initiated by critical events or decisions in the process were characterized by hidden conflicts brought to the surface. This was the FAST case when the ownership changed structure, when Storcks Industrier bought Toringe-Hus. Together with a disappointment in the progress of the project, this change induced Fribohus to leave FAST.

The entire process can be regarded as a number of individual parallel processes, where each process can be of different importance for the total process at a particular moment. Those parallel processes with the highest degreee of potential conflict seem to be latent for the longest time. They are only brought to surface in critical situations.

The total JV process has here been divided hierarchically into three parallel processes. The criterion for the division is the degree to which the partners' individual goals are involved in the process. Each parallel process gives an outcome. The different processes are related to each other as illustrated in figure 12.3 below. The three processes, ordered from low to high involvement of individual goals, are:

1. The task process

2. The strategy development process

3. The distribution process

The least complicated process in the hierarchy is *the task process*. This mode consists of all those decisions and activities aimed at fulfilling the joint goals of the JV. The content of the task process depends on the business aims of the JV and can vary extensively from case to case. The outcome of this process can be measured in terms of costs and benefits, i.e. economic result.

In our case study this involved activities such as market investigations, product development, construction of test houses, the development of a catalogue, the creation of a net of contacts, internal management, administration etc.

The next process in the hierarchy is *the strategy development process*. Here, the choice of products for each market and the manner in which the system is to work internally and externally are developed and confirmed. The business aims are determined, and the means available to the JV system are established. In this process the partners may have opposing interests depending on internal conditions. They may assess opportunities and obstacles in the environment in different ways.

Cyert and March outline three major methods in which the objectives of a coalition are determined (Cyert & March, 1963, pp. 29 ff); a bargaining process, an internal organizational control process and a process of adjustment to experience. These three approaches can also explain how the goals of a JV are determined for the co-operation system.

However, when a new organization enters the market, there exists no earlier experience. The internal control process is not yet developed. Because of this, their development of goals differs from that in a functioning organization (Ibid, p. 33; Simon, 1953). The first development of objectives in a JV process seems therefore to involve a great deal of negotiations and bargaining. The outcome of this process are established goals and means of the JV system, which in turn control how the system is to be managed.

In this case study, strategy development questions were particularly intensive at the outset and when offers from international business agents were discussed. In these discussions several board members maintained that independent agents could be useful in regard to connections with customers. Other board members believed that such agents just wanted money, preferably in advance, and asserted that they would be of no help at all. These different opinions were based among other things, on differences in attitudes to single orders. The two financially weak companies were most interested in fast, single orders. The other two companies argued instead for long term export activities. During the planning of the product development and from time to time in shorter discussions, strategy development activities also took place.

The examples demonstrate the type of negotiations which can take place during parallel processes. Indeed, introduction of the JV process consists, to a great extent, in seeking and considering a unified strategy for partners with sometimes similar, sometimes dissimilar goals.

The third and last parallel process is *the distribution process*. This involves those elements which are most closely related to the individual goals - for example, how ownership, power, and results should be divided among the partners as well as between the partners and the joint organization.

The outcome of the distribution process is a distribution norm (a division of ownership and power) and rules for how to change this norm. Articles of partnership and decisions at shareholders' meetings are documents which indicate these distribution norms. This process also determines how the result of the activities should be divided among the partners, and between the partners and the joint organization.

In our case, the distribution process was latent during the main part of the total introduction period. However, some members were disappointed with the results of the first distribution norms. Individual members expressed opinions such as »something must be done about this», »let's wait and see», and »the first agreement ought to be permanent». Negotiations about the distribution norms took place openly on only two occasions, the first at the beginning and the second when Fribohus left the system. After the new situation developed in December 1976, when just two equal partners remained, there were also a few more limited discussions about personnel and material contributions to the JV.

Figure 12.3 shows these parallel processes, their outcomes, and their main interrelations.

In contrast to the strategy process, the distribution process is mainly concerned with dividing a fixed amount, for example, 100 %, of ownership. This concern, together with the close relationship of this process to the individual goals, makes strategy development the most crucial part of the progress and survival of the JV. In this process the goals and means of the JV are discussed and confirmed. This outcome provides the framework within which the

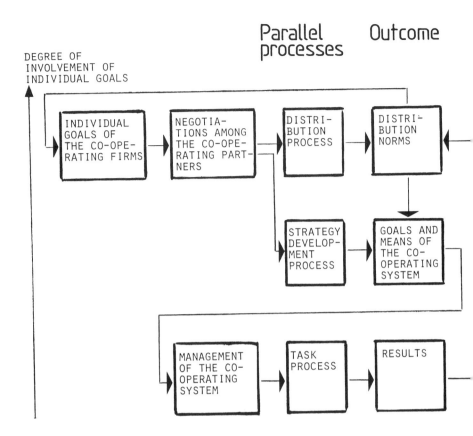

Parallel processes | Outcome

DEGREE OF
INVOLVEMENT OF
INDIVIDUAL GOALS

INDIVIDUAL GOALS OF THE CO-OPE-RATING FIRMS

NEGOTIA-TIONS AMONG THE CO-OPE-RATING PART-NERS

DISTRI-BUTION PROCESS

DISTRI-BUTION NORMS

STRATEGY DEVELOP-MENT PROCESS

GOALS AND MEANS OF THE CO-OPERATING SYSTEM

MANAGEMENT OF THE CO-OPERATING SYSTEM

TASK PROCESS

RESULTS

Figure 12.3 Parallel processes in the introduction of a JV.

management of the JV can perform the task process, whose outcome is distributed in accordance with the distribution norms. It is clear that the three parallel processes are clearly integrated.

In the two higher processes there may be conflicting interests due to differences in the partners' individual goals, differences in their access to resources, and constraints on each partner's ability to act. The usual way to treat such conflicting interests during the birth process of a JV is bargaining. Later on in the process, when rules for conflict resolution have been developed, the elements of bargaining decrease in number and importance.

4. Discussion

Two models of the introduction of a JV process have been generated, mainly from a longitudinal case study. Besides this real-time data collection from an ongoing process, the birth of JV has been examined in historical studies of other cases, and in interviews with experts. The first of the two models generated divides the birth process into five sequential phases. The second model divides the process into three parallel processes. In this final section some tentative conclusions regarding these models are discussed.

The two models are considered to be general. Every birth process of a JV, which is not interrupted during the introductions, seems to include elements from all five sequential phases and all the parallel processes. The number and length of each sequential phase may, however, differ greatly from case to case.

The sequential phases and the parallel processes are related in several ways. For instance, the activities in one of the processes seem to be more common in one particular phase than in another. The most important relations are noted in figure 12.4.

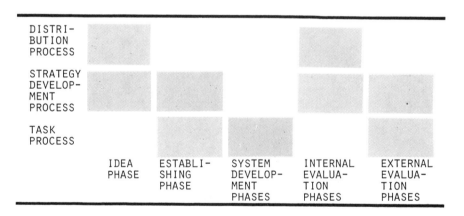

Figure 12.4 Relations between sequential phases and parallel processes.

The distribution problems must always be discussed before a co-operation agreement can be reached. Later, this process can be activated at any time. During the internal valuation phase, the achievements up to that phase are assessed. In this judgement even the distribution norms may be put into question.

In this case, the partners reached a preliminary agreement during the idea phase, which then was changed and made more precise during the establishing phase. The distribution norms were again more actively and openly discussed and evaluated during the first internal valuation phase. In this case the changed ownership of FAST was a factor causing the onset of the latent distribution process.

The strategy development process can be more or less active during the whole introduction. It is actually the very first activity, and it starts the idea phase. This process is latent only when the task activities are dominant during the system development phase.

Because the task process involves the activities related to those decisions made in the strategy development process, these two processes are highly interrelated. The task process normally dominates the system development phases.

Such was the case in FAST. In the first system development phase the reference group was active and met frequently. The test house was built, and there were many trips and activities for internal control. In the same way, the task process dominated the subsequent system development phases. Task activities also played a role in all the other phases as well; in other words, the decisions made were carried out. In the establishing phase, for instance, the main task activity performed was the market investigation.

Events external to the JV process can affect the focus and acitivities of particular parallel processes. Critical events, outcomes, and decisions inside the process can also shift the focus from one parallel process to another. It seems generally true that a critical event in an earlier process can give rise to activities in a later parallel process.

In our case, for example, the distribution process came to the fore as a result of the change in ownership of FAST. Different opinions on how to perform task activities activated the strategy development process. This process was also set in motion by external discussions, for instance when members of the co-operating system had been in contact with possible customers and other individuals in the environment.

The most critical process is the distribution process. Unsolved problems in this area can destroy an otherwise successful JV when a critical situation appears. The distribution norms will be evaluated by the partners when they are to be put into practice.

In the establishing phase and the system development phases, commitment grows among the partners, a commitment which is required for success in a JV. The greater the commitment is, the greater the number of difficulties and pressures the JV can withstand. Therefore, it is important that commitment is established and developed as early as possible.

During the establishing phase the partners begin to identify with the JV. If the partners themselves perform activities later in the process, they develop commitment by involvement. System development normally demands commitment by involvement. System development normally demands commitment by investments. These three methods illustrate possible approaches to the establishment of commitment to the JV.

In the case of FAST, not all the participants had met before the JV was formed. This meant that they needed a good deal of time to get to know each other and to develop a commitment of identification with the JV. In a case where the partners know each other very well before the formation of the JV, the establishing phase will probably be shorter and will be concerned only with the new situation itself and not with the establishment of trust between the partners.

The partners in FAST acted in the first phases in a manner which built up commitment and identification. They did not stress their conflicting interests. In contrast, the commitment by involvement did not develop as positively as expected. None of the partners could regard FAST as his sole occupation. Besides, some activities were performed by external agents. The market investigation, for instance, was conducted by a consulting firm. This lack of internal involvement resulted in passive and slow development. The internally performed task activities are particularly important when it comes to building up the co-operation system, for example its resources, control systems and experience.

In other cases, the task process can consist of joint purchasing, joint logistics, joint sales trips and so on. All these joint activities require different system development approaches. The product development in FAST may seem rather complicated when compared with other joint activities, and this may be one explanation for the large amount of time spent on system development in this case.

Through co-operation with larger firms possessing more resources, it is possible that a system development phase can be expedited. Larger firms are usually capable of greater investments in analysis and examination of high risk projects and do not have to be as careful as the firms in this case. The fact that larger firms have access to many forms of personal skills may also make them less disposed to hire external experts system development assignments.

The control of FAST was not transferred from the board to the manager until rather late, and then only successively, after the main questions of strategy development had been solved. In a case where the strategic difficulties are smaller, the manager would probably assume control earlier. This would presumably facilitiate the process.

One of the more significant factors in the birth process of FAST was support from the government agencies, both as »marriage broker» and as financier. It must once again be noted that the financial support must be paid back if and when the project makes a profit.

This official support initiated the entire process and pulled it into the system development phase, but it also caused the system to try to use as much as possible of that help. That led to periods of passivity on the part of the members themselves and to delays in the process. If the partners had financed the JV on their own, it is possible that they would have pursued the project more energetically, if at all.

It is probable that government support is likely to increase the number of JV cases started, but it is also possible that government support can cause the JV's to be passive and intermittently inefficient.

In the opinion of one board member, there was only one situation in which the presence of the researcher could have influenced the process, and that was during the discussion of their relationship with STU. (It is possible that some members of the board were somewhat worried about officially declaring that they would like as much support as possible from STU.) In other unofficial and more personal conversations much »off the record material» was given to the researcher, both from the board as a group and from its individual members.

The models developed for the introduction of a JV process have not yet been tested systematically against a random choice of JV cases. The tests performed are of less significant value. One test was to compare the researcher's interpretation with the involved board members' private independent experience of the process. A case-internal longitudinal test was also performed by using the earlier mentioned recoded tapes in later phases of the process. These tests have made new and better interpretations possible.

External validity tests have been performed in two ways. First, results have been discussed with other researchers in this field, and with persons who have been or are involved in co-operation processes. Second, the knowledge generated from this case has been compared with knowledge acquired in the researcher's earlier studies of co-operation cases (Andersson et al., 1976). These tests seem to give credence to the concepts, models and statements which have been presented here as a conceptual basis for understanding the introduction of a JV process.

5. References

Aiken, M. and Hage, J., 1968
»Organizational Interdependence and Interorganizational Structure». *American Sociological Review, Vol 63, 912-930.*

Andersson, R.G.A., et al., 1976
»Regional samverkan inom materialförsörjning och fysisk distribution.» *STU, slutrapport 74-3146.* Företagsekonomiska institutionen, Högskolan i Växjö.

Andersson, R.G.A., 1978
Samverkan mellan småföretag. Avhandlingsutkast. Institutionen för ekonomi och administration, Högskolan i Växjö.

Ballon, R.J., (ed), 1967
Joint Ventures and Japan, Tokyo: Sophia University.

Benson, J.K., 1975
»The interorganizational Network as a Political Economy.»
Administrative Science Quarterly, Vol. 20, 229-249.

Berg, S.U. and Friedman, P., 1977
»Joint Ventures, Competition and Technological Complementarities; Evidence from Chemicals.» *Southern Economic Journal,* Vol. 43, No. 3, 1330-1337.

Bivens, K. and Lovell, E., 1966
Joint Ventures with Foreign Partners. National Industrial Conference Board, New York.

Boswell, J.S., 1972
The Rise and Decline of Small Firms. Plymouth: George Allen & Unwin.

Brodén, P., 1976
Turbulence and Organizational Change. Department of Management and Economics, Linköpings University, Linköping.

Buchanan, B., 1974
»Building Organizational Commitment: The Socialization of Managers in Work Organizations.» *Administrative Science Quarterly,* Vol. 19, 533-546.

Butler, R.J., Hickson, D.J., and McCullough, A.E., 1974
»Power in the Organization Coalition.» Internal paper, University of Bradford.

CEPES, 1968
Grenzüberschreitende Unternehmenskooperation in der EWG. Stuttgart.

Cyert, R.M. and March, J.G., 1963
A Behavioral Theory of the Firm. Englewood Cliffs, N.J.: Prentice Hall.

Edström, A. and Gullander, S., 1975
»Co-operation Agreements in Swedish Industry 1963-72.» University of Gothenburg, Department of Business Administration, *Research Report, 1975-38.*

Friedmann, W.G. and Beguin, J.-P., 1971
Joint International Business Ventures in Developing Countries. New York: Columbia University Press.

Glaser, B.G. and Strauss, A.L., 1967
The Discovery of Grounded Theory: Strategies for Qualitative Research. Chicago: Aldine Publishing Company.

Gueztkow, H., 1966
»Relation among Organizations.» In R. Bowers (ed). *Studies on Behavior in Organizations,* University of Georgia Press, 13-44.

Gullander, S.O.O., 1975
 An Exploratory Study of Inter-Firm Co-operation of Swedish Firms. Ph.d. thesis Columbia University, New York.

Ibielski, D., 1974
 »Managing the Smaller Firm in Times of Change.» Paper presented at the Fourth International Small Business Seminar, September 6-8, Oslo, Norway.

Litvak, I.A. and Maule, C.J., 1973
 »Some Characteristics of Successful Technical Entrepreneurs in Canada.» *IEEE Transactions on Engineering Management,* Vol EM-20, No 3, 62-68.

Litwak, E. and Hylton, L.F., 1962
 »Inter-Organizational Analysis: A Hypothesis in Co-ordinating Agencies.» *Administrative Science Quarterly,* Vol. 7, 395-420.

Neilsen, E.H., 1974
 »Contingency Theory Applied to Small Business Organizations.» *Human Relations,* Vol. 27, No 4, 357-379.

Pettigrew, A.M., 1977
 »The Creation of Organizational Cultures.» *EIASM Working paper 77-11,* Bryssel.

Rydén, B. 1971
 Fusioner i svensk industri. Stockholm: IUI.

Said, K.E., 1976
 »The Industrial Coalition of Small Firms - Key to Small Business Survival?» *Journal of Small Business Management,* Vol. 14, No. 3, 6-11.

Schermerhorn, J.R., Jr., 1975
 Determinants of Interorganizational Co-operation.» *Academy of Management Journal,* Vol. 18, 846-856.

Shapero, A., 1975
 »Entrepreneurship and Economic Development.» Paper presented at International Symposium on Entrepreneurship and Enterprise Development, Ohio, USA.

Sheldon, M.E., 1971
 »Investments and Involvments Mechanisms Producing Commitment to the Organization.» *Administrative Science Quarterly,* Vol. 6, 143-150.

Simon, H.A., 1953
 »Birth of an Organization: The Economic Co-operation Administration.» *Public Administration Review,* Vol. 13, 227-236.

Slipsager, F., 1967
Eksportsamarbejde mellen industrivirksomheder, Copenhagen: Einar Harcks Forlag.

Small Firms, 1972
Report of the Committee of Inquiry on Small Firms. Chairman J.E. Bolton, Her Majesty's Stationary Office, London.

SOU 1975:89,
Långtidsutredningen 1975. Stockholm: Liber.

Stanworth, M.J.K. and Curran, J., 1976
»Growth and the Small Firm - An Alternative View.» *Journal of Management Studies,* No. 2, 95-110.

Starell, L. and Lundell, P., 1975
Prissättningen på monteringsfärdiga trähus. Statens Pris- och Kartellnämnd, Dnr B I:2/74.

Starkweather, D.B., 1971
Health Facility Merger and Integration: A Typology and Some Hypotheses.» In White, P.E. and Vlasak, G.J., (eds.), 1971, *Interorganizational Research in Health.* Conference Proceedings, Washington D.C.,: U.S. Government Printing Office O-421-532.

Steers, R.M., 1977
»Antecedents and Outcomes of Organizational Commitment.» *Administrative Science Quarterly,* Vol. 22, 46-56.

Stopford, J. and Wells, L., 1972
Managing the Multinational Enterprise - Organization of the Firm and Ownership of the Subsidiaries. New York: Basic Books.

Susbauer, J.C., 1975
»Nyföretagarens olika skeden.» *Refererad i Ekonomen* nr 8, 13-15.

Thompson, J.D. and McEwen, W.J., 1958
»Organizational Goals and Environment: Goal Setting as an Interaction Process.» *American Sociological Review, Vol. 23, 23-31.*

Tomlinson, J.W.C., 1970
The Joint Venture Process in International Business. Cambridge, Mass.: MIT Press.

Wainer, H.A. and Rubin, I.M., 1969
»Motivation of Research and Development Entrepreneurs. Determinants of Company Success.» *Journal of Applied Psychology,* Vol. 53, 178-184.

Watkins, D.S., 1976
»Entry into Independent Entrepreneurship: Toward a Model of the Business Initiation Process.» Paper presented at EIASM seminar in Copenhagen.

13. THE IMPACT OF CORPORATE MERGERS ON INDUSTRIAL AND LABOR RELATIONS

Howard Aldrich and Clare P. Sproule
New York State School of Industrial and Labor Relations,
Cornell University
and International Institute of Management, Science Center, Berlin [1]

1. Introduction

Mergers have been an active corporate strategy in the U.S. for almost a century, but conglomerate-type mergers represent a more recent development. This new organizational form is often alleged to have eroded union power and disrupted the industrial relations process. This chapter examines the organizational-level consequences of mergers, focusing on the role that industrial relations issues play in the merger process. We review changing patterns of merger activity since the 1880's, describing the legal and organizational context within which mergers occur. After identifying some consequences claimed to result from mergers, we test these claims against results from a small survey of corporations involved in mergers or acquisitions. We show that mergers and acquisitions made very little difference to the industrial relations and collective bargaining processes of the surveyed firms.

Mergers, joint ventures, and acquisitions are forms of interorganizational relations arising from the dynamic interplay of environmental constraints and organizational strategies. Interorganizational arrangements may be strategies for coping with uncertainty and avoiding dependence, but they may also reflect the imposition of powerful external actors' logics of action (Aldrich, 1979, Chapter 11). Mergers are often motivated by diverse considerations and the complexity of the merger process produces many unforeseen consequences. Most explanations of merger activity focus on motives (and consequences) concerning capital and product markets. Rarely have investigations focused on labor market considerations, a curious omission when viewed against the background of the labor-management conflicts characterizing our industrial era. »Industrial relations», as a corporate activity and academic subfield, arose in the context of large firms' efforts to cope with labor as a problem in the early decades of this century (Bendix, 1949; Edwards, 1979). We would thus expect industrial relations and collective bargaining issues to be taken into account by persons involved in merger activity, but little research has focused on this expectation.

[1] We wish to thank Tom Kochan and Michael Gold for their advice at various points in this research.

This chapter examines the organizational-level consequences of mergers, focusing on the role that industrial relations issues play in the merger process. After reviewing the changing pattern of mergers during the past 75 years, we examine the legal and organizational context within which mergers occur. Industrial relations problem areas that have been identified by previous investigators are discussed. These speculations are examined more closely through examining results obtained from a pilot survey of corporations involved in mergers in 1975 and 1976. To anticipate our major findings, we˙show that mergers have had surprisingly little impact on industrial relations departments and other aspects of the collective bargaining process.

2. A Historical Overview of Merger Patterns

Although the number of mergers is small in absolute terms, compared to other forms of interorganizational activities, mergers have had a major impact on the distribution of assets and market power in the population of business organizations (Aldrich and Mueller, 1981). A massive wave of mergers toward the end of the 19th and beginning of the 20th centuries substantially altered market structures in England and the United States. Another wave of mergers after World War II, continuing into the 1970s, created a new form of organization - the conglomerate - and contributed to the increasing concentration of corporate assets in the hands of the largest firms.

Three great waves of merger activity have swept the United States in the past century: An initial period of massive horizontal mergers between competitors in 1887-1904, a transitional period of increasing vertical integration and some mergers for diversification in 1916-1929, and an explosion of conglomerate mergers after World War II (Scherer, 1970). The early wave was sparked by major economic and social structural changes in the fabric of U.S. society, and was paralleled to a large extent by a similar pattern of mergers in the United Kingdom. It ended with the severe recession of 1903-1904 and a federal government crackdown on mergers having anti-competitive effects. The shape of the post-World War II merger wave was also marked by major structural changes in the United States economy and was heavily influenced by selective government prosecution of vertical and horizontal - but not conglomerate - mergers.

In the years immediately following World War II, most corporate mergers were still of the horizontal or vertical type, with conglomerates not accounting for half of the large mergers until the early 1950s. (Large mergers are acquisitions involving 10 million or more in assets.) Counting all mergers recorded by the Federal Trade Commission, there were 16,601 mergers from 1945 through 1968. Over one-fourth of the manufacturing firms ranking from the 501st to the 1,000th largest in size were acquired through mergers between 1950 and 1962, with very large firms accounting for most of the assets acquired during this period. Indeed, almost all of the firms on *Fortune* magazine's list of the top 500 industrial corporations participated in the merger movement. Large organizations' dominance of merger activity continued into the 1970s, as 961 of the 1,919 acquiring firms in 1973 had assets of 50 million or more while 1,580 of the acquired companies had assets of less than 1 million. Merger activity by large firms was partially responsible for the increase in aggregate concentration of industrial assets within the largest 200 firms, although industry-specific concentration ratios were only modestly affected.

By 1967-68, conglomerate mergers totaled 83 percent of all large manufacturing and mining firm acquisitions recorded by the Federal Trade Commission (FTC). Thus, by the 1970s, conglomerate mergers had become the dominant form of acquisition involving assets of 10 million or more. Given the importance of such mergers, the Federal Trade Commission distinguished between three subtypes:

1. Product extension, when both firms are functionally linked in production and/or distribution, but sell in different product markets;

2. Market extension, when both firms manufacture the same products but sell in different geographic markets; and

3. »other» types, which includes firms with neither a buyer-seller nor a division of labor direct relationship. Product extension mergers are now the most numerous of all conglomerate mergers.

The shift to conglomerate rather than horizontal or vertical mergers was heavily influenced by governmental constraints. The Celler-Kefauver amendment in 1950 to the Clayton Anti-trust Act gave the FTC and the Justice Department strong weapons against the traditional forms of merger, but left a large gray area through which conglomerate mergers could slip (Alexander, 1971). The Celler-Kefauver amendment extended the Clayton to prohibit the acquisition of assets rather than just stock, and also liberalized the definition of what constituted competition in »any line of commerce in any section of the country.» With a stronger act to work from, the FTC and the Justice Department challenged a high proportion of mergers in the two decades after 1950, with almost all of these being challenges to either the traditional horizontal and vertical or more recent market extension mergers. The agencies challenged only 3 percent of the product extension and none of the »other» conglomerate mergers. The obvious strategic choice for organizations seeking to escape or mitigate the impact of competitive interdependence was to diversify, thus contributing to the development of a new organizational form.

3. Mergers and Industrial Relations

3.1 The Problem

After World War II, a rapid increase in corporate mergers led some specialists to speculate about the impact of mergers on industrial relations and the collective bargaining process. Apart from an increased frequency of mergers and the large amount of assets involved, the rise of conglomerate mergers as a new organizational form provoked speculation that union power was eroding (Alexander, 1971). Hendricks (1976) investigated whether conglomerate mergers had a negative effect on union wage levels, and found no evidence to support such a claim. In addition to wage levels, mergers potentially could effect many other aspects of industrial relations: the size of a personnel or industrial relations department, the degree of autonomy delegated to local bargaining representatives, or the nature of union-management conflict itself.

Our research focuses on the consequences of mergers for the collective bargaining process and on changes in the structure and functioning of industrial relations and personnel department. Management authority to modify relations with the employees of newly acquired firms is circumscribed by legal constraints laid down by the National Labor Relations Board (NLRB) and the Supreme Court. There are a number of areas of discretion, however, and our review will focus on these. Much of the literature on the consequences of mergers focuses on the situation of white collar rather than blue collar workers, and the white collar literature is mainly concerned with top executives. Discussions of the work force tend to be fairly general and thus we are limited in our ability to form empirical generalizations from this literature.

3.2 Legal Constraints

Collective bargaining is an area heavily bound by laws and precedence. Many of the potential options open to organizations resulting from mergers have been foreclosed by the NLRB or the Supreme Court. Thus, the impact of corporate mergers on collective bargaining is more limited than one might first imagine. The same legal constraints also apply, of course, to the ability of unions to respond to merger situations. Perhaps most important, the National Labor Relations Board (NLRB) has limited the prospect of unions creating a single bargaining unit across the various establishments of a single conglomerate employer. If the NLRB ever decides to require parties to bargain over the establishment of bargaining units across the operation of a single employer, it would substantially increase the likelihood of creating coalitions of unions isomorphic in structure to the form of conglomerate corporations.

The major collective response unions have made to conglomerate mergers has been to attempt coalition or coordinated bargaining. The Industrial Union Department of the AFL-CIO has served as a clearinghouse for enlisting the cooperation of various unions bargaining with a single employer. The Industrial Union Department has generally not taken the initiative, but rather has waited until an international union has come to it suggesting the formation of a coordinated bargaining committee. In 1977, there were still less than 100 such committees, despite the widespread prevalence of the conglomerate corporation.

Obviously, coordinated bargaining is not the same thing as creating a new bargaining unit, with which an employer *must* bargain. As Alexander (1971, p. 365) noted

> »Unions are restricted in their attempts to redress the tactical shift in bargaining power. They cannot bargain to an impasse or strike to change the bargaining unit. The appropriate bargaining unit is to be determined by the board.»

As this issue is extremely complex and was not addressed in our research, we will not attempt to deal with it further in this chapter.

An issue that is central to our research, however, is the question of whether an acquiring company must recognize the union of the company being acquired. The simplest case, of course, is when the purchasing firm is organized by a union but the acquired firm is not. In this case, management is not obligated to extend the union agreement to cover the new employees. If the union wished to organize the new employees, it would have to try to gain support from at least 30 percent of the proposed unit to call for a labor board election.

If the acquired company has a union, two doctrines - successor and accretion - of the NLRB are relevant in determining whether the acquiring company must recognise it. These doctrines grow out of a series of decisions in the past several decades: *Wiley, Wackenhut, Reliance, Burns,* and *Howard Johnson.* Spelfogel (1970, p. 578) summarized the NLRB's *successor doctrine* as follows:

> »The NLRB, with court approval, has consistently held that where there is a substantial continuity in the 'employing industry', the 'successor' must assume the former employer's obligation *to bargain* with a labor organization representing a majority of the employees. In determining whether there is sufficient continuity for this purpose, the Board has considered such factors as whether the same plant was used; whether the same or substantially the same work force was employed; whether the employer did the same jobs under the same working conditions; whether the supervisor personnel remained the same; whether the same machinery, equipment and method of production were employed; and whether the same products or the same services <were > performed. If a sufficient amount of these factors exist to establish a 'successor' relationship, the successor has been held obligated to bargain with the union upon request, even though the sale and the transfer of assets specifically excluded any assumption of the obligations of the pre-existing union contract.»

The *accretion doctrine* of the NLRB is a set of principles specifying the conditions under which continuity in the pre-existing bargaining unit of the acquired firm is upheld. The central question is whether the old organization continues more or less intact, or has been absorbed so totally into the acquiring firm's structure that it has ceased to exist. Logically, the accretion doctrine.covers three possibilities:

1. Both pre-existing units were destroyed and an entirely new unit has been created;

2. Both pre-existing units, the acquired firm and the acquiring firms, persist unchanged; and

3. The acquired firm is totally absorbed into the larger firm and ceases to exist as an independent entity.

In determining which of these three possibilities has occurred, the NLRB weighs a number of factors including:

>The size of the units and character of jobs involved, and the degree - if any - of functional integration of operations such as interchange of employees, common wage and benefit patterns, and centralized managerial and labor relations control».

If condition one is deemed to apply, then the existing contracts are deemed abrogated and a new bargaining unit must be determined. If condition two is found, then nothing changes and the acquiring company is obligated to recognize and deal with the unions making up the historical bargaining units. If the third condition is found, then the unions in the acquired firm no longer have claim to the bargaining unit and the acquiring company's unions are deemed to represent all the employees of the new organization.

Although a »successor» company has a strong obligation to recognize and bargain in good faith with unions representing the acquired company's employees, the Supreme Court in its *Burns* decision ruled that

>neither the successor nor the union could be held involuntarily to the predecessor union contract, and both were free to negotiate new employment terms and conditions. The high court also stated that even the limited obligation to recognize and bargain with the union which represented the predecessor's employees was contingent on whether the bargaining unit remained essentially unchanged and whether the union continued to represent a majority of employees in that unit»
(Spelfogel, 1978, pp. 299-300).

In it's 1974 *Howard Johnson* decision (417 US249; 94 Supreme Court 2236) the Supreme Court reaffirmed its *Burns* ruling and further clarified the extent to which the *Burns* decision narrowed the earlier *Wiley* decision. Essentially the Supreme Court held that a successor has no obligation to hire the old employees of the acquired firm. Although the law is much more subtle than we can possibly convey in these few pages, it should be clear that NLRB and Supreme Court doctrines regarding the impact of mergers on collective bargaining are still evolving.

A central strategic implication of the *Burns* and *Howard Johnson* rulings should be noted. From a labor relations point of view, the simplest course to take for a conglomerate firm is to allow the continuation of both units unchanged. If the acquired company is allowed to operate as an autonomous division, and is thus not fully integrated into the parent corporation, the conglomerate's labor relations situation is essentially unchanged. It will continue to recognize the union of the acquired company as well as unions previously recognized in the parent company. Any other course of action would complicate its labor relations situation. Destroying the acquired company by integrating it or by creating an entirely new organization out of the acquired and acquiring companies would require a reorganization of the bargaining unit and a possible contest over representation. This is not to say that corporate strategists will take this as a central premise in their merger activities, but only that it is another constraint pushing corporations toward making pure conglomerate mergers. The simplest course of action is to acquire a company and allow it to operate more or less autonomously within the framework of the overarching corporate shell.

3.3 Potential Problems Accompanying Mergers

The literature on potential personnel problems in mergers during the 1960s reflected two concerns:

1. Problems resulting from ignoring personnel issues prior to mergers, in the planning stage; and

2. Coping with problems in the post-merger phase which arise from inadequate planning.

Many articles in the 1960s argued that human factors often make the difference between success and failure in a merger. Schoonmaker (1969, p. 39) noted that »one of the most common merger mistakes is to overemphasize financial considerations and underemphasize human problems». In a study of 50 companies involved in mergers during the first half of 1969, Boland (1970) found that the personnel or industrial relations manager was consulted less frequently than other key executives concerning potential merger problems. Only 38 percent of the companies consulted their personnel relations departments before the merger. When chief executives were asked how much consideration was given to 26 marketing, manufacturing, financial, and personnel aspects during a premerger evaluation of the acquired company, labor relations history and climate ranked fifteenth, union contract ranked sixteenth, and employee benefit programs ranked nineteenth. In all three cases, the majority of chief executives said that they gave only routine consideration to these areas. When personnel factors were mentioned, they tended to focus on top management and the professionals in the acquired and acquiring companies. As in most studies of business success, a successful merger was attributed to the talent of the company management and to effective communication at the outset of a merger.

Many articles pointed to the range of problems in the personnel area that could result from mergers. Consideration of the responsibility of personnel and industrial relations departments points up the scope of potential problems: recruitment of employees, transfers of employees between work groups or departments, compensation and benefit programs, dismissal of employees, layoffs, structure of work tasks, disciplinary measures, safety measures, holidays and vacations, retirement and sick leaves, personnel records, profit sharing, employee stock purchase plans, employee activity programs, and organization change and management development. Problems could potentially arise in any of these areas after a merger.

Certain kinds of problems were mentioned more often than others, however. Three areas in particular were mentioned often and were included in our questionnaire study: disparities in wages and benefits, differences in seniority and pension plans, and differing organizational policies regarding operations. Spealists recommended that corporations try to plan ahead and anticipate or eliminate as many problems as possible, instead of waiting for them to occur. They argued that such problems should be evaluated in premerger assessments because they can turn out to be quite costly to adjust after the fact. If wages differ between organizations, for example, the corporation ought to consider how much it will cost to equalize them. Corporations should also be aware of the hidden costs of benefit programs, such as unfunded pension liabilities and poor group insurance, that the acquired company may have. If new people are given benefits equal to the present labor force, it may turn out to be much more costly than anticipated (Butler, 1965, p. 74).

A dominant theme in the literature in the 1960s was a warning to corporate executives that if they were planning a merger, part of their time and effort should be put into the personnel function. Some recommendations were given for specific methods to overcome problems associated with mergers, but more often it was left for individual executives to evaluate and solve their own personnel problems. McLagan (1965, p. 30) argued that broad corporate operating policies should be established in such areas as finance, personnel, and public relations, but only if the organizations were relatively similar. Beattie (1970) recommended that organizations develop a master benefit plan. This would make it relatively easy to compare the benefits of the acquired firm to current benefits paid by the parent firm and then evaluate where discrepancies occurred.

Given the extensive emphasis on planning ahead for potential personnel problems, it is curious that a course offered by the American Management Association recently on »Mergers and Acquisitions» contained no reference to industrial or labor relations. In a brochure describing the comprehensive, four-day seminar, the course outline listed the following areas to be covered: financial analysis, accounting aspects, pacts and legal aspects, financial packaging, and modern financial concepts. Even though one of the catch-phrases told participants that they would learn how to »prevent potential headaches», and that they will also learn how to deal with »post-acquisition problems», no mention was made of unions or the NLRB. Perhaps the seminar's lack of concern regarding industrial and labor relations reflected a feeling that such problems are secondary compared to the primary problems of financial and legal considerations. In any event, the American Management Association's lack of attention to personnel problems mirror the dearth of articles in the 1970s concerning the same topic.

3.4 Organizational Level Changes

We expected mergers to effect the industrial relations process in a varity of ways. First, we felt that mergers may have some impact on the size and authority of a personnel or industrial relations department. Merger increases the size of the corporation, and thus might lead to a need for a larger clerical staff in the personnel department. If new unions are added to the number already dealt with by the personnel department, then a larger negotiating team might be required along with more personnel specialists. If the acquired companies are allowed to operate as autonomous divisions, it may mean that greater delegation of authority has to be allowed for local level bargaining. For companies not having a separate personnel department, mergers might lead to the creation of such a full-time function.

Second, a merger might disrupt the pattern of industrial relations established in the acquired firm. This might lead to increased voluntary turnover, higher levels of absenteeism, or other signs of dissatisfaction such as an increased number of grievances, strikes, or charges of unfair labor practices. Some of the changes required by a merger might heighten management's attention to personnel relations and lead them to devote more time than previously to managing such relations. For example, some acquired companies may not have formal wage and salary programs or formal job classification programs.

Third, mergers might require changes in union contracts, although as we have seen this is most likely to be the case when the acquired unit has been totally absorbed into the parent company. In cases where the acquired company is allowed to operate autonomously we would expect fewer problems.

Fourth, a merger might increase union militancy. This could take the form of increased efforts toward coordinating bargaining or resistance to further merger efforts. These four issue areas were included in the survey questionnaire we sent to our sample.

4. Study Design

In studying the impact of mergers during the 1975-76 period, we used samples from two sources: the National Industrial Conference Board Report on Mergers and Acquisitions, and the Federal Trade Commission Report on Mergers and Acquisitions. Our first sample was drawn from the National Conference Board Report and was limited to corporations with headquarters in New York State. Initially, we tried phoning the personnel directors of these companies, but we found that they were reluctant to discuss labor problems over the telephone, and most asked us to mail the questionnaire to them. Thus, we changed our strategy and sent them an eight-page questionnaire. The response rate, however, was so low from this initial sample that we had to draw an additional sample. It appeared that many of the corporations in our first sample were not unionized and thus many felt our questionnaire was not appropriate to them. Our second sample was drawn from the Federal Trade Commission Report and included only industrial corporations. Ninety corporations were chosen in the second sample, again all with headquarters in New York State. Given the nature of the reporting services used, it is clear that the samples were biased towards large corporations.

A majority of the firms contacted either did not reply or sent letters indicating their refusal to participate. A common reason for refusing to participate was a corporate policy prohibiting participation in any outside survey. Others felt that our questionnaire was not relevant to them because they were so large that any information given would be on an aggregate basis and thus would not bear directly on the merger that we were asking about. (The questionnaire we sent asked about a particular merger that had occurred during the past two years.) Finally, another reason for refusing to take part was the problem of confidentiality. Many executives argued that we were asking for information that was sensitive and not released to any outside person. We received completed questionnaires from 18 firms and partial information from a number of others. In this report, we will focus mainly on the completed questionnaires. Thus, our study is in every sense a pilot study. We can make no claim to having a representative sample, but it does appear, given the consistencies in the reports received, that there are some patterns deserving further exploration.

5. Results and Discussions

5.1 Caveat

Since the number of cases in our pilot study is so small, we report the results primarily in terms of raw numbers rather than percentages. After describing the types of mergers included in the sample and some general characteristics of the corporations involved, we present information supporting our contention that the mergers these corporations entered were basically non-problematic for them. Most appeared not to have done much planning for the industrial relations subsystem before the merger, and it appears that few consequences ensued for the industrial relations department. Most corporations had no trouble with the contracts and, in general, few problems occurred in the industrial relation subsystem.

5.2 Characteristics of the Corporations and Mergers

Even though we did not receive completed questionnaires from all corporations, we did receive enough information either in questionnaires or letters to classify the type of merger in 28 cases. In only 2 cases could we classify the merger as a »real merger»: that is, in only two instances did the acquiring corporation completely integrate the acquired company into its structure. In four cases what was reported as a merger in the Conference Board report on FTC report turned out to involve simply the purchase of a product or service - no employees were involved and there were no changes in corporate identities. One merger was overseas and, thus, had no impact on the corporation's United States operations. In another case, a company completed the acquisition of an already partially owned firm. In two instances a plant was purchased but there was no merger as such. Finally, in the 18 cases which make up the bulk of the cases analyzed in our study, the action taken was actually an *acquisition* that is, the acquired company continued to be operated as an autonomous unit. For example, one corporate labor relations director noted that he was in a decentralized organization - subunits had complete autonomy and profit responsibility at the division or subsidiary level. Indeed, a

302

number of the persons filling out the questionnaire went out of their way to stress that the acquired company continued to be operated as an autonomous unit within the overall corporate structure. Some pointed out that the acquired company had completely different operations, served a different market, with a different product, and operated in a different geographic location. A number also noted, however, that with the passage of time there would be some integration of the acquired company into the parent corporation structure.

As previous literature on mergers would lead us to expect, the acquiring firms were substantially larger than the firms they acquired, with the average size of the acquiring firms just over 6,000 employees, while the average size of an acquired firm was about 230 employees. Parent companies that were unionized were quite a bit larger than the non-unionized companies, with the former averaging 7,760 employees and the latter 2,800. The size of acquired firms did not differ significantly by the type of corporation acquiring them, with the average firm acquired by a unionized parent company having 240 employees, and the average firm acquired by a non-union parent having 211 employees.

For almost all parent corporations then, the acquired firm represented only a small increment to its total labor force. This differed, however, by whether the parent firm was unionized or non-unionized, as in only 2 of 11 cases for which data is available did the acquired firm's employees represent as much as 10 percent of the total employment of the unionized parent company. For the non-unionized firms in the six cases for which data is available, the size of the acquired firm was roughly one-quarter of that of the parent company before it acquired the new unit. In two cases it was insignificant and in the other case it represented about one-fifth of the labor force of the acquiring firm.

All but two of the 18 firms returning completed questionnaires were in the manufacturing sector, and, thus, as one might expect, almost all were unionized; thirteen of the eighteen were unionized in part or totally. By contrast, only ten of the eighteen acquired firms were unionized. In only one instance did a non-unionized parent company acquire a unionized corporation. Four of the five non-unionized parents acquired non-unionized subsidiaries, suggesting a desire to maintain some consistency in the labor relations subsystem of the corporation.

5.3 Planning for the Merger

We asked the personnel directors in what ways their company took premerger industrial relations situations into account; for example, by setting up committees using special staff or taking other steps. Six of the seventeen corporations said they did nothing to take premerger industrial relations into account, while five did attempt to review existing labor agreements in the acquired corporations. Four others mentioned informal procedures, such as comparing benefits informally in the finance office, or informing the union that the contract would be honored.

Perhaps a better indicator of premerger planning lies in answers received to the question of how much consideration, if any, was given to the industrial relations situations of the parent company and the acquired company. Respondents were given the choice of checking three categories: none at all, some consideration, and a great deal of consideration. Four respondents said none at all, nine said some consideration, and only five said a great deal of consideration. Four of these five were unionized firms. The one non-unionized firm that mentioned giving a great deal of consideration to the industrial relations situation remarked that it was done to assure the parent company that no substantial problems were involved in the merger. Perhaps the greater tendency of the unionized companies to give a great deal of consideration to industrial relations stems from their much larger size and their greater experience with diverse labor relations situations. Seven of the eleven dealt with ten or more unions, and thus had extensive experience with the collective bargaining process.

5.4 Lack of Change in the Personnel Department

Respondents were asked what changes, if any, there had been in the personnel or industrial relations department as a result of the merger; for example, changes in staff size, larger negotiating teams, or more authority given to local level bargaining. All eighteen respondents replying to this question said there had been absolutely *no* change. All but one of the corporations had a separate personnel department and all of them said that this department existed before the merger. Although this finding might appear surprising, given our earlier expectation that mergers would have an impact on the industrial relations process, in retrospect it is not. At least for the unionized firms, the acquired firm represents a very small addition to a substantial labor force. Most of the problems involved in dealing with personnel and industrial relations were solved before the corporation engaged in the merger we studied. Four of the six non-unionized parent corporations acquired a non-unionized firm, and one only partially unionized corporation acquired a similarly partially unionized subsidiary. For the non-unionized corporations, half the acquisitions did result in a substantial increase in their labor force. Nonetheless, it appears to have been handled without any major changes in the personnel department.

In ten of the acquisitions, the acquired company retained its separate personnel departments. In five of the remaining seven cases, the acquired firm did not have a separate personnel department. Thus, in only two cases was the personnel department of an acquired firm abolished or integrated into the parent company's personnel department. This is another indication that most of the mergers we studied were conglomerate mergers, where the acquired company retained a great deal of its own identity within the corporate structure. We believe this accounts in large part for the lack of any changes experienced by the corporations in their employee relations, subsequent to the acquisition.

5.5 Lack of Impact on Union Contracts

For the eight acquisitions which involved a union contract and for which information is available, only three involved changes in the contract itself. In one case, the parent company renegotiated some contractual conditions prior to the merger. In a second case, the pay formula spelled out in the contract was changed and in a third case, some unspecified but minor changes were made.

5.6 Few Problems Occurred in Industrial Relations

Personnel and industrial relations directors were asked if their industrial or personnel relations were considered a problem after the merger, and how much of a problem they were. Five of the six non-unionized firms reported no problems with their industrial relations. The one firm reporting a problem said that there were some small pay and benefit differentials to be worked out. Six of the eleven unionized firms reported no problems, and another two reported only small problems. Of the three reporting fairly difficult problems, one actually involved external conditions over which the firm had no control - namely, high turnover because of the tight labor market situation. Of the remaining two cases, one involved an historical relationship of the acquired company's unions dealing directly with the managers of the company and working on side deals which were outside of the contract. The acquired firm's contract language was ambiguous and did not seem to cover the provisions which employees had come to expect. Finally, in the third case reported of a difficult problem, the respondent was referring mainly to difficulties in reconciling benefits between the parent company and acquired company's wage and compensation systems.

In another attempt to determine whether industrial relations had become a problem after the merger, respondents were asked whether top management now paid more or less attention to industrial and personnel relations than before the merger. All of the non-unionized companies reported that the same amount of attention was paid as before the merger. However, five of the twelve respondents in unionized companies reporting said that top management paid more attention than before, in one case *much* more attention than before.

Further examination revealed that in all cases where a respondent said that management paid the *same* attention as before, he had also reported that industrial and personnel relations were considered to be *no* problem after the merger. By contrast, in all cases where the manager reported that more attention was paid than before the merger, he had also reported that there was a small or fairly difficult problem with industrial relations after the merger. Thus, in not quite half the unionized firms, the presence of problems - however small - were alleged to have led management to pay more attention to industrial relations than before the merger. The problems, of course, were quite small.

All of the non-unionized firms reported that there had been no change in the number of strikes, number of grievances, and that there had been no charges of unfair labor practices after the merger. All of the unionized firms also reported no change in the number of strikes and no charges of unfair labor practices. However, in two instances there was an increase in the number of grievances. The picture painted here is one of strong continuity in the pattern of industrial relations within the corporations.

Finally, for the unionized firms we were interested in whether the merger had an impact on possible union tactics. Six of the eleven managers replying to the question said that unions in their company knew about the merger before it took place. In only two cases did it appear that there was some formal mechanism by which the corporation made known that the merger was going to occur. All of the industrial relations managers said that unions had made *no* objection to the merger. Some specialists have argued that mergers will eventually lead to increased attempts to impose multi-plant or multi-union bargaining. However, all of the managers replying to our questionnaire said this had *not* occurred in their corporation. Two said that they were aware of some efforts toward coordination of the union's efforts and communication between the unions, but this had not led to multi-plant bargaining. Given a lack of change on the management side, it is reasonable to expect that unions would not try to change the bargaining structure, since there is no incentive to do so. Only if management policy became centralized, as in the case of a true merger, would unions have a strong incentive to seek coordinated bargaining.

6. Conclusions and Implications

Corporate mergers and acquisitions evidently do not pose the sorts of personnel and industrial relations problems that specialists in the 1960s had alleged. While there is some indication that top management is paying more attention than before to industrial and personnel relations, there were few problems ensuing from the mergers and acquisitions we studied. Ideally, we would like to obtain information about the actual process of the merger. Do corporations shy away from mergers or acquisitions that might involve labor problems? If this was the case, then our results might simply reflect the wisdom of corporate acquisitions experts in choosing merger or acquisition targets that will not pose industrial relations problems for the parent company. Alternatively, corporations many have learned from the literature of the 1960s and now handle mergers so well that personnel and industrial relations problems are avoided.

We must emphasize that all but one of the mergers we studied were actually closer to pure conglomerate acquisitions, in the sense that the acquired company continued to operate as a more or less autonomous division or subunit within the corporate structure. This meant that the acquired company's personnel department could continue to operate as before and that until its contracts expired, the parent company would not intervene to change relations with unions. As we noted above, pure conglomerate mergers may represent the simplest solution to the industrial relations problem, for matters continue as they traditionally have within the company until some point at which the parent company moves to absorb more fully the acquired firm into its structure. Perhaps the investigated corporations followed a long-term strategy in this area. They may acquire another firm, leave the industrial relations situation unchanged for a while, and then slowly integrate the two and impose the parent company's policies on the acquired firm. This would, it appears, reduce some of the immediate problems of mergers and give the corporation more time to plan for the long-range problems that might result. Thus, a followup study should investigate the longer run impact of mergers on management personnel, the degree of centralization of management decision making, and changes in the wages, fringe benefits, and working conditions of salaried and hourly employees. Perhaps the total effects of mergers and acquisitions on industrial relations cannot be determined until a corporation has gone through the hights and lows of a complete business cycle.

7. References

Aldrich, Howard, 1979
    Organizations and Environments. Englewood Cliffs, N.J.: Prentice-Hall.

Aldrich, Howard and Susan Mueller, 1981
    »The Evolution of Organizational Forms: Technology, Coordination, and Control.» In Barry Staw and L.L. Cummings (eds.), *Research on Organizational Behavior,* Vol. III. Greenwich, Conn.: JAI Press.

Alexander, Kenneth, 1971
    »Conglomerate Mergers and Collective Bargaining.» *Industrial and Labor Relations Review,* 24, (April): 354-374.

Bendix, Reinhard, 1949
    Work and Authority in Industry. New York: Harper.

Beattie, Andrew, 1970
    »How to Handle Benefits When Your Firm Merges.» *Administrative Management* 31, (April).

Boland, Richard, 1970
    »Merger Planning: How Much Weight Do Personnel Factors Have?» *Personnel,* 47, (March): 8-13.

Butler, John, 1965
    »Maximizing Personnel Potential in a Merger.» *Mergers and Acquisitions,* Fall.

Edvards, Richard, 1979
    Contested Terrain. New York: Basic Books.

Hendricks, Wallace, 1976
»Conglomerate Mergers and Collective Bargaining.» *Industrial Relations,* 15, February: 75-87.

McLagan, Bruce, 1965
»Why Mergers Go Wrong.» *Management Review,* 54, January: 30-33.

Scherer, Frederick, 1970
Industrial Market Structure and Economic Performance. Chicago: Rand McNally.

Schoonmaker, Alan, 1969
»Why Mergers Don't Jell.» *The Critical Human Elements,* 46, September: 39-48.

Spelfogel, Evan, 1970
»Labor Liabilities in Purchases, Acquisitions, and Mergers.» *Labor Law Journal,* 21, September: 577-581.

Spelfogel, Evan, 1974
»Corporate Successor's Obligation to Honor His Predecessor's Labor Contract: Howard Johnson Case.» *Labor Law Journal,* 25, May: 298-304.

14. THE MACRO MANAGEMENT OF SUPPLY: A PROCESS OF INTERORGANIZATIONAL LEARNING

Les Metcalfe
International Institute of Management,
Berlin
and
The London Graduate School of Business Studies
London

1. Introduction

The political economy of pluralism requires a new form of industrial policy making. Increasing organizational interdependence is creating complex, multi-level structural problems. Failure to resolve these problems creates low trust institutional conditions, resulting in productivity traps and preventing macro structural change. Industrial restructuring depends on the evolution of new policy making capabilities for the macro management of supply. The macro management of supply is an interorganizational learning process through which alternative industrial futures are designed and implemented. The role of network organizations in facilitating macro structural change is discussed.

The theme of this chapter, the macro-management of supply, implies that Keynes was only half right. Problems of industrial restructuring and economic development require a new level and form of policy making. Explicit processes for the macro-management of supply as well as the macro-management of demand are required, because deepening interdependence among business organizations, and between business and other segments of society, are generating complex problems of macro-structural change. Existing policy-making institutions were not designed to deal with problems of this order and their failure to resolve emergent conflicts is undermining the capacity of societies to guide their development. A common observation on current problems is that while political decision is rapidly displacing market choice, the capacity of political processes to handle an increasing volume of ever more complex problems has not developed in parallel. The problem of governmental overload this gives rise to has been discussed elsewhere (see, e.g. Scharpf, 1977; Rose, 1977). But it is only one facet of wider changes that is difficult to interpret within conventional characterizations of the business/government relationship. The symptoms of malfunctioning are obvious, but there is disagreement about the underlying causes (see, e.g., the collection of papers on the business/government relationship in the US, edited by N. Jacoby, 1974).

The classic laissez-faire concept of an economic system operating within a minimum framework of rules laid down by government and regulated by competition, is obviously out of touch with contemporary realities. The size and scope of governmental activities, the scale of business enterprise, the extent of industrial concentration, the prevalence of mergers, joint ventures, consortia and other forms of interorganizational co-operation, make this schema an inappropriate one. Equally, the notion of a mixed economy with more or less distinct private and public sectors is misleading. Government intervenes in numerous ways, as regulator, planner, purchaser, promoter, protector, to influence the structure, conduct and performance of industrial organization. In the other direction economic interest groups increasingly encroach into traditionally governmental areas of decision-making, raising fears of corporatism - fears which must be tempered by a specification of what is meant by corporatism (Schmitten, 1974; Lehmbruch, 1974, 1976).

Not all the problems cluster around the government industry interface. Businesses also face new societal demands for industrial democracy and new forms of participation, effective corporate responsibility, and the representation of community and amenity groups in strategic decision-making. Conflicting demands and competing pressures are part and parcel of organizational life. But current problems are straining the adaptive capacities of organizations and stretching interorganizational relations to the breaking point. Challenges to the values organizations serve and the legitimacy of organizational power reflect broad irreversible environmental changes that cannot be prevented but are extremely difficult to steer in preferred directions. The suboptimal outcomes of ad hoc crisis management have recently been documented in Brenner's (1976) analysis of the politics of international monetary reform. The energy crisis has also focussed attention on the imprudence of assuming the stability of existing interorganizational relations and the difficulties of effecting macro-structural change in productive activities as complex as those concerned with energy supply. The danger is, that failure to resolve structural problems will create turbulent industrial environments which defeat further adaptive efforts (Emery & Trist, 1965; Metcalfe, 1974).

2. The Political Economy of Pluralism

The gap between problems of structural change and the available means of dealing with them is symptomatic of the emergence of the political economy of pluralism. High degrees of interdependence - co-operative and competitive - among large, functionally and culturally differentiated organizations are the rule rather than the exception. Co-ordination of productive activities depends on the management of intricate and often fragile interorganizational networks. This institutional framework of production and supply is usually taken for granted. But in phases of structural change it begins to disintegrate. The process of disintegration is unwittingly accelerated by the piecemeal efforts of individual organizations to protect their own interests, while collective responses are slow to develop and frequently directed at preserving an established structure rather than designing a new one.

The lopsidedness of economic policy-making - the neglect of macro-structural problems on the supply side - is attributable to the fact that we have not yet come to terms with the political economy of pluralism. The problems generating capacity of interorganizational networks frequently exceeds the problem solving- capacity of their component organizations. Because the institutional conditions of supply are neither stable, well understood nor effectively managed, a new basis for analysis and description, diagnosis and prescription is required. This paper seeks to meet these needs by showing how problems of macro-structural change arise and how they can be dealt with. The inability to deal with structural problems creates productivity traps which reduce short term efficiency and narrow the range of politically feasible long term options. On the basis of this analysis the kinds of new policy processes needed for the macro-management of supply will be outlined. It will be shown that designing alternative industrial futures and guiding the transformation of large, complex interorganizational systems depends on the development of interorganizational learning processes to create societal flexibility and safeguard its use.

An underlying theme of this paper is that the behaviour of pluralistic systems in process of structural change is governed by an economics of flexibility. Emergent structural problems rapidly exhaust adaptive capacities because the combined effect of successive qualitative changes of them is multiplicative not additive (Bateson, 1963). Designing the evolution of advanced societies (Jantsch, 1975) requires the capacity to discriminate among different classes of structural problems and to formulate policy responses appropriate to them.

3. Structural Change and Organizational Interdependence

To understand how productive traps arise and explain how they may be dealt with it is necessary to be clear about what is meant by structural change and structural problems. Change, to coin a phrase, is and is not constant. Change is constant in the sense that stable organizational structures are maintained in dynamic equilibrium by the continous interaction among social processes, sustained by the mutual adaptation of individuals and groups. But these interacting processes and mutual adaptations do not necessarily maintain the larger structural context of day to day interaction. By accident or design, they can change it. A useful distinction can be drawn, therefore, between interaction among the participants within a given structural context and interaction which changes the context itself.

Policy makers and planners may seek to influence outcomes directly by intervention in the given action situation, or indirectly by altering the perceptions, values, opportunities, and decisions procedures, creating a wider range of policy options through structural change. Structural problems occur when conflicts of interests and values arise which prove irreconcilable at the interaction level. Their resolution depends on the participants' perceiving their structural origin and devising ways of dealing with them. Thus, depending on the perceptiveness and political skills of the participants - including policy makers and planners in that term - structural problems present them with important opportunities to reconsider established relationships and guide change, or the danger of creating traps from which they are unable to extricate themselves.

The situation is further complicated because social systems experience more than one kind of structural change. As Hernes (1977) pointed out:

> »In analysing structural change, it is crucial to note that we are dealing with structures at different levels, and that these levels are interrelated in such a way that the structure at one level is the output of a process which itself has a structure.» (Hernes, 1977, p. 519).

To which it may be added that there are also feedback effects from system performance that may promote either stability or change at each level.

Hernes distinguished three interrelated levels of structure, *output* structure, *parameter* structure, and *process* structure.

Output structure is the pattern of relations and activities that deliver a particular set of outputs. The level and composition of outputs depends not only on the output structure but also on the values of the parameters within which it operates and the form of the process that combines the parts into a functioning whole. Because of the possibility of stability or change at each level, four patterns of social system behaviour of increasing complexity can be identified: simple reproduction, extended reproduction, transition and transformation. *Simple reproduction* denotes a system in general equilibrium, exhibiting zero structural change and maintaining a constant level of performance. *Extended reproduction* encompasses growth and decline in output structure but stops short of altering parameters and process structures. *Transition* denotes a more complex pattern of behaviour in which output structure changes in response to parameter changes, while *transformation* denotes the still more complex case in which process level changes prompt successive changes in parameter and output structures.

These distinctions are relevant from two different standpoints. First they reveal the complexity of structural problems. Growth or decline in system performance may be directly attributable to changes in output structure or it may be due to the indirect effects of higher level structural changes operating on output structure. Actions directed towards redesigning output structure may well be misconceived if the sources of problems are elsewhere in the industrial environment. A detailed longitudinal comparison of the performance of manufacturing industry in the United Kingdom and West Germany between 1954-1972 documented the considerable differences in performance, with German industry outperforming British industry across the board (Panic, 1976). Yet, one of its main conclusions was that industrial structure in the two countries was very similar and that the failure of UK industry was not attributable to structural problems. The definition of structure employed - the sectorial distribution of output and factor inputs, as well as the size structure of companies and plants - leaves out of account differences in the capacity of industry institutions to handle changes in parameter structure and process structure, however. The omission is important because there are marked differences between the well-developed and integrated infrastructure of West German industry and the weak and fragmentary institutional infrastructure of British industry (Shonfield, 1965; Lehmbruch, 1974, 1977; Metcalfe and McQuillan, 1977a). This suggests the utility of comparative studies designed to discover whether such institutional differences actually do facilitate development by increasing the effectiveness of co-ordinated responses to crises of structural change.

Besides revealing the potential complexity of current problems of industrial restructuring, the distinctions among levels of structural change are significant from a second standpoint. As Table 14.1 shows, there is a parallel between them and a set of distinctions among the causal textures of organizational environments (Emery & Trist, 1965; Metcalfe, 1974).

Table 14.1   Structural change and organizational interdependence.

Levels of structural change	Types of organizational environment
TRANSFORMATION, CHANGE IN PROCESS PARAMETER AND OUTPUT STRUCTURE	TURBULENT
TRANSITION, CHANGE IN PARAMETER AND OUTPUT STRUCTURE	DISTURBED REACTIVE
EXTENDED REPRODUCTION, CHANGE IN OUTPUT STRUCTURE	PLACID CLUSTERED
SIMPLE REPRODUCTION, ZERO STRUCTURAL CHANGE	PLACID RANDOMISED

The conceptual equivalence suggests a way of formulating complex problems of structural change and poor performance as problems of organizational design and interorganizational learning. The causal texture of organizational environments is a function of the interdependencies among a set of organizations which form an interorganizational system. Treating the causal texture of the environment as conceptually distinct implies the existence of constraints to organizational behaviour which are independent of particular organization and characteristic of the system. These systemic constraints may be orderly, predictable and stable at low levels of interdependence but at high levels of interdependence they are unpredictable and unstable. In turbulent conditions micro level organizational strategy formulation becomes confused because the macro level rules of the game become ambiguous and even contradictory. The resulting uncertainty defeats adaptive efforts, polarizes policy issues and promotes pervasive factional disputes. Instead of solving structural problems, interorganizational dynamics lead to productivity traps.

4. Turbulence, Trust and Productivity Traps

Productivity traps, causing stagnation, reducing performance, and restricting flexibility arise when organizational interdependence results in turbulent environmental conditions. Macro structural conflicts undermine the conditions of trust and mutual confidence on which adherence to the rules of the game and hence, system performance depend - whether the system in question is privately run industry, a publicly provided service or, as for instance in banking, a combination of the two.

In principle the problem of turbulence is familiar enough. It is simply one form of the classic problem of public policy; a situation in which individually rational actions combine to produce unintended and undesired aggregate outcomes. Co-ordinated collective action could achieve positive widely recognized benefits but opportunities are missed because of a climate of mistrust and intergroup hostility borne of previous failures to resolve structural problems. What is not familiar is the application of this type of analysis to interorganizational problems of supply management. Yet, the link between supply and production problems and those of organizational design is quite a close one:

> »Like all behavioral systems, the true boundary or definition of a system is linked to its purpose and design. This concept of the boundary of a system should not seem strange to economists, because they are used to speaking of an economic system as being defined by its production function, i.e. its behavioural design.« (Dunn, 1971:191).

Even though production functions are among the behavioural foundations of economic theory, insufficient attention has been paid to their organizational characteristics. This is particularly true of macro production functions. While accepted as necessary theoretical constructs, they are often regarded as constructs with no real world institutional reference of management implications. In situations of structural stability the dependence of micro activities on the information and co-ordination inputs provided by the socio-political environment is easily overlooked. Yet the fundamental premise of economic theory, that self-seeking individuals can gain from trade implicity assumes compliance with an elaborate framework of social constraints.

> »Although depicted as the perfect example of the beneficial outcome of purely private, individualist activity in the absence of government, the invisible hand theorem presumes a system of collective choice comparable in sophistication to the market system it governs.« (Mueller, 1976:397)

This said, it appears to be increasingly the case that the existing processes of public or collective choice are not up to the tasks of maintaining a stable environment for economic activity, nor are they capable of managing change in an orderly way. In complex, pluralistic social systems there is too little mutual awareness among organizations of the extent of their interdependence and too little appreciation of the systemic effects of »go it alone» policies. Interorganizational networks of the order of complexity of, say, a financial system, with subtle distinctions of status among different types of banks and financial intermediaries or an industry consisting of firms, with extensive links with trade unions, suppliers of components and raw materials as well as with customers, cannot be explained only in terms of the values and objectives of the parts. Specialization creates patterns of mutual dependence that structural problems threaten to disrupt. Short term particular interests are more obvious than the well being of the system as a whole and there are few incentives or opportunities for individual organizations to contribute to the resolution of long term problems. However, if these problems are neglected, all suffer.

The impact of macro structural problems on the quality of interorganizational relations and, so, on the productivity of pluralistic systems can be illustrated by mapping a prisoner's dilemma game matrix into a production possibility diagram as in figure 14.1.

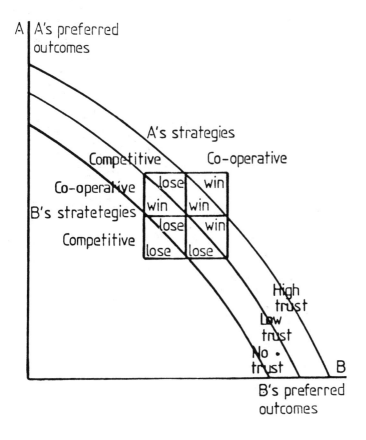

Figure 14.1 Productivity and interorganizational relations.

The same resource inputs are associated with different levels of productivity depending on the confidence each participant has in the readiness of the others to take their interests into account in making decisions (Fox, 1974). The interaction of strategic choices in this simplified case leads to three production possibility boundaries. If integrative co-operative strategies are chosen, the outcomes are located on what may be termed a high trust boundary. If one participant chooses a co-operative strategy while the other chooses a competitive strategy, the outcomes are located on a low trust boundary at a lower level of system performance. Still less productive outcomes forming a no trust boundary result from the mutual selection of competitive strategies.

In mixed motive games of this kind, it is realistic to assume an initial low trust situation and it is easy to see why distributive concerns and therefore competitive strategies predominate. Failure to develop integrative strategies to resolve structural problems leads to no trust situations or productivity traps in which disintegrating relations immobilize organizational resources in activities where they are ineffectively employed. As performance falls short of expectations, vicious circles of mutual recrimination and withdrawal of co-operation are established which amplify the effects of the initial decline. The downward spiral leads to polarization of attitudes, reduces effective communication and leads to confrontations and crises of legitimacy which prevent the process being reversed.

The frustrations that fuel intergroup rivalry and industrial conflict are frequently attributed to unrealistically high expectations of economic performance and demands for income shares that in aggregate are beyond what can be satisfied. The problem is defined as a distributive one. This analysis offers an alternative explanation of the gap between expectations and performance by formulating the problem as one of integration, which if unresolved triggers destructive intergroup competition. The two explanations are not mutually exclusive. The point is simply that disparities may originate because of unresolved structural problems on the supply side and if they do, demand management measures will not solve them.

Once initiated the degeneration of supply conditions is likely to persist. Progressive deterioration has characterized the evolution of British industrial relations for many years and in some respects was reinforced by the recommendations of the Donovan Commission of Industrial Relations (Fox and Flanders, 1969). Three problems have formed the background for the arguments of many advocates of industrial relations' reform. These are, the problem of increasingly frequent unofficial and unconstitutional strikes; the problem of restrictive practices resulting in inefficient labour utilization and the problem of wage drift, the uncontrolled upward movement of earnings and labour costs due to piecmeal bargaining (Goldthorpe, 1974). The habits of thinking and political skills learned and valued within the constraints of this disintegrating situation cannot easily be pressed into the service of designing new frameworks for dealing with long-term structural issues.

5. The Macro Management of Supply

Advanced societies do not, as yet, have the capacity for frequent restructuring that would enable them to discard old institutional arrangements as they build new ones, better suited to changed circumstances and new tasks (Schon, 1971; Michael, 1973). In situations of declining productivity special, private interests tend to dominate general, public concerns and if they are unable to resolve structural conflicts organizations are forced to act defensively to try to safeguard their own positions. Their perceptions are bounded by the range of their existing responsibilites, the threats of the immediate situation and suspicions about the motives and intentions of others. Lacking the confidence to co-operate in the task of removing structural sources of ambiguity, they select short term courses of action which lead to the worst of all possible worlds. The outcomes of this self-fulfilling prophecy lend credence to initial misconceptions and perpetuate a reign of error (Merton, 1968), which increases the likelihood of large and costly policy failures in the future.

But, »a trap is a trap only to creatures which cannot solve the problems that it sets» (Vickers, 1970, 15) and there are no grounds for assuming that the damaging consequences of productivity traps cannot be circumvented. The crucial question is, how can interorganizational policy processes be redesigned to provide advance warning of higher order structural problems and facilitate their resolution? Awareness of the origins of productivity traps points to the need for macro level interorganizational learning processes to manage change in the supply environment. Since the unco-ordinated activities of subsystems are more likely to exhaust adaptive capacities than increase systemic flexibility, learning processes are needed to establish a shared perspective on problems and achieve agreement on ways of dealing with them.

Conceptually, the form and functions of the macro management of supply can be specified quite clearly. What is required is a multi-stable system (Ashby, 1960) in which subsystems interact directly with each other to provide the system as a whole with higher level self-organizing capacities. The manifest function of this learning process is to facilitate orderly transformations from one set of productive activities to another, implying, of course, significant changes in the purposes to which social resources are put and the values organizations serve. Underlying this substantial contribution to societal guidance is the latent function of making more effective use of exisiting adaptive capacities and promoting their development. In so far as the economics of flexibility is multiplicative rather than additive, the organizational development implications of the process are extremely important, because successive qualitative changes may have unexpectedly sharp disintegrative effects on pluralistic systems that were previously quite stable. Indeed, it may well be the case that in order to cope with an increasing pace of structural change pluralistic systems will require a deutero learning capacity that will enable them to formulate alternatives to the existing rules of the game, rather than represent them as a norm from which any departure threatens total disintegration.

The compound character of structural problems calls for methods of problem solving and conflict resolution that give due weight to the interrelatedness of policy proposals. The importance of the integrative aspects of interorganizational learning exposes a deficiency in one frequently proposed method of resolving complex and contentious conflicts - breaking the problem down into its component issues and dealing with them one by one. The underlying theory is that by keeping close to questions of detail, negotiations are less likely to degenerate into irresolvable debates about issues of principles (Fisher, 1969; Rapoport, 1974; Thomas, 1976). But in situations of macrostructural change it is emphatically not the case that looking after the pennies is an effective way of looking after the pounds. Without denying the usefulness of ensuring that all participants to negotiations have a thorough knowledge of the substantial issues and each others positions on them, the process of fractionation is, at best only an initial stage in managing turbulence. Equally important is the synthesising process of creating a new definition of the situation based on a set of mutually compatible and generally acceptable ground rules. No blueprint or formula could possibly be devised spelling out how organizations should behave under all conceivable circumstances. Instead, this integrative phase of interorganizational planning produces process designs which describe the procedures required for the effective regulation of the system as a whole and the problems organizations should expect to encounter and have to resolve in working out a mutually acceptable pattern of roles and relationships.

The application of this approach to problems of industrial restructuring suggests ways of dealing with difficult and important policy issues. Since the oil crisis, with its direct impact on fuel costs, and far reaching social and political implications poses such a severe test of the adaptive capacities of advanced societies it is appropriate to examine the macro management problems it presents.

A recent study of energy policy in Sweden, sponsored by the Swedish Secretariat for Future Studies, has drawn attention to the institutional obstacles to widening the range of politically feasible policy options and ensuring that strategic decisions are democratically made (Lönnroth, Steen, and Johansson, 1977):

> »The main thrust is to understand the mechanisms that lock us up to the one or the other supply alternative and (...) how to change such mechanisms and keep several doors open.» (Lönnroth **et al.**, Page 4).

This study examines the historical evolution of energy problems and policy responses. It illustrates some of the main problems encountered in designing interorganizational learning processes for the macro management of supply.

The particular difficulties encountered in the electricity supply sector are not untypical of planning problems that seem likely to become more prevalent. Planning horizons are long term, say 20 years. Policy decisions are of major importance, both from the point of view of society as a whole, because the energy sector is so closely interwoven with other facets of social life, and to the various interests directly involved because decisions have important differential impacts upon them. Policy decisions are not made at one point in time and then implemented according to well-defined rules. Policy is the outcome of a stream of decisions, which are the subject of constant negotiation and debate. But the most active and attentive participants in the policy formation process are precisely those established interests with most to lose from substantial change in the methods of energy supply. The interoganizational system of rules governing the behaviour of the electricity supply industry has a built in bias towards expansion in established directions, and against the consideration of a wider range of options. In consequence, new technologies are judged according to how well they fit the existing interorganizational structure and the possibilities of building new institutional structures to meet new circumstances have few advocates and little effective support.

This case shows the disparity between organizational investments in policy processes designed to maintain an increasingly unviable status quo, as against policy processes designed to anticipate structural problems and generate alternative ways of dealing with them. Organizations define their functions and interpret macro policy issues in terms of their roles in the existing output structure. Changes in parameter and process structures are resisted as long as possible. Departures from the status quo are seen as threats to be warded off and not as symptomatic of more deep-seated changes. In organizations geared to growth, stagnation and decline are more likely to lead to regression than development (Hedberg, 1974; Hedberg, Nystrom, and Starbuck, 1976).

This view of the interorganizational system of rules as a complicated filter constraining the range of policy options is congruent with the analysis of productivity traps. Macro structural conflicts, whether manifest or latent, are conflicts about the rules of the game. But processes of multi-stability needed to deal with them involve an inversion of the normal concerns of policy makers - an ability to participate in designing new processes and parameters to support the operation of alternative output structures.

Just a game theoretic concepts are useful in distinguishing among conflicts of interest which arise from different sources, so they are helpful in indicating ways of dealing with them. If policies are devised on the basis of super-game and meta-game analyses, the participants are led to consider a wider range of options than those presented by the immediate situation.

Super games assume that the current game is one of a series of games and in formulating their strategies, the participants consider the effects of their strategic choices on the future behaviour of other participants. In a purely zero-sum competitive situation, such expectations make no difference, of course. But in non-zero sum games, analysis of the present situation in the light of a series of similar future situations, has the very important function of preventing a low-trust situation. The successful operation of a voluntary incomes policy seems to hinge on the acceptance by participants of a perspective of this kind. In fact, in the British context, it can be seen quite explicitly in the negotiations conducted by the Government with the trade union movement last year. The approach has short term utility but there is doubt about its long term adequacy. The merit of super-game analyses is that by making present and future interdependencies manifest, they restrain degenerative tendencies. They do not, however, provide the means of promoting transformations.

Meta-game analyses provide a more fruitful means of planning development, because they permit wider consideration of alternative sets of rules of the game. Two contrasting empirical studies analyzing this process have shown macro-level interventions, achieved agreement, and concerted action where the unco-ordinated interaction of micro-level forces had failed to resolve structural problems. These studies, focused on the work of the British National Economic Development Office, have been reported elsewhere (Metcalfe, 1976; Metcalfe and McQuillan, 1977b).

In one instance, the wool textile industry, the problem was designing a viable future for an old-established industry whose internal structure prevented movement away from declining traditional markets. The adaptation of the industry as a whole was obstructed by excess capacity and weak selling by numerous small businesses with poor long-term prospects. In the other case, the problem was recognizing the existence of a new industry, where the intersecting interests of organizations involved in the manufacture and construction of chemical plants, power stations and other types of large industrial plants created a turbulent environment.

A common factor in these cases was the formation of a network organization (Berry, Metcalfe, and McQuillan, 1974) to which macro structural problems could be referred and through which extensive participation in problem solving and implementation was facilitated. Their general importance is, initially providing a wider and more open forum for the diagnosis of structural obstacles to change and subsequently a focus for building the trust and mutual confidence that are the pre-requisites for the successful management of industrial change.

Unlike organizations which define their functions in terms of an existing pattern of output structure, network organizations' functions are defined in terms of promoting interorganizational co-operation to deal with potentially disruptive changes in process structure. The contributions they make to promoting integrative planning processes include, providing a focus for defining problems to be solved in systemic terms, prompting participation in redifining the objectives and structure of the system as a whole and monitoring the process of implementing change.

6. Conclusions and Implications

The pluralistic structure of modern economies, characterized by high levels of organizational interdependence, require new processes for managing change which can be conceptualized as the macro management of supply. Sluggish responses to complex macro structural problems contain the danger that productivity traps may reduce performance and flexibility. The macro management of supply as a process of redefining the purposes and redesigning the structure of interorganizational networks brings to the fore a range of issues that make new demands on existing political and economic institutions, and calls for the creation of new ones.

In the first place, the macro management of supply is an integrative planning process in which government participates with other interests but not one that government controls. Extensive participation in restructuring the ground rules of organizational interaction is important, not only to ensure that the interests of all affected groups are taken into account, but also prepares the way for implementation of agreed structural changes.

Secondly, governmental and non-governmental representative organizations are called upon to fulfil new design functions on a regular basis. These include defining roles, devising arbitration and conciliation procedures to resolve predictable conflicts of interest, assisting in formulating performance criteria and establishing appropriate mechanisms for social control, account-ability, and corporate responsibility.

Finally, a key element in the management of changes in process structure is the formation of network organizations. Network organizations co-opting individuals from all the interests involved in a system provided a focus for the analysis of industry-wide problems and a context for producing coherent and politically-feasible ways of dealing with them. Network organizations do not have executive powers. Their contribution to the macro management of sup-ply is as a catalyst establishing a common perspective on current structural problems and involving other organizations in the process of dealing with them.

7. References

Ashby, Ross W., 1960
    Design for a Brain. London: Chapman and Hall.

Bateson, Gregory, 1963
    »The Role of Somatic Change in Evolution», in Bateson, 1973, *Steps to an Ecology of Mind.* St. Albans, England: Paladin.

Berry, Dean F., Metcalfe, Les, and McQuillan, Will, 1974
    »Neddy: An Organizational Metamorphosis», *Journal of Man-agement Studies,* February, pp. 1-20.

Brenner, Michael J., 1976
    The Politics of International Monetary Reform. Cambridge, Mass.: Ballinger Publishing Co.

Dunn, Edgar S. Jr., 1971
    Economic and Social Development. Baltimore and London: John Hopkins Press.

Emery, F.F., and Trist, E.L., 1965
    »The Causal Texture of Organizational Environments», *Human Relations,* 18, pp. 21-32.

Fisher, R., 1969
    International Conflict for Beginners. New York: Harper and Row.

Fox, Alan, 1974
Beyond Contract: Work, Power and Trust Relations. London: Faber and Faber.

Fox, Alan, and Flanders, Allan, 1969
»The Reform of Collective Bargaining: From Donovan to Durkheim», *British Journal of Industrial Relations,* Vol. 7, pp. 151-180.

Goldthorpe, John H., 1974
»Industrial Relations in Great Britain: A Critique of Reformism», *Politics and Society,* Vol. 4, No,. 4, pp. 419-452.

Hedberg, Bo L., 1974
»Growth Stagnation as a Managerial Discontinuity», International Institute of Management, Preprint No. 1/41-74, Berlin.

Hedberg, Bo L., Nystrom, Paul C., and Starbuck, William H., 1976
»Camping on See-Saws: Prescriptions for a Self-Designing Organization», *Administrative Science Quarterly,* Vol. 21, pp. 41-65.

Hernes, Gudmund, 1977
»Structural Change i Social Processes», *American Journal of Sociology,* Vol. 82, pp. 513-547.

Jacoby, Neil H., (ed.), 1974
The Business Government Relationship: A Reassessment. Santa Monica: Goodyear Publishing Co.

Jantsch, Erich, 1975
Design for Evolution. New York: George Braziller.

Lehmbruch, Gerhard, 1974
»Consociational Democracy, Class Conflict and the New Corporatism», I.P.S.A. Round Table on Political Integration, Jerusalem.

Lehmbruch, Gerhard, 1976
»Liberal Corporatism and Party Government», I.P.S.A. World Congress, Edinburgh.

Lönnroth, Måns, Steen, Peter, and Johansson, Thomas B., 1977:
»Energy in Transition», Secretariat for Future Studies, Stockholm.

Merton, Robert K., 1968
Social Theory and Social Structure. New York: The Free Press.

Metcalfe, Les, 1974
»Systems Models, Economic Models and the Causal Texture of Organizational Environments: An Approach to Macro Organization Theory», *Human Relations,* Vol. 27, pp. 639-663.

Metcalfe, Les, 1976
»Designing Industrial Futures». Paper presented at the E.G.O.S. Colloquium on Social Change and Organizations in Contemporary Society, Denmark.

Metcalfe, Les, and McQuillan, Will, 1977
»Corporatism or Industrial Democracy?», *Political Studies,* Vol. 27, pp. 266-282.

Metcalfe, Les, and McQuillan, Will, 1977
»Managing Turbulence», in: *Prescriptive Models of Organizations,* TIMS, North Holland, and, *Studies in Management Sciences, Vol. V.,* Nystrom, Paul C., and Starbuck, William H. (eds.), North Holland, Amsterdam.

Michael, Donald, 1973
On Learning to Plan and Planning to Learn. London: Tavistock Publications.

Mueller, Dennis C., 1976
»Public Choice: A Survey», *Journal of Economic Literature,* Vol. 24, No. 2, pp. 395-433.

Panic, M., (ed.), 1976
»The U.K. and West German Manufacturing Industry 1954-72», NEDO Monograph No. 5.

Panitch, L., 1978
Corporatism in Canada. European Consortium for Political Research Workshop. Corporatism in Liberal Democracies. Grenoble

Rapoport, Anatol, 1974
Conflict in Man-made Environment. Harmondsworth, England: Penguin Books.

Rose, R., 1979
»Ungovernability: Is there Fire behind the Smoke?» *Political Studies,* Vol. 27, pp. 351-370.

Scharpf, Fritz W., 1977
»Public Organization and the Waning of the Welfare State», *European Journal of Political Research,* V.

Schmitten, Phillipe C., 1974
»Still the Century of Corporatism?», in: Pike, Frederick B., and Stritch, Thomas (eds.), *The New Corporatism,* London: Notre Dame Press.

Schon, Donald A., 1971
Beyond the Stable State. London: Temple Smith.

Schonfield, Andrew, 1965
Modern Capitalism, Oxford University Press.

Thomas, Kenneth W., 1976
  »Conflict and Conflict Management», in: Dunnette, Marvin (ed.) *The Handbook of Industrial and Organizational Psychology,* pp. 889-935. Chicago, Ill.: Rand McNally.

Vickers, Sir Geoffrey, 1970
  Freedom in a Rocking Boat. Harmondsworth, England: Penguin Books.

Subject Index

A

absenteeism, 301
accretion doctrine, 297
acquired company, 297-298, 301-302
acquired firm, 207-208, 297, 301, 303-304, 307
acquiring firm, 207-208, 297, 299, 302-303
acquisition, 25, 57, 87, 217, 293, 295
actors, 210
adoption of means, 140
advertising intensity, 182
after sales servicing, 180
agreements, 14
airplane industry, 170
allocating performance, 178
allocating resources, 140, 178, 185
allocation, 174, 177
American Hospital Association, 138, 143
American Management Association, 300
anti-competitive effects, 294
apparel industry, 170
arbitration, 321
Arla, 39, 44
artificial systems, 136
Ashridge Management Center, 217, 237
association of producers, 133
associations of independent economic units, 131
asymmetrical interdependence, 196, 200
automobile industry, 136
autonomy, 296

B

bargaining power, 207, 297
bargaining unit, 299
beer industry, 170
benefit programs, 300
birth process, 211, 269, 271, 276
Bismarck, 114
blue collar workers, 296
Blue Cross, 138
board composition, 114
Bonini Syndrome, 12
branding, 180
British, 319
business idea, 210

C

capacity reduction, 211-212, 239
capital market, 293
capital transfer, 30
car industry, 170
cartel, 178
cash register industry, 170
Celler-Kefauver amendment, 295
centralization, 43, 162
CEPES, 269, 276, 289
cereal industry, 170
change agent, 212
checklists, 15
chemical industry, 170
chief executives, 299
cigarette industry, 170
Clayton Anti-trust Act, 295
clothing industry, 170
co-operation, 67, 81, 83, 87, 91-92, 94
co-operative agreement, 194, 197
co-operative factories, 125
co-operative suppliers, 200
co-operatives, 35, 37, 40-41
co-optation, 14
coalition, 282
codetermination, 247
coercion, 107, 111
collective bargaining, 293-296, 304
combines, 100, 123-125, 127, 131
COMECON, 123
commercial interdependence, 197, 200
commitment, 236, 270, 286-287
common messengers, 110, 115
communication of information, 174
company performance, 207
competition, 295
competition control, 16
competitive interdependence, 54, 91, 208, 295
competitiveness, 212
computerized axial tomography, 141
concentration, 100, 117, 174, 186, 207-208, 294-295
concentration of production, 130
concentration ratio, 181
concerted action, 177, 180, 185
conciliation, 321
conflict, 210, 212, 217-219, 225, 232, 235, 257, 309
conflict avoidance, 210
conflict of interest, 234
conflict resolution, 211-212, 217, 236, 239
confrontation, 235
conglomerate corporation, 296
conglomerate firm, 294, 298
conglomerate merger, 15, 17, 25, 30, 52, 207-208, 294-296, 299

congruence, 210
consensus seeking activities, 266
consolidated ownership, 176, 178, 180-181
consolidation, 208
consortium, 4, 101, 138, 144, 152, 157
construction, 190
construction industry, 128
consumer durables, 180
contextual conditions, 210
contingencies, 210
contingency theory, 136
contracts, 14, 68
contractual agreements, 197
cooptation, 107, 110, 111
coordinated bargaining, 296
coordination, 174, 177, 185, 310
corporate labor relations director, 302
corporate management system, 101, 139, 149
corporate operating policies, 300
corporate system, 153
corporation taxes, 178
cost containment, 163
cross-sectional approach, 270
customer preferences, 198

D

decentralization, 249
decentralized organization, 302
degeneration, 316
delegation of authority, 301
Denmark, 272, 274
Department of Industry, 236
dependence, 293
determination of goals, 140
development of institutional links, 200
direct investment, 102, 189-191
dis-joint purchasing, 102
disintegration, 310, 317
disparities in wages and benefits, 300
dissatisfaction, 301
distilled liquors industry, 170
distributing units, 177
distribution of assets, 294
distribution phase, 212
distribution process, 210, 282-283
diversification, 11, 18, 30, 53, 107, 139, 169, 173, 209, 294
diversifying merger, 18
divestitures, 174
division of labor, 295
document analysis, 271
domain of a firm, 68
dominance, 9
Donovan Commission of Industrial Relations, 316

downstream firms, 57
duPont, 139
dynamic equilibrium, 311

E

earnings, 208
ecological approaches, 13
ecological characteristics, 136
economic efficiencies, 207
economic environment, 207
economic exchange, 195-196
economic rationality, 209
economics of flexibility, 311
economies of multiplant operations, 173
economies of scale, 9
effectiveness ratio, 157
electrical machinery industry, 170
employing industry, 297
employment maintenance, 211
engineering industry, 128
enterprise associations, 100, 126
entrepreneurship, 210,269
environmental determinism, 135
equipment and supplies industry, 170
equipment supplier, 189
equity, 10, 209
establishing phase, 276-277, 286
European Communities, 15
Evan dynamic organizational effective indicators, 158
export consortia, 193, 202
export-promoting, 190
extended reproduction, 312
external evaluation phase, 276, 280
external experts, 287
external validity, 288
externalities, 175-176

F

factories, 170
failing firm&industry hypothesis, 208
farmers' co-operatives, 13
Farmers Milk Co-operative (LMC), 39
Federal Trade Commission (FTC), 295, 301
federation, 176
Federation of Dairy Co-operatives (VMC), 39
federations, 5, 173
financial analysis, 300
financing, 190
flexibility, 314, 317, 320
focal organization, 106, 107
food processing industry, 170, 197
France, 172
franchising, 174

free riders, 180
fringe benefits, 307
functional integration, 139, 162, 298
furniture industry, 125, 170

G

geographic location, 303
geographical diversification, 170
geographical expansion, 140
German Democratic Republic (GDR), 129
Germany, 163, 172, 272
General Motors (GM), 139
goodness of fit, 136
government regulation, 142
governmental constraints, 295
Great Britain, 137, 212
green-field plants, 10
grievances, 301
group insurance, 300
growth, 9
Grängesbergs Industrier (Gränges), 241, 245, 247

H

harvester industry, 170
health systems agency, 150
heterogeniety, 198
hierarchical organization, 169, 173, 179
hierarchical process analysis, 210
horizontal expansion, 209
horizontal integration, 127
horizontal interdependence, 108-109, 111-112, 115
horizontal merger, 15, 52, 54, 110, 125, 207-208, 217, 294-295
hospital industry, 101, 114, 136
host country, 138
household appliance industry, 170
human problems, 299

I

idea phase, 276, 286
identification, 225, 287
ideologies, 13, 44
implementation, 213, 263
independent entity, 298
individual goals, 210
industrial and labor relations, 212, 295, 298, 300, 304-306
industrial associations, 100, 124-126, 130
industrial concentration, 208
industrial conflict, 316
industrial groups, 174
industrial policy, 190, 309
industrial relations department, 294, 296, 300, 302, 304
Industrial Union Department of the AFL-CIO, 296

information impactedness, 180
insider opportunities, 11
institutional choices, 178
institutional competition, 178, 185
institutional economics, 175
institutional links, 197
integration, 123, 155, 173, 233, 235, 294
integrative planning process, 320
integrator, 220-221
inter-hospital coordination, 142, 160
inter-hospital strategy, 160
interaction, 311
interchange of employees, 298
interdependence, 108, 176, 309, 313
interfirm co-operation, 67, 71
intergroup competition, 316
interlocking directorates, 4, 99, 105-106, 111
interlocking stockholdings, 174
internal evaluation phase, 276, 278-280
international capital market, 190
International Iron and Steel Institute, 240
international resource transfer, 189
international trade, 189
interorganizational dynamics, 313
interorganizational interdependence, 105
interorganizational learning, 309, 311, 313, 317-318
interorganizational networks, 310
interorganizational system, 155, 311, 313, 319
involvement, 278, 287
Iran, 275, 277
IRS Source Book of Corporation Income, 182
Italy, 16, 264

J

Japan, 163, 240, 274
job classification programs, 301
job protection, 239
joint actions, 181
joint decision making, 174
joint facility, 146
joint interests, 281
joint venture, 4, 14, 73, 101-102, 138, 146, 157, 189-190, 269, 275-276,293
Justice Department, 295
Jämtlands Läns Mejeriförening, 40

K

key industries, 125

L

labor board election, 297
labor market, 293
labor relations: see industrial and labor relations

laboratories, 170
LAMCO, 241
large economic organization, 124-125
large mergers, 294
leather industry, 170
legal arrangements, 269
legal constraints, 296
Leiterunternehmen, 124
levels of analysis, 107
leverage., 207
licensing, 189-190
light industry, 170
liquidity, 11
local bargaining representatives, 296
longitudinal case study approach, 211, 217, 270, 285
loose coupling, 99

M

machinery industry, 170
macro management of supply, 309, 317-318, 320
macro-structural change, 309
malpractice suits, 141
management contracts, 102, 189-190
management development, 299
management of conflict, 233-235
management organization, 174, 181, 190, 209, 278
managerial skills, 10
manufacturing industry, 170
market contracting, 178
market extension mergers, 295
market power, 9, 11, 207-208, 294
market share, 9
marketing, 125, 180, 190
marriage broker, 276, 287
master benefit plan, 300
meat industry, 170
Medicaid, 137
Medicare, 137
merger implementation, 211, 249
merger management, 139, 148, 174, 209-210, 293-294
merger motives, 15, 267
merger negotiation, 245
merger policy, 16
merger protection, 16
merger-as-search, 17-18
metal products industry, 170
Middle East, 272, 275, 278
Milk Co-operative (MC), 39
milk industry, 170
mode of transfer, 201
monitoring, 174, 177, 185
monopoly profits, 9
monopoly situation, 198
motives, 6, 9, 11, 17, 91, 210

multi-divisional structure, 139
multi-hospital system, 138 141, 149, 158, 163
multi-industry operations, 182
multi-unit establishment, 156, 169
multinational corporation, 138
multiplant associations, 124
multiplant enterprises, 100, 125-127, 130, 181-182, 186
mutual dependence, 56
myth, 13, 44, 211

N

National Farmers' Union (RLF), 35
National Health Planning and Resources Development Act, 137
National Industrial Conference Board (NICB), 301
National Labor Relations Board (NLRB), 296, 298, 300
National Science Foundation (NSF), 183
natural systems, 136
Nedre Norrlands Producentförening (NNP), 40
negotiated environment, 53
negotiations, 74
network organizations, 309, 321
non-acquiring firms, 209
non-diversified firms, 179
non-integrated firms, 179
non-profit organizations, 101
non-unionized companies, 304-305
norms, 210
Norway, 273

O

obligation to bargain, 297
OECD, 15
official goals, 160
operative exchange, 195-196
operative goals, 160
organizational autonomy, 142
organizational climate, 219
organizational effectiveness, 105, 143, 157
organizational environments, 313
organizational interdependence, 313-314, 320
organizational strategies, 293, 300
organizational structure, 155, 299, 313
organizational visions, 44, 47
outcome quality, 143, 156
outcroppings, 114
output structure, 312
overarching corporate shell, 299
ownership control, 11

P

parameter structure, 312
parent company, 298, 303

participation, 212
pension liabilities, 300
pension plans, 300
performance, 312, 314, 316, 320
performance measures, 159
personnel department, 296, 299-300, 304
personnel issues, 299
personnel policies, 245, 249
petroleum industry, 170
planning horizons, 318
pluralistic structure, 311, 317, 320
Poland, 124
policy responses, 311
political economy of pluralism, 311
political effectiveness, 114
portfolio theory, 19
post-merger integration, 6, 212, 217-219, 300
power, 235
power generator industry, 170
pre-merger phase, 6, 207-208, 212, 217, 304
primary metal industry, 170
printing industry, 170
process modell, 211
process research, 210
process structure, 143, 156, 312
processed foods, 180
product diversification, 140
product extension, 295
product market, 293
production sharing, 189-190
production-concentration, 123
productive outcomes, 316
productivity traps, 314, 317, 320
Professional Standard Review Organization Law, 137
profit-pooling, 176, 178
profitability, 9, 25, 207-208, 242, 271-272
project organization, 249-250
psychiological pit, 213
public relations, 300
public sector, 14
purchase interdependence, 190, 207

R

R and D expenditures, 125, 179, 182, 252
rationality assumption, 9
recession, 294
redefining the purposes, 320
refrigerator industry, 170
regulated industry, 137
reorganization, 217, 299
representation, 299
representative organizations, 321
resource commitment, 153
resource exchange, 208

resource interdependence, 71, 94, 135, 207-208
restructuring, 255
risk minimization, 14

S

SAAB-Scania, 263
sales dependence, 207
sales offices, 170
sales taxes, 178
sales uncertainty, 207
Saudi Arabia, 275-280
Sears-Roebuck, 139
Securities and Exchange Commission, 10
security, 10
selection of partners, 269
seniority, 300
sequential phases, 276
service contracts, 189-190
Seven Countries Study, 4, 6, 207-209, 264
sewing machine industry, 170
shared service organization, 141
shareholders, 207-208
sharing profits, 174
shirking, 178
simple reproduction, 312
single function firm, 171
single product firm, 171
single region firm, 171
size, 12, 207
small firms, 270, 272, 291
social exchange, 195-196
societal flexibility, 311
socio-political context, 13, 35, 42, 44, 48, 211-212, 239, 264-265,269
SOU, 291
Soviet Union, 130, 240
specialization, 100
spreading of risks, 207
stagnation, 314
Standard Oil of New Jersey, 139
standardization, 155, 162, 180, 272
State Enterprise Holding Corporation, 247
static performance, 161
steel industry, 170, 243
stock market performance, 11
stock prices, 209
strategic decisions, 140, 210, 212, 219, 282-283
strategic exchange, 195
strikes, 301
structural change, 294, 309, 311-313
structural-complexity model, 94
structure, 140, 143-156
STU Swedish Board for Technical Research, 277, 280, 288
successor doctrine, 297
supplier networks, 189, 190, 193, 198

supplier provided information, 179
Supreme Court, 296, 298
Sweden, 137, 240, 264, 275
Swedish Centre for Working Life Studies, 239
Swedish Dairy Association (SMR), 35, 39
Swedish Farmers (LRF), 35
Swedish Farmers' Associations (SL), 35
Swedish Industrial Board, 236
Swedish model, 265
Swedish Steel Inc., (SSAB), 245
symbiotic interdependence, 54, 108, 208
system development phase, 276, 278-279, 286-287
system performance, 312, 316

T

Taft-Hartley Labour Law, 138
task development process, 210, 282
techno-economic contingencies, 13, 35, 42, 44, 48, 209, 212, 239,264
technological diversification, 200
technological interdependence, 197-198
technology transfer, 189
telephone industry, 170
temporal approach, 210
textile industry, 170
tight coupling, 99
tobacco industry, 170
top management, 207, 296
transaction costs, 52, 115
transaction-specific investment, 177, 180-181
transfer modes, 190
transformation, 312
transition, 312
transportation equipment industry, 170
trial-and-error learning model, 95
turbulence, 314
turbulent conditions, 313
turn-key projects, 102, 189-191, 197-198
turnover, 301
typewriter industry, 170

U

U.S. Census of Manufacturers, 182
U.S. Congress, 117, 121
uncertainty, 14, 51, 54, 177, 180, 208, 293
unfair labor practices, 301
union contracts, 301, 305
union militancy, 301
union power, 293, 296
union wage levels, 296
union-management conflict, 296, 304
unions, 243
United Kingdom, 172, 294
United States, 137, 170, 173, 240, 264, 294
upstream firms, 57

V

W

Authors Index

Brunsson, N., 258-259, 261-263, 267
Buchanan, B., 289
Bunting, D., 114, 119
Burns, 297-298
Butler, R.J., 277, 281, 289, 300, 307

C

Cable, J., 13, 17, 111
Cannedy, L.L., 150, 166
Casson, M., 189, 206
Chandler Jr., A.D., 101-103, 136, 139, 160, 162, 164, 170, 173, 186
Channon, D.F., 101-103, 136, 160, 162, 164
Child, J., 94-95
Coase, R.E., 173, 175, 186
Comanor, W.S., 110, 113, 119
Conn, R.L., 25, 31, 208, 214
Cummings, L.L., 307
Curran, J., 269, 291
Cyert, R.M., 31, 51, 53, 64, 69, 95, 282, 289

D

Daems, H., 99, 101, 169, 174, 186
Dale, A. 44, 48
Danielsson, C., 48
Davis, L.E., 175, 186
Demsetz, H., 175, 181, 186
Denzin, N., 37, 48
Dewey, D., 25, 31
Dewing, A.S., 208, 214
Dill, W.R., 105, 119
Dodd, P.R., 208, 214
Domhoff, G.W., 106, 119
Donabedian, A. 143, 156, 164
Dooely, P., 112, 119
Dunn Jr., E.S., 314, 321
Dunning, J.H., 189, 206

E

Edgren, J.-O., 218, 237
Edström, A., 13-14, 67, 69-70, 95, 99, 211, 217, 220, 237, 269, 289
Edvards, R., 307
Ellert, J.D., 28, 31
Elling, R.H., 114, 118
Emery, F.F., 310, 313, 321
Esposito, F.F., 113, 119
Esposito, L., 113, 119
Evan, W.M., 53, 64, 101, 106, 108, 119, 135-136, 143, 157, 164

F

Fama, E.F., 19, 32
Firth, M.A., 208-209, 214
Fisher, R., 318, 321
Flanders, A., 316
Forrest Jr., W.H., 143, 167
Fottler, M.D., 138, 165
Fox, A., 316, 322
Franko, L.G., 70, 96
Freeman, C. 180, 186
Freeman, J., 106, 119,
Freidson, E., 166
Freitag, P.J., 118
Friedman, P., 269, 289
Friedmann, W.G., 269, 289

G

Galbraith, J., 136, 165
Georgopolous, B., 166
Glaser, B.G., 271, 289
Glaser, R., 37, 48
Glinski, B., 124, 134
Gogel, M., 112, 116, 119
Gold, M., 293
Goldberg, W.H., 5, 14, 99, 103, 211, 218, 239, 240, 264, 268
Goldthorpe, J.H., 316, 322
Goodman, P.S., 109, 120
Gorecki, P.K., 26, 32
Gort, M., 17, 26, 32, 208-209, 214
Gouldner, A.W., 136, 165
Graham, J.B., 141, 165
Granovetter, M.S., 117, 119
Greenfield, S. 164
Guetzkow, H., 70, 96, 281, 289
Gullander, S., 70, 96, 269, 276, 289-290

H

Haberich, K., 70, 96
Hage, J., 70-71, 90, 95, 270, 288
Halpern, P.J., 28, 32
Hammarström, O., 268
Hannah, L., 26, 32
Hannan, M., 106, 119
Hawkins, K.H., 110, 119
Hedberg, B.L., 268, 319, 322
Helmich, D.L., 107, 119
Hendricks, C., 118
Hendricks, W., 296, 308
Hernes, G., 312, 322
Heydebrand, W.V., 137, 143, 165
Hickson, D.J., 289

Livermore, S., 208, 215
Lorsch, J., 105, 219-221, 237
Lovell, E., 269, 289
Lundell, P., 272, 291
Lönnroth, M., 318, 322

M

Mahajan, V., 152, 166
Maier, A., 258, 262, 268
Maier, N.R.C.F., 258, 262, 268
Mandelker, G., 28, 32, 113, 120, 208, 215
Mann, H.M., 113, 120
Manne, H.G. 25, 33
Mansinghka, S.K., 25, 34, 208, 216
March, J.G., 31, 45, 48, 51-53, 64, 69, 95, 219, 237, 282, 289
Marcus, M., 181, 186
Marcus, P., 208, 215
Mattsson, L.G., 99, 102, 189, 193, 206
Maule, C.J., 269, 290
McCullough, A., 289
McEwen, W.J., 277, 291
McLagan, B., 300, 308
McNeil, M.C., 139, 167
McQuillan, W., 313, 320-321, 323
Means, G.C., 106, 118
Meeks, G., 208, 215
Merton, R.K., 48, 317, 322
Metcalfe, L., 212, 309-310, 313, 320-323
Michael, D., 317, 323
Mindlin, S., 94-95
Mintz, C., 118
Mintzberg, H., 114, 120
Morgenroth, W.M., 109, 121, 207, 216
Mueller, D.C., 3-4, 8, 17, 26-27, 33, 52, 64, 208, 215, 236, 264, 268, 314, 323
Mueller, S., 294, 307
Murphy, N.B., 113, 118

N

Narver, J.C., 26, 33
Neilsen, E.H., 270, 290
Nelson, R.L., 26, 33
Neuhauser, D., 143, 166-167
Norbäck, L.E., 13, 67, 95-96, 99
Normann, R., 48, 91, 96
North, D.C., 175, 186
Nowak, P., 54, 64, 69-71, 89, 96, 112, 116, 121
Nyström, H., 13, 35, 42, 49, 211-212, 239
Nystrom, P.C., 319, 322

O

O'Connor, J.F., 113, 120
Olsen, J., 45, 48
Osborn, R.C., 181, 186

P

Palouzek, F.P., 141, 165
Panic, M., 312, 323
Panitch, L., 323
Pennings, J.M., 13, 99-100, 105, 108-109, 117, 120
Penrose, E.T., 17, 33, 208, 215
Perrow, C., 152, 160, 166
Perrucci, R., 106, 120
Pettigrew, A.M., 270, 290
Pfeffer, J., 5, 8, 14, 16, 53-54, 57, 60, 64, 69-71, 89, 96, 101-102, 107, 109, 111-112, 114, 116, 120-121, 135, 163, 207-209, 215
Pilisuk, M., 106, 120
Poensgen, O.H., 5, 8, 99, 102
Pointer, D.D., 150, 166
Porter, M.E., 180-181, 186-187
Portner, F.E., 9, 16, 237
Portnoy, S., 138, 166
Pugh, D.S., 140

R

Radcliffe, R., 110, 119
Radner, R., 33
Radosevich, H.R., 9, 16, 237
Rafferty, J., 139, 150, 166
Rapoport, A., 318, 323
Reid, S.R., 26, 33, 208-209, 215
Reid, W., 70, 96
Richardson, G.B., 174, 187
Rose, R., 309, 323
Rotschild, M., 33
Ruback, R., 208, 214
Rubin, I.M., 269, 291
Ruchlin, H.S., 150, 166
Rumelt,, R.P., 101-102, 113, 121, 136, 139, 160, 162, 166
Rydén, B., 218, 237, 269-270, 276, 290

S

Said, K.E., 270, 290
Salancik, G.R., 5, 8, 69, 96, 207-209, 215
Sarnat, M., 17, 32
Scharpf, F.W., 309, 323
Scherer, F.M., 3, 53, 64, 113, 121, 208, 215, 294, 308
Schermerhorn, J.R., 270, 290
Schmidt, S., 53-54, 64
Schmitten, P.C., 310, 323